27

DATE DUE

APR 1 1 1997			
MAR 2 5 REC'D			
GAYLORD			PRINTED IN U.S.A.

A GREAT AND NECESSARY MEASURE

Reproduced by permission of The John Carter Brown Library, Brown University.

A GREAT AND NECESSARY MEASURE

GEORGE GRENVILLE AND THE
GENESIS OF THE STAMP ACT

1763–1765

John L. Bullion

University of Missouri Press

Columbia & London, 1982

Library of Congress Cataloging in Publication Data

Bullion, John L., 1944–
    A great and necessary measure, George Grenville
    and the genesis of the stamp act, 1763–1765.

    Bibliography: p. 290
    Includes index.
    1. Finance, Public—Great Britain—1688–1815.
    2. Finance, Public—United States—To 1789.
    3. Great Britain—Colonies—America—History.
    4. Taxation—United States—History.
    5. Grenville, George, 1712–1770. I. Title.
    HJ1013.B84   336.2′00973   82–2775
    ISBN 0–8262–0375–2   AACR2

For Jack's Grandparents and for Laura

Acknowledgments

Every student of British politicians and the American question owes a considerable debt to the remarkable British historians who have labored in that vineyard before him. I am no exception to this rule. As I finished this book, I realized all the more fully that the questions I have asked could not have been answered without the assistance of the painstaking research and careful interpretations of Sir Lewis Namier, John Brooke, Ian R. Christie, and P. D. G. Thomas. It will be obvious to anyone who reads this book that I have disagreed with these men on points both major and minor. I hope that my reliance on and respect for their work will be equally obvious.

My work in this general area began fourteen years ago, in the form of research for a paper for Philip L. White's graduate seminar on the American Revolution at the University of Texas. Since that time, his interest in that topic and in me has never flagged. He encouraged me to research an impossible dissertation topic that covered British imperial policy from 1760 to 1776, and then as I began to write, he helped narrow my focus to George Grenville. Throughout my work on Grenville, he has remained a sympathetic and discerning critic. Moreover, his recommendation was crucial in helping me to find academic employment and thus in providing the financial and psychological reserves I drew on to complete my study. It is no exaggeration to state that I would have finished none of my work without Phil's guidance and friendship. I can only acknowledge this debt; I cannot repay it.

I owe substantial debts to other historians as well. Standish Meacham and Richard Alan Ryerson read my dissertation closely and critically; many of their suggestions have been incorporated into the present work. I have also benefited from discussions with John Shy, David Syrett, Ira Gruber, Charles Mullett, E. A. Reitan, W. R. Fryer, and William D. Liddle. Just before I began writing this book, Gerard H. Clarfield advised me to concentrate on Grenville and taxation and to leave a complicated survey of British commercial policy for another book, a suggestion that vastly shortened and considerably simplified the organization of the present work. I would also like to thank an anonymous reader of an earlier version of this work for his trenchant and helpful comments. My approach to the problems of thinking and writing about politicians and policy making has been strongly influenced by Roger J. Spiller. Finally, my colleagues at Southwest Texas State University and the University of Missouri-Columbia provided congenial and stimulating atmospheres in which it was easy to teach and write history. For that, I thank them as well.

As is always the case with historians, my obligations to archivists and librarians are legion. I have never encountered anyone in a library on either side of the Atlantic who was not courteous and helpful. Many in England went well beyond the call of duty by advising me on hotels, train schedules, and, in one case in Stafford, on the National Health Service. And two became active participants not only in my search for documents but also in my efforts to understand the period: Carolyn Sung of the Library of Congress and John C. Dann of the William L. Clements Library. To Carolyn and John, and to their counterparts at other archives, go my heartfelt thanks. I also would like to thank those individuals and libraries that have given me the following permissions: the Keeper of Public Records, for permission to quote from Crown copyright material at the Public Record Office; the Trustees of the British Library, for permission to quote from materials in Additional Manuscripts and to reproduce Charles Jenkinson's memorandum; the Henry E. Huntington Library, for permission to quote from the Stowe collection and to reproduce a paper by Henry McCulloh and a letter by Nathaniel Ware; the Trustees of the Fitzwilliam (Wentworth) Estates and the Director of the Sheffield City Libraries, for permission to quote from the Rockingham and Burke Papers; the late Earl Fitzwilliam, for permission to quote from the Burke Papers at the Northamptonshire Record Office; the Marquess of Bute, for permission to quote material from the Bute Papers; the Earl of Dartmouth, for permission to quote from the Dartmouth Papers at the Staffordshire Record Office; the Trustees of the Will of Matthew Fortescue-Brickdale, Deceased, for permission to quote from the Brickdale Diaries, which they hold the copyright to; the Keeper of Western Manuscripts at the Bodleian Library, for permission to quote from the North Papers; the Principal of Manchester College, Oxford, for permission to quote from the William Shepherd Manuscripts; the National Library of Scotland, for permission to quote from the Minto Papers; and the William L. Clements Library, for perssmission to quote from the Shelburne, Townshend, and Knox Papers.

My typists, Phyllis Kaser and Norma Castleman, were swift, accurate, and—most important of all—unfailingly tolerate of the frequent amendments and changes I made in the book as it progressed. I know that I tested their patience on a number of occasions, and I did so at times when one was looking for a new job and another was caring for a seriously ill husband. I admire them for the skill, patience, and good humor with which they handled the manuscript and its author under those trying conditions. I was indeed fortunate that they typed my book.

I would also like to thank several people who rarely discussed Grenville with me, and never found documents or read drafts for me, but whose example and support I have cherished. They are Faye Callan, Bob Crunden, Martha and Bill Dolman, Lynn and Steve Gentzler, Larry Goodwyn, Lisa and Curley Griffin, Ruth and Jack Hexter, Pat Hearden, Jim Hopkins, Karen Janes, Ann and Eddie Mears, Howard Miller, Fordyce Mitchel, Jim Pohl, Rex Polser, Arch Puddington, Bob Rosenbaum, Ann Schlumberger, Alice and Bob Smuts, Bob Somers, Cindy and Tom Stewart, Everette Swinney, and—most of all—Anne and Max Green, Phil Hewitt, and Irene Spiller.

The people to whom I owe the most I have remembered in the dedication. My gratitude to them is much more easily acknowledged than described. Still, I believe they know what I am referring to, and that is enough.

John L. Bullion
Columbia, Missouri
May 1982

Contents

Abbreviations, *xiii*

Introduction, *1*

CHAPTER I

The Background of Colonial Taxation
October 1760–February 1763, *11*

CHAPTER II

A Cautious Beginning: Bute's Ministry and
American Taxation, January–March 1763, *27*

CHAPTER III

"The Particular Habits of His Life":
Some Implications of Grenville's Political
and Administrative Character, *43*

CHAPTER IV

"The First Great Object": Obstructing the
Clandestine Trade to America, April–November 1763, *62*

CHAPTER V

Taxing Molasses, July 1763–March 1764, *78*

CHAPTER VI

The Search for New Sources of Revenue
July 1763–March 1764, *99*

CHAPTER VII

The Politics of Postponing the Stamp Tax
March–December 1764, *114*

CHAPTER VIII

Preparing and Passing the Stamp Act
December 1764–February 1765, *136*

CHAPTER IX

Dispensing Places "of Emolument and of Influence"
December 1764–July 1765, *164*

CHAPTER X

Thoughts and Hopes about Future American Revenue
March–July 1765, *181*

CHAPTER XI

"The Author of all the Troubles in America"
August–December 1765, *193*

APPENDIX A

Henry McCulloh's "General Thoughts," *211*

APPENDIX B

Nathaniel Ware, *220*

APPENDIX C

Charles Jenkinson's Memorandum, *224*

Notes, *230*

Bibliography, *290*

Index, *310*

Abbreviations

Additional Grenville Papers. Additional Grenville Papers, 1763–1765, ed. John R. G. Tomlinson (Manchester, 1962).

Add. MSS. Additional Manuscripts in the British Library, London.

Adm. Admiralty Papers at the Public Record Office, London.

BL. British Library, London.

Bowdoin-Temple Papers. The Bowdoin and Temple Papers, Collections of the Massachusetts Historical Society, 6th ser. 9 (Boston, 1897).

Burke Correspondence. The Correspondence of Edmund Burke, ed. Thomas Copeland et al., 10 vols. (Cambridge, 1958–1970).

Bute Letters. Letters from George III to Lord Bute, 1756–1766, ed. Romney Sedgwick (London, 1939).

C.O. Colonial Office Papers at the Public Record Office, London.

Commons Journals. Journals of the House of Commons.

Dodington Journal. The Political Journal of George Bubb Dodington, ed. John Carswell and L. A. Dralle (Oxford, 1965).

EHD. English Historical Documents, vol. 9. *American Colonial Documents to 1776*, ed. Merrill Jensen (New York, 1955).

Fitch Papers. The Fitch Papers. Correspondence and Documents During Thomas Fitch's Governorship of the Colony of Connecticut, 1754–1766, Connecticut Historical Society Collections 18 (Hartford, 1920).

Franklin Papers. The Papers of Benjamin Franklin, ed. L. W. Labaree et al., vols. 10–14 (New Haven, 1966–1970).

Gage Papers. The Correspondence of General Thomas Gage with the Secretaries of State, 1763–1775, ed. C. E. Carter, 2 vols. (New Haven, 1931).

Grenville Papers. The Grenville Papers: being the Correspondence of Richard Grenville, Earl Temple, K.G., and the Right Honourable George Grenville, their friends and contemporaries, ed. W. J. Smith, vols. 1–4 (London, 1852–1853).

Hardwicke Correspondence. Philip C. Yorke, *The Life and Correspondence of Philip Yorke, Earl of Hardwicke, Lord High Chancellor of Great Britain.* (Cambridge, 1913), vol. 3.

Harris Diary. The diary of James Harris, which is no longer available to scholars, and thus can be studied only from extracts in published works.

HEHL. The Henry E. Huntington Library, San Marino, California.

Ingersoll Papers. "A Selection from the Correspondence and Miscellaneous Papers of Jared Ingersoll," ed. F. B. Dexter, in *Papers of the New Haven Colony Historical Society* 9:201–472 (New Haven, 1918).

JCTP. Journal of the Commissioners for Trade and Planatations . . . Preserved in the Public Record Office, 15 vols. (London, 1920–1938).

Jenkinson Papers. The Jenkinson Papers, 1760–1766, ed. N. S. Jucker (London, 1949).

Lennox Letters. The Life and Letters of Lady Sarah Lennox, 1745–1826, ed. Countess of Ilchester and Lord Stavordale (London, 1902).

MHSC. Massachusetts Historical Society, Collections.

Namier and Brooke, *House of Commons.* Sir Lewis Namier and John Brooke, eds., *The House of Commons 1754–1790. The History of Parliament,* 3 vols. (Oxford, 1964).

OED. Oxford English Dictionary.

Parliamentary History. W. Cobbett and T. C. Hansard, eds., *The Parliamentary History of England from the Earliest Period to the Year 1803* (London, 1806–1820).

PRO. The Public Record Office, London.

P.R.O. Special Collections, Gifts and Deposits, at the Public Record Office, London.

Regulations. [Thomas Whately], *The regulations lately made concerning the colonies, and the taxes imposed upon them, considered* (London, 1765).

Ryder Diary. "The Parliamentary Diaries of Nathaniel Ryder, 1764–1767," *Camden Miscellany Vol. XXIII,* ed. P. D. G. Thomas, Camden 4th ser. 7: 229–351.

Shelburne Correspondence. Lord Fitzmaurice, *Life of William, Earl of Shelburne, Afterwards First Marquess of Landsdowne, with extracts from his papers and correspondence,* 2d rev. ed., vol. 1 (London, 1912).

S.P. State Papers at the Public Record Office, London.

ST. Stowe Collection at the Henry E. Huntington Library, San Marino, California.

Statutes at Large. The Statutes at Large from Magna Charta . . . , ed. Danby Pickering (Cambridge, 1762–1807).

STG. Stowe Collection, George Grenville Papers, at the Henry E. Huntington Library, San Marino, California.

T. Treasury Papers at the Public Record Office, London.

Walpole, *Memoirs of George III.* Horace Walpole, *Memoirs of the Reign of King George the Third,* vols. 1–3, ed. G. F. Russell Baker (London, 1894).

Walpole's Correspondence. The Yale Edition of Horace Walpole's Correspondence, ed. W. S. Lewis, 40 vols. (New Haven, 1937–1980).

WLCL. The William L. Clements Library, Ann Arbor, Michigan.

A GREAT AND NECESSARY MEASURE

To establish the right of
Parliament to impose
these [taxes], and to
produce an American
revenue, is a great
and necessary measure.

—Thomas Whately
12 June 1765

I have ever said, I wish
to see a plan and a
system. I framed a
plan. I framed a
system.

—George Grenville
26 April 1770

Introduction

Perhaps more so than historians of other eras, scholars who study the formulation and execution of British imperial policy during the 1760s have felt the tug and pull of historical inevitability. To borrow Sir Lewis Namier's evocative phrases, the decisions of British politicians and the reactions of American colonists seem to follow the same fixed laws and irresistible impulses as "the revolutions of planets, . . . the migrations of birds, and . . . the plunging of hordes of lemmings into the sea."[1] Most British politicians of the time shared a strong commitment to the absolute sovereignty of Parliament in imperial government. Therefore, they also shared a strong commitment to Parliament's right to tax the colonists, directly or indirectly. Furthermore, most politicians who thought at all about the conditions of the empire agreed that the home government should exercise its constitutional authority. They agreed it was necessary for Britain to control colonial smuggling. They agreed it was necessary for Britain to raise a revenue from the colonies. And they all felt—some, of course, more strongly than others—that the American colonies were dangerously free from effective control and should be returned to their proper, subordinate, position. Given this basic agreement on the theory of imperial government and on the definition of imperial problems, much can be said for concluding, as Ian R. Christie has, "The logic of the situation [in 1763] drove events strongly forward in the direction they were to follow."[2]

Still, one must realize that this agreement on the structure of the empire's government and on the nature of imperial problems did not provide specific answers to the practical question of how to proceed. For instance, George Grenville could have upheld Parliament's sovereignty, raised a revenue, reduced smuggling, and asserted British control over the colonies by lowering the duty on foreign molasses imported into America from sixpence to one penny per gallon. One penny, men familiar with the contraband trade assured him, was the bribe smugglers customarily paid corrupt customs officers to enter their foreign molasses as domestic. Surely illicit traders would have gladly paid the same amount into the King's purse and thus gained absolute security against any possibility of prosecution for bribery or smuggling.[3] But Grenville chose to set the duty at threepence instead, thereby irritating the mercantile community in the colonies. To take

1

another example: Grenville could have tried to raise a revenue in America by issuing paper currency, charging interest on it, and applying the interest to the costs of the army defending the colonies. Benjamin Franklin suggested that he do this; so did Henry McCulloh, a man of many ideas for reform and with some influence at the Treasury. Both argued that colonists so needed a reliable medium of exchange that they would happily pay the interest. But Grenville rejected the suggestion because—according to Franklin—he was "besotted with his stamp scheme."[4]

Would setting the molasses duty at one penny and collecting interest on paper currency have inspired Americans to resist parliamentary tyranny? Perhaps they would have; perhaps not. It does seem certain, though, that if resistance to these policies had occurred, it would have been a resistance shorn of substantial support from merchants, the agricultural elite of the northern colonies, and the planters of the South. In any crisis that might have arisen, Britain would have enjoyed far more support from these powerful groups in American society than she in fact did during the 1760s and 1770s. Thus, different decisions by Grenville might have totally prevented, considerably delayed, or essentially changed the American Revolution.[5] How and why Grenville and his colleagues reached the fateful decisions are questions I examine in this book.

Various Influences on the Treasury's Decisions

Early in the course of my examination, I discovered that the men at the Treasury did not make these decisions on fiscal grounds alone. Convinced that Britain might be confronted with serious financial and commercial crises during the aftermath of the Seven Years' War, and equally convinced that the trade with the colonies might provide the best way of mitigating the seriousness of the two emergencies, they knew that they had to weigh carefully the possible commercial impact of any taxes Parliament might impose on Americans. These convictions inspired Grenville's statement to the House of Commons that "the great object" of his proposals relating to the colonies was "to reconcile the regulation of commerce with an increase of revenue."[6] The awareness that this was "the great object" always influenced the Treasury's deliberations on American taxation.

Moreover, their perceptions of political realities in Britain and in America always played important, and sometimes decisive, parts in the decisions of Grenville and his colleagues. From the beginning of his tenure at the Treasury, Grenville read reports that insisted, "The inhabitants of the maritime provinces . . . already begin to entertain some

extraordinary opinions concerning their relationship to and dependence on their Mother Country."[7] The First Lord also quickly learned
that the cost of collecting customs duties in America exceeded the
collections themselves and concluded that "through neglect, connivance, and fraud, not only is the revenue impaired, but the commerce of
the colonies is diverted from its natural course, and the salutary provisions of many wise laws to secure it to the Mother Country are in great
measure defeated." As men at the Treasury well knew, this development
had a significance beyond the mere evasion of laws, no matter how
serious that might be. The neglect, connivance, and fraud that defeated
the purposes of the Acts of Trade and Navigation had permitted
colonists, as a colleague of Grenville observed, "to contemn [those
laws] with impunity."[8] When colonists regarded the very most important imperial legislation contemptuously, they demonstrated that their
respect for the authority of the Mother Country had seriously eroded.
This questioning of British authority and evasion of British law had
profound implications for the planners of American taxation. Within
Britain itself taxation was frequently controversial. As Grenville
observed, "A matter of revenue . . . was of all things the most interesting to the subject."[9] And in Britain, the people freely conceded the right
of Parliament to impose taxes, generally respected the authority of the
government, and, though many taxes were covertly evaded and some
were openly defied, had the experience of paying some duties on a
regular basis. Financiers clearly would have none of these advantages
when planning taxes for America. This reality of politics across the
Atlantic determined the Treasury's choice of the taxes to be imposed
and shaped many of the details of the legislation that enacted them.

Resistance in the colonies to British authority and laws had another
significance for Grenville and his colleagues: Americans did not believe
that Britain would govern them in their best interests, but would take
selfish and inequitable advantage of them whenever she could. To
counter this perception, Grenville never missed an appropriate opportunity in Parliament, in meetings with the colonial agents, and in a
pamphlet written in January 1765 by Thomas Whately, Grenville's
friend and assistant, to insist that Britain's self-interest would compel
her to use the force of her authority and laws to govern the colonies
justly and moderately. As for himself, Grenville always took care to
speak "of the colonies in general in terms of great kindness and
regard."[10] In particular, he took pains with the agents, telling them in
February 1765, "He took no pleasure in giving the Americans so much
uneasiness as he found he did—that it was the duty of his office to
manage the revenue—that he really was made to believe that consider-

ing the whole of the circumstances of the Mother Country and the colonies, the latter could and ought to pay something, and that he knew of no better way than that now pursuing to lay such tax, but that if we could tell of a better he would adopt it."[11] That he was so desirous of convincing colonists that they had nothing to fear from the exercise of British authority should not surprise historians of eighteenth-century Britain. As Douglas Hay has perceptively observed, the rulers of that society spent much of their time gauging opinion, for they "were acutely aware that their security depended on *belief*—belief in the justice of their rule, and in its adamantine strength." Grenville was well aware of the general rule that "the respect and affection of its subjects is the basis on which every wise government must be founded." He was also keenly cognizant that "if that foundation has been once overturned, it is not the work of a day to temper the materials so as to unite and re-build them."[12] The cracks in that foundation in America created serious political problems, ones Grenville had to take into account as he planned American taxation.

Grenville did not expect that his words alone would reverse years of distrust and disobedience. His taxes, therefore, would have to be enforced in an unfavorable atmosphere. Moreover, they would have to be enacted in such a way as to give American politicians no pretexts for claiming that limits had been established on British authority, for these men would certainly seize upon any concessions he might inadvertently give them while trying to reassure them of his and the Mother Country's goodwill. Yet at the same time he was exercising such care, Grenville felt obliged to take actions that would help convince colonists that they could trust a Britain with unlimited authority. To avoid failure in his efforts to achieve both political goals, he maneuvered carefully during the planning and enactment of the new taxes on colonists.

Finally, the political significance of collecting parliamentary taxes in the American colonies influenced decisions at the Treasury. "In other countries," noted Whately, "custom house duties are for the most part little more than a branch of the revenue; in the colonies, they are a political regulation, and enforce the observance of those wise laws to which the great increase of our trade and naval power are principally owing."[13] Insofar as the taxes were not collected and the laws not obeyed, the connection between Britain and her colonies was proportionately weakened. Publicly, the Treasury proclaimed that this really harmed the colonists by "depriving the Mother Country (so far as such practices extend) of those resources, which the commerce of the colonies secured to herself would constantly furnish, for their benefit and her own; when her trade and her manufactures by these means decline, her people decrease, and her power and revenues diminish, her efforts must be so much the fainter for general or partial good."[14] Privately, though, the Treasury worried that Britain might find herself unable to reverse the recent trends and strengthen the connection between the two countries. The colonies' "vast increase in territory and population," Grenville and his colleagues told the King in October 1763, "makes the proper regulation of their trade of immediate necessity, lest the continuance and extent of [these] dangerous evils . . . may render all attempts to remedy them hereafter infinitely more difficult, if not utterly impracticable."[15] This sense of political urgency spurred on and intensified the search at the Treasury during 1763–1765 for effective taxation and successful exertion of British authority in America. Grenville and his colleagues were well aware that "to establish the right of Parliament to impose these [taxes], and to produce an American revenue, is a great and necessary measure."[16] They were no less aware of the political consequences of failing to reach these goals.

Sources and Methodology

Contemporary documents relating to the American policies of the Grenville administration are, to say the least, limited in quantity. The Newcastle papers, a primary resource for scholars of the eighteenth century, contain little relevant material because the Duke was far from being a confidant of Grenville's and had little interest in America during these years.[17] The Earl of Bute, George III's favorite, was in seclusion during these years. Evidently he and the King did continue to carry on a frank and full correspondence, but the two men, aware of the sinister significance the political world attached to their friendship, prudently destroyed these letters.[18] Two of the most skilled reporters of parliamentary debates, Horace Walpole and Sir Roger Newdigate, concentrated on the debates concerning general warrants, John Wilkes, and— especially in the case of Newdigate's diary—local affairs. Grenville was estranged from his brother Richard, Earl Temple, and his brother-in-law, William Pitt, during these years, so he passed along none of his thoughts to them. William Knox had not yet established his close relationship with Grenville, so his papers reveal little about the workings of the Treasury during these years. The Earl of Buckinghamshire was a close friend of the First Lord's, but he spent most of 1763–1765 as Britain's ambassador to Russia, and most of his correspondence with Grenville dealt with domestic politics. Within the ministry itself, the Earl of Egremont not only was Grenville's brother-in-law, but he also served as the Secretary of State responsible for the colonies. Unfortunately for historians, he died on 25 August 1763. The papers of his successor, the Earl of Halifax, have been lost. The President of the Board of Trade, the Earl of Shelburne, resigned on 2 September 1763 after a few months in office. His papers have survived. Those of his successor, the Earl of Hillsborough, a man who respected Grenville and was his political friend, are scattered and incomplete.

This dismal litany could go on to list and explain the dearth of material on Grenville's American policies in other major collections of eighteenth-century politicians. The point, however, seems clear enough: Men one might ordinarily expect to have known and recorded information on these matters did not. This fact, plus the state of the records that have survived, has forced historians of Grenville's Treasury to search long and hard merely to describe the narrative of his tenure in office. Moreover, once documents are discovered, it is often necessary to try to attribute and date them; historians of this Treasury have constantly had their ingenuity and knowledge tested by unsigned, undated documents. Scholars have also been cursed by more than their share of elliptical sentences, passive constructions, and references to undescribed meetings. These challenges have, I suspect, caused them to focus on chronology and description. No historian has before completely separated and analyzed the tangle of motives at the Treasury. Nor has anyone ever described in detail how Grenville's fiscal, commercial, and political goals, at times singly and at times in combination, affected the Treasury's decisions during 1763–1765.[19]

I have not uncovered a substantial cache of new material, although I have found several pieces of evidence whose significance historians have overlooked. (Three of the most important of these may be found in the appendixes.) Rather, my findings rest upon a careful reading of the language of the familiar sources and an analysis of them based upon the political and administrative context of the times. I decided to follow this course because I discovered that however limited in quantity these sources were, they were of exceptional value.

Part of this value derives from the character of Grenville himself. A tireless worker, "a man born to public business, which was his luxury and amusement," he certainly read and digested the materials on America preserved in his personal papers and in the Treasury's official records. Doubtlessly he mastered them as well, if the testimony of a close friend may be believed: "His strength and his memory served him to recollect every argument that had been used, and to suffer scarce a word of any consequence to escape his notice" in parliamentary debates.[20] One need not speculate on whether Grenville read reports, or whether he was attentive to them, or whether he understood them. Contemporary testimony removes those areas from doubt.

Moreover, most of his contemporaries, with the exception of a few carping remarks made by men who had been particularly wounded by him in partisan battles, pointedly commented on his candor when he made public remarks.[21] Grenville had no reputation for deceit. Nor did he have any for the sort of eloquence that blinds men to the thoughts and reasoning, or lack of the same, beneath high-flown sentiments. Rather, he prided himself on his ability to explain his position fully and logically, to impress his audiences with his command of the subjects at hand. At this stage of his career, he usually avoided "passion and reproaches," even on occasions when "there was the justest occasion for both." He also followed the advice that he gave Charles Jenkinson: "Modesty and firmness are the two points I shall have in view; I shall draw no conclusions myself, but shall do all I can to make others draw them."[22] When one reads the words of Grenville, one finds the sentiments of a man with a reputation for careful honesty and for painstaking explanation. A reading of Grenville's thoughts on America confirms what his contemporaries said of him: He was not the sort to use words ignorantly, carelessly, imprecisely, or deceptively.

His closest friends did notice, however, that Grenville was not so perfectly honest as to discuss every consideration on his mind. Indeed, one of them admired "his wariness never to suffer himself to be drawn out beyond the line he had prescribed to himself."[23] When Grenville felt discussion of a subject was politically unwise, he remained quiet. Thus Grenville's careful silences before certain audiences—particularly on matters he was well-versed in, such as finance, commerce, or the precedents of government and the House of Commons—frequently are as useful an indicator of his motives as his comments are.

Fortunately, a substantial number of Grenville's comments on American matters have survived. At Grenville's request, Whately wrote two pamphlets that explained the Treasury's decisions in great detail and attacked the opposition's policies with equivalent vigor. One of these, *The regulations lately made concerning the colonies, and the taxes imposed upon them, considered,* was published in January 1765; the other, *Considerations on the trade and finances of this kingdom, and on the measures of administration with respect to those great national objects since the conclusion of the peace,* was published after the Rockingham ministry had undone many of Grenville's policies in the parliamentary session of 1765–1766. Both offer valuable insights into the motives of British ministers during this period, and *Regulations* demonstrates as well the Treasury's determination to convince the public in Britain and America of its goodwill toward the colonies. In addition to these two pamphlets, an M.P. named Nathaniel Ryder kept shorthand notes on Grenville's major addresses on American taxation during 1764–1765. While Ryder's accounts of the debates are occasionally ambiguous and are not so complete as Henry Cavendish's records of speeches during the sessions between 1768 and 1774, they are invaluable. Ryder was obviously interested in American affairs and therefore had an incentive to pay close attention to Grenville's remarks. Moreover, Ryder was a very conscientious diarist; he even noted when he failed to "much attend" to speeches.[24] Finally, the First Lord inadvertently provided reporters of his speeches and remarks the advantage of his tendency toward repetition. As his friend Thomas Pitt, Jr., explained, Grenville "never had done with a subject after he had convinced your judgment till he wearied your attention." A less friendly observer commented on Grenville's 9 March 1764 speech in this way: "Mr. Grenville spoke for two hours and forty minutes, much of it well, but too long, [and with] too many repetitions."[25] Whatever torments Grenville's audiences in the House of Commons suffered, though, the historian is the beneficiary from a speaking style so repetitious that a conscientious listener could hardly help but grasp his major points and recall the language he used to make them.[26]

Moreover, Grenville's comments about the colonies were recorded carefully by the colonial agents for their employers. Unfortunately, many of their reports about their meetings with him at the Treasury and their observations of him at Westminster have been lost. Still, many of the letters that have survived are from agents who were clearly conscientious and unusually well connected at Grenville's Treasury. Richard Jackson, the agent for Connecticut and Pennsylvania, served informally as Grenville's private secretary and was consulted by him on American policies in 1763–1764.[27] Charles Garth, the agent for South Carolina, was an extremely active agent who took his duties seriously. It is clear from his correspondence that the duty he took most seriously was "to procure the best intelligence possible" and to convey it as accurately as he could to his employers. Moreover, he was known at the Treasury as a supporter of government in the House.[28] And Jared Ingersoll, who sent home to Connecticut the longest reports of any agent, was personally close to Thomas Whately, discussed the stamp tax in detail with him several times during January 1765, and met at least once with Grenville, who respected his abilities.[29] These men not only carefully recorded Grenville's words, but they also sent to their employers their personal impressions about the First Lord's attitudes toward the colonies. It is significant that the agents' narratives of and reactions to their meetings with him are in essential agreement. As a result, their letters give a vivid, factually accurate, and emotionally sensitive picture of a persuasive, powerful man trying to convince Americans of his goodwill, yet artfully avoiding subjects that might give them an opportunity to take advantage of his kindness.

In addition to these various records, the papers of Charles Jenkinson, one of the Secretaries to the Treasury, and of Whately, the other Secretary, have survived. Jenkinson's files are extensive, reflecting his prodigious energy, wide-ranging interests and assignments, and dedication to duty. Like Grenville, he used words cautiously and precisely in public writings and debate.[30] His private papers display the same cautious precision and close reliance on facts and logic. Moreover, they reveal a man who resented colonial claims to independence from direct parliamentary taxation and who urged the necessity of nipping these pretensions in the bud, before the colonies became powerful enough to resist British authority. His frank correspondence with Benjamin Hallowell, the comptroller of the customs at Boston, offers interesting and valuable insights into the thoughts at the Treasury about taxing the colonies and establishing British authority. Whately's papers are much less extensive. Most of them may be found in Grenville's papers, a testimony in itself to his influence on the First Lord. Keenly interested in the colonies and deeply involved in the planning of American taxation, Whately maintained a close relationship with Jared Ingersoll and exchanged detailed and frank letters with John Temple, the surveyor-general of the customs for the northern district of colonies in America. Whately never betrayed anger with colonial claims, as Jenkinson did, and was particularly sensitive to the necessity of preventing, as much as possible, political "outrage" in the colonies at British taxes. Like Jenkinson, however, he was thoroughly committed to collecting an American revenue and to strengthening Britain's power in the colonies. Also like his colleague, he served Grenville energetically and well. His use of the language was sufficiently precise and careful, and his personal and political connection with Grenville so close, that the First Lord chose him rather than Jenkinson to write pamphlets defending the ministry's policies.[31] Because Grenville rewarded both men with his confidence, Whately's and Jenkinson's papers together provide reliable access to the Treasury's planning and implementation of American taxation.

These collections do more, however, than merely give some of the details and some of the motives behind the planning of American taxation. Together with Grenville's papers, the files of Jenkinson and Whately offer scholars numerous examples of the art and science of politics and government as practiced by Grenville. These examples further illuminate his reactions to the fiscal, commercial, and political problems of raising a revenue from the colonies. As one becomes aware of Grenville's fondness for calculating the political odds closely, maneuvering people into positions that sharply limited their freedom of action, and taking decisive gambles, one can understand more fully many of his tactics and much of his confidence as he plotted the course of colonial taxation. In a similar fashion, an appreciation of Grenville's wariness of inadvertently creating precedents that would bind Britain's freedom of action in dealing with the Irish Parliament makes some of his decisions on handling the subordinate legislatures in America much more comprehensible. His attitudes toward smuggling in British waters, and the tactics he followed to fight it there, give valuable clues to the decisions he made regarding the clandestine trade in the colonies. And the criteria the Treasury used during the planning of new taxation in Britain allow inferences to be made confidently about some of the processes of determining the "proper" taxes for Americans.[32] There is a danger, certainly, of using this material to make arguments by analogy and thus stretching interpretation beyond the limits justified by the evidence. Still, a knowledge of Grenville's attitudes and behavior in British politics and government can usefully supplement knowledge gained from a close analysis of the evidence relating to his choices on American matters during 1763–1765.

In sum, the offices, the connections, the relationships, and the personal and political characteristics of the authors of these various documents, combined with these men's intense interest and deep involvement in the decision to tax America, prove that their evidence, though limited in quantity, is the product of well-informed, responsible people who used words as carefully as they could. As such, if studied closely, the evidence affords an opportunity to describe Grenville's actions more completely and to sort out his motives more fully than ever before. This book is an attempt to take advantage of that opportunity.

Chapter I

The Background of Colonial Taxation
October 1760–February 1763

During the fall of 1762, Richard Rigby had an important duty. His friend and patron, the Duke of Bedford, was in Paris, serving as the British plenipotentiary to the French court for the purpose of negotiating peace. Before he left England, the Duke had asked Rigby to keep him informed about the internal politics of the Cabinet. He knew that a critical struggle was going on there between one of the Secretaries of State, George Grenville, and the First Lord of the Treasury, the Earl of Bute. Grenville was willing to fight on for another year in hopes of gaining more territorial concessions in the Caribbean; Bute feared that even one more year of war would result in national bankruptcy and impotence. As a fervent believer in the necessity of an immediate peace, and as the man charged with the negotiations, Bedford wanted fresh and accurate news on Bute's successes and failures at persuading other men in the government. Rigby worked hard to provide him with that intelligence. On 16 September, he reported to Bedford that Bute was tempting Charles Townshend, the Secretary at War and a brilliant orator in the House of Commons, with the position of President of the Board of Trade and a vote in the Cabinet. He also noted, "I believe Charles Townshend has a promise for his favorite American plan."[1]

For at least a decade, Townshend had believed that Parliament should impose duties on those imports into the colonies that did not "facilitate and extend our American commerce." He further believed that Parliament should appropriate the money collected for two purposes. The first was defense; this revenue could help defray those charges and thereby lighten the Mother Country's fiscal burdens. The second was the establishment of a permanent revenue for the support of the executive in American governments; this money could help defeat the assemblies' "settled design of drawing to themselves the ancient and established prerogatives wisely preserved in the Crown as the only means of supporting and continuing the superintendancy of the Mother Country, . . . by their annual bills of supply."[2] Thus, even before he knew whether peace would be made that year or not, Bute had informally learned about the potential fiscal and political advantages of taxing America. Moreover, he had apparently given informal assurance to an influential proponent of taxation of his approval and support for such a scheme.

On 3 November, Bedford signed the preliminary articles of peace. For the next five weeks, men in government immersed themselves in the effort to win, by as huge a majority as possible, a favorable address on the preliminaries from the two houses of Parliament. That goal they achieved on 9 December. Probably soon afterward, some men began to discuss informally among themselves ideas about colonial taxation, for the King noted in a letter he wrote to Bute in March 1763, "The subject was new to none, having been thought of the whole winter."[3]

The Men Involved

Very little contemporary evidence relating to these meetings exists. Fortunately, the letter George III wrote to Bute in March does reveal the men who were familiar with the subject. The Lords of the Treasury, unsurprisingly, had talked about taxing America. Bute probably expressed a desire to George III to hold preliminary discussions on this matter. After getting the King's approval, he brought up the subject with his colleagues. Sir Francis Dashwood, as Chancellor of the Exchequer and the man responsible for introducing and explaining Treasury legislation to the House of Commons, doubtlessly took part in the discussions. Because neither Bute nor Dashwood knew much about details of finance and taxation, they probably insisted that James Oswald, the member of the Treasury Board who was most knowledgeable on these subjects, play a prominent role. The fourth member, Lord North, was so intrigued by the business at the Treasury that he refused appointments to sinecures at Court to remain there. North was also determined to establish a reputation as a speaker on fiscal affairs in the Commons. His interest and ambition probably led him to pay close attention to the discussions and perhaps to enter into them fully. The remaining Treasury Lord, Sir John Turner, though usually indolent, was energetic and able when his interest was aroused. Whether America interested him at this time is unknown. The two Secretaries to the Treasury, Samuel Martin and Jeremiah Dyson, were present when an American tax was discussed at formal meetings of the Board. Martin's fiscal knowledge and acumen were on a par with Oswald's, and he had not hesitated to intervene in policy questions when the Duke of Newcastle was First Lord. Moreover, in 1759 he had recommended to Newcastle the imposing of a stamp tax on colonists. Still, there is no indication that he was active in these discussions. Finally, Bute's private secretary, Charles Jenkinson, knew about the Treasury's interest in colonial taxation. He could not take a direct hand in any meetings, of course, but he was busy collecting material for the First Lord's information.[4]

The King's letter mentioned by name two other men who had thought about American taxation. One was Henry Fox, the paymaster-general and the Leader of the House of Commons. Fox had almost no experience in devising new taxes; rather, he had specialized for many years in improving his own fortunes by skillful investment of the public's money. Still, the Leader of the House of Commons, who would have to defend the government's fiscal proposals, had to be kept informed about the Treasury's plans and offered a voice in their formulation. Furthermore, Fox had recently proved himself an expert at predicting the reactions of the House and managing its members. Called on in October 1762 to replace Grenville as Leader by a desperate Bute, he had steered the preliminaries triumphantly through the House. At the time of his appointment, Newcastle had accurately forecast, "He will begin by sounding everybody and turning out some for examples. He has agents working everywhere. He knows whom to employ, and how to work upon different dispositions and constitutions." Newcastle complained, moreover, that "No man knows better than he does the weakness and wickedness of mankind, or [how] to make the best use of it."[5] Such knowledge was obviously useful to men considering whether to impose a new tax or not.

The other politician from outside the Treasury whom the King mentioned was the man who had lost his place as Secretary of State and his position as Leader of the House in October 1762, George Grenville. At that time, Grenville had agreed to become First Lord of the Admiralty, the post he still held when men began to study the possibility of taxing America. He was proud of his understanding of the intricacies of trade and finance, and equally proud of his ability to communicate his understanding to less well informed people. Indeed, he was the ministry's principal spokesman on those subjects in the House of Commons. Not because the King, or Bute, or Fox trusted him; he had fought too hard and too long to defeat Bute's wishes during the peace negotiations for any of those men to do that. But Dashwood's ignorance of finance foretold his limitations in debate, and Oswald, whose expertise and oratory were comparable to Grenville's, suffered from the political liability of being as Scottish as the unpopular Bute. The First Lord had no choice but to inform Grenville about the discussions and to solicit his opinions. He also planned to keep a close eye on his colleague.[6]

In addition to the men he named in his letter, the King also noted that men in "every branch of government" had considered taxing America. Discussion of the subject with Welbore Ellis could hardly have been avoided, for he had replaced Townshend as Secretary at War in December and therefore became the minister responsible for telling the House how many troops were to be stationed in America, where they would be posted, and how much they would cost. Certainly Bute assumed that Ellis would be asked who would be paying for them, because he chose Ellis to announce in march 1763 that "the American force was intended to be paid for a future year by America."[7] At the very least, Ellis was privy to the decision the Treasury finally reached. Charles Townshend accepted the presidency of the Board of Trade on 23 February, having already expressed to Bute his views on colonial taxation. He too was aware of the decision to delay any imposition for the present. Townshend seems to have concurred in the original decision, for when he suddenly introduced a tax bill in mid-March, George III was furious at "this insidious proposal."[8] Undoubtedly, Bute also solicited the informal opinions of the two Secretaries of State, Egremont and the Earl of Halifax. As the Secretary for the Southern Department, Egremont was formally responsible for the colonies. Protocol demanded that he be asked for his opinion on colonial taxation. Moreover, because Egremont was responsible for devising a scheme for the settlement and governance of the new acquisitions and because this would necessarily entail some thought on taxation, his would not be a careless, ill-informed judgment from a minister whose attention was on other duties. Nor would that of Halifax. The other Secretary of State, during a long tenure at the Board of Trade, had established a reputation as an expert on colonial affairs and as an advocate of imperial reform. Bute had probably guessed, if he did not know for sure, that Halifax had convinced Charles Townshend of the necessity of establishing a permanent revenue. Impressed by his background, Egremont thought Halifax would be a useful man and planned to consult with him. Bute probably felt the same way.[9]

Bute and Egremont shared another adviser as well. Egremont had asked the Earl of Mansfield, the Lord Chief Justice and the preeminent jurist on the bench, to study the preliminaries, to examine French proposals for the definitive treaty, and to suggest any changes that seemed advisable. Mansfield had applied himself to the job with vigor, aiming at a clarity of expression that would admit of only one interpretation, and that one favorable to British interest. Like any good lawyer, he assumed that the other party to a contract would always be looking for ways to twist its language to his advantage. Mansfield accordingly advised certain precautions. Some of his precautions seemed excessive to Bute. Other comments seemed "indecent" to George III, proving again to his satisfaction Mansfield's "disinclination

to government, and his own opinion of his superiority of abilities over the rest of the world." Still, Bute wanted to include the Lord Chief Justice in the discussion on American policy, so when he discovered that Mansfield had become interested in matters concerning commerce in America and the new acquisitions, Bute asked the King to invite him into the Royal Closet. Mansfield began this session by praising highly Bute's "conduct in having prevented the Duke of Bedford from spoiling the peace by making too many concessions." The King responded on cue by "dropp[ing] that the work was not yet finished, that the making a good use of what we had gained was a difficult though agreeable affair." Thus encouraged, Mansfield divulged his idea that the Cabinet should agree on a plan for establishing the new colonies *before* asking the Board of Trade for advice. After "the properest plan [was] fixed on, then the Board of Trade should be written in a public letter for their advice (but privately instructed what they should say)." If not, he explained, "The Board of Trade would probably send, for want of lights, a plan that would be improper, which would be a very unpleasant affair."[10] Lawyer Mansfield was delicately telling his royal client not to trust Charles Townshend. He was also diplomatically but firmly advising King George that decisions on America were political decisions of the highest import for the nation and should be made by the men holding the great offices and bearing the responsibility for the conduct of public affairs— not by minor politicians, clerks, and other functionaries at a subordinate board. Finally, he was quietly warning the King that seeking and maintaining unanimity within the government on American policies would be highly desirable. Bute must have found this advice familiar and pleasing. He had been basing his investigation into the merits of taxing the colonies on similar procedures and principles.

Common Assumptions: The Significance of the National Debt

The investigation evidently proceeded as calmly and as unanimously as Bute could have wished. Had there been serious disagreements, men who held the minority opinions would surely have recorded their views, then or later. Some might have protested publicly at that moment. In any case, quarrels in Bute's administration usually became public knowledge, because keen observers like Rigby, aware that many of the ministers disliked others personally and distrusted them politically, kept alert for signs of discord. Such signs appeared often. Bute and his colleagues frequently fought among themselves over policy questions, political alliances, and patronage arrangements. Reports from Rigby to Bedford normally contained intelligence like this from a February 1763 letter: "The Cabinet as usual are not harmonious."[11] Yet despite the close scrutiny of Rigby and others, despite the touchy feelings among the participants and their readiness to dispute with one another publicly, no document exists describing the substance of any informal talks, let alone one detailing disagreements. This startling absence of evidence suggests the strong probability that these men easily reached consensus, that they found the answers to many basic questions to be so obvious as to preclude argument and, almost, discussion.[12] It is unlikely that Bute bullied, or bribed, or begged these men into this agreement. Any extraordinary efforts by him to coerce or persuade would have been noted in public records or private papers, and no documents fitting this description exist either. More likely, these men found they were reaching similar conclusions more or less independently, just as Mansfield and Bute did.

Apparently the consensus on taxing the colonies was based on certain assumptions that these men strongly believed in and held in common. Among the assumptions that created consensus, one of the most important was these men's fear that making payments on the national debt might undermine Britain's power and prosperity. This worry had taken firm root in their minds long before the war was over. Almost as soon as Britain committed herself in 1756 to a European war against France, Bute and his pupil, the future George III, began to worry about the consequences financing that war would have on the country's future. In 1757, the Prince had hoped that he and Bute would one day "free [the nation] from her present load of debts."[13] As the war dragged on and the debt burgeoned, that hope dimmed, and both men became more alarmed. Neither knew much about the intricacies of finance, but both had learned enough to know that the government was paying for the war by borrowing money. They also understood that the government's creditors usually demanded, and received, pledges that it would devote future receipts from specific taxes to paying the interest and principal of the loan. The greater the debt, therefore, the heavier the tax burden on Britain's people would be and the longer they would have to bear it. And, as the Prince and Bute knew, the people would have to bear this burden faithfully. Failure to meet interest and principal payments would expose the nation as a poor risk, and in future emergencies creditors either would refuse to loan her money or would try to protect their investment by charging her high interest rates. Yet maintaining the nation's credit rating, Bute and George learned, exposed Britain to another serious danger. A government desperate for revenue could not merely tax the land and luxuries of the propertied classes; it would have to impose heavy duties on the coal, candles, windows, salt, beer, and other necessities of the industrious poor. If these duties were too heavy, employers would have to raise wages, or their laborers could not afford these bare necessities. Manufacturers would respond to the rising cost of labor by raising the price of finished products. As they did so, their goods would become less competitive in international markets. Sales of British manufactures would decrease. The amount of money this most valuable commerce brought back to Britain would dwindle. The country's economy would proportionately decline. Manufacturers would be forced to let people go. The industrious poor would either emigrate or forget about marrying, reproducing, and leading useful lives and devote themselves instead to riot and begging. Thus, a government necessarily struggling to preserve Britain's credit with heavy taxation would necessarily be running the risk of generating serious economic and social crises. Neither Bute nor George III felt that this point had been reached when George II died in October 1760. They did, however, readily agree to include in the new King's first speech to Parliament a statement indicating, "The greatest uneasiness which I feel at this time is in considering the uncommon burdens necessarily brought upon my faithful subjects."[14]

Around the same time, Grenville was advising William Pitt to disapprove of the Treasury's plan to increase the tax on each barrel of beer by three shillings. Because the revenue collected from this tax would be *"cruelly wrung from the briny sweat of industry,"* it would effectively force wages and prices upward and ultimately injure the nation's trade. He was so convinced of this, he told Pitt, that his conscience would not permit him to let the tax pass unopposed. When Pitt refused to intervene, Grenville did speak against it in the House. It was the first time he had ever publicly contradicted Pitt. Newcastle fretted that Bute had caused this apostasy by promising to make Grenville the Chancellor of the Exchequer. This fear was probably unfounded, though surely Grenville did expect that his speech would be received favorably at Court. Still, his ambition should not obscure his genuine opposition to this particular tax; he saw to its repeal after he became First Lord of the Treasury. Like Bute and the King, Grenville was becoming increasingly uneasy at the growth of the debt and the possible effects that paying it would have on the country's economy.[15]

This uneasiness mounted during 1761–1762 as the war dragged on. Britain's deep involvement in the war in Germany had frustrated the King, Bute, and Grenville for years. None of these men thought the nation derived much benefit from the monstrous expense of subsidizing allies and sending an army there. In December 1761, in his first major address as Leader, Grenville reminded the House of his past opposition to Britain's participation in the continental war, stated his continued opposition, and declared that he supported the maintaining of that involvement only "upon the principle of *honor*." He also took care, however, to tell the House that honor did not demand that the nation destroy itself and to list circumstances that would require abandonment of allies. Grenville included among them a situation in which "the taxes upon your commerce, agriculture, and manufactures . . . run in a circle until they became impossible" and the nation's goods became too expensive to compete effectively in international markets. He did not claim that this situation was about to occur, but he made plain his feeling that subsidizing German allies should cease soon.[16] James Oswald made similar points, bluntly telling the House that "he hoped it would be known abroad that it was duty and not interest that made us pursue" the war in Germany.[17] Bute and the King applauded these sentiments and persuaded Charles Townshend to change his views on the wisdom of continuing the German war to conform with theirs.[18]

The concern of these men about the national debt and the taxes necessary to service it increased rapidly during 1762. In January, Townshend expressed in the House his fear that "we should sink from a dream of ambition to a state of bankruptcy." With Spain's entrance into the war, Townshend argued, Britain must limit her involvement in Germany.[19] In February, Mansfield speculated that reneging on the promise to pay Prussia £670,000 might avert bankruptcy.[20] In May, Grenville and Oswald, aided by accounts Samuel Martin clandestinely sent them, accused Newcastle, the last defender of the German war in the government, of needlessly increasing the public debt. After they persuaded the King and Bute that the government needed a vote of credit for only £1,000,000 rather than the £2,000,000 the Duke wanted, Newcastle resigned, with the King's parting hope that his accounts "would be full" ringing in his ears.[21]

After the parliamentary session ended in June 1762, Jenkinson coolly summarized the financial status of the nation in a paper, "Observations on the money faculties of the state." He pointed out that before the war taxes raised £8,400,000 annually; now they raised £9,800,000. "The increased burden on the people" was £1,400,000 annually; consequently, the nation's power to collect additional revenue was significantly diminished. Before the war, he went on, the Treasury could borrow £1,000,000 and pay only £27,000 in yearly annuities; now, to get £1,000,000, the Treasury was promising to pay £50,000. To raise this money, the government had to impose many new taxes. These new taxes diminished the produce of the older ones whose surplus was appropriated to the sinking fund. As a result, the sinking fund now produced £1,750,000 annually, rather than the £2,400,000 it would have generated had the war not occurred and interest on the public debt been held at 3 percent. "While the extent of the public services is continued," Jenkinson observed, "the necessity of performing them by loans must continue also, and the mischiefs attending that method must go on increasing." He hardly needed to conclude formally that the nation's capacity to raise more revenue and her ability to pay off debts "are very considerably impaired."[22] Bute could see that for himself. By late July, his vision of "the long train of calamities that the continuation of this war [will] bring" convinced him that Britain had to make peace that year. The King agreed. "In a year or two," he told Bute, "from being brought to a state of beggary we shall be forced to sue for peace" and be in "the shameful situation of setting down with what [we] may be permitted to keep by the French."[23]

Grenville, however, dissented from this gloomy conclusion. He believed Britain could safely fight on for at least another year, if she limited her expenses by engaging only in defensive warfare in Portugal and in naval operations elsewhere. Moreover, he believed she should continue the war until France ceded enough Caribbean territory to insure that Britain would dominate the sugar trade. During the summer of 1762, he fought Bute tenaciously and well, converting a majority of the Cabinet to this goal and forcing Bute and Egremont to negotiate secretly with the French in an effort to circumvent the Cabinet's instructions. George III angrily explained Grenville's persistence by calling it political timidity. Grenville was so afraid of defending a treaty against Pitt's attacks, reasoned the King, that he unrealistically wanted France to cede everything. This accusation was unfair. Before Pitt left the Cabinet, Grenville had sympathized with "the opinion of many [that Guadeloupe] is the most important [conquest] of all." He had also felt that, if possible, that island would become even more crucial to Britain's postwar interest if France retained fishing rights off Newfoundland. By 1762, the Cabinet had decided that France could fish, and Guadeloupe, Grenville bitterly recalled, had been "given up at an extraordinary council called when [I] was ill in bed, and not able to attend it."[24] Apparently he thought that dominating Europe's sugar supply would enable Britain to maintain her favorable balance of trade with the Continent, even if the weight of taxes increased the price of British manufactures to the point that they competed much less successfully there. Sugar, therefore, was of crucial importance to the nation's power and prosperity. He believed this deeply enough to make a barely veiled ultimatum to Bute in September. Britain had to demand compensation for Havana, preferably Florida and Puerto Rico, or he would be unable to defend the preliminaries in the House. Even with these concessions, he added, the political situation was so volatile that the best course for the government to take would be "laying the preliminaries of the ensuing peace before Parliament for [its] opinion previous to their being signed."

Grenville did not point out that this would give him as Leader a good chance to veto every article he disapproved of. Nor did he call attention to the fact that if the House discussed articles in great detail, the debate would take so long that Britain in effect would have to continue the war for another year. Bute, however, did not miss these implications. He was willing to demand Florida or Puerto Rico as compensation, but he could not agree to the rest without giving up control over the negotiations to Grenville. If he gave up control, the war would go on, and the country would be ruined. With George III's reluctant approval, Bute asked Fox to become Leader. For all of Fox's cynicism, he did believe peace had to be made and was confident he could persuade the House to approve it. Halifax, another man who appreciated the necessity of an immediate peace, took Grenville's place as Secretary of State. Stunned by the ruthlessness of this coup and isolated politically, Grenville accepted as consolation the post of First Lord of the Admiralty and agreed to support the preliminaries. The King signed the articles, and Fox began working on arguments and inducements that would persuade members to make a favorable address on them.[25]

As Fox's campaign began, he and Bute also started to face the first consequence of the war. As many men had predicted, the end of the war did not mean the end of heavy taxation. The Treasury decided that Parliament needed to retain the most productive tax, the one on the assessed value of land, at the wartime level of four shillings in the pound.[26] Other taxes would have to remain at the same rate as well. Bute had toyed with the idea of reducing the tax on beer when peace came, but this, he now realized, was impossible. When he and Fox drew up the King's speech that would open Parliament, they included a reminder, "We must expect, for some time, to feel the consequences of [the most vigorous and expensive efforts] to a very considerable degree."[27]

Thus, all the men involved in the informal consideration of whether to tax America had believed for a long time that the war was severely straining Britain's financial system. Most of them were convinced the nation had come perilously close to fiscal bankruptcy and diplomatic impotence. Although Grenville had doubted that such a crisis was imminent, he could feel no more confident in 1763 than his colleagues about Britain's future, for he was painfully aware that his country had failed to secure domination over the fishery and sugar trades, two commerces he regarded as vital to its prosperity after the war. None of these men disagreed with Bute's diagnosis that taxation would remain heavy in Britain for years to come. Nor would any of them have been surprised if this heavy taxation raised the price of British manufactures to less competitive levels and caused a disturbing slump in commerce. Members of the Cabinet did not at that time make explicit the source of their apprehensions about the advantages foreign competitors would enjoy, probably because they found it politically inexpedient to do so while they were keeping taxes at wartime levels. But Whately did provide—after he and Grenville left office in 1765—a brief explanation of the reasoning at Whitehall as peace began. Whately began his account by asserting, "That the wealth and power of Great Britain depends upon its trade is a proposition which it would be equally absurd in these times to dispute or to prove." During the war, the high levels of taxation increased the price of labor and materials in Britain. At the same time, the high interest rates the government was willing to pay for loans made it much more difficult and expensive for private subjects to borrow money. Finally, the collapse of the French carrying trade made extraordinary and depleting demands on the British merchant marine. The full effects of these factors that raised the price of British goods would be felt after the war: "Rival nations (not before rivals) may undersell us at foreign markets in many items and even become competitors at our own." Moreover, taxes would have to remain high to maintain interest payments, and "the taxes necessary for paying the interest of so large a [debt] must sooner or later be detrimental to many branches of the manufactures, produce, and trade of this Kingdom." Whately concluded by noting that this "evil was unavoidable when the expense [during the war] was so great." During peacetime, though, the government had to take measures to soften its effect, or Britain's commerce, and thus her power, would decline.[28] To say that Bute and his colleagues were deeply interested in 1763 in finding any way of safely lightening the burden on British taxpayers would be an understatement.

Common Assumptions:
The Necessity for a Larger Military Presence in America

According to the King's speech on 25 November 1762, "Lay[ing] the foundation of that economy which we owe to ourselves, and to our posterity, . . . can alone relieve this nation from [her] heavy burdens." This foundation could best be laid, George III and his advisers agreed, by reducing the amount of money spent on the armed services. The King plunged vigorously into the discussions on converting the army and navy to peace establishments, urging his ministers to finish the job and remarking with some asperity to Bute on 6 January 1763, "If we go on deferring [the return of men and ships from India], God only knows to what extent our debt will still increase." His passion for economy was genuine, as was his Cabinet's.[29]

Still, these men knew that the height of foolishness was an economy that shortsightedly sacrificed security. Even before making any inquiries, they took for granted that the military establishment in America would be much larger than it had been before the war. Canada, the Floridas, and the land west of the Appalachians had populations that had been hostile to Britain for nearly a century; large contingents of regular troops would have to be stationed there, and in areas adjacent to them, in order to secure these new colonists' loyalty and help British civilians administer their government. Once the colonies were secured, their defense probably would still require the presence of regulars. The French, after all, had in 1762 suddenly seized Newfoundland, and many other new conquests were equally as vulnerable and potentially as valuable. As early as December 1761, Grenville had speculated that guarding new conquests might prove almost as burdensome as making them. Neither he nor the other ministers knew until Ellis calculated it in February that the pay of the troops in America would be £224,903, but none seemed surprised by this figure.[30] Moreover, this sum did not include extraordinaries, contingencies, and the cost of transport. Nor did it include the increased cost of the fleet that the government would have to station in American waters. Before the preliminaries came before Parliament, Jenkinson had in his files a plan for the disposition of the navy's ships that projected that a fleet of twenty-six ships, manned by 3,290 sailors, would be sufficient when peace came. In 1750, the totals had been seventeen ships and 2,360 men.[31] No one among the powerful in government objected to the idea of a larger fleet in North America, probably because the possibility of French vessels carrying on an extensive smuggling operation in the Gulf of St. Lawrence had so disturbed the entire Cabinet during 1762.[32] No one doubted, either, that the cost of securing and defending America by land and sea would be high.

This new peacetime expense in a time of financial and commerical crisis, plus the fact that these forces would be defending Americans, naturally raised the question of American assistance in paying for them. One need not speculate much over the answer George III and his advisers inclined toward; one need only recall their behavior once they determined that the security of the British Isles also required a larger peacetime army. This decided, Halifax devised an appealing plan for painlessly supporting that force. The King could now pay out of Irish revenues up to 12,000 soldiers in Ireland during peacetime, without any special vote or appropriation for that purpose by the Irish Parliament. Suppose His Majesty, in the lawful exercise of his prerogative, increased that force to 18,000: Could he then take enough money out of Irish revenues, again without vote or appropriation, to support the fifteen extra regiments? Halifax said he could. Tempted by the prospects of having a larger army without expense to Britain, the King and Cabinet agreed. Halifax had served as Lord Lieutenant of Ireland, the rest of the Cabinet were experienced politicians, Bute and the King were not fools—all of them could accurately predict an adverse political reaction in the Irish House of Commons to this. Moreover, this plan had dubious claims to legality. When George III solicited the opinion of the Attorney-General, he quickly replied, on 27 December 1762, that sixty years of precedents indicated that during peace the King could not use his prerogative to increase the size of the army in England or Ireland above 12,000 men. In 1756, he went on, George II had obtained an address from the British Parliament before he enlarged the army in Ireland. This opinion had no immediate effect on the ministry's determination to go ahead with the plan. The ministers probably anticipated that it would be very popular in England; they perhaps believed that "no measure [could] be more universally agreeable to, or more ardently desired by" the Anglo-Irish than one that promised even greater control over the Roman Catholic majority.[33] Whatever their reasoning, the weight of precedent and the certain opposition of a subordinate parliament did not deter them at all. Their primary concern was to relieve the British taxpayer whenever possible, and thus protect as much as they could the nation's fiscal strength and commercial prosperity. If this could be done in Ireland, or, for that matter, in America, it should be done.

Common Assumptions: The Prosperity of America

No one in the Cabinet doubted that the Irish could afford the additional expense. Could colonists? How prosperous were Americans? No one in Bute's administration paused long over these questions. They had answered them before the parliamentary debates over the preliminaries and then stated their conclusions to the two Houses.

During the debates, the administration's supporters flatly predicted, "North America alone would supply the deficiencies of our trade in every other part of the world." They noted that customs records clearly showed that "the exports to North America for some years past [have] been one quarter of the British trade." "The greater part" of these exports were "our manufactures." Sales of those manufactures represented "a clear profit to the nation." In the past, these sales had increased as the colonies' population grew. In the future, it was reasonable to assume that "our American planters would by the very course of their natural propagation in a very short time furnish out a demand for our manufactures as large as all the working hands of Britain could possibly supply." Moreover, the planters would continue to pay for these manufactures as they had in the past, with products that could be reexported to foreign markets, and with flax seed, "naval stores, indigo, iron, and furs, which may be deemed materials for manufactures, and therefore bring returns from foreigners equal to their value." At present, the commerce to and from the colonies "may be fairly said to yield full half the national balance Great Britain [gained] by trade." After colonists developed the riches of the new acquisitions, it would doubtless yield more. The American colonies would "increase population and of course the consumption of our manufactures, pay us for them by their trade with foreigners, and thereby [give] employment to millions of inhabitants in Great Britain and Ireland." Thus, the ministry concluded, they "are of the utmost consequence to the wealth, safety, and independence of these Kingdoms and must continue so for ages to come."[34]

To be sure, Fox and his cohorts were to a certain extent indulging themselves in political hyperbole when they made these statements. They could be sure that Pitt would stress the value of the sugar trade, and they reasoned that a good offense would be the best defense. Did they believe all they said, or were they consciously exaggerating? Grenville certainly must have felt uncomfortable as he sat silent and listened to colleagues attack the sugar trade as essentially unprofitable. If he spoke on that matter, he probably noted that the French islands were less defensible than before and that they now had only British sources for food and lumber, and he probably expressed the hope that Britain could use these advantages to gain more of the sugar trade.[35] Grenville may have also felt that his colleagues were exaggerating the future value of the American commerce. But he certainly knew that their description of its present state was accurate, for he had access to the same customs statistics that they did. In 1751, these statistics revealed, Americans had imported £1,376,204 worth of goods from England. In 1760, they imported goods valued at £2,688,815. These figures showed by themselves an immense expansion of the American market; moreover, a man as well versed in commercial affairs as Grenville knew that the numbers were too low, because they did not include any smuggled goods. The trade had slumped in 1761 to £2,041,884, but this decline did not alter the overall impression that the figures gave.[36] British colonists in

America were prospering. Even if one doubted that Americans would soon buy *all* the manufactured goods British laborers were capable of making, there seemed to be no reason to fear that they would stop prospering and that the market would stop growing. A people so prosperous certainly could afford to contribute something to their own defense.

Common Assumptions: The Necessity for Coercing Americans

None of the men who considered taxing the colonists believed that they would voluntarily assume some of the fiscal burden of their defense. Halifax and Townshend had long since noticed and decried the colonial assemblies' refusal to part with any money except on their own terms and for their own purposes. During 1762, Egremont had frequently heard about colonists who traded with the French and assemblies that balked at supporting the war effort with money, men, and supplies. When the Earl looked through his files, he quickly discovered that this conduct had gone on in other years as well. In 1762, the King publicly expressed his disapproval of undutiful refusal by the Pennsylvania and North Carolina assemblies to raise troops and commanded Egremont to inform them officially of his displeasure.[37] Grenville had no direct connection with the colonies during the war. Before it, though, his brother Henry had served as governor of Barbados. "There is such an indisposition in the people of this island to provide properly for their defense," he wrote Grenville in 1751, "that I should be heartily sorry to have [its] protection . . . in my hands in the day of danger."[38] In 1760, George Bubb Dodington, a close political friend of Bute's, observed that the colonies "contribute but little themselves, and in any necessaries that are to be provided, or furnished for the defense of other brethren that are in danger, they make their bargain as well, and keep it as ill, as if it was made between the Cabinet Council here and their great support, the Common Council of London."[39] Bute may never have heard Dodington's opinion on the colonies' conduct during the war, but he certainly knew about the bargain some colonies had made. During the war, Pitt had felt compelled to promise that Parliament would reimburse colonies that levied, clothed, and paid provincial troops. On 14 January 1763, the Treasury began calculating how much money Britain owed for one year. The bill eventually came to £133,333.[40]

Agreement

These experiences taught Bute and his colleagues that Parliament would have to force the colonists to contribute to their defense. The method of coercion that came most readily to mind was some form of taxation. None of these men ever doubted that imposing a tax on the colonies was well within Parliament's constitutional rights. Probably most of them expected some protest against the exercise of that right. Certainly no one in Britain liked to pay taxes, and, as a paper that circulated at the Treasury, the Board of Trade, and Egremont's office during the early days of Grenville's administration noted, "The inhabitants of the maritime provinces . . . already begin to entertain some extraordinary opinions concerning their relation to and dependence on their Mother Country."[41] This anticipated protest deterred the Bute administration no more than did the expected outcry in Ireland against paying for 18,000 troops. Indeed, Halifax, Townshend, and possibly Egremont thought that the existence of such "extraordinary opinions" was a good reason to tax Americans and appropriate some of the revenue for the support of civil government. Others, most notably Grenville, did not approve of any such use of the money.[42] All agreed, though, that large military forces must be stationed in Ireland and America. All agreed that the two peoples could help pay for their own defense. All agreed that the two peoples should help pay, because British taxpayers needed every relief their government could find for them, in order to avoid overburdening the nation's finances and overpricing her manufactured goods. Finally, all agreed that the Treasury and the Board of Trade should look for "proper" ways to raise money in America. By late January 1763, the Treasury had begun. In February, Egremont began preparing to ask the Board of Trade "in what way, least burdensome and palatable to the colonies, can [Americans] contribute towards the support of the additional expense which must attend their civil and military establishments upon the arrangement [for the new settlements] which your Lordships shall propose?"[43]

Chapter II

A Cautious Beginning: Bute's Ministry and American Taxation, January–March 1763

None of the men from outside the Treasury who participated in the preliminary discussions interfered very much in the initial search for a "proper" American tax. Charles Townshend was out of office from mid-December to mid-February. Although Ellis consulted with him on War Office business, and thus kept Townshend au courant on the ministry's plans for the army in America and Ireland, the bargaining over the powers he would have if he accepted the presidency of the Board of Trade consumed most of his time. Converting the army to a peace establishment fully occupied Ellis. "To have the principal hand in reducing a large army," Rigby pointed out to Bedford, "is a most irksome and unpleasant task."[1] Equally burdensome was the job of reducing a large navy. Grenville had to make difficult decisions quickly about the navy's men and material. Which officers to keep on active duty, which to put on half-pay, how many sailors should stay, which ships should be repaired, which ships should be decommissioned, where fleets should be stationed and in what force, which instructions should be amended—the First Lord of the Admiralty had to make a good beginning on answering these questions by late January 1763, when the House would discuss the naval estimates.[2] If Grenville thought of taxation at all, it was probably briefly and in the most general terms. At the same time, Halifax, Egremont, and Mansfield were having "some dark suspicions about *French faith*" and trying to write into the final treaty language that would guarantee British fishermen access to the best banks and coves off Newfoundland. Constructing securities against French treachery in this and other areas kept these men busy. Their thoughts did not turn toward the details of colonial policy until after the signing of the definitive treaty on 10 February.[3] Like their colleagues, they could not spare much time from their immediate concerns. Moreover, after Parliament reconvened from the Christmas vacation on 20 January, the business of the session was added to their other duties.

Jenkinson had fewer and less pressing concerns than these men. He also had the advantages of being highly dedicated and apparently tireless. But Jenkinson's activities and influence were determined by Bute, and Bute's dedication and stamina were fast waning. Had Fox desired to, he probably could have persuaded Bute to take an active role when the Treasury discussed possible taxes. Before Fox became Leader of the House, the King and Bute had been reacting to the oncoming parliamentary discussion of the negotiations passively. They had not been canvassing members in advance of the House's meeting and were responding to criticism of the terms of peace by "rest[ing] the whole singly upon this, the impossibility of our carrying on the war." By example and argument, Fox had changed their attitude. His "already foretelling victory is most comfortable," the King observed on 11 October. Soon George III and Bute were helping Fox make political contacts and were aggressively stressing the merits of the cessions they had gained, rather than defensively referring to Britain's fiscal straits.[4] Bute respected Fox's abilities and felt a debt of gratitude to him after their victory on 9 December. But Fox did not try to cash in that debt on the issue of American taxation. His burst of energy during the fall had tired him and made him ill. His wife was reminding him of his determination to quit active politics. He wanted to be made a peer, and he was willing to serve as Leader for the rest of the session to insure that the King would grant that wish. But he did not intend to get involved in matters of policy.[5]

Bute, also, desperately wanted to retire. "I feel every day," he wrote on 28 November 1762, "how little nature has formed me to practice those arts by which ministers support themselves." Moreover, he felt that the strain of handling "the extravagant demands of every person who [came] near [him and] the base ingratitude of numbers whose situation [he had] made" was wearing him out physically and mentally. Once the definitive peace was signed, Bute reasoned, he could honorably quit office and public life. He concentrated his energies on reaching that date without revealing his weakening will to govern. After resigning, Bute admitted that "he had thought little of taxes; his object was the Peace."[6]

Men at the Treasury therefore had little interference from within the government during December and January. They also enjoyed a freedom from any pressure from outside the administration. To provide them with that sense of freedom, Bute and his colleagues did not publicly discuss their preliminary thoughts and decisions on American taxation. Clearly, the ministers saw no reason to give Pitt and Newcastle time to prepare arguments and drum up support against any proposals for new taxation that the ministry might make. There may have been another reason for the ministry's silence, one that the Treasury would particularly appreciate. The ministers may have been trying to protect against the possibility that the Treasury would be forced to make a hasty decision.

In their preliminary, informal discussions, Bute and the others had decided *in theory* in favor of raising a revenue in America. Whether this decision actually would be translated into a new tax, or into more vigorous collection of existing revenue legislation, or into some more binding form of requisition, had not been decided. Nor had they decided whether they would begin raising an American revenue this year, wait until next year, or defer it for years to come, or, even, whether they would decide against the entire scheme. Without doubt, a great deal of information and extremely persuasive arguments would have been required to convince these men that they should postpone indefinitely any attempt to raise money in America. Still, all of them were probably aware, to varying degrees, of the peculiar difficulties of taxing colonists. No colonial tax, for instance, could seriously impair Americans' ability to buy more and more British goods in the future. As Egremont noted in his 5 May 1763 letter to the Board of Trade, he was interested in discovering "in what way least burdensome . . . to the colonies, can they contribute towards the support of the additional expense which must attend their civil and military establishments?" If a tax was burdensome, the market that these men believed was essential to preserving British manufacturing and commerce from the worst effects of the national debt would shrink, with potentially disastrous results. Moreover, no colonial tax would depend for its execution upon a presumption that the taxpayer would voluntarily pay it out of habit, as was essentially the case with the land tax in England. Even men nearly ignorant about the colonies knew that the government would have to assume that the taxpayer would look for ways to dodge the tax. With this in mind, Egremont commanded the Board of Trade to look for ways of tapping the colonists' wealth that were not only the "least burdensome," but were also "palatable to the colonies." It was clear that devising a tax to meet both criteria would not be easy and that a "proper" tax could not be established without "much information."[7]

It was also clear that in theory an American tax would be as popular in the House as it was to Bute and his colleagues. As early as January 1760, men were saying in London that the colonies "for whose protection [an army] will be established" would have to "bear at least the greatest share of charge for it . . . ; this will occasion a tax." In December 1762, one of Newcastle's followers responded to news about the government's plan to station 18,000 men in Ireland by telling the Duke that the colonists should be immediately forced to pay a "considerable" part of the expense of their defense. "If we once take upon ourselves the whole burden," warned Lord Kinnoul, "it will be every year more and more difficult to throw any part of it on them."[8] The ministers may not have known that Kinnoul held this opinion, but surely they guessed after nearly three years of rumors that some people did. Prematurely revealing the results of their informal discussions might encourage those people to pressure the Treasury in and out of the House to tax the colonies this year. Unsure that they wanted to do that, yet fearful of the pressures that might be brought to bear, Bute and his colleagues kept quiet. They succeeded in keeping the preliminary discussion secret for some time. Neither Rigby nor Newcastle heard anything about the discussions on taxing America until 19 February. At that time, they learned from an unknown source that when the Secretary at War discussed the army estimates, he would state "that the troops for North America will, it is hoped, be paid another year by the colonies themselves."[9]

The Treasury: Administrative Reform and a Linen Tax

There is no evidence directly linking this statement of hope with any activities at the Treasury. Indeed, there is little evidence that suggests that board was investigating possible American taxes before mid-February. Dashwood considered at least three proposals for new British taxes seriously enough to collect papers on them, but his files evidently contain no comparable papers on colonial taxation. North saved a paper examining the state of the King's prerogative revenues in the plantations, including quitrents in royal colonies and the 4.5 percent ad valorem tax on exports from the British West Indies. The report was critical of some colonial practices, particularly land speculation, and concluded with this advice: "Many regulations are now become absolutely necessary with regard to the government of the colonies, as well as the King's particular revenue; some . . . [may] be obtained through the rules of offices of government at home; others not attainable without the authority of Parliament." Throughout their careers, North and Dashwood were attracted to administrative reforms. Perhaps the paper's presence in North's files indicates that during 1762–1763 he was principally interested in reforming the procedures of collecting and managing revenues already being raised in the colonies.[10] Certainly he and Dashwood voted with the rest of the Treasury on 16 February to ask the customs commissioners which customs officers were absent, with or without leave, from their posts in America. In part, this interest in ending sinecures in the American customs service was a sign of the Treasury's growing interest in the possibilities of collecting a larger revenue by enforcing the plantation duties and the tax on foreign molasses imported into the colonies. Still, the Treasury did not express an official interest in either tax until March 1763.[11]

James Oswald probably caused this delay by concentrating the Treasury's energies and time on a proposal of his. At some time before the end of January, he had realized that his influence with Bute, plus the obvious desire of other ministers for a "proper" American revenue, gave him a unique opportunity to realize goals he had had since 1744. Oswald had long believed that duties on foreign linens imported into Britain should be higher. He had also felt for many years that the government should stop granting liberal drawbacks (that is, repayments) of those duties to British merchants who reexported foreign linens to the colonies. The implementation of these policies, he hoped, would give British manufacturers of linen a competitive edge in domestic and colonial markets. Even if they could not take advantage of the government's assistance, the nation could console herself with the additional revenue. In the past, linen merchants had had enough influence in Parliament to keep the full drawback in force and duties reasonably low.[12] By 1763, though, men in Parliament had heard from the opponents of the peace treaty dark references to a "want of trade" in the future, references that had not been disputed by the ministry, except to say, "There was . . . no reason to dread that want of trade which their adversaries insinuated, since North America alone would supply the deficiencies of our trade in every other part of the world."[13] Thus a proposal that offered the prospect of either increasing the trade in British goods to America or indirectly raising money from Americans would be very appealing to them. The merchants would be at an unprecedented disadvantage; supporters of the manufacturers would have the most powerful arguments on their side.

Oswald began his campaign by meeting privately with William Tod, an experienced lobbyist at Whitehall for British linen manufacturers. Together the two men worked out a proposal for "the linen tax, etc." Then Oswald took it to Bute for his private consideration. The First Lord approved of the scheme.[14] On 31 January, Samuel Martin wrote to the customs commissioners, telling them that Dashwood wanted them to compile two accounts. The first was an account of "linens imported into Britain in the last seven years, distinguishing the sorts and the quantity of each in every year"; the second account was of "duties received for each sort of linen, and the sums which have been drawn back upon the reexportation of the several kinds of linen respectively." Martin added that Dashwood wanted the accounts as soon as possible, a sign that the Chancellor of the Exchequer wanted the information available before he recommended Oswald's proposal to the House on Budget Day in early March.[15]

But Dashwood never introduced the linen tax. "The subject was complicated," Bute later recalled, "and mixed with our treaties with Russia." As a result, "his friend, Sir Francis (a very good man) found difficulties in stating it." The Earl of Shelburne recounted this episode less diplomatically: "Dashwood . . . could not be made to understand a tax on linen, which was first intended, sufficiently to explain it to the House, and it had to be laid aside in consequence."[16] The papers describing the proposal stayed in the hands of Samuel Touchet, a financier who evidently was coaching Dashwood, and have been lost.[17] Some aspects of the proposal, however, may be inferred from other sources.

Clearly, Oswald did plan to change some of the duties on imported linens. The reference to the Russian commercial treaties reveals his intention to revise duties on Russian broads and drapes. Furthermore, the subject matter of the accounts that Dashwood asked for on 31 January suggests that Oswald was planning some sort of changes in the drawbacks. Surely Oswald did not intend to tamper with drawbacks on foreign linens reexported to foreign nations. Such a step would harm the British carrying trade without providing any compensating benefit to the nation. On the other hand, lowering or removing the drawback on foreign linens reexported to the colonies could not help but benefit Britain, if colonists could afford to pay more for linen and if they would neither smuggle it nor manufacture it themselves. Oswald did not doubt that they could afford more expensive linen. He later calculated, "The laborer throughout all North America earns upon an average a dollar a day, equal to four shillings and sixpence," which was well above the average English laborer's wage.[18] He probably held this same opinion in 1763. The high cost of labor not only indicated the presence of a market for higher-priced linen, but it also insured that colonists would not try to manufacture it themselves. Oswald surely discounted the danger of smuggling, thinking that the profit to be gained by selling contraband linen was too small to entice men into risking loss of their goods or ship.[19] Thus, lowering or removing the drawback would either increase sales of British manufactures in America or allow the Treasury to keep the sixty to seventy thousand pounds now paid yearly in drawbacks as revenue from what one commissioner of the customs later called a way "indirectly to raise a revenue from the plantations."[20] This indirect tax was attractive for several reasons. It would not diminish the colonists' buying power; it could be collected by the existing customs establishment and therefore would create no additional overhead; it would be collected in Britain by British officers, not in America by officers who had a reputation for corruption; and Americans could resist it most successfully by buying more British merchandise, which would in itself provide another benefit to the nation. In sum, it would not be burdensome, and, if unpalatable to colonists for some other reason, it could not be resisted.

Dashwood's failure to master the details of the proposal did not mean that the Treasury gave up on the tax. To the contrary, the Treasury asked on 4 March for an account of "the drawbacks upon all goods exported to America for four years immediately preceding the war and also a like account for the space of four years during the war."[21] Nothing more could be done in 1763 than gathering more information; by 4 March, men at the Treasury were preparing to propose in the House new taxes on cider, on wines, and on insurance policies and bills of lading.[22] They thought, however, that in 1764 they might be very interested in getting a revenue from America indirectly by reducing the drawbacks.

For the present, they settled on a policy of administrative reform that, they probably hoped, would have significant results rather quickly. Grenville recalled in September 1763 that many complaints had been made in Parliament during the previous session about the miserable state of the revenue from customs in America: "This, it was urged, arose from the making all these offices sinecures in England." That analysis probably appeared first at the Treasury, inspiring the order of 16 February for a list of officers absent from duty there. Indeed, another order, dated 4 March, asking for an account "of payments of plantation duties paid in the plantations, with the several places distinguished," may have been an effort to prove this point beyond any question and to justify strict disciplinary action against individuals.[23] Coming on the same day as the request for the figures on drawbacks in the colonial trade, this order suggests that the Treasury was leaning toward a program of reform in the colonial customs service and of revisions in the system of drawbacks. It was a cautious, conservative way to raise revenue from the colonies. No new taxes would be collected in America; no new officers would be appointed there. Perhaps these developments might occur later, but only after the gathering and sifting of more information. For the immediate future, the Treasury felt most comfortable with a cautious approach. It would raise some more revenue, perhaps much more, without risking the nation's commerce with her American colonies.

Introducing Colonial Taxation in the House

By 19 February, Bute and his colleagues had decided that Ellis would announce, "The troops for North America will, it is hoped, be paid another year by the colonies themselves."[24] Perhaps the Treasury had communicated enough optimism about the prospects of administrative reform and Oswald's scheme to make that decision. If such was the case, the men at the Treasury also communicated their caution along with their optimism. The words *"it is hoped"* suggest a tentative aspect to the plan, just as the words *"another year"* are conveniently vague about the precise time that colonists would begin shouldering the burden of their defense. At first glance, the report Rigby sent Bedford on 23 February seems more definite. "I understand," he wrote, "part of the plan of the army is . . . to make North America pay its own army." Rigby may have understood this to mean that Americans would pay for the army in 1764 or in 1765, but clearly, whoever informed him about the plan left this matter open to differing interpretations.[25] When Ellis introduced the estimates for the army, he observed, according to Jenkinson, "that the American force was intended to be paid for a future year by America." Again, the government had been careful not to determine which future year. One should note at this point that it is doubtful that Jenkinson was taking notes on Ellis's statement out of casual interest. Four other members took notes on this debate, and only Sir Roger Newdigate, a Tory country gentleman who passionately hoped for a reduction in taxes and government expenditures, mentioned Ellis's comment in his description. Rather, Jenkinson was probably performing a service that he continued to fulfill as Grenville's assistant: keeping track of the exact nature and specific language of any pledges for future action that the Treasury might make or seem to make.[26] Evidently, he did not regard this as a promise to raise enough money in America to pay completely for the army there after the next year; he did not apologize for missing this goal during the debates in 1764 and 1765. Neither did Grenville. Neither did Ellis. Indeed, no one who had served in the Bute ministry apologized. Moreover, no one from the opposition or from the ranks of the Tories accused them of breaking a promise. Bute and his colleagues had broken the news of their intention to raise an American revenue circumspectly and cautiously.

The response of their friends and foes in Parliament is interesting. During this session, the administration was challenged frequently on the details of its military and fiscal programs. Yet apparently no one, on hearing about the government's intent, pressed for specifics about the administration's plans. For instance, the Tories and the country gentlemen in the House of Commons, who had as a group supported the address on the preliminaries, were deeply disturbed by the scheme to station 6,000 more troops in Ireland and pay them without any special appropriation. To them, such a step would dangerously increase the powers of the Crown. They asked the ministers to give up their scheme. Fox and Bute agreed that the administration could not afford to lose the Tories' support and scrapped the plan. At the same time, they asked the Tories to support the rest of the peace establishment, including the twenty regiments scheduled for America. Both sides publicly accepted this deal at a meeting between Dashwood, Fox, Ellis, Townshend, and the Tories on 24 February. In the accounts of this meeting, there is no record of anyone having quizzed the ministers present on how they planned to pay for the army in America. Surely some of the leading Tories knew about the government's vague intentions; those intentions must at least have been mentioned during the session.[27] But no one probed deeper, even though this same group of men had just been upset by the constitutional implications of a tax that would not have fallen on them. Perhaps they were so happy with their bargain that they did not want to endanger it. Perhaps the Tories felt so ignorant of American affairs and the existing bureaucratic and legislative arrangements for dealing with them that they believed they could not frame intelligent questions. They must have mentally reserved the right to oppose any scheme for raising an American revenue that seemed likely to give the Crown too much unchecked power. Whatever the Tories' reasons, though, the administration was now sure of their support on this year's establishment. It could also be confident that the independent members favored the idea of Americans paying for their own defense.

In the House on 4 March, only two members referred to Ellis's statement of intent. According to Jenkinson, Charles Townshend's brother, George, stated his admiration for "the plan of making the American army to be paid by the Americans." Intent on "lavish[ing] . . . encomiums on the peace and peace-makers," Townshend did not go on to ask how the ministers planned to raise the money. Nor did William Beckford, the Lord Mayor of London and a firm ally of Pitt. Beckford argued that the army should be reduced, not augmented, then added, "America can pay an army but *that* [is] no inducement to keep one there. The money [raised by American taxes] may be transmitted to England and applied to uses here."[28] Even had Townshend and Beckford demanded further details, the House might not have listened too closely to any response, for the day's grand event was Pitt's speech on the proposed establishment of the army. Pitt began by damning at some length the peace treaty as "inadequate, precarious, and hollow" and predicting "it would soon be broken." For that reason, he supported the administration's plan for the army, with one exception: "He wanted greater numbers in America."[29] He had nothing to say about any American revenue, an omission that he presumably expected would leave him the opportunity to praise or condemn specific proposals in the future. To the ministers, his silence on that point signaled that he was not unalterably opposed to the idea and might even support a proposal openly if he thought the money raised would be used to improve or enlarge the American army. The comment by his friend Beckford on colonial taxation, which Jenkinson noted, probably strengthened the impression that Pitt would not object to American taxes. The administration doubtlessly also noticed how Pitt's speech had demoralized Newcastle's followers, leaving them silent. The Duke objected to the proposed military establishment in general and to "the American plan" in particular. His reasons for opposing them were not related to the American revenue; rather, he based his opposition on grounds that would appeal to Tories: "such an extensive plan of power and military influence as never thought of before in this country." When Pitt scorned these arguments and asserted that "the Crown can acquire no influence by means of that force," none of Newcastle's friends in the House had the nerve to contradict him.[30] Neither did they have any inclination to challenge Ellis about the intended American revenue.

Thus the administration had learned by the morning of 5 March two lessons about parliamentary reaction to raising an American revenue. First, considered in principle, it was a noncontroversial idea. The strong tendency of members was toward approving a "proper" tax or "proper" administrative reforms. Second, the idea could most easily become "improper" and controversial if the method of raising the revenue appeared to increase dangerously the prerogatives of the Crown. By avoiding this mistake, the administration would probably have little trouble maneuvering its proposals through Parliament. Just how little trouble it would take became more apparent to the ministers two weeks later.

Charles Townshend and the Molasses Duty

The fourth of March was the last good day for ministers in the House of Commons for some time. When Dashwood introduced the budget, "he performed so awkwardly, with so little intelligence or clearness, in so vulgar a tone, and in such mean language, that he . . . said himself afterwards, 'People will point at me, and cry, *"there goes the worst Chancellor of the Exchequer that ever appeared."* ' "[31] He was certainly one of the most complaisant. In private conferences and in the committee on ways and means, he and his colleagues agreed to drop their proposal to put additional stamp duties on insurance policies and bills of lading. They also allowed the country gentlemen to pressure them into changing the tax on cider from a ten shilling per hogshead duty to be paid by the first buyer, to a four shilling per hogshead duty to be paid by the maker. From the standpoint of efficiently collecting the tax, this change had merit; from the standpoint of politics, making the duty on cider an excise tax was disastrous. No one could object, as Bute pointed out, to taxing cider "upon a principle of equality"; if the poor in one part of England paid heavy taxes on beer, the poor in another part should bear a like burden on their favorite beverage. Many people, however, were prepared to object to excises. Newcastle's friends were desperate for excuses to oppose the government, and this issue had shaken Walpole's power thirty years before. As for Pitt, he was sufficiently inspired to assert a certain relationship between an Englishman's home and a castle.[32]

The ministry that responded to these charges and stayed alert for divisions on the bill was more than usually distracted and divided. On 2 March, Bute had confidentially told Fox that he intended to resign as soon as he could and asked Fox to succeed him at the Treasury. Understandably, the Earl's full attention was not on current events. As for Fox, on 2 March Grenville and Dashwood openly implied that his handling of the paymaster-general's accounts during the war would require serious and thorough investigation. Infuriated, Fox blurted out to a member of the opposition that "he was not to be so used; that *he* [Fox] had no power," and that he might resign.[33] As the pressures on the ministry from within and without were increasing, the House committee inquiring into laws soon to expire recommended on 9 March that the Molasses Act of 1733, set to expire at the end of the first session of Parliament after 29 September 1763, was "fit to be continued."[34]

Jenkinson was on the committee. If he studied that law at all—and there is no reason to suspect him of laziness or inattention—he cannot have failed to see the possibilities of raising a considerable revenue from a duty of sixpence sterling on each gallon of foreign molasses imported into the American colonies. If Jenkinson did not know already that a thriving trade in French molasses had gone on before the war, he needed only to ask Rose Fuller, the chairman of the committee and a merchant from Jamaica who specialized in the West Indian trade, to find out. The Bute administration had stressed in December that America's population was expanding at a rapid rate and that Americans' appetite for goods was growing apace. Jenkinson could reasonably assume that the American demand for molasses would increase with the population, too. In the future, moreover, one crucial aspect of the trade would be different. As Jenkinson had pointed out in December, the peace treaty left the French West Indies utterly dependent on British North America for food and lumber. America's monopoly of these essential goods would enable her to dominate markets in the French islands. American merchants could drive favorable bargains with the French, perhaps so favorable that the French, in effect, would be paying the sixpence duty. Fuller could have also told Jenkinson, if he did not already know or guess, that this duty had raised little money in the past. This news would not have discouraged him. A change of enforcement procedures or a reduction of the duty, or both, and Britain would have a means of raising a considerable revenue now, and a more lucrative one later, without injuring American commerce or impairing Americans' ability to buy more British manufactures. The chance of accomplishing this compelled Jenkinson to favor continuing the act. Probably there was little danger it would lapse; the British West Indians, who had favored its passage 1733 and had successfully worked for its continuance five times since, would not have allowed that to occur. This time, though, continuing it would not simply mean keeping a dead letter on the statute books. The Treasury would be interested in investigating how to make it raise a revenue.[35]

Soon after Fuller moved to continue the act, the Treasury revealed its interest in the molasses duty. On 15 March, the men at the Treasury asked the legal officers of the government whether revenue from this duty "is to be considered as public money, unappropriated to any particular service, or as money disposable by His Majesty in like manner as the prerogative revenue of the Crown."[36] Two concerns motivated this inquiry. One was administrative: Could this revenue legally be used to pay for the army in America? The other was political: Would the administration have to defend this act against charges that using money raised on its authority would dangerously strengthen the Crown's prerogatives? No one at the Treasury wanted to be caught unprepared by a sudden accusation from the parliamentary opposition that might, in an atmosphere heated by debate on the cider tax, jeopardize the continuance of the Molasses Act.

Where the Treasury saw danger, Charles Townshend saw opportunity. Like Fox, he believed the "greatest and most necessary of all schemes [was] the settlement of America," and he intended to play the premier role in determining policy on the new acquisitions. To that end, he had been maneuvering for months to expand the powers of the

President of the Board of Trade at the expense of Egremont's office. His efforts had not been wholly successful, but at least he had gained a position in the nominal Cabinet. Making a spectacular and successful intervention in the discussion of the Molasses Act, he must have hoped, might establish his preeminence on other American matters.[37]

Townshend's earlier service on the Board of Trade had familiarized him with the act, and his service on Fuller's committee had alerted him to the fact that the House would discuss its continuance this session. So when he asked John Bindley, a friend of his, several questions about illicit trade to and from America, he included some on the molasses trade. Bindley consulted with "sundry merchants who have not only traded to the respective settlement in North America but who have actually resided there, and may be depended on for truth." They estimated that there were seventy-three large distilleries in America, producing close to twenty-five thousand tons of spirits a year, "chiefly distilled from French molasses." Almost all that molasses entered America illegally. Bindley accounted for this illicit commerce by pointing out that "the extent of coast, which is near 3,000 miles, has but few officers, and these [are accustomed] to connive at a clandestine trade, when they see their interest in it." They saw their interest often enough to establish a set rate for bribes "to our governors and custom house officers of twenty guineas for a vessel of one hundred tons, or in proportion." Merchants were so willing to pay the bribe that the collector at Boston realized around three thousand pounds a year in bribes and fees. Because of the long coast and the habit of connivance, Bindley concluded, "The government perhaps would find it a very difficult task to put the collectors . . . on a better footing." He suggested that "perhaps some of the small ships of war properly authorized and instructed would be the most effectual check."[38] Townshend had a different idea. The molasses trade was extensive, important, and well established. Masters did not drop their cargoes off in remote coves; they went to major ports. Merchants did not sneak the cargoes into town; they avoided this bother and expense by bribing officers. What would they care if the bribe went into the public's purse rather than the officer's? Indeed, for the security of legality they might be willing to pay a little more than the established douceur. Townshend calculated that American merchants would pay a tax of twopence sterling per gallon. On 18 March, he moved in the committee on ways and means an amendment to the Molasses Act that would lower the duty from sixpence to that figure.[39]

Jenkinson's account of Townshend's speech that day has not survived, but one can surmise from the response of the House and of the ministers present that it was an impressive performance. Townshend probably used some of the information Bindley provided to buttress his case. He certainly made "heavy complaints . . . [about] the state of our revenues in North America." He may even, if he had the information, have noted they "amount between £1,000 and £2,000, the collecting of which cost . . . between £7,000 and £8,000 a year."[40] Doubtlessly he concluded with a statement similar to one he made on 30 March: "The high duties produce nothing by driving all people to smuggle from the enormity of the gain."[41] Townshend may also have stressed the experimental nature of his proposal. He evidently recommended that the Molasses Act as amended be continued only to the end of the parliamentary session that met after 29 September 1764.[42] Thus Parliament would have to check the results of the amendment soon and could discover quickly whether any revisions of the rate, either up or down, were advisable.

The committee approved Townshend's motion. The ministers present, including Fox, Grenville, and the Lords of the Treasury, made no effort to block it. Indeed, they kept silent throughout. This "much hurt" George III, who felt they could hardly plead surprise, since "this subject was new to none." Indeed, "All ought to have declared," the King fumed to Bute, "that next session some new tax will be laid before the House, but that it requires much information before a proper one can be stated, and thus have thrown out this insidious proposal." He also thought that Townshend's conduct "deserve[d] the dismissing him or [at] least the making him explain his intentions."[43]

Fox, Grenville, and the rest were probably as angry as George III at Townshend's behavior, and for the same reasons. Without warning, Townshend had breached the informal agreement within the ministry to proceed cautiously on raising an American revenue, and he had done so without providing any good reason for discarding that policy. No one could tell for certain yet whether or not administrative reforms might strengthen the American customs service to the point at which it could collect the sixpence duty. Even if one conceded the need to cut, no one could be sure that twopence was the highest duty that could be collected. One could assume, however, that raising a duty precipitately right after cutting it precipitately would create commercial, administrative, and political difficulties. The molasses duty seemed to ministers in the House, as well as to George III, a classic case for careful investigation. Unlike the King, however, the more experienced men in the House sensed a trap. Why was Townshend making this particular proposal, which he could guess would be popular, at this particular time, when the Treasury was struggling to preserve the excise tax on cider? Perhaps he wanted to pressure the Treasury into accepting his proposal; perhaps he only wished to elicit a definite pledge of a future tax, the very sort of pledge George III would have given him. Whatever his immediate purpose, beneath it lay his desire to establish before the House his influence over American affairs. The safest course, the ministers apparently decided, was to deceive him, then kill the bill procedurally.[44]

On 19 March, the select committee that usually drew up tax legislation began work on a bill continuing and amending the Molasses Act. The committee, dominated by men from the Treasury, worked quickly. Hearing of this, and recalling the Treasury's silence on Townshend's motion, Jasper Mauduit, who assisted his brother in carrying out the latter's duties as agent of Massachusetts Bay, predicted, "Short as the term is, [Townshend] will probably carry it through before the rising of Parliament."[45] Others probably made the same mistake. On 24 March, the select committee presented the bill to the House. That same day, it passed its first reading, and the cider tax was given final approval. On 26 March, during a rare Saturday session, the amended Molasses Act passed its second reading, and the Speaker scheduled the committee stage on the bill for Monday, the twenty-eighth. But that day, the ministers suddenly asked for a postponement of the committee until Wednesday.[46] When the House agreed to this, Townshend must have realized that things were not what they seemed. The Treasury had strung him along past the third reading of the cider tax. There had been no debate on the second reading of the bill because debate at that stage was customarily reserved for discussion of the principle of a bill, not its details, and the government approved of this bill's principle.[47] Now, having successfully postponed the committee stage once, the ministers could be sure that they could continue postponing it until the session was over. On the thirtieth, Townshend made one final try either to secure the bill's passage or to force the government to commit itself. He repeated his arguments for lowering the duty to twopence. In reply, Grenville spoke "against lowering them."[48] Nothing else is known about his remarks. At that moment, he was helping write a bill that significantly increased the authority and power of naval officers to assist in "the prevention of the clandestine running of goods into any part of His Majesty's Dominions," so perhaps he argued that this improvement would make smuggling so much more hazardous in American waters as to incline men to pay the sixpence duty.[49] Perhaps, too, he countered Townshend's points about the weakness of the American customs service by arguing that the weakness lay in allowing Englishmen to hold these offices as sinecures.[50] If this proved to be the case, then reforming the situation might lessen the need to reduce the duty. Whatever he said against lowering the duty, he made no promises of future action. Had he done so, surely his friend James Harris would have recorded it in his diary. After this exchange between Townshend and Grenville, the House voted to postpone the committee meeting for a month, a date that all members knew was well after the time for adjournment.[51]

So the government had once more acted cautiously on the question of raising an American revenue. The Treasury now had a year to examine the molasses duty and to make its recommendations without being bothered by formal votes or verbal commitments for or against the sixpence duty, or the twopence, or, for that matter, any duty at all. Of course, the Treasury would only have that one year. Postponing consideration of the amended Molasses Act would cause it to expire when the next parliamentary session ended. Thus, a decision would have to be made by the Treasury and Parliament by April or May 1764. Still, this deadline probably did not seem like cause for serious concern in March 1763.

Indeed, the administration had reason to be pleased with its accomplishments on colonial taxation since making peace. A consensus within the government in favor of looking for a "proper" means of raising an American revenue had been reached. The Treasury had found three promising possibilities worth serious inquiry: revising the system of drawbacks, reforming the officers in charge of enforcement, and collecting some tax on molasses. Parliament had shown that it would follow the Treasury's recommendations on taxing America. The administration's opponents had made no serious objections to these policies; indeed, though James Oswald anticipated that "the settlement of America . . . [would] certainly be the chief point upon which all future opposition [would] attempt to throw its colors and raise its battery," he did not expect equivalent opposition to American taxation.[52] Finally, the members who supported the government had frustrated Townshend's efforts to seize more control over American affairs. In sum, there was no reason for men in government to be pessimistic about the chances of finding and passing through Parliament "proper" taxes that would help considerably in supporting the army in America. Few of them guessed, though, that George Grenville, not Bute, would be the First Lord of the Treasury who would find and pass those taxes.

Chapter III

"The Particular Habits of His Life": Some Implications of Grenville's Political and Administrative Character

Most of Grenville's contemporaries in Britain and America believed that he had contributed a great deal to the worsening of imperial relations during the 1760s. The role they generally assigned to him was that of first mover; as Grenville himself reflected in 1770, "All the troubles are supposed to have originated with my Administration."[1] Modern scholarship, however, has diminished his part in the drama. "Conceivably Grenville was the wrong man in the wrong place at the wrong time," Ian R. Christie has written, "yet the logic of the situation drove events strongly forward in the direction they were to follow." P. D. G. Thomas has pointed out that "much of what Grenville's administration did with regard to imperial problems would have been done by any ministry in office from 1763." And Thomas C. Barrow has concluded, "Grenville's role in these events has been exaggerated at the expense of the truth. The movement towards reform—and even the direction chosen—had a deeper base than the whims or fancies of one man."[2]

The work of these scholars has been a valuable corrective. They have called attention to the consensus on many matters of colonial policy and to the continuity of personnel and planning from Bute's administration to Grenville's, and thus they have enabled others to see Grenville in a more accurate light. Yet even these historians are reluctant to give up completely the old image and to regard Grenville merely as the captain of a ship on a preordained, disastrous course. "Grenville's character," Christie has noted, "displayed both strengths and weaknesses which may have contributed to the growing friction within the Empire." Thomas summed up, "After all qualifications have been made, there can be no doubt that Grenville left his personal mark on American policy." Barrow judged that "perhaps more than any other man Grenville was horrified by the size of England's debt." Among the aspects of Grenville's personality that these men found interesting and perhaps significant were his lack of broad vision and sensitivity in politics, his preoccupation with enforcing the law, particularly trade laws, his love of economy, his persistent conscientiousness, and his tireless industry.

Because these traits left him in complete agreement with the course of British policy, historians have concluded that he drove the ship onto the rocks more aggressively than others might have done.[3]

Their description of these characteristics of Grenville is accurate, as far as it goes, but still incomplete. Three aspects of his character set him apart from almost all of his contemporaries in British politics. The first of these was his penchant for risking all politically when he felt the odds were in his favor and the prize worth the gamble. He did not take wild leaps of faith; indeed, he calculated the chances of success as carefully as he could. But if the odds favored him, he was not afraid to act decisively. The second unique trait, which deeply colored his administration of the Treasury, was his obsessive hatred of smuggling. Stating without much elaboration that he favored strict enforcement of the customs laws obscures the fervor of his feelings. Such a statement also oversimplifies his reaction to contraband trade. He regarded smuggling not only as a threat to the nation's commerce and finances, but also as a symptom of serious political problems. Because he believed smuggling posed a serious economic threat, he wanted to defeat it; because he believed it had political roots, he prepared himself to use a variety of attacks. Finally, to an unusual degree for an eighteenth-century politician, Grenville was skeptical about both the value of the opinions of official boards and the wisdom of their established administrative practices. During his tenure in a variety of offices before coming to the Treasury in 1763, he displayed on many occasions a readiness to make his own investigations of problems, reach his own conclusions, and attempt to implement new approaches—even in the teeth of expert opinion and opposition. In part, this tendency was a symptom of his prodigious energy; the man was simply incapable of sitting idly in an office and permitting his subordinates to run without supervision even the most routine and mundane of a department's affairs. But it resulted in part from self-confidence: He knew that he could devise better and more efficient ways of doing business. Far from being afraid of reform, he was inclined toward it. To understand completely why Grenville made certain decisions as he planned American taxation, it is necessary to describe more fully his distinctive inclination toward reform, as well as his readiness to take gambles and his determination to curb smuggling.

Grenville in Politics, 1761–1763

When Bute broke the news of his retirement and Grenville's appointment to the Treasury to Bedford, he described his successor as "the only person in whom [the King] can confide so great a trust: Mr. Fox having taken the King's word when he first entered on the management of affairs that, the peace made, he might be permitted to go to the House of Lords."[4] Had Grenville ever read this letter, he would have regarded it as the final vindication of his political strategy. Since late 1761, he had been trying to recognize exactly when Bute had no choice but to do as he wished and then to take the maximum advantage of the Earl's helplessness.

Grenville had finally decided to accept the appointment as Leader of the House in October 1761 after considerable soul-searching. On 2 October, his elder brother, Temple, and his brother-in-law, William Pitt, declared that they would resign from the Cabinet over the issue of war with Spain. Grenville learned this at 2:00 A.M. the next day, at the same time he learned that Bute wanted him to leave his country seat immediately and come to London. By 4:00 A.M., he was on the road. On the way he met Temple, and stopped to inform him of Bute's summons and to ask his opinion about what he should do. Although Grenville agreed with the majority of the Cabinet that war with Spain was unnecessary, he loyally told his brother that he too would resign if Temple wished it. Perhaps fatigued by the events of the previous day, and perhaps surprised to be holding such a conversation at dawn on the London road, Temple assured his brother that he "saw no other person in the Kingdom that ought to resign upon that measure other than Mr. Pitt and himself." Grenville traveled on to London, where he discovered that Bute had sent for him with the intention of offering him Pitt's office. This he "absolutely declined, though earnestly pressed to it by Lord Bute from the King, by every argument that could be suggested." Grenville's "delicacy" of mind, as he later explained it, prevented him from serving at this time as Secretary of State. He suggested instead that the Earl of Egremont, his wife's brother, be appointed to the office.[5] Finally convinced, Bute and the King agreed to this proposition but made Egremont's appointment contingent upon Grenville's becoming Leader of the House of Commons. Grenville's immediate reaction to this is unknown. Within a few days, he saw several objections to this scheme and begged to be permitted, as he had planned for some time, to become Speaker of the House. Yet in his notes on Bute's letter to him, dated 13 October, there is a cryptic reference to the "generous offer made *by* me to go into the present situation; the King's acceptance; the manner of his reception of it in his closet; . . . my own opening this plan; the delivery of [the seals] to [the] Earl of Egremont."[6] But whether Grenville asked to be Leader or not, he revealed his favorable inclination toward accepting the position soon after the offer was made. By 7 October, he, Bute, and Newcastle had begun discussing who should be the next Speaker.[7]

At this point, a new crisis arose for Grenville, one that threatened more than his political future. Before Temple returned to town on 8 October, he changed his mind about his brother's remaining in office. Perhaps Temple was infuriated that his brother would take the lead in the House; in any case, he became "most hostile and outrageous [saying] that [Grenville] had deserted his family, [and] that he would never let him come within his doors nor see his face more."[8] Here was serious news indeed, for Temple had enough power over Grenville's life to punish him severely. He controlled the votes of the borough that sent his brother to Parliament. He also had an unusual and potentially crushing advantage in the economics and politics of the Grenville family. Most family estates in eighteenth-century England were bound by strict settlements; a large proportion of the Grenvilles' property was not, however, and Temple could disinherit his brother. Even if he did not take this extreme step, he could damage the interests of Grenville's children, who stood to inherit the childless Temple's title and the bulk of the property, by selling or willing land to others. In the past, Temple had occasionally suspected that Grenville wished "to divide the family, and put [him]self at the head of a party in it."[9] Grenville's twin apostasy—not resigning, then accepting the leadership—might cause Temple to take a terrible revenge. Against this grim possibility, Grenville weighed his knowledge that society would judge Richard guilty of highly indecent and unjustifiable behavior if he punished his brother too severely for being in the King's service.[10] If Grenville stayed in office, he would be gambling that this consideration would sufficiently deter Temple from reacting extremely or irrevocably.

Perhaps Grenville thought that this risk was too great; perhaps the isolation from his family underscored for him the chance that the King and Bute might someday leave him isolated politically as well. Whatever his fears, when Grenville spoke with Bute on 13 October, he described to him his family's reaction and asked to serve not as Leader but as Speaker of the House. Grenville argued that this post "was on many accounts far the most eligible to him" and cited as evidence for this argument "the disjointed state of the ministry, his own want of support, [and] the danger His Majesty ran of being obliged to abandon a faithful servant whom he would leave in the midst of his enemies, and by that means deprive [him] of the power of being useful to him." Grenville then closed the conference by asking Bute to think carefully about these objections.[11]

Bute did, then wrote an extraordinary letter to Grenville, "laying down a plan of his future conduct." Because it was so frank, and because it referred to Newcastle as a "crazy old man," Bute understandably wanted the letter to remain in his possession and accordingly asked that Grenville merely read it, then return it immediately via its bearer. With equal caution, Grenville dictated the major points of the letter to his wife.[12] In his abstract of it, he noted the King and Bute's "regret . . . upon the barbarous usage of my family" and Bute's remark that had he forseen Temple's reaction, he would have insisted that Grenville accept Pitt's old office.[13] Then he summarized Bute's understanding of the conditions under which Egremont became Secreary of State, noting that according to Bute the present arrangement "could not have been done but upon this plan," that there was "general acquiescence of everybody to it," and that there would be "difficulty attending the King in departing from it."[14] The Earl then observed that others might regard Grenville's doubts as the result of "wavering, and irresolution or timidity," but that he did not, and he proceeded to try to quiet Grenville's fears about being abandoned. He referred to Newcastle as a timid man who would not give any trouble and who would be punished if he did. Bute also noted that he "had certain information that after the peace [Newcastle] would resign when called upon, [and he] thought it therefore better to let this old man tide over a year or two more of his political life." He promised that Grenville would have access to the King and that Grenville would have daily proof of the King's resolution to support him. Finally, according to Grenville's notes, Bute closed by pledging his utmost support to the ministry and by observing, "The King was upon the same ground, would support me to the utmost, my honor was his honor, my disgrace his disgrace."[15] These expressions pleased Grenville and encouraged him to feel more secure about both his political prospects and his isolation from his family. He began to think more positively about becoming Leader.

No doubt Grenville was further encouraged toward this decision by a letter Newcastle wrote him on 13 October. In it, the Duke expressed his concern "at what I saw and heard this day" about Grenville's doubts and pledged his determination "in all events to give you all the little assistance in my power." Newcastle also acquiesced in Grenville's choice for Speaker, Thomas Prowse, thus retracting his objections of a week earlier.[16] This concession made the chances of political isolation more remote by seemingly confirming Bute's analysis of Newcastle. Nevertheless, Grenville required one further proof of Bute's support. The Earl had assured him that Henry Fox would not oppose the ministry in the House. To Grenville, this was welcome news, but it raised a disturbing question about his own position as Leader. "What . . . figure shall I make?" he complained to Newcastle. "Mr. Fox has superior parliamentary talent to me; . . . [he] has a great number of friends in the House

. . . attached strongly to him; . . . [he] has *great connections*. I have none; I have no friends; I am now unhappily separated from my own family." Bute negotiated with Fox and extracted a promise that "he was ready to take a part or not [in the House on] public business, according as Mr. Grenville should wish and think best for the King's service."[17] Thus Grenville obtained not only Fox's support but his silence as well. He then settled down to the business of being Leader, confident that he had reduced to almost nothing the chance of his being isolated politically and cast away unrewarded to face Temple's wrath alone.

Grenville could be confident of something else as well. Bute, who suffered from naiveté at many crucial points in his political career, may have felt in October 1761 that his words and acts had won Grenville's undying loyalty. To the contrary: They had instead fully revealed to Grenville how desperately the King and Bute needed him. Indeed, Bute had admitted this openly in his 13 October letter, then confirmed it in his subsequent negotiations with Fox. Grenville's cautious, suspicious mind would not permit him to believe that George III and his favorite had cultivated him for months, then offered him the leadership, out of any longstanding affection for him personally. They had to find a man who was willing to be Leader and who could speak about trade and finances knowledgeably and effectively enough to hold his own against Pitt. Such men were rare, and the King and Bute had obviously narrowed the field a great deal by absolutely refusing to consider Fox or any of Newcastle's followers. This left them with Grenville, Charles Townshend, and Bute's friends. Grenville could safely assume that they had balked at making the erratic Townshend Leader. He could also be sure that they believed none of Bute's friends measured up to the job; if they had they would have offered it to one of them. He was, therefore, not only their choice as Leader; he was their *only* choice. If he did well, he would be in a good position to improve his office and power within the administration. When Newcastle was eased or forced out of the Treasury, moreover, his chances for obtaining better office and more power would improve even further. These insights probably helped determine him to stay on as Leader. Certainly he began trying to take advantage of his situation almost immediately.[18]

Grenville did well in the House. In the Cabinet, he helped force Newcastle's resignation. Furthermore, he had taken—or so he thought—Bute's measure. Bute had "so fluctuating a mind, nobody could answer what" he would think from one hour to the next.[19] At one moment, he opposed renewing the subsidy to Prussia; at the next, he had given in to Newcastle's importunings. At one time, he pressed Grenville to use the Treasury accounts to undermine the Duke; at another, he hesitated to accept Grenville's recommendations.[20] These vacillations not only signaled to Grenville that he and Bute probably disagreed on some policy issues, but they also convinced him that Bute might be vulnerable to bullying. After Newcastle resigned in May 1762, Bute offered to make Grenville Chancellor of the Exchequer, a position he had wished for in 1761. Grenville refused it. "I don't doubt," the King observed, "but if he could he would have some office where he could in his opinion figure more, than as an assistant in a board." George III cautioned Bute "not [to] let slip what we had lately in our eye, the placing him in the Admiralty, there he could be easily spurred on, and would be out of the way."[21] Bute pressed Grenville again. Again he refused, for he wanted a position where he would definitely be in the way: Bute's old office, the Secretary of State. Bute was appalled but powerless. He could not "point out to [the King] a good Chancellor of the Exchequer" other than Grenville, let alone a new Leader.[22] Grenville became Secretary of State.

At this point, Bute, who had been feverish and distraught, apparently recalled that Egremont, the other Secretary of State, was Grenville's brother-in-law. He also remembered that Grenville had suggested that Egremont succeed Pitt in that office. Afraid that this relationship and Egremont's obligation would increase Grenville's power, he decided to ask Egremont and Halifax, the First Lord of the Admiralty and Lord-Lieutenant of Ireland, to exchange offices. The excuse for this, he decided, would be that the King feared that "two brothers [as] Secretaries, having the same office, will not be relished." Perhaps this scheme might have worked, but Bute and the King were sufficiently afraid of Grenville's possible reaction that they discussed it with him before acting. After "a night's meditation" by Grenville, Bute was distressed to see what he had "often observed before": "millions of fears and difficulties, and above all a refinement that this must proceed from a jealousy infused in me." Grenville had claimed that Bute must not really want him to be Secretary of State, for after Egremont was affronted and removed, he could hardly stay in that office. If Bute had no confidence in him as Secretary, how could he have confidence in him as Leader? Was the Earl planning to leave him without support, to abandon him at the first opportunity? Should he leave the leadership now? Bute felt he could not stand up to this implied threat. He denied any hostile intention toward Grenville and even admitted to him, "If I was at all susceptible [to that idea], I should be of all men the maddest in the plan I am now following." Then Bute surrendered. Egremont would stay Secretary.[23]

Beneath the veil of polite language, delicate expressions of family loyalty, and pained accusations of betrayal, this was a power play, pure and simple. Grenville could not flatly state that he wanted to be Secretary because of the additional money, the higher prestige, and the greater influence he would have on the peace negotiations any more than he could bluntly tell Bute to find another Leader if he did not get that office. Honor would require that Bute resist demands couched in that language, and above all else, Grenville did not want to incite resistance. Indeed, given the uncertain future of his family, he would have to yield if Bute insisted. Polite, oblique discussions that skirted the real issue would not force the Earl to resist and would give him time to think and worry about the difficulties of finding another Leader. Grenville bet that Bute was too timid to call his bluff. He was correct.

After this triumph in May 1762, Grenville fought all summer and into the fall to maneuver Bute and the Cabinet into demanding from the enemy substantial concessions in the Caribbean. To be sure, he was persistent because he thought that the nation would vitally need those possessions to cushion the shock of declining sales of manufactured goods after the war. He was also persistent, however, because he thought that he could again bluff Bute into accepting his terms. His tactics were the same. When other men had one objection to a point in negotiation, "Grenville," Bute discovered, "had twenty."[24] The most telling of these arguments to the Cabinet was political. Grenville was the Leader; therefore, he could plausibly claim to know the mood of the House about various concessions better than anyone else. Moreover, since he would be staking his reputation on a successful defense of the treaty there, his opinions had the additional credibility of being those of self-interest. At first, his comments were phrased diplomatically.[25] Later, his opinions became more openly threatening. Grenville wanted the right to approve all patronage requests from members of the House, a right Bute had withheld from him since he became Leader. As the parliamentary session of late fall 1762 approached, Grenville hinted broadly that he might not be able to defend the peace successfully without this additional power. After news of the fall of Havana reached London on 29 September, he flatly stated that he would not defend the peace unless it included compensation, preferably Florida and Puerto Rico, for that conquest. With these acts, he pressed Bute too far. Grenville never anticipated that the Earl might turn to Fox—the King hated Fox, and Grenville himself had been made Leader to thwart his power. Thus he had failed to gauge just how desperate Bute was for peace. On 4 October 1762, Bute wrote to Fox, telling him the King "was in great distress on finding Mr. Grenville unwilling or unable (or perhaps half one, half the other), to go on as his minister in the House of Commons," and begging him to come to London.[26]

Grenville had no choice but to accept Fox as Leader and the Admiralty for himself. As he confessed to the King, his family relations remained the same: He could not even be sure that Temple would permit his reelection from Buckingham. Understandably, after Grenville made this announcement, the King reported, "He seemed on parting very low."[27] Still, Grenville optimistically recorded Bute's statement to him "that he . . . knew my zeal and attachment to the King, and had therefore always wished to see me at the head of the Treasury; that he knew my talents and fitness for that great department, and felt thoroughly how unfit he was for it." Grenville also recorded Bute's wish to retire from that position.[28] However improbable this may have seemed to him, Grenville must have clung to this hope as he defended the preliminaries and worked at the Admiralty. In March 1763, Bute retired and offered to make Grenville First Lord of the Treasury.

The King and Bute offered the position, however, subject to Grenville's agreement to some extraordinary conditions. Bute would name the entire administration, including Grenville's own Treasury Board. Bute's brother would control Scottish patronage. Grenville could neither attack Fox's friends nor seek alliance with opponents of the preliminaries. Moreover, though Bute pledged he was retiring forever from politics, George III bluntly told Grenville that he hoped "to keep [Bute] near me" for "many, many years," presumably giving advice that he would follow no matter what Grenville said.[29] Grenville accepted these conditions, but he immediately began working to modify them. He persuaded the King and Bute not to replace Egremont.[30] He got appointments for two of his friends, James Harris, at the Treasury, and Thomas Pitt, Jr., at the Admiralty.[31] Finally, he talked the King, against George III's own wishes, into granting the reversion of a Teller's place a the Exchequer for his son and a pension of £3,000 a year for himself, to begin after he left the Treasury.[32] This decision was more than a financial cushion for Grenville's family against Temple's revenge. It was a signal for him to go on chipping away at Bute's influence.

Thus Grenville continued doing what he had done for two years: risking the consequences of opposing the wishes of his family, of Bute, and of the King. In the past, he had won some gambles and lost others. Despite those losses, he had realized his life's ambition. Unsurprisingly, the events of March 1763 did not teach him that he should be more cautious in the future. Instead, they converted him all the more completely to the conviction that calculated boldness in politics was often the best policy and convinced him that he should not despair at temporary setbacks. His rise to the Treasury may have had another effect on him as well. Grenville had succeeded against what would have seemed to be long odds in 1761. Perhaps the memory of that success persuaded him that he was a man of destiny, a man who could triumph no matter how difficult the situation. Certainly that memory encouraged him to act when he calculated that he was betting on a sure thing. The Stamp Act would seem such a sure thing to him that, as he later confessed to the House, "I had not a doubt in regard to the success of it, [and] . . . I would have pledged my life, . . . I would have pledged a thousand lives."[33]

Attacking Smuggling from Without

Grenville did not seek power merely to gratify his own ambition or to protect his children. He saw the commercial and fiscal disasters that Britain might be swept into, and he was determined to serve the King and nation well during this time of crisis. Grenville would never have openly boasted, as Pitt did, that he could save the nation and no one else could. Still, beneath modest disclaimers of genius lay a confidence that his energy and his knowledge of trade and finance were ideally suited for the situation. "The extension of the commerce . . . , the improvement of the advantages we have obtained, and the increase of the public revenue," he wrote in April 1763, "are the proper works of peace."[34] He planned to excel at all three.

A common enemy threatened his success in all three areas. In America and Britain, smugglers were actively competing with fair traders in several commerces. Since smugglers did not have to pass customs duties along to their customers, they competed at a substantial advantage. As they drove lawful merchants and masters out of trade, or into smuggling, they wrenched the nation's commerce out of its proper course and "defeated the salutary provisions of many wise laws."[35] At the same time, of course, they defrauded the nation of large sums of money. Grenville came to the Treasury knowing that smugglers could do considerable damage to the country's trade and finances at a moment when she needed every penny and all the legal trade she could get. He began his new duties knowing also that illicit traders were openly selling contraband tea in London. Soon after he became First Lord, the Treasury bluntly ordered the commissioners of excise to stop those sales.[36]

The commissioners complied, but neither they nor Grenville were very sanguine about the results of using excisemen to enforce trade laws after contraband had entered Britain. Smugglers offered popular goods at low prices; therefore, they were popular themselves. Excisemen received little help from the populace at the best of times; in a case like this, they could count themselves lucky if they were only passively resisted. Moreover, because smuggling was profitable, those involved in clandestine trade included well-to-do men who were either politically powerful themselves or well connected. This fact multiplied the difficulties of internal enforcement. Jenkinson, who became a Secretary of the Treasury in late April 1763, once received some "hints to prevent smuggling," which included a proposal for a penal law that called for the transporting of all people found guilty of importing or removing contraband. He laid it aside with the observation that it was difficult enough to get convictions when penalties were much lighter. Moreover, he noted, "In the maritime counties in particular, it would affect too many of the inhabitants, in other respects very useful and necessary subjects as sailors or husbandmen, not to mention merchants or gentlemen, ever to expect or even to wish so severe a law should be carried into execution."[37] These objections killed the proposal.

In making these objections, Jenkinson assumed for argument's sake that smugglers would resist only by thwarting legal proceedings. He and Grenville knew better than that. The members of Parliament from the West Country cider counties had been openly pressured by their constituents into resisting all compromise and causing as much trouble for the government as they could over the excise on cider. The intentions of the people, great and small, in those counties had been made clear by an amendment their members offered, requiring that all trials under that act be tried in the county where the alleged offense occurred. After this failed and the act passed, leading men in the West Country began whipping up popular resistance both to the tax and to the excisemen.[38] The interests of smugglers might be defended less openly, but indeed no less vigorously. The excise commissioners were already reluctant to try to enforce the duty on silver plate "against a great number of persons, many of them of great consideration, [who are] liable to, [but] do not pay this duty."[39] Quite probably, they would be equally reluctant and ineffectual against smugglers.

This left Grenville with two options. He could determine the prices smugglers were charging for their goods and lower the appropriate duties to the point that the profit illicit traders made was not worth the risk they took. Those who argued for this course claimed that the volume of the legal trade would increase so much that the nation's revenue from customs would not suffer, and might even grow. In March 1764, Grenville conceded in the House of Commons that it was "a beneficial work to review the public taxes and make proper alterations." He also speculated that "Customs House Laws may be further reformed with time." Revising taxes, however, "must be done with care." For the present, he would not propose any reductions or reforms in British customs law.[40] If they did not already know, his listeners realized then that Grenville had no intention of doing either until he had tried in every way to collect the present duties.

The second option, and the one Grenville had favored since his days as First Lord of the Admiralty, was to increase the difficulties smugglers faced in running their goods into Britain. He could not hope to stop all smuggling; considerations of economy limited the number of men and vessels he could use to enforce the law. But if he could increase the risk of detection and seizure past a certain point, the fainthearted might leave the trade, and the bold might raise their prices as a hedge against loss of a ship and cargo. Thus the volume of smuggled goods would decrease and their price would increase. Buying contraband would become less easy, less attractive, and less popular. As fair traders claimed a greater share of the market, the revenue would increase in proportion.

Grenville's first step toward reaching this goal was using some navy ships in the enforcement of the revenue laws. The Hovering Act, passed before he went to the Treasury, applied to Britain as well as to the colonies, and Grenville insisted on vigorous execution of its provisions. The Admiralty stationed fifty-three ships, manned by 2,630 officers and sailors, around Britain and Ireland, and even after he went to the Treasury Grenville kept track of their stations and their successes.[41] In September 1763, Jenkinson asked the customs commissioners to send an account of the net produce of customs during the same quarter in 1762 and 1763 "so the produce may be compared." While the Treasury waited for this information, the excise commissioners sent news that the East India Company had sold an unusually large amount of tea between April and October 1763, noting that this increase resulted "chiefly" from "the cruisers . . . stationed round the coasts to prevent smuggling." In January 1764, the Treasury heard that customs collection in 1763 had exceeded the previous year's total by £391,186. "Stationing ships," Grenville joyfully concluded in the House, "has been of service."[42]

Grenville had also heard by January 1764 that "some people imagine[d]" that customs collections would decline in the future.[43] Whether these predictions irritated him or not, he seems to have become determined to do everything he personally could to improve on the record of 1763. The Treasury had already been exchanging information about smugglers' ships and destinations with the Admiralty. In July 1764, Grenville tried to improve the quality of the intelligence. The

Treasury asked the Secretary of State to order British consuls in northern European ports to send comprehensive reports on smuggling operations in their areas. Which British subjects were involved? What were their methods? Which were their ships? What were their favorite cargoes? What were the size and value of these cargoes? What were their business arrangements in Britain and Europe? The consuls were also asked to send immediately any news they might learn about sailing dates, so the Treasury could pass on the intelligence to the Admiralty. Grenville himself in 1764 studied the reports from the most thorough of the consuls, Thomas Mortimer, in an effort to learn more about his adversaries and how to fight them on the sea.[44]

Grenville had also been paying attention to his line of defense on land, the customs service. He did not doubt that customs officers' "neglect, connivance, and fraud" made smuggling appreciably easier in many places, and he intended to dismiss any officers who did not do their duty.[45] To be sure, he was aware that these men were frequently well connected; indeed, Jenkinson kept in his files a list of officers, with observations on when they were appointed and, in some cases, by whose influence.[46] Still, these men were peculiarly vulnerable. They served at pleasure, and the customs commissioners could discharge them after an administrative hearing. Moreover, no patron could legitimately challenge Grenville's desire "to do justice [to] . . . [his] duty to secure the public revenues" by insisting on the removal of an inefficient or corrupt officer.[47] He could therefore safely pressure the customs commissioners to keep their officers in line. In February 1764, the Treasury demanded that the commissioners investigate allegations that the Liverpool agents were negligent. If they were, "Was it due to . . . connivance"? In April, the commissioners were ordered to stop their officers from admitting French silks as Italian. Also in April, the Treasury wanted an investigation of the alleged negligence of officers in Kent and Sussex in seizing boats and vessels. In June, Grenville and his colleagues heard that officers at Dover and Harwich were exacting and accepting gratuities in return for admitting huge quantities of French goods. The commissioners were to stop "this scandalous practice." They tried but apparently failed, for in October, the Treasury again warned them to check the Dover packet boats carefully. In August, Grenville personally demanded to know why the commissioners had not informed him about a fight between officers and smugglers at Deal. Also in August, the Treasury planned to add officers at Whitehaven without consulting the commissioners. In September, the commissioners, at Treasury insistence, dismissed seventeen tidewaiters. In October, the Treasury demanded that the commissioners dismiss negligent com-

manders of customs vessels at Leith. By the end of the year, the
commissioners had also discharged eleven collectors.[48] No one
doubted, least of all the customs commissioners, that the First Lord of
the Treasury was responsible for this activity. And Grenville could see
no end to his interference in the administration of the customs service.
At the end of 1764, he wished aloud to Jenkinson that he had "men of
business at his Board of Customs."[49] Grenville wanted men who
worked hard and who were knowledgeable about taxing the legal and
suppressing the illegal trade. He clearly was a man of business, as a letter
of his to Jenkinson, discussing responses to "the outrageous insult" at
Deal in August 1764, demonstrates.

> There seems to me but three things to be done. The first is to have the
> offenders prosecuted and punished as severely as the law will allow. The
> second is to reinforce the lieutenant of the cutter by a sloop and a man of war
> who may be fully sufficient to keep that gang in order. The third is to send
> troops, particularly dragoons, upon that part of the coast. . . . Add to it the
> advertisement which you mention of a reward for discovering and
> apprehending the offenders. . . . I desire to know what the [smuggler's] ship
> is, the name of the captain, and what steps can be taken in this business with
> the Directors of the East India Company. I asked Mr. [Thomas] Pitt
> whether any orders had been sent to the Admiralty to reinforce [the]
> lieutenant . . . , which most certainly should have been done immediately
> from any of the neighboring stations, as the whole ship might otherwise be
> unloaded in a few days . . . [and he] told me he would write to Mr. Stephens
> about it today. . . . You should write to the Secretary at War to hasten [the
> troops there] with the greatest expedition. What I have traced out above
> will, I hope, be sufficient to restrain so daring an act of violence under our
> eyes, which it imports to repress effectually in the first instance, if we mean
> to preserve, much more if we mean to increase, the revenue of customs. I am
> much surprised we have not heard from the Commissioners on this
> subject.[50]

This extraordinary concern about customs officers' behavior was not
Grenville's only intervention in the details of customs business during
1763–1764. The Treasury also ordered a survey to be made of English
ports. Grenville followed the progress of the survey closely, reading
occasional memoranda and on one occasion studying the full surveys
"to see the form of them, and the infinite variety of official matter."
Pleased with the results, Grenville planned a similar survey of all Scottish ports.[51] He also inquired into the way the commissioners of
customs for Scotland conducted their business. On 26 June 1764, the
Treasury noticed in the account books that no goods from France or
Italy legally entered Scotland between 1756 and 1762. The Scottish

commissioners' explanation was unsatisfactory, and the Treasury bluntly asked them whether it was usual in Scotland "to allow entry of French produce or manufactures under other names and as from other countries."[52] After that, Scottish customs officers knew that they would not be immune from Grenville's deep interest in the customs service.

Attacking Smuggling from Within

Grenville tightened his defenses against smuggling in British waters in another way. During the parliamentary session of 1763–1764, members had asked what the Treasury planned to do about smuggling from the Isle of Man into Ireland, Scotland, and England. Smuggling from Man presented special problems for the customs service. This island in the Irish Sea was part of the realm, but the family of the Duke of Atholl had received a parliamentary charter during the reign of James I confirming an earlier royal grant of all the powers and privileges of government. Atholl appointed the governor, named the bishop, coined money, constituted all the courts on Man, heard final appeals from them, and kept all the revenues from the island. Customs officers could not legally search or seize vessels there. As a result, the island became a haven for smugglers, who took advantage of its location to run tea into all three countries.[53] Because Parliament "expected" the Treasury to "pursue every legal method for the prevention of this evil," Grenville instigated an investigation of the contraband trade, particularly of "any commodity of the growth or manufacture of the East Indies," on 20 May 1764. Soon afterward, the Treasury discovered that customs officers estimated that the trade from Man cost the revenue two hundred thousand pounds a year.[54] The Treasury also learned how difficult it would be to stop this illicit commerce. The customs commissioners of Scotland pointed out "the impossibility of the cruisers to keep the seas in the season the smugglers choose for their illicit practices"; they complained about the broad waterways of Scotland and the flat coasts of England; and they noted the popular support for the smugglers both on Man and in Scotland and England.[55] Only customs officers on Man itself could effectively reduce the volume of the island's clandestine traffic. The Crown would have to purchase the rights of government. Grenville agreed. On 25 July, the Treasury opened negotiations with Atholl. In the meantime, Grenville planned to station some ships and customs officers in the waters off Man.

Atholl did not bargain from a strong position. He could guess that Grenville planned to use the authority of a parliamentary act on the Isle of Man passed in 1725 to force sale, so he probably counted himself lucky in 1765 to get £70,000 for his rights. The price probably satisfied

Grenville, too. He knew it was something of a gamble, for he could not reasonably expect that the officers could immediately stop all the clandestine trade from Man.

In fact, his efforts in other areas during 1764 had not borne the expected fruits. In October 1764, the customs commissioners had sent him the depressing news that receipts for this year were down one hundred ten thousand pounds from the previous year.[56] Still, any reduction in smuggled tea from Man would help make up that deficit, so the effort seemed worthwhile. He had not expected his war against the smugglers to be easy. If they developed new tactics, so must he.

Buying the rights of government on the Isle of Man was a new tactic for Grenville to use in his efforts to control smuggling in British waters. He chose to interfere in the existing political arrangements on Man, rather than trying to stop smuggling outside the country as he had in the cases of England and Scotland. This was not, however, an entirely new situation for him. In North America, too, the King's authority was distant, and his officers' powers were weak. Smuggling was rampant there for similar reasons: The inlets and coasts invited clandestine trade, and the people supported the smugglers. In North America, as in the case of the Isle of Man, this situation convinced Grenville that he had to take extraordinary measures to diminish smuggling. In both places, he also felt compelled to gamble that he could devise ways not only of enforcing the law, but also of changing the internal political climate.

Grenville and Administrative Reform

In his famous speech on American taxation, Edmund Burke gave an intriguing explanation of Grenville's ill-fated decision to go ahead with a colonial stamp tax. Grenville's error, Burke argued, was not due to any defect in character, nor to any shortcoming in mental ability, nor to any inattention to detail, nor to any failure in his dedication to duty. In all these respects, Grenville deserved his reputation as "a first-rate figure in this country." Burke therefore concluded that "if such a man fell into errors, it must be from defects not intrinsical." The source of Grenville's mistakes "must rather be sought in the particular habits of his life," habits that "do not alter the groundwork of [a man's] character, yet tinge it with their own hue."[57]

According to Burke, one of the most important of these "particular habits" was his service for most of his adult life in one government office or another. Such men were "apt to think the substance of business not to be much more important than the forms in which it is conducted." As a result, they ascribed too much importance to correct procedures and precedents and too little to a broad "knowledge of mankind, and . . .

[an] extensive contemplation of things."[58] Burke summed them up thus: "Men in office go on in a beaten track."[59] They were unable to respond flexibly "when a new and troubled scene is opened, and the file affords no precedent."[60]

Perhaps Burke's criticism of most of officialdom in eighteenth-century Whitehall was accurate; it was not, however, a just charge against Grenville. Grenville had not merely "studied practically the several duties and services of most offices"; he had studied them with an eye toward improving their services when it seemed necessary.[61] In his first office, as a junior Lord of the Admiralty during 1744–1747, he soon felt confident enough to question the deployment of ships made by veteran admirals. He interested himself in particular in the regular and efficient cleaning of ship's bottoms. In 1745, he persuaded the other Lords of the Admiralty to order the Navy Board "to take all possible care to put everything at that yard [at Kinsale] into order immediately for the cleaning of ships."[62] Soon afterward, he fretted that "we [might] spoil all our line-of-battle ships, by keeping what formed the Western Squadron in the Downs all winter, instead of cleaning them, and putting them in order for the spring," and thus be vulnerable to a French invasion.[63] In 1746, during the planning of a Canadian expedition, Grenville insistently reminded the First Lord of the Admiralty, the Duke of Bedford, of the absolute necessity of making preparations early and of sending news of the plans to America as quickly as possible.[64] This burst of energy came to naught, as the mission was scrubbed, and Grenville's efforts to create greater efficiency in the planning and execution of a major expedition in America bore no fruit. This must have seemed a typical development to Grenville, for as time passed he became less and less enchanted with his colleagues at the Admiralty (and they with him) and more and more eager to become a Lord of the Treasury. Finally, after a frustrating wait, he achieved that post in June 1747.[65]

Grenville's service at the Treasury was, however, equally frustrating. Henry Pelham, the First Lord, did not trust him, and he, in turn, disliked Pelham. On at least two occasions, Pelham broke promises he had made to Grenville, and the embittered Grenville later referred to his activities at the Treasury during 1747–1754 as "giving what support I was able to those who never gave any to me."[66] Despite these personal frictions, however, Grenville had a deep appreciation for the boldness and calculation with which Pelham accomplished the reduction of the national debt. However much it may have galled Grenville to do so, in his first speech on the budget to the House of Commons, he praised Pelham's reform and at the same time hoped that his parliamentary opponents would be as public-spirited in assisting him with necessary reforms as Pelham's had been.[67]

For most of the time between 1754 and 1762, Grenville served as Treasurer of the navy. He devoted much of his energy during that period to devising and attempting to enact legislation that would enable the navy to mobilize much more quickly in times of emergency. In his view, the principal reasons that the navy could only reach full strength over a period of years rather than months were the shortage of trained seamen in the service at the beginning of war and the difficulties of recruiting them. To solve these problems, he proposed to make the navy more attractive to skilled volunteers, and to make it more attractive, he planned to provide for "a regular method for the punctual, frequent, and certain payment of [seamen's] wages; and for enabling them more easily and readily to remit the same for the support of their wives and families; and for preventing frauds and abuses attending such payments." These, he had discovered, were among the principal grievances of seamen. Remedy them, he assumed, and the navy could be manned more easily. He drafted a bill that established budgetary and administrative restraints and procedures that he believed would accomplish these reforms. Ultimately, he not only succeeded in getting passed the Navy Act of 1758, "arguably the most single important piece of legislation attempting to grapple with [these problems] between 1696 and 1835," but he did so in the teeth of opposition from the Navy Board itself.[68] The next year, Grenville again attempted a major reform. Grenville's and Pitt's allies introduced legislation that would have required all skilled British seamen to register with naval authorities. In time of war, the navy would determine how many seamen it needed, and names would be chosen by lot off this list. The bill also limited seamen's service to three years at the usual wages, requiring the navy to pay them threepence per day extra if it chose to keep them a fourth year and sixpence per day extra thereafter. If the bill had passed, the major reasons that few men volunteered—low pay and indefinite service— probably would have been removed to a considerable degree. But the merchant community at large rallied against the bill and finally defeated it in March 1759.[69] Thus the program for naval reform remained incomplete.

Also during his tenure as Treasurer of the navy, Grenville maintained his earlier interest in the operation of the navy's yards. When he heard about an investigation into a fraud at the Deptford yard, he intruded himself into it, even though such an investigation lay outside his official duties.[70] This particular matter continued to concern him during his brief service as First Lord of the Admiralty, October 1762 to April

1763. When he discussed the expense of maintaining the fleet in good condition with his successor at the Admiralty, he noted, "The most reasonable and knowing part of the world have long been persuaded that all the naval money is by no means applied in the most frugal manner." Furthermore, he continued, "I have thought so myself, [and] I did resolve when I had the honor to be in that office, to make the strictest and most careful examination into a matter of this great moment, and had taken some steps toward it, but my short continuance in that station prevented me from carrying it into execution."[71]

Thus, when Grenville began work at the Treasury, he had had long experience at personally examining the usual practices and procedures of important offices, testing their efficiency and usefulness, and changing them when he felt change was necessary for the service of the country. Arguments from officials and from interested parties did not deter him from these investigations, any more than their opposition to his proposals frightened him from attempting reform. Had he lived long enough to hear Burke's description of him as a follower of the "beaten track" of office, no doubt he would have laughed. On a variety of occasions in his official career, he had attempted to beat his own track. His failures at doing so did not discourage him; his successes acted as inspirations to go on in his own way when necessary. During his tenure at the Treasury, this "particular habit of his life," his willingness to take political gambles, and his determination to crack down on clandestine trade were to encourage him along the path toward imperial disaster.

Chapter IV

"The First Great Object": Obstructing the Clandestine Trade to America, April–November 1763

Grenville had begun worrying about the contraband trade to America while most of his colleagues were still concerned about the terms of peace. In 1762, the Cabinet had decided to give France possession of two islands in the Gulf of St. Lawrence, St. Pierre and Miquelon, to serve as shelters for French fishermen, on condition that France fortified neither, erected no buildings except for the convenience of the fishing fleet, kept no more than fifty men there, and permitted periodic British inspections. On 26 July 1762, Grenville noticed that the counterproposal from Versailles "left out . . . the words relating to the inspection," so he "proposed that they should be inserted again in our answer." The military potential of these tiny islands did not frighten him much. It was their potential for becoming depots for an illicit trade between France, the nation's great enemy, and the North American colonies that disturbed him. Grenville knew about the illegal commerce in the Caribbean; he did not want to create a similar area in the fishing waters. At first, "all the other Lords," however, "seemed not inclined to" insist on inspection. Undismayed, he wore down their reluctance. When Bedford left for France, the Cabinet instructed him to insist upon an *"inspection raissonable"* of St. Pierre and Miquelon.[1]

Grenville also wanted to keep the French fishing fleet as far from Cape Breton as possible. In this case, military considerations were important to him. The inhabitants of Cape Breton probably would not change their allegiance from France to Britain just because of a treaty. The French, therefore, must not be given the chance to appeal to old loyalties in a future war. Inhibiting the development of a clandestine trade also concerned him, though. If Cape Breton was British, then Britain should monopolize its trade. Moreover, the thought that ports on this island were conveniently located for illicit commerce between France and the American colonies may have crossed his mind. He wanted to forbid the French fleet from sailing closer than thirty leagues. When the French objected, he agreed with the rest of the Cabinet that

Bedford could "give way, and reduce this distance from the coast of Cape Breton, within which the French are not to be allowed to fish, to twenty or to fifteen leagues, relaxing however as little as you possibly can on this head."[2]

Ultimately, Britain had to yield on both points. The preliminary articles did not include provisions for British inspection of St. Pierre and Miquelon. Eager for peace, Bute's administration had settled for the French king's word that his nation would abide by the terms of the cession and for only a fifteen-league limit off Cape Breton.[3] These developments clearly disturbed Grenville. When Egremont asked on 8 March 1763 for instructions to the commander of naval ships stationed at Newfoundland, Grenville and his colleagues produced a draft in less than two weeks.[4] When Charles Townshend, as President of the Board of Trade, reported to the King on 15 March on the dangers presented by the smuggling of French goods from Labrador, the coast of Canada, Acadia, and St. Pierre and Miquelon (islands, according to the report, "convenient for carrying on an illicit trade with North America"), Grenville copied the report. Within two weeks, the Admiralty had written further instructions for all naval officers in the waters from Newfoundland south. The tenth instruction read, "In case any endeavors shall be used to carry on an illicit trade from . . . St. Pierre and Miquelon with the island of Newfoundland, or with any other part of His Majesty's dominions in North America, you are to be particularly attentive to the same, and to prevent (if possible) all communication whatever between the said islands . . . and any part of His Majesty's dominions in America." The Admiralty also ordered its officers to keep French vessels outside the fifteen-league limit.[5] Townshend and Grenville's concern that these waters would become havens for smugglers probably helped convince the Treasury to recommend extending the provisions of the Hovering Act to North America. The Admiralty then revised its instructions to captains in American waters to conform with this act and sent the final draft to the King on 27 May. Six days later, Grenville and the rest of the Cabinet approved the instructions, advising that they be "forthwith transmitted" to America.[6]

Townshend's arguments for reducing the molasses duty probably deepened Grenville's concern about contraband trade in America. Whatever Grenville may have said in rebuttal to Townshend in the House on 30 March, in his heart he accepted as true the assertion that the deficiencies in the American revenue were due to smuggling. "It will, I am afraid, be necessary for us to make many regulations with regard to the officers of the customs in North America," he wrote to the Earl of Bath on 30 April, "which may probably stop for some time the appointment of new officers there."[7] He did not elaborate on the regulations, nor the reason for them, but clearly he was intent on strengthening the enforcement of laws against illicit trade. Three weeks later, Grenville officially committed the Treasury to reforming the American customs service. On 21 May, Jenkinson wrote to the customs commissioners, ordering them on behalf of the Treasury to consider the state of the revenue in America, find out why it "was not equal to the sums it should be," and "report as soon as possible your opinion thereupon to the Treasury Lords." Furthermore, he added, "Take into your consideration in what manner the same revenue may be better collected for the future, and as soon as you have drawn up a plan for that purpose, . . . transmit it with all expedition to their Lordships for their approbation."[8]

Grenville had been First Lord of the Treasury for only five weeks when the commissioners received this letter. As yet unaware of his determination to reduce smuggling drastically in Britain and America, they dawdled. On 14 July, Jenkinson wrote again. The Treasury, he announced, planned to consider their report on the customs revenue in America on 22 July. The commissioners made the deadline with one day to spare.[9] By that time, Grenville had already begun considering the implications of some information he had received from two men outside the government. He was also preparing to act on some of their suggestions for reform.

The Advice of McCulloh and Ware

At first glance, it may seem strange that Grenville was ready to reach some conclusions about colonial trade and willing to make some decisions about the best ways of attacking colonial smuggling before receiving expert opinions from the customs commissioners. Such readiness was, however, typical of the skepticism he had often displayed during his career about the value of official boards' opinions and the wisdom of their established administrative practices. Given his past record in office, and given the record of inefficiency and corruption revealed by the dismal customs receipts from America, it is not surprising that Grenville and his colleagues had begun their own inquiries before the Customs Board reported to the Treasury. Given the apparent quality of the information and suggestions those inquiries produced, it is not surprising that Grenville was prepared to make some decisions as well.

Soon after 5 July 1763, Jenkinson received a letter with enclosures from Henry McCulloh. The two men may have met previously, for, as McCulloh's son later noted, "My father's political connections are far from contemptible." Moreover, McCulloh had addressed a memorial on the subject of colonial reform to Bute while Jenkinson was the Earl's secretary. If they were acquainted, Jenkinson knew that McCulloh had been a merchant and land speculator in North Carolina, still owned thousands of acres there, and had served as a special commissioner inspecting quitrent payments in the Carolinas. But even if they were strangers, Jenkinson recognized that Grenville would be interested in McCulloh's plan for a stamp tax on the colonies estimated to yield sixty thousand pounds a year. Jenkinson forwarded that plan to the First Lord, sending with it McCulloh's proposal for using the proceeds from the tax as security for exchequer bills of union in America.[10] He may have also enclosed a paper by McCulloh with the cumbersome title "General thoughts with respect to such regulations as are humbly conceived to be necessary in America and in the islands in the West Indies lately ceded to us by France."[11] In this paper, McCulloh briefly described the colonial trade in contraband products and goods and offered some thoughts on how to curb it.

Around the same time, someone at the Treasury was in contact with Nathaniel Ware, apparently to discuss his views of the colonies' clandestine trade, for Ware referred in a 22 August 1763 letter, included in Grenville's files, to an estimate he had made earlier of the amount of molasses annually smuggled into America. As the men with whom he discussed the illegal trade realized, he was ideally suited to describe it, having served as comptroller of the customs at Boston from 1750 until 1757. Indeed, he still held that post, though he had been on leave in England for the past six years.[12] Officially, Ware had obtained leave because of his "perpetual want of health in America through the extreme severity of that climate," and he had been asking Treasury officials since 1757 to grant him an equivalent place in England in exchange for his American office in order to preserve his physical well-being.[13] He had also, according to the story he told Bute in July 1762, described to H. B. Legge, Chancellor of the Exchequer from 1757 to 1761, "both in words and writing, several practices in the American trade apparently hurtful to the manufactures and commerce, and consequently to the revenue of Great Britain, if not disgraceful to the Mother Country and to His Majesty's Administration, where the subjects by their extreme remoteness are prevented from judging of either except from the specimen[s, the corrupt customs officers] before their eyes."[14] Ware, during his extended leave, had also discussed the clandestine trade with Newcastle, who promised him an English place, and with Halifax, "to whom [after] I had presumed to offer some imperfect observations on the present state of the Northern colonies, was likewise pleased to honor me with his countenance." None of these expressions of approval and promises of reward had resulted in a place, however, and thus Ware approached Bute in 1762, closing one plea with an eloquent appeal:

> If national industry be the true principle of this empire, and commerce rather than conquest its most interesting object; if Great Britain in return for so much blood and treasure can never derive any advantage from these American colonies, whatever vague ideas may be conceived of their value, except by their trade; if in the amazing growth of the British settlements upon that continent the seeds of a future independency be already discoverable; if the time approaches when any force the Mother Country shall be able to apply at such a distance may prove very ineffectual, should the authority or reputation of her government be unhappily lost; and if that opinion or reputation of that must really after all depend, among the inhabitants as it were of another world, upon the conduct of such as are appointed over them from hence, your lordship will best judge whether His Majesty's future service . . . may not in those distant parts probably be affected by the apparent discouragement of an officer who endeavored to act upon the above principles, and was notoriously known to reject the usual methods of accumulating.[15]

Evidently, Bute's response to Ware's letter has not survived. Certainly Ware was ready, if called on, to describe the clandestine trade in detail, analyze both specific and general weaknesses in the supervision and governance of the colonies, and propose a series of reforms. He had already prepared a lengthy report on these subjects and presented it to the Earl of Halifax.[16] Whether Bute ever spoke with Ware, or read a copy of his report, is, however, unknown. It is intriguing to note that years later John Almon recalled from the political gossip of the early 1760s that Bute had studied closely "a plan . . . by a naval officer from Boston, of new modeling the governments of that country" and had begun "this scheme . . . in idea, before the conclusion of the peace in 1763."[17] Whatever the fate of Ware's report in 1762, its survival allows the historian to know what his ideas were.[18] That he changed his mind before the Treasury contacted him in 1763 is highly unlikely.

At least two men in Grenville's Treasury were familiar with Ware and his particular claim for a place, but who contacted him is unknown. Lord North knew about Ware; one of Ware's petitions to Bute for a job in England is in North's files. Charles Jenkinson also knew about the comptroller of Boston, for Jenkinson, in his capacity as Bute's secretary, read, endorsed, and apparently filed the letter Ware wrote to Bute on 6 July 1762.[19] The hints that Ware threw out in that letter about his intimate knowledge of smuggling and corruption in the colonies, and his transparent desire to gain a place by suggesting ways of hindering the one and ending the other, could not have escaped Jenkinson's attention. When the clandestine trade became an item of important business at Grenville's Treasury, Ware was an obvious source of information.

There were no signs of collaboration between McCulloh and Ware. They had different ideas about proper ways of raising a revenue in America, and, if they knew about one another, they probably regarded each other as rivals for favor and position. So Grenville must have been disturbed by their essential agreement about colonists' clandestine trade with European nations. Both McCulloh and Ware were sure that such a trade existed. Both believed that colonists illegally bought large quantities of East Indian piece goods and tea from foreigners. Both asserted that colonists also smuggled substantial cargoes of foreign linen, cambrics, woolens, and other textiles. McCulloh informed the Treasury that before the war the center of this trade was Cape Breton; Ware noted that Louisbourg on Cape Breton had been "the rendezvous of a great trade," but he also observed that each year ships sailed from Boston, Rhode Island, and New York to Holland and Hamburg, then returned directly to their home ports.[20] McCulloh and Ware both pointed out that most of the contraband initially entered British America through ports in the charter colonies, where the peculiar political institutions of those provinces and the dominant popular sentiment against enforcing British commercial legislation reduced customs officers' effectiveness to almost nothing. From the charter colonies, merchants reshipped the goods south. Once the contraband was in an intracolonial, coastal trade, it was impossible under the present system to detect its illegal entry. Thus, foreign products and goods circulated easily and safely through all colonial markets. How much contraband was involved in this trade? McCulloh told the Treasury, "Men acquainted with the trade computed [it] at upwards of £500,000 per annum." Ware did not set a figure on this illicit commerce. Instead, he invited the Treasury to remember what a "general consumption" tea was in America, then ask the British East India Company how much tea it sent there. He also reminded the Treasury that in 1754 white American colonists spent on an average twenty shillings apiece for British goods. "If it be considered," he argued, "that the very lowest orders . . . there are really better fed, clothed, and every way accommodated than the most industrious and discreet of our journeymen artificers in London, . . . can the smallness of the export be otherwise accounted for, than by supposing the people to be farther supplied either by a clandestine trade or their own manufacturers?" Most manufacturing enterprises in America were still tiny. "The great point," the one in which colonists "are really culpable, is their clandestine trade."[21] Finally, McCulloh and Ware agreed that reducing the volume of this trade should be, as McCulloh argued, "the first great object to be taken into consideration" by the government. "The profits are excessive, [and] should the people generally rush into it, what adequate remedy to apply, except fleets and armies, might be difficult to conceive."[22]

Grenville did not question the accuracy of this information. In the House on 9 March 1764, he stated that "a trade has been opened by three or four colonies with France to the amount of £4 or 500,000 a year," an estimate he repeated in private correspondence after he left office.[23] It is not surprising that he accepted McCulloh's and Ware's statements as correct. The two men's descriptions of the clandestine trade were remarkably similar. Moreover, they independently confirmed what Grenville already suspected: The waters around Cape Breton had been havens for smugglers. And, aside from these considerations, Grenville probably gave particular weight to information provided by McCulloh and Ware because they had not only been in America, but they had probably been involved, McCulloh as a southern merchant, Ware as a charter-colony comptroller, in the evil they described. Even if they did not participate in or connive at this trade, they were informing on fellow merchants and brother officers. "The character of an informer is so contemptible, [and] especially when the information is supposed to proceed from a mercenary motive," Grenville had observed before, "that . . . very few choose to run the risk of having such a character fixed upon them, . . . unless it be such an atrocious crime as entitles the prosecutor to the thanks of mankind in general, as well as to a reward from the society to which he belongs."[24] That McCulloh and—particularly—Ware would run such a risk probably enhanced their credibility with Grenville. Certainly he agreed with them that smuggling goods into America was an atrocious crime, if not in the eyes of mankind, then surely in the opinion of a nation dependent on colonists' buying more and more British goods. As Whately later noted, the clandestine trade "was all stolen from the commerce, and part of it from the manufacturers, of Great Britain, contrary to the fundamental principle of colonization, to every maxim of policy, and to the express provision of the law."[25] The Secretary's choice of verbs doubtlessly conveyed the emotions felt at the Treasury when that illicit commerce was contemplated there.

Grenville not surprisingly agreed with McCulloh and Ware that the government should take immediate steps against the clandestine trade. He had been a member of an administration that had confidently and publicly predicted in December 1762 that there was no need "to dread that want of trade which their adversaries insinuated, since North America alone would supply the deficiencies of our trade in every other part of the world."[26] Grenville probably qualified this sweeping statement in his own mind, but his words and acts throughout his tenure at the Treasury leave no doubt that he always believed that this trade was of great economic significance to Britain. As Whately commented after leaving office, it was from the North American colonies, and particularly the new ones, that "we must . . . chiefly expect compensation from the disadvantages under which our trade will labor in the European and other markets, where we have competitors to encounter."[27] If Britain's competitors had penetrated colonial markets, they had to be attacked, and attacked vigorously. Moreover, Grenville and his colleagues also agreed with the warning from McCulloh and Ware that the presence of European competition in the North American colonies signaled political difficulties as well: Smuggling European products and goods into America was a greater problem than smuggling into Britain "and the consequences of it more pernicious, as tending to break the connection between the Mother Country and the colonies."[28] For both economic and political reasons, the news from McCulloh and Ware was so deeply disturbing that it spurred action.

McCulloh and Ware had useful ideas about how to accomplish what Grenville later called the "particularly desirable" end of preventing the "intercourse of America with foreign nations."[29] McCulloh believed that the trade was potentially more vulnerable where it was now safest. All merchants should be required, he suggested, to list at the port of entry "the different species or qualities or quantities of goods imported from Great Britain." When merchants shipped goods to other colonies, the collector would list in a cocket "what part or proportion of the said goods so imported from Great Britain are [being] shipped coastways by them." When a ship entered another port, the collector there would check cocket against cargo. If the cocket did not describe the cargo accurately, or if it did not show that the goods were legally imported, the collector would seize and condemn the goods. Officers in Britain, McCulloh pointed out, used this form to prevent frauds in the shipment of debenture goods. "In America, it is absolutely necessary for the preventing of smuggling that all goods whatsoever should be subjected to this regulation." Using the cockets in this way would prevent any "great quantity of prohibited goods . . . [from being] carried to the Southern colonies, in which the far greater part of the said goods are at present consumed." Such a provision might also be useful in enforcing the collection of a reduced molasses duty. "Consequently," this reform would "increase the exportation of our home manufactures and other goods usually shipped from this Kingdom, and may also be the means of raising a fund for the use of America."

Ware had a more elaborate program of reform. He suggested that the government reconcile and codify the various statutes dealing with the customs in America. He noted that the customs commissioners needed to write clearer, more up-to-date instructions. He argued that the home government should provide a standardized set of fees for officers, a move that would prevent both gouging and dependence on local assemblies. Officers should not be allowed to hire substitutes, as that encouraged corruption. The surveyors-general in America should inspect all ports in their districts every two years and report to the Treasury on them. Moreover, the Treasury should require all collectors "to keep two books, the one for foreign, the other for coasting trade," and to enclose "general accounts of all exports whether, and of all imports whence," with their quarterly accounts of customs receipts. The customs commissioners could then compare accounts from every port in America and England and, according to Ware, at "a single glance . . . discover any fraud that may arise, and in what ports." If any officers dared to be corrupt or proved to be inept under this surveillance, the Treasury could expeditiously remove them, thereby increasing the fear of the others and encouraging further conscientiousness. Ware confidently predicted that if the Treasury implemented his reforms, the men there would soon see a remarkable growth of British trade to America.[30]

McCulloh's and Ware's suggestions impressed Grenville. They seemed to be practical and promised to be effective. If customs officers in Britain could follow similar procedures and use similar documents, then officers in America could do the same. Requiring cockets and making officers keep comprehensive records on all commerce would at least put smugglers and their corrupt accomplices to more trouble. As the records became more complete, moreover, the Treasury would have a fuller picture of the movement of commodities in trade within the British empire. Such comprehensive plans would not only put smugglers in greater jeopardy, but they would also allow the home government to regulate both the customs service and imperial commerce even more effectively. Finally, the plans would be inexpensive to implement. The Treasury would not immediately have to appoint new officers in America to execute these reforms, an appealing point to men who watched every shilling.

Reforming the Customs Service

The customs commissioners' report on 21 July confirmed and supplemented the observations and suggestions made by McCulloh and Ware. Noting that this report referred to one dated 10 May 1759, the Treasury retrieved that document from its files and read it as well on 22 July. The 1759 report cited extensive trade between the colonies and Holland and Hamburg. The more recent document confessed that the officers in America often served interest rather than duty, suggested that all absent officers be ordered to their stations, and advised that some frauds might be more easily detected "by farther checks and restraints to be imposed by Parliament, whereby the identity and quantity of goods shipped in the West Indies, and the duties paid there, may be better ascertained, and determined upon their arrival at the port for which they cleared out."[31] Grenville acted with his customary dispatch on the recommendations from his official and unofficial sources.

On 25 July, Jenkinson informed the commissioners that the Treasury wanted them to order all officers to their stations. If customs officers did not depart by 31 August, the commissioners were to dismiss them. Then Grenville and his colleagues issued a number of instructions to the Customs Board regarding officers in America and record keeping of dutied and undutied goods. The commissioners had not advised that the Treasury make these orders in their 21 July report, nor had they attempted to inspire them with deliberate hints. That the men at the Treasury devised these instructions themselves, however, is highly unlikely. Such was not the usual procedure of eighteenth-century Treasuries, which rarely formulated specific reforms of commercial regulations, preferring instead to rely on the expertise of outside authorities. Moreover, in 1763 Grenville and his associates knew very little about the procedures and papers of customs officers, an ignorance that ultimately so disturbed the First Lord that he tried to educate himself by studying reports from English ports.[32] The detail of these instructions, and the Treasury's obvious confidence in their efficacy, leaves scant room to doubt that Grenville and his colleagues had listened to experts on the subject. The congruence of these instructions with reforms advocated by McCulloh and Ware strongly suggests that they were those experts.

The Treasury began by directing the commissioners to send proper instructions to all customs officers, "enforcing in the strongest manner the strictest attention to their duty," and commanding them to maintain regular correspondence with London, describing their proceedings, the conduct of their subordinates, and any obstructions they met with. This order was probably inspired by one of Ware's suggestions, as was the next, which dealt with all goods in colonial trade, not just the dutied ones that the commissioners had confined their attention to in their 21 July report. Officers in America were to "transmit . . . exact accounts of the imports and exports of the several ports, and what may from time to time be the state of the revenue in consequence of these directions."[33] Three days later, the Treasury again considered the reports of 10 May 1759 and 21 July 1763 and again meshed them with a suggestion from outside. Jenkinson informed the commissioners on 1 August that the Lords of the Treasury had noted their comments about the need for future parliamentary legislation to determine "the identity and quantity of goods shipped *in the colonies,* and the duties paid there."[34] The Treasury wanted a report on the nature of those parliamentary "checks and restraints." By substituting *in the colonies* for *in the West Indies,* Jenkinson was diplomatically suggesting that the Customs Board consider regulations to determine the identity and quantity of goods in the colonial coastal trade, as well as in the commerce between the British West Indies and mainland America. Thus the customs commissioners began studying the feasibility of McCulloh's proposal.

The commissioners produced their report and their draft of the new instructions to American officers on 16 September.[35] On 21 September, the Treasury inspected the commissioners' work. The report, which included a recommendation to use cockets to prevent the circulation of smuggled goods in the colonies, received approval from the Lords of Treasury. Grenville and his colleagues immediately ordered the Customs Board to prepare a bill enacting their proposals. The Board's draft of instructions, however, was too vague on one crucial point. Officers in America, the Treasury commanded, were "to extend their care not only to the improvement of the revenue, but also to the prevention of that clandestine trade."[36] Taking no chance of misunderstanding, the commissioners amended their instructions to require officers to prevent "the clandestine trade in foreign manufactures."[37]

Before they did this, however, the commissioners finally admitted what Grenville doubtlessly suspected: "The present increase and importance of our American colonies [demanded] that a proper person of experience and skill in business . . . be appointed Plantation Clerk" and devote all his time to matters affecting the colonies. The Treasury quickly approved this request. On 5 October, Grenville appointed Henry Hulton, a man whose probity and skill at examining accounts of British expenditures in Germany had impressed him, to the position.[38]

Hulton would receive all letters from America, prepare and dispatch the commissioners' answers, pay close attention to the conduct and correspondence of the officers, and "take care of the whole business in the plantation department relating to the revenues." He would place his observations on the state of the revenue before the commissioners, but he was outside their direct supervision. Indeed, when he accepted the job, Hulton assumed that he would be under Grenville's scrutiny, a prospect that delighted him, for he was ambitious and eager to please.[39] As for Grenville, he was happy to have a man at customs who would expedite American business.

The Treasury completed its efforts to "remove the causes to which the deficiency of [the American] revenue and the contraband trade with other European nations are owing" by preparing a memorial asking the King for assistance from other departments. "Strict orders," advised Grenville, "should be given to the governors of all colonies to make the suppression of the clandestine and prohibited trade with foreign nations, and the improvement of the revenue the constant and immediate objects of their care." Troops and ships in America should be placed in such stations that would enable them to assist in realizing these goals and in protecting the customs officers "from the violence of any desperate or lawless persons." In particular, the Treasury expected the navy to be as effective in American waters as it had been at home. Grenville and his colleagues therefore "earnestly wish[ed]" that sea patrols might "not only be continued, but even extended and strengthened as far as the naval establishment will allow." Finally, the Treasury recommended "that a uniform plan be prepared for establishing the judicature of the courts of admiralty in [America] under persons qualified for so important a trust." Impartial administration of justice, the Treasury explained, would insure the execution of British laws.

Drafting and completing this memorial took six days. Grenville and his colleagues signed it on 4 October and sent it immediately to the Privy Council where it was approved. By 10 October, the appropriate offices began taking measures to support the American customs service. At the Treasury, the period of concentration on discovering the causes and planning the obstruction of the clandestine trade in foreign products and goods had come to an end. Only the execution of that plan remained.[40]

The Significance of Customs Reform for American Taxation

During this period of concentration on smuggling, Grenville initiated an investigation into the advisability of reducing the molasses duty. He also ordered the drafting of a bill that would impose stamp duties on colonists. These cannot be coincidences of timing. That Grenville assigned Ware to help investigate the molasses duty and used McCulloh to help prepare the stamp bill suggests that he saw some relationship between reforming American commerce and reforming colonial taxes.[41] The agents of the colonies would have been happy to advise the Treasury on setting the molasses duty. Other men had suggested a colonial stamp tax; moreover, the Treasury could assume the availability of both the legal expertise of the stamp commissioners and whatever information on colonial documents was in the files at the Board of Trade. Indeed, Grenville included these other sources in his inquiries. But his respect for the knowledge and judgment of Ware and McCulloh, and probably his assumption that these men interpreted as he did the significance of the causes and extent of American smuggling for planners of American taxation, demanded that they be involved in these other investigations.

To Grenville, the volume of the clandestine trade had an arresting implication. If Americans imported four to five hundred thousand pounds worth of goods more than the records of their legal trade indicated, they could hardly claim exemption from parliamentary taxation on the grounds of poverty. Grenville probably never believed that colonists could not afford to pay any tax at all. He may have insisted in the House on 30 March 1763 that they were capable of paying a duty of sixpence on molasses. But after hearing McCulloh's estimate, he could never give credence to that claim. This did not mean, of course, that he would not be careful to avoid harming a specific colonial trade. In general, though, he could be sure that the population was prosperous enough to help support its own defense. Planners of taxation would need to be careful but not timid.

The size of that illicit commerce also indicated to Grenville that planners could dismiss the argument that because colonists spent all their money in Britain for manufactured goods, and thus supported the Mother Country, Parliament should not tax them. Indeed, assertions that the colonists traded exclusively with Britain must have seemed to Grenville as evidence of ignorance or knavery. He might answer them politely, as Whately did, that "some [taxes] are absolutely necessary, though 'all the produce should go . . . for [British] manufactures,' " but in his heart he would add, as Whately did, "which I wish more the case than it is." The existence of a huge clandestine trade, in fact, made it the Treasury's duty to find some means of taxing this wealth that was supporting the nation's rivals. Grenville noted in the House on 9 March 1764 that the Treasury's reforms had succeeded in somewhat reducing the volume of smuggling: "The proportion from England has increased." The increase was insufficient, however; Britain still needed to "collect the revenue from the plantations."[42]

McCulloh had noted that "the people settled [in America], especially in the charter governments, have always given great opposition to any [duties] passed here, and . . . conceived very wrong notions of their privileges." Ware shared the same sentiments. To Grenville, this must have been the natural consequence of years of uninhibited smuggling. Moreover, as he stated in the Treasury's memorial of 4 October, "Their vast increase in territory and population makes the proper regulation of their trade of immediate necessity, lest the continuance and extent of [these] dangerous evils . . . may render all attempts to remedy them hereafter infinitely more difficult, if not utterly impracticable."[43] Similar arguments held true for taxation. The longer Britain went without imposing and collecting a tax, the harder it would be to begin. Grenville's knowledge of a cause and an effect of smuggling—the willingness of large numbers of colonists to disobey British laws and their confidence that they could do so successfully—combined with his realization that the colonies were growing more powerful led him to believe that the government should tax Americans effectively and quickly.

The key word for him, however, was *effectively*. The accounts of McCulloh and, especially, Ware cannot have given him much confidence in the customs officers in America. Even if the Treasury did force them to go to their stations and to keep accounts of all imports and exports, the officers would still be the same men who before had either neglected their duties or connived with smugglers. Surely they would continue to look for opportunities. Surely they would find some. Ware's system of accounts might eventually detect the corrupt, but one or two seasons of an officer's issuing fraudulent cockets could permit the importation of considerable amounts of contraband. Less than a month after issuing the memorial of 4 October, the Treasury received complaints that illegal settlements "are frequently entered into for the duties at the ports in America."[44] Grenville ordered the commissioners to do their utmost to prosecute the offenders and to prevent similar occurrences in the future, but he cannot have been sanguine that the commissioners could prevent every artifice in advance. Nor could he solace himself with the thought that the Treasury would from now on identify and send only the best officers to the colonies. It would be "difficult," he knew, "to find good officers who will go to North America."[45] Too much confidence could not be placed in the navy, either. As a former First Lord of the Admiralty, he was aware of the navy's tight budget. As First Lord of the Treasury, he was aware that that budget had to stay tight. He might hope that the sea guard in

America would be "extended and strengthened as far as the naval establishment [would] allow," but he soon learned that was not very far. In November 1763, the Treasury asked the Admiralty to station "a competent number of sloops" off Rhode Island to prevent the clandestine trade there. The Admiralty replied that it could not "at present spare any others for that station"; the best it could do was send orders to the two ships in the area to be particularly attentive to Rhode Island.[46] Despite his best efforts, Grenville was certain that "smuggling . . . [would] continue." He therefore concluded, "As this will diminish the revenue, some further tax will be necessary to defray the expense [of defending] North America." That "further tax" could not be collected by customs officers or be dependent for its execution on a competent number of sloops. It would have to be an internal tax. McCulloh had suggested imposing a stamp tax on the colonists in early July. That sort of tax, Grenville reasoned, was "the least exceptionable" that Parliament could place on colonists, "because it requires few officers and even collects itself; the only danger is forgery." By September he was decided. McCulloh and the solicitor to the commissioners of stamps, Thomas Cruwys, began drafting a bill.[47] The Stamp Act of 1765 was to become the most significant legacy of Grenville's preoccupation with colonial smuggling.

It was not the only legacy, though. Another was a feeling of urgency, an urgency so strong that it overrode his training and experience in fiscal matters and compelled him to act quickly on American taxation. As a man knowledgeable in finance and taxation, Grenville knew that it was "a beneficial work to review the public taxes and make proper alterations, but it must be done with care."[48] Ill-advised, hastily executed changes could harm the nation's finances and trade at a time when neither could stand much damage. Moreover, the political dangers of precipitate tax reform had recently been brought home to him during the passage of the cider tax. He also had before him the example of the previous ministry's caution in approaching the taxation of colonists, a caution that he had publicly supported. As P. D. G. Thomas has pointed out, "Grenville is known to history as the man who taxed America; but his first speech on the subject [on 30 March 1763] was a successful intervention to stop such a tax."[49] Certainly Grenville did not lack excuses in 1764 for again delaying taxation. On 10 January 1764, William Wood, the veteran secretary to the customs commissioners, expressed to Jenkinson his wish "that every [th]ing which may have been thought of respecting the plantations may be deferred to another year." He continued, "You want information of several things from the plantations, especially in 'Account of what duties are payable by an act of assembly . . . on the importation and exportation of Negroes, wine, rum, or other liquors' or on any goods, or merchandise, and shipping."[50] But if Grenville ever heard this advice, he disregarded it. Aware that colonists were wealthier than their legal trade indicated, believing that taxation might be the most effficient and sure way of tapping that wealth, and certain that Parliament must impose taxes quickly, Grenville thought that the riskier gamble would be hesitation, not action. Grenville's administration, Henry Hulton observed late in 1763, had raising a revenue in America "much at heart."[51] This was the administration's goal, in large part, because the First Lord of the Treasury was determined to counteract the financial, commercial, and political effects of a huge clandestine trade.

Chapter V

Taxing Molasses, July 1763–March 1764

When Grenville began work at the Treasury, no one could be sure of his reaction to the idea of reducing the duty on molasses. Therefore, the customs commissioners, who traditionally did not like to lead where First Lords were unwilling or unable to follow, hedged their bets in their report of 21 July.[1] After admitting that colonists smuggled a huge amount of molasses and repeating their 10 May 1759 conclusion that "so long as the high duties imposed on [molasses] continue, the running the same in His Majesty's colonies will be unavoidable," the commissioners avoided directly advising a change. Instead, they observed, "It is but justice to say that many [officers] have suggested to us the expediency of introducing the produce of foreign colonies into North America in exchange for our fish and lumber [on the payment of] lower duties in British ships only." The officers advised this, the commissioners continued, because "the molasses particularly, being necessary to the distillers in New England, will continue to be run . . . , if not permitted to be entered at an easy rate, even if our officers were more active in their duty in defiance of all temptation or opposition." This was hardly a bold statement, though it represented a considerable change from their questioning in 1759 "how far it may be expedient to attempt to remedy this evil by an alteration of this law, which was passed at the request of the British planters [in the West Indies] as an encouragement to their trade."[2] Doubtlessly, the commissioners recalled that in the House on 30 March, Grenville had opposed lowering the molasses duty. They probably hoped he would see the wisdom of this step, but they could not be sure. If he held to his former opinion, it would be better for the American officers to bear the onus of making the suggestion.

When the customs commissioners reported on 16 September, they evidently did not doubt the direction of Grenville's policy. They confidently predicted that the necessities of British colonists in America and French colonists in the West Indies would increase the trade between the two areas. "Our colonies . . . , being now augmented, will require very great additional quantities of sugar, rum, and molasses for their own necessary consumption." They would buy most of these goods in the French West Indies, "where these commodities will be likely to be obtained at the cheapest rate." For their part, the French would require "far greater quantities" of provisions and lumber from British colonies, since they could no longer buy from French colonists in North America. They would pay for their products with the rum, sugar, and molasses that their suppliers demanded. "The flux of these commodities . . . being thus likely to be greatly increased, the establishing . . . proper duties thereon at a lower rate than at present, so as to diminish the temptation to smuggling, and the securing the just collection of these duties, seems to be an object at this juncture of importance to the revenue."[3]

The commissioners' confidence was surely based upon their assumption that Grenville would agree with their reasons for wanting to lower the duty. Because molasses was a commodity necessary to continuing prosperity in New England, colonists would not react to a moderate duty on it by withdrawing from the trade and looking for other, untaxed commerces. Instead, they would import legally, or they would smuggle. A moderate duty would encourage them to trade legally. Moreover, the French utterly depended on British colonies for their food and lumber. Colonists would seize the advantages monopolizers traditionally enjoyed, and either charge their customers enough more for American products or pay them enough less for their molasses to cover the amount of the lowered duty. Few men would run the risk of smuggling in order to evade a moderate tax they were not really paying. But if the tax remained too high, men would run that risk if they could find buyers for molasses that was substantially cheaper than that brought in by legal traders. In America, the odds that smugglers would escape detection and prosecution were high. It was impossible to guard the whole coast, and it was difficult to distinguish foreign from British molasses. Also, as the commissioners regretted, American customs officers were well aware of their "distance from inspection . . . in a country where the strict observance of [their duty] is rendered highly difficult and obnoxious." The twin temptations of profiting personally and avoiding trouble "too easily led [them] off from their duty to their interest." They could be trusted to collect a moderate duty on molasses, however, because no one would try to bribe or bully them. They would probably collect a significant sum from the beginning, too. The trade from America to the French West Indies, according to "common fame," was already sizable.[4] Whatever was collected could hardly be smaller than the revenue raised by the sixpence rate, which "has been for the most part either wholly evaded or fraudulently compounded."[5] Furthermore, as the colonies expanded and their trade increased, so would this revenue. For these reasons, the commissioners concluded that Parliament should reduce the molasses duty.

The Decision to Lower the Duty

If the commissioners assumed that men at the Treasury agreed with their analysis of the molasses trade, they were correct. Grenville repeated on 9 March 1764 in the House of Commons their point that "certain commodities from the French islands . . . are absolutely necessary" to the colonies. Two weeks later, he also told the House that, in effect, the French would pay the tax, because "they want our lumber as much as North America does their molasses."[6] The two Secretaries to the Treasury, Jenkinson and Whately, made the same points later in 1764. "The French, who have no other method of disposing of their molasses," Jenkinson confidently asserted, will be "forced to pay the duty and not the people of the colonies who purchase the molasses." Whately advanced another reason for reaching the same conclusion. French planters "depend on North America for the subsistence of their produce, as they can no where else procure in any quantity, or at any tolerable price, the casks and other materials that are necessary for that purpose."[7]

Still, the commissioners were not being overly timid when they phrased their recommendation to lower the molasses duty in oblique terms on 21 July. In theory, at least, if the French could be forced to pay a moderate duty, why could they not be forced to pay sixpence a gallon? Moreover, it was reasonable for the customs commissioners to assume that a minister who had declared in the House on 30 March that sixpence could be collected and who had responded to reports of smuggling in Britain and America by strengthening the water guard would be predisposed to enforce the existing rate. The question remaining for historians is, was the commissioners' caution misplaced? Put another way, did Grenville ever seriously consider the possibility of trying to enforce a sixpence duty?

One piece of evidence has survived that suggests he did, a letter written to someone at the Treasury by Nathaniel Ware on 22 August. Ware reported the result of a careful investigation into the volume of French molasses annually smuggled into the colonies and gave his opinion on ways by which "the old duty . . . [may] be exacted." That Ware himself settled on these lines of inquiry is unlikely; he personally favored doing away with all British duties on molasses. Such duties were, he believed, "prejudicial to British navigation," and thus economically harmful. He also saw some political benefits arising from repeal of the Molasses Act. "Nothing could more effectually palliate any necessary severity in putting an effectual stop to future clandestine importation from Europe" than ending this tax.[8] That Ware held these opinions, yet made this investigation, indicates that he did so at the Treasury's behest.

The text of the letter itself further strengthens this interpretation. Ware began his report abruptly, with no explanation of why he was making these inquiries, a mode of address he would not have adopted with the Treasury had Grenville and his colleagues not already been aware of the subjects he planned to report on. Moreover, Ware explained the delay of his report, which indicates that Grenville had been expecting Ware's answers. Also, after Ware enumerated the ill effects that would ensue if the full sixpence duty was collected, he excluded from his discussion of ways to mitigate those undesirable consequences the most logical and practical of all solutions: reducing the duty. This omission suggests that the Treasury asked him to consider only the feasibility of collecting the sixpence duty.[9] Finally, Ware was a desperate man when he penned this report. Because his health had suffered cruelly during Boston's winters, he had tried since 1756 to obtain an equivalent place in England. Furthermore, he had an additional reason to dread returning to New England. As he observed to Bute in 1762, he felt keenly "the necessity of being protected . . . , and rather than return among a people who must of course disapprove any attempts to throw light upon their transactions, I prayed to be removed elsewhere, even though it were to an appointment of less value." If he felt this way before his collaboration with the Treasury in 1763, his apprehensions must have increased apace as he used "various shifts and pretenses" during that year to extract information from Americans in London. If he still could not get an English place, Ware at least wanted to continue to receive his salary while remaining in absentia. The Treasury's order that officers absent from America be on their way to their posts by 31 August or face dismissal all but foreclosed this hope.[10] It is unlikely that any man in this situation would have spent his time making an inquiry and writing a report on matters that ordinarily would have seemed unessential to him without feeling certain that the First Lord wanted a report on those subjects. In Ware's case, it is much more probable that he rushed to complete his answers to questions that Grenville had asked him to investigate.[11]

From Grenville's standpoint, Ware was the ideal man to make such an investigation. He had served as comptroller at a port where, as the First Lord knew, ships reputedly brought in vast amounts of French molasses. He might, therefore, know how the trade operated and at what prices smugglers bought and sold molasses. Even if he did not know everything, he would know how to find out additional information. In making inquiries, he would have the knowledge and experience necessary to recognize improbable rumors and estimates, no matter how plausible they might seem to the uninitiated. Finally, Grenville could be certain that Ware's eagerness for an English place would impel him to deliver accurate information to the Treasury as quickly as he could. On this last point, the First Lord was not disappointed. Ware had his report ready by 22 August, nine days before he was required to leave for America.

In the course of his investigation, Ware discovered that men in London firmly believed that "the importation of foreign molasses has increased greatly during the war to the amount of . . . sixty thousand hogsheads annually." He did not accept this figure, which was much higher than his conservative estimate of twelve thousand hogsheads, at face value. And, after investigation, he discovered that the higher figure was based on conjecture and thus was "too vague to be depended upon." He decided that a more accurate estimate could be obtained by determining how many distilleries were in America, then by finding out how many hogsheads of molasses the average distillery would use every year. To this total, he planned to add an estimate of the amount of molasses Americans consumed in their beer and food. Moreover, he decided to collect his data only from those Americans in London who were familiar enough with that country's commerce to give reliable answers. Unsurprisingly, he found these colonists "extremely cautious of giving any light into their own affairs," but through his patient use of "various shifts and pretences" he ultimately succeeded. On 22 August 1763, he reported to Grenville that American distilleries probably consumed at least 38,625 hogsheads of molasses per year. In addition to this total, colonists added to their food and beer "five thousand hogsheads more than is said to be imported from all the British islands, so that, if our calculations be just, the foreign only must exceed 43,625 hogsheads."

Could sixpence per gallon be collected on this molasses? Ware's research indicated that the trade was thriving despite costs of bribes and provincial taxes that totaled around that figure. He cautioned Grenville, though, that the trade would not survive an additional British duty of sixpence. The margin of profit, already fairly slender, would absolutely vanish, and "that trade must totally fail." Ware did not think that this was desirable. Not only would the provinces most deeply involved in it be ruined, but other colonies would quickly feel the contraction of their market for lumber. Moreover, the French were dependent on America for supplies, and "in case of a rupture, what use may not be made of such advantage?" The advantage would be lost if commerce with the French

West Indies ceased. The sole solution, therefore, was to collect the sixpence duty only if "all provincial duties are taken off."

This was not the only change the Treasury should make, according to Ware. He warned Grenville that taxing foreign molasses heavily without placing some duty on British molasses would encourage illicit traders to try to bribe customs officers in the British West Indies to certify foreign molasses as domestic. Such efforts, he predicted, would be successful to the point that the amount of British molasses imported would "probably be doubled by collusion of the people in our islands," although this, he added, "is no more than has formerly been practiced." Even if the Treasury did put some duty on domestic molasses, it would be necessary to tax rum produced in the Caribbean as well. "Was the duty to extend to molasses only, the foreign islands would manufacture theirs into rum for the use of the continent, as in part they do already; or, which would be much the same in the end, our own islands would do it for them." Ware did not insult the First Lord's intelligence by drawing the obvious conclusion. If Grenville wanted to avoid disrupting the American colonies' commerce in molasses and to collect much money at all from this duty, the Treasury would have to take these steps.

Ware closed with a final recommendation. He anticipated that collections of the molasses duty would "fall short of expectation," because "there must . . . after all be a large deduction for frauds, under the term 'leakage.' " So he suggested that the Treasury tax some other goods and services that the assemblies had successfully taxed. These included a duty on all sugar imported into America, excises on wine and Mediterranean fruits, and a tonnage duty on ships entering American ports. Because Britain paid for the defense of the American frontier, the assemblies could not reasonably protest to the Mother Country's tapping of these sources of income. On this note, Ware ended his report.[12]

Ware's report, combined with considerations Grenville could reach independently, probably ended the First Lord's hope that the Treasury could collect the existing duty. Ware had tacitly assumed that the new system of law enforcement in the colonies would work perfectly; Grenville could not realistically make that assumption. Nor could he dare to hope that colonial assemblies would cooperate with the government by voluntarily repealing their taxes on molasses. To the contrary: Since, as McCulloh had observed earlier that summer, "the people settled there, especially in the charter governments, have always given great opposition to any" British tax, and since "they conceive very wrong notions of their privileges," he could expect strong resistance to such a proposition.[13] The resulting uncertainty about the total weight of taxes would assist smugglers and impede the legal trade. Moreover, Grenville believed it was desirable that colonists continue paying for the costs of their civil governments, so he was probably wary of diminishing their ability to do so.[14] He may have also been reluctant to take the chance of inadvertently encouraging French distilleries in the West Indies. Once established, such a manufactory might damage New England's economy to the point that colonists there could afford fewer British manufactured goods.[15]

Ware's report thus lengthened the odds against any attempt at collecting the sixpence duty. Around the time Grenville received it, he was also waiting to look at documents "on some American subjects respecting the customs . . . from the Customs House, which [Edward] Hooper [a commissioner of the customs] was then engaged in collecting." Whether these materials ever arrived is unclear. If they did, they must have supported the recommendation the commissioners made on 16 September to lower the duty. Even before these materials were due to arrive, the First Lord made arrangements to discuss them with Richard Jackson, the agent for Pennsylvania and Connecticut. Grenville could hardly have wondered about Jackson's reaction to a proposal to enforce the sixpence duty; the only question Grenville could possibly have had to ask Jackson was his opinion on how much it should be reduced.[16] Thus the commissioners' report of 16 September probably confirmed a decision that was already well in the process of being made in Grenville's mind: He would have to lower the molasses duty. Any effort to enforce collection of the sixpence rate would harm the empire's trade, without increasing the revenue or improving political relations between the Mother County and the colonies.

Setting the New Duty

The commissioners did not recommend what the new duty should be, and Grenville never asked for their advice on this point. He obviously regarded this decision as his responsibility. Besides, he and they knew that the customs house would not have precise information about the size of the bribe that smugglers usually paid their officers or about the amount of foreign molasses entered as the duty-free domestic product. Again, the First Lord had to look outside the official world of Whitehall for the intelligence he needed to make a decision.

Determining the approximate size of the usual bribe was not difficult. Ware told Grenville on 22 August that "about one penny sterling [went] to the officer for connivance." Apparently McCulloh also set it at this figure, for he advised lowering the duty to a single penny in "General thoughts."[17] Another informant, however, was certain that the bribe was at least five farthings (one and one-fourth pence) per gallon, and perhaps even higher.[18] During the fall of 1763, Richard Jackson discovered that one and one-half pence "seems by the best lights I can get the nearest the measure." Jackson probably passed this intelligence on to the Treasury. This, in his opinion, was a strong argument in favor of lowering the tax from sixpence to one and one-half pence, a sum that he proposed to Grenville. Moreover, he was not at all reluctant to introduce Jenkinson to a colonist who could provide him with "material information on the state of the customs, and manner of collecting them in that country." It is unlikely, then, that he would have withheld the fruits of his investigation from the First Lord.[19] Whether Jackson was the source or not, the men at the Treasury came to believe that smugglers were paying one and one-half pence per gallon.[20]

Finding out the size of the illicit trade was more difficult. Grenville cannot have expected that it would be easy, but he needed to settle upon some reasonably accurate estimate so he could calculate the probable produce of the tax and measure from the actual receipts whether much smuggling continued. Rumor in London had it, as Ware noted, that the illicit trade had risen during the war to sixty thousand hogsheads, or 6 million gallons (at the official standard of 100 gallons per hogshead), annually. Ware thought this "conjecture as to quantity [was] too vague to depend upon."[21] Grenville evidently agreed and asked Ware to investigate its accuracy.

The results of that investigation must not have heartened Grenville much. Calculating that there were 117 distilleries in America, assuming that each used "at a medium between 100 and 550 hogsheads each" every year, and adding the "farther consumption of molasses in beer and in their food throughout all that continent," Ware concluded that "the foreign only must exceed 43,625 hogsheads." He was unwilling to be more specific than that, obviously believing that 60,000 was an inflated figure. McCulloh made a similar estimate, guessing that smugglers brought in 43,200 hogsheads per year.[22]

Estimates made for Jenkinson and Whately were more promising. Jenkinson learned that the illicit trade probably amounted to ninety thousand hogsheads a year. Whately's information indicated that "the consumption of [foreign] molasses in North America is about eighty thousand hogsheads." Whately did, however, calculate that a duty of threepence would reduce consumption "in the proportion of 9 to 7," and thus "the quantity to pay the duty will be but 62,222 hogsheads." From these various sources, Grenville sensibly concluded that "the quantity [was too] doubtful [to] form any certain estimate" of the produce of a tax. Still, the preponderance of the evidence confirmed to his satisfaction that the volume of the trade was probably between forty-eight and seventy-two thousand hogsheads per year.[23]

A trade of that size could yield a considerable revenue, if the proper tax were discovered and imposed. Grenville began by asking for advice on this point from men outside the administrative offices of government. He seems to have started with merchants who traded with the West Indies, for "the sum first thought of by the Treasury was four pence," the figure the West Indians mentioned to Grenville.[24] He probably consulted with them first as a matter of political caution and courtesy. The West Indians, after all, had originally asked that Parliament impose a duty on the trade. Also, when the act came up for renewal, they were the men who advised continuing it. In his talks with them, though, Grenville learned they did not oppose a reduction in the duty. Their willingness to see the nation collect a greater revenue indicated that the commerce in French molasses did not overly concern them. This cannot have surprised him much. As an investor in sugar land in Barbados, he knew that British planters and traders in the West Indies were far more concerned with keeping French sugar out of American and British markets than they were with regulating the colonial trade in molasses. Any duty, or no duty at all, on foreign molasses would protect their interest in the American markets, for the very good reason that they had little interest in selling molasses there.[25] Indeed, some of the West Indians may have expressed privately to Grenville the hope Rose Fuller and William Beckford later stated publicly in the House, that the duty would raise a considerable revenue. So long as Grenville satisfied them by increasing the tax on foreign sugar and by preventing any contraband trade in sugar, he could lower the molasses duty. Equally important, by showing that they had no significant interests in these matters, the West Indians must have signaled to Grenville that they made their recommendation of four pence in the spirit more of a suggestion than of a demand. If he decided to lower it even further, it was not likely they would raise serious objections.[26]

When the agents for the American colonies learned about the West Indians' recommendation, Grenville indicated to them that he was seriously considering it. Whether this was true or not is unknown. On the floor of the House in 1766, he implicitly denied ever considering keeping the tax that high. He definitely did not discuss with the agents the greater importance that the West Indians placed on stopping the clandestine trade in sugar than on ending the commerce in molasses. There was no sense in giving the agents that bargaining advantage. Instead, in order to force the colonial agents to come up with what they believed was the highest realistic duty, he allowed them to remain mistaken about the West Indians' real concerns. He also told them bluntly that they should not waste their time with petitions for removal of this tax. "All agree," the agents learned, "that a practicable duty should be laid, and the payment of it enforced. To attempt to controvert either of these, would be to no manner of purpose."[27]

The agents responded "in conjunction" to this news. They advised that the duty be reduced to one penny.[28] As they may have observed to Grenville, experience had shown that this rate would not overburden the trade and could be collected. The First Lord's lack of enthusiasm for this proposal must have been obvious to Richard Jackson, the agent who knew him most intimately, for Jackson observed to Benjamin Franklin, "Though I wish the duty on foreign molasses was but one penny I shall not oppose a duty of twopence." The reason for Grenville's lack of enthusiasm is also obvious: At least one person had told Jenkinson that the bribe was higher than that. Given the fiscal crisis of the nation, he could hardly agree to a lighter tax than the one corrupt officers regularly imposed and collected. Perhaps in response to Grenville's reaction to a penny tax, Jackson proposed a duty of one-half penny more. He did so, he told Franklin, "because it seems by the best lights I can get the nearest the measure."[29] This proposal did not win Grenville's favor either, and again for obvious reasons. Whether or not Jackson informed Grenville of the reason for his suggestion, the First Lord knew that this figure was either close to or identical with "the measure," and he and his colleagues at the Treasury accepted as "certain" this maxim: "A duty may always exceed the expense of smuggling," so long as the difference was not too great.[30] According to a paper in Jenkinson's files, the difference between even five farthings and twopence was not too great. If the duty was twopence, "There [would] be no temptation to smuggle" molasses.[31] Grenville was clearly of a similar mind. So for fiscal reasons he rejected the agents' suggestions that he set the molasses duty below twopence per gallon; the nation would lose revenue at such low rates.

Political considerations also influenced this decision. The steps that Grenville and his colleagues took during the fall of 1763 against the smugglers of European goods certainly show no willingness to compromise with clandestine traders in American waters. To the contrary: Those decisions reveal a determination to attack smugglers aggressively and to force them to obey the law whenever possible. Setting the molasses duty below twopence per gallon, at the amount of the bribes paid to corrupt officers, "while a general relaxation of laws against [smuggling] prevailed over all that continent" and when measures had been taken to hamper clandestine trade, would be a surrender to the smugglers of molasses.[32] To be sure, they would pay the duty, but that payment would not teach them obedience to the law. Rather, it would symbolize the success of their previous resistance. If possible, Grenville wanted to remove such symbols from their memories by compelling merchants to pay a duty higher than the measure after he had increased the risk of detection, seizure, prosecution, and condemnation to the point that their self-interest would force them to obey the law.

Could the trade bear the collection of a twopence duty? Apparently no one at the Treasury ever doubted this. Their confidence was surely reinforced by the agents' response to the possibility of setting the tax at that rate. Neither Mauduit nor Jackson, agents who represented colonies deeply involved in the molasses commerce, objected to that sum, and, as Whately later observed, "thereby acknowledged their trade could bear" it.[33] Thus, a twopence duty had the advantages of being unburdensome and of being higher than the bribe and therefore no surrender to clandestine traders, but not so much higher as to offer great incentives to smugglers to continue in the illicit trade. By late 1763, the Treasury had decided to lower the tax to twopence. The person who during December 1763 drew up the "estimate of the tea, sugar, and molasses smuggled into North America" assumed that the duty would be twopence.[34] Moreover, on 30 December, Jasper Mauduit told his correspondents in Massachusetts, "Mr. Grenville seems now to be satisfied with twopence." In his next sentence, Mauduit flatly predicted that the duty "will not be more than twopence."[35]

Mauduit wrote to Massachusetts again on 11 February. He reported that "the West-India gentlemen have been at the Treasury Board, and the thought of laying threepence a gallon on the foreign molasses has been again resumed" by Grenville and his colleagues. Mauduit and his brother counterattacked, arguing that this duty would force Americans to offer French planters too low a price for their molasses. Rather than pay it, the French would establish more distilleries, make their own rum, sell it to the fishing fleet, and receive in return the refuse fish that was the staple of their slaves' diet. Americans in turn would have to choose between competing with their new rivals by paying more for French molasses and then trying to smuggle it into the colonies or by giving up the trade and reconciling themselves to buying fewer British manufactures and making their own. Either development would harm Britain; both could be avoided only by lowering the duty to twopence.[36]

The Mauduits formulated their argument skillfully. They had heard, Jasper explained, "many of the merchants" comment "that it is a common concern with both [Americans and West Indians] to discourage the French, Dutch, and Danish distilleries, and for that purpose to allow the foreign islands to sell us their molasses." Making this argument would, they hoped, allow them "to avoid, as much as possible, the committing ourselves in any dispute" with the West Indians.[37] The Mauduits probably also assumed that Grenville would be leery of taking a step that might destroy a foreign market for American agriculture and diminish the colonial market for British manufactures. This assessment was correct. Grenville did not, however, choose to protect British interests in the way the Mauduits desired. Instead, the Treasury decided to prohibit the importation of foreign rum into any British colony in America. Anyone caught trying to smuggle the prohibited liquor in would face a harsh penalty, the loss of the spirits and the ship that carried them.[38] Confident that this measure, enforced by a more active customs service on the mainland and a water patrol around Newfoundland, would discourage development of French distilleries and deter smuggling, Grenville did not allow the Mauduits' plea to influence his decision on the molasses duty. After inserting into the minutes a brief summary of the Mauduits' argument as "representing against the imposition of a higher duty than twopence on French molasses, as destructive of the distilleries [in Massachusetts], a heavy burden on the fisheries, and a means of promoting the distilleries lately set up by the French," the Treasury took no action on the brothers' recommendation. With this act, Grenville marked his final decision to set the duty at threepence.[39]

Reasons for Setting the Duty at Threepence

Jasper Mauduit never doubted that the "West-India gentlemen" deeply influenced Grenville's opinion, and many historians have believed the same. Grenville encouraged this interpretation himself. In the House on 30 April 1766, he described the threepence duty as a compromise: "The West Indians were for lowering it from sixpence to four pence, the North Americans to twopence, . . . [I] had proposed the middle way." No one contradicted this version at the time, so he probably explained his decision to the interested parties in the same way in February 1764.[40] Indeed, he could easily portray the decision as a compromise of economic interests. The West Indians thought four pence was "necessary to secure the preference due to British molasses"; the Americans "desired it might be no more than twopence, which they thereby acknowledged their trade could bear." Both sides had legitimate points, but neither could override the fact that the strained financial resources of the Mother Country required assistance from the colonies. Therefore, it would seem fairest that both sacrifice some to attain that essential end. As Grenville put it to the House on 9 March 1764, "You must collect the revenue from the plantations. . . . [My plan would] allow certain commodities from the French islands which are absolutely necessary, but . . . give a preference to our own colonies' manufactures by paying duty."[41]

In their own minds, the Mauduits and other agents knowingly added to this talk of economic compromise what they perceived to be the realities of West Indian political power. Grenville, they were sure, was trying to avoid antagonizing these powerful men. The First Lord did not need to hint at this interpretation with them; he could be certain they would reach it on their own. He may have reflected that at times no one is easier to deceive than men who pride themselves on being realistic, for when he described his decision as a compromise, Grenville was being more politic than frank. The West Indians were not sacrificing much, and he knew it. They distilled almost all their molasses into rum and then shipped it to Britain, where the upper classes drank it. The main interest of producers of molasses in the British islands was not keeping foreign molasses from Americans; it was reducing the duty paid on rum distilled in the British West Indies when it entered Britain. That tax, they believed, "always [has] and ever must prevent rum from getting to the lip of the common people." Its repeal, merchants trading to the West Indies argued in a petition to the Treasury on 18 February 1763, would both expand the rum's British market and "meet the French brandy, and in great measure prevent smuggling." One of the signers of that petition was Peregrine Cust, a man politically close to and respected by the First Lord, so much so that Grenville accepted advice on the nation's finances from him. When Grenville planned the reduction of the molasses duty, he consulted with Cust. If he did not already know about the economic facts of life in the islands, Cust could have told him.[42]

Grenville also knew he had no reason to fear the West Indians' political power. He had given them what they wanted, by increasing significantly the duty on foreign sugar imported to the colonies, from five shillings to twenty-seven shillings per hundredweight, and by prohibiting the importation of French rum.[43] Equally important, Grenville could be confident that he controlled a majority in the House of Commons. On 18 February, the administration had won a close vote over the question of general warrants after the opposition had been industrious "beyond all example and belief." Grenville counted almost fifty defections on this question of principle from the usual ranks of the government's supporters and expected that "most of them, if not all, will in all probability come back again . . . at the next division" to the side of the administration. Besides, raising a revenue in America was certainly more popular than serving general warrants.[44] Moreover, had Grenville been truly concerned about domestic politics when he decided on the molasses duty, he would have chosen twopence. Charles Townshend was not only the best debater the opposition had in the House, but he was also its leading spokesman on colonial affairs and a man whom "unfortunately [the opposition] . . . could neither do with . . . nor without."[45] Putting the duty at twopence would have insured at least his silence and probably his support. Grenville did not feel the need of that support, however. Indeed, by choosing threepence, he practically guaranteed Townshend's opposition.

So Grenville's decision was not the result of compromise, but the fruit of other considerations, one of which was surely fiscal. The First Lord believed that a threepence duty would yield more money than a twopence tax. Moreover, as will be seen, Grenville could not anticipate any political advantages from imposing twopence rather than threepence or from first setting the tax at the lower figure, then raising it later. It is worth pausing, however, to speculate why he bothered to describe it as a compromise. He probably did so to give the agents and their employers the impression that he was sufficiently concerned about their interests to resist the proposal of the West Indians. To people who accepted the power of that interest as an article of faith, his apparent willingness to compromise would seem proof positive of his goodwill toward the colonies. This interpretation becomes still more plausible when one remembers that Grenville was always careful during 1764 and 1765 to reassure the agents of his regard for Americans and his determination not to overburden them. Indeed, on 11 February 1764, he took advantage of a conversation with Israel Mauduit on the molasses duty to make precisely these points. "Mr. Grenville," reported Jasper Mauduit, "after the kindest expression of regard to the colonies, assured my brother that whatever were the distresses brought upon the revenue by the extravagant expenses of the war, [he] did not mean to draw anything from America for the relief of them." Grenville only desired, he continued, "that it should bear the charges of its own government and defense, and nothing more."[46]

Precisely what caused Grenville to decide between 30 December and 27 February that threepence would bring in more money than twopence will never be known. Certainly he never talked about this point with the agents. Some clues, however, have survived. At some time before 27 February, Whately calculated that threepence would raise £77,775 a year, even after the weight of that imposition reduced the volume of the trade. The Secretary's figures also indicated that the most twopence could raise would be £66,667. To men who referred to the saving of £8,000 on the collection of stamp duties in Scotland as a substantial gain for the Treasury, this sum was not to be despised, and Grenville may have been impressed by these estimates.[47]

Another clue may be found in his remarks to the House on 9 March, when Grenville argued that paying a threepence duty would have little effect on the colonists' trade because they could force their customers to pay it. He was referring not only to the French planters, but also to the Africans who consumed New England rum. He had learned, the First Lord told the House, that when American merchants abruptly raised the price of their rum in 1763 in anticipation of a strict enforcement of the sixpence duty, their Guinea trade did not suffer at all. Later in the debate, Peregrine Cust, whom members of the House regarded as an expert on the African trade, spoke "about the price of molasses being increased on the coast of Africa, by which he confirm[ed] what Grenville had said."[48] Cust had served as Bristol's representative on the governing committee of the African Company since 1755. In early 1764, that committee received word from the governor of Cape Coast that it must begin sending other spirits, for the Africans would not drink English brandy. The news that "English brandy will soon be absolutely unsaleable" may have caused Cust to deduce that New England rum was selling as well as ever despite its higher price, or he may have received this information privately.[49] Once Grenville heard this intelligence from his trusted friend, he must have quickly grasped its significance. As he told the House, this news proved that a significant part of the molasses trade could bear a threepence duty.[50] Moreover, as New England merchants realized that they could pay a threepence tax without losing their Guinea trade, smuggling molasses would lose much of its attraction. Would experienced traders dare detection and loss of ship and cargo to a more vigilant customs service in order to evade a duty they could expect to pass on to the consumer? Grenville could reasonably assume they would not. They would complain about paying the duty; that he could count on. But the odds were that they would pay.

Finally, a third clue may be found in Whately's pamphlet, *The regulations lately made concerning the colonies*. Whately claimed that smugglers had been paying one and one-half pence per gallon in bribes "while a general relaxation of laws against [smuggling] prevailed over all that continent." Once the laws were enforced, he predicted, "that charge will be higher in proportion to the additional risk of seizure." It was "certain," he also noted, "that a duty may always exceed the expense of smuggling," provided it did not exceed it so much as to encourage men to risk their reputation and property by smuggling goods and selling them at a substantial profit. Whately concluded that "these reasons concur to prove that a duty considerably higher than [one and one-half pence] per gallon may be imposed on molasses without being, by its excess, an inducement to smuggling."[51] Nothing exists to suggest that these statements, made in January 1765, do not accurately recount conclusions reached at the Treasury a year earlier. It remains unknown what information, or which informants, convinced the Treasury that the measures taken against smuggling in American waters would be sufficiently intimidating to raise the expenses and increase the uncertainty of the clandestine trade to the point where officers could collect a threepence tax. The dearth of information on these matters suggests that this analysis may have been the fruit of Grenville's determination to attack smugglers successfully, rather than of any outside source. Later in 1764, one friend of America was sufficiently impressed by Grenville's genuine and obvious outrage at smuggling to write to correspondents in New York, "The ministry, as well as the whole House, appear determined, at any expense or trouble, to attempt to put a stop to illicit trade." He warned them, furthermore, that this goal "will be most certainly attended to with the utmost vigor."[52] Perhaps Grenville, heartened by the successes of his campaign against smuggling in Britain during 1763, was optimistic about the equally vigorous actions in America, and thus decided on threepence.[53] Clearly, the feeling at the Treasury that the new measures would drive up the bribe, the news that American merchants could pass on the tax to some consumers of their rum, and the encouraging estimates of the produce of a threepence tax had an important influence on the decision to make the duty threepence.

The Uses of a Perpetual Revenue

Grenville was determined to make this duty and the other provisions of the American Revenue Act of 1764 (commonly called the Sugar Act) perpetual. In part, he must have wished to save future Treasuries and Parliaments the trouble of renewing it. Moreover, he probably wanted to spare merchants and customs officers recurring periods of uncertainty about trade conditions in the years ahead. Doubtlessly, he did not want to give colonists the impression that these reforms and taxes were temporary expedients, ones Americans could persuade the British government to repeal or reduce in the near future. Such hopes could lead them only to disappointment and frustration, for Grenville had no intention of modifying the threepence duty until he had given it a fair trial—over a number of years. He did not plan to be discouraged by small collections at the beginning; he had confidence that they would improve.[54] Furthermore, he desired that colonists come to terms as quickly as possible with what he expected to be a perpetual fact of life, that they would have to pay parliamentary taxes "for defraying the expenses of defending, protecting, and securing" the American colonies.[55]

Grenville had also decided that the revenue raised in America by parliamentary taxation would be used only for defense. As early as 6 January 1764, he had argued against Halifax over the merits of using the revenue for other purposes. Halifax was "extremely heated and eager" that part of the money should pay colonial officials' salaries. "Mr. Grenville," recounted Mrs. Grenville's diary, "would not consent to their having salaries from England."[56] P. D. G. Thomas has speculated that Grenville balked at Halifax's proposal "through political caution or financial economy." The more likely explanation is that both influenced his decision. In conversations with colonial agents, Grenville stressed that it was in the colonies' self-interest to assist in supporting the army that had defended them so capably in the past and remained on guard in the present. Because the Mother Country's straitened finances would not permit her to maintain an army in America without assistance, the colonies would have to make some of their own fiscal sacrifices if they wanted to continue to enjoy the full extent of British protection. Grenville could hardly have made such an artful appeal to self-interest had he been raising money by parliamentary taxation to support the existing civil establishment. The First Lord's awareness of this political advantage may also be seen in his vehement denials to the American agents in February 1765 of any intention of usurping colonial assemblies' legitimate functions, which to his mind included the support of civil government in the colonies. Jenkinson, too, was sensitive to the political implications of this decision. He noted in early 1765 that Britain had the right to use taxes collected in America for purposes other than defense but chose not to. "The discretion we use," he explained, "should . . . be a matter of comfort to the colonies, as it clearly points out that where necessity does not call upon us, where their own assemblies can sufficiently answer the purpose, we do not mean to exercise" the right. Grenville never used this argument publicly in the House or privately in conversations with the agents; by calling attention to Parliament's right, Grenville might cause unease in the colonies. Still, Jenkinson's comment, and Grenville's reaction to it, demonstrates again the Treasury's appreciation of the need for political caution in the use of American taxes.[57]

In his letter of 11 February 1764, Jasper Mauduit wrote that Grenville "desired . . . that [America] bear the charge of its own government
and defense." Some historians have interpreted this statement as an
indication that the Treasury was then considering authorizing the King
to use part of the money for the salaries of civil officers.[58] This plan was
discarded, one scholar has argued, when Grenville realized that the
receipts would not cover the full expense of the army, let alone that of
the civil establishment, too. The strength of this argument is diluted by
the fact that well before January 1764, Grenville could tell from the
discrepancy between Ware's and McCulloh's calculations and those of
Whately and Jenkinson that "the quantity of molasses [was] so doubtful
that he [could not] form any certain estimate" of its potential revenue.
No estimate placed the revenue above £77,775. McCulloh had guessed
in July 1763 that stamp duties would yield some £60,000 annually.
Grenville may have been more optimistic than that, for in May 1764 he
privately "conjecture[d] it might probably raise from £80 to 100,000."
Still, before he talked with Israel Mauduit on this subject, he was aware
that the two most productive colonial taxes would fall considerably
short of covering the army's pay, which had been estimated in 1763 at
£224,000.[59] If Grenville was considering the use of American money
for purposes other than defense, he would have taken into account
before 11 February the limited revenue available. Perhaps the Mauduits
misunderstood him. Perhaps Grenville intended to make clear that the
assemblies would have to continue paying for their own government.
Or perhaps he was deliberately trying to acquaint the Mauduits with the
most extreme position in the ministry, so when the truth of Grenville's
intentions emerged, they would portray him in letters to Massachusetts
as a moderate man whose mind could be changed. It is interesting to
note that in later letters, Israel Mauduit did call attention to Grenville's
moderation, pointing out in one instance, "He did not expect that
America should bear more than a good part of this expense [of the
army], whereas other leading Members not of the ministry said it ought
to bear the whole."[60] Whatever explanation is correct, that Grenville
seriously thought about using receipts from the molasses duty to defray
royal officials' salaries is doubtful.

The Debate in the House

Grenville had no trouble winning the House's approval for the
threepence rate. His speech on Budget Day, 9 March 1764, was probably his best performance ever, the work of a confident politician who
had just won a major triumph in the difficult debate over general
warrants and was now dealing with subjects on which he was an

acknowledged expert. He also had the advantage of speaking to an audience that entirely agreed with him on basic principles. After Jasper Mauduit watched the debates on colonial taxation during March, he did not think there was "a single man in Parliament who thought that the conquered provinces ought to be left without troops, or that England, after having run so deeply into debt for the conquering of these provinces, by which stability and security is given to all the American governments, should now tax itself for the maintenance of them."[61] The opposition did contend that a tax of twopence would raise more money, but with faint hearts and little hope of success. When Charles Townshend attended the debate in committee on the molasses duty, on 22 March, he found "the opinions impressed on [9 March] too strong to be shaken, and resistance useless, if not imprudent." He therefore took no active part, though he suspected that threepence was too high to yield much revenue, and divided the House only in courtesy to Sir William Baker, who had borne the main burden of debate for the opposition. By a vote of 147 to 55, the House supported Grenville's recommendation of threepence.[62]

The Advantages of Beginning at Threepence

Baker raised some intriguing points during the debate, however. He noted that the tax was "rather too high at threepence per gallon. . . . It will throw the trade into other channels." He then suggested, "We had better begin with twopence and raise it afterwards." Grenville countered by repeating his reasons for believing that customs officers could and would be able to collect the threepence tax: stricter discipline of the officers, changes in the system of bonds and cockets, more extensive use of the navy, and a more impartial administration of justice in the Admiralty Courts. The First Lord also reiterated why he thought that the French and the consumers of New England rum would pay the tax. These reasons convinced the House, just as they had convinced Grenville earlier.[63] Still, to the historian the issues Baker raised are interesting, and particularly so when one studies the private papers at the Treasury. According to Whately's calculations, collecting a threepence duty would probably reduce the volume of French molasses imported into North America by 22 percent.[64] Why did the men at the Treasury shrug this off at a time when they regarded American markets as crucial for British manufacturers? In December 1764, moreover, Whately referred to the possibility of the Treasury pursuing in the Stamp Act "the general principle . . . of laying all duties lighter at first than they are intended to be raised hereafter." This "might be proper," he observed, "in North America." At the same time, Whately commented, appropos of a stamp tax on grants of land, "Like all other new duties, . . . it should begin low."[65] A duty on molasses might not technically be a new tax, but any duty that in the immediate past had raised the paltry sum of £430 in a year and now was expected to raise £50,000 or more annually would certainly appear new to the taxpayer.[66] Jenkinson recognized this fact when he observed to a correspondent in Europe that "the beginning to execute [plantation laws] afresh made them have the appearance of new laws, though they had subsisted in reality for a great many years."[67] Surely these general principles and considerations were not suddenly discovered by men at the Treasury in late 1764. So why did Grenville refuse to start with twopence, a sum that customs officers could collect, and then raise it later, when Americans were habituated to the payment of the duty?

The reason the Treasury was unconcerned about a reduction in the molasses trade was publicly expressed by Whately in the pamphlet he wrote in early 1765. The Secretary pointed out that if the duty diminished the sales of American distillers in some markets, the gainers would be British distillers. "If the effect of this duty should be to diminish that quantity," he noted, "I cannot see any great national mischief that would attend it, because I cannot admit that any manufacture should be encouraged in the colonies to the prejudice of those established in the Mother Country."[68] In the Treasury's opinion, then, the gain to manufacturers at home would compensate for any decline in sales of goods to Americans caused by the threepence duty.

The reason for not doing as Baker suggested, setting the duty first at twopence, then raising it to threepence, is obvious. Had Grenville done so, he would have given away for no political advantage the additional revenue that threepence would bring in. Putting the duty at twopence would not please the smugglers. The Mauduits had made it clear that the merchants of Massachusetts wanted a one penny duty.[69] "Indeed," Whately observed, "whatever rate is fixed will in all probability be censured by those whom it affects," for they would prefer no tax at all.[70] So twopence would yield less revenue while still being the focus of political attacks. The Treasury might as well solace itself for the continued complaints with the additional revenues.

Also, whatever goodwill Britain might reap from apparent moderation in taxing a people who "are inclined to object to all taxes" would be lost when the time came to increase the tax.[71] Because the initial duty was so close to "the measure," moreover, paying it would not have accustomed potential smugglers to obedience. They would make the same efforts to evade the threepence duty that they currently made, but with this difference: Time would have passed, the colonies would be more populous and prosperous, and enforcing unpopular laws would be that much more difficult. Once Grenville was certain the trade could bear a threepence tax without collapsing, he intended to collect it. If a struggle was to occur over the duty on molasses, he preferred that it occur at that time, when men at the Treasury were ready for it. Soon after the duty went into effect, the Treasury acted to prevent masters from obtaining false clearances from corrupt officers in the British West Indies.[72] Alert for signs of new tricks from smugglers and determined to defeat them, Grenville and his colleagues would test thoroughly the practicality of the threepence duty.

The struggle between smugglers and the British might harm collections at first. As Whately noted, only experience could reveal weaknesses in the enforcement of the law and the revised tactics of smugglers.[73] That dimunition would prove worthwhile, nonetheless. When defending the Sugar Act, Whately noted, "In other countries, custom house duties are for the most part little more than a branch of the revenue." He added that in Britain's American colonies, however, "They are a political regulation." Enforcing the duties in turn "enforce[s] the observance of those wise laws to which the increase of our trade and naval power are principally owing."[74] The struggle to raise an American revenue, the struggle to defeat smugglers of European goods, and the struggle to control contraband traders in molasses were parts of a larger battle to maintain political control over an increasingly rich people. Grenville never lost sight of that fact.

Chapter VI

The Search for New Sources of Revenue
July 1763–March 1764

Grenville also never lost sight of the fact that he had to fight the battle of taxation on ground where he held most or all of the advantages and colonial lawbreakers had few or none. This insight guided him in the planning of the molasses duty, and it continued to guide him as he considered other possibilities for taxation during the fall and winter of 1763–1764. He always tried to create a situation in which taxes would virtually enforce themselves because men would realize that it was in their self-interest to obey, a good practice to follow, in all places, at all times, for men imposing new taxes.

In planning American taxation, Grenville was particularly careful to observe this practice. In the distant past, colonial smugglers might have been conscious that they were breaking the law, just as assemblymen might have been aware that they were defying the Mother Country. But as Britain failed to act effectively against these attacks on her authority—so frequent, so open, and so successful for so long—an ominous change occurred in colonial attitudes. A contemporary of Grenville's colorfully explained the process thus: "Critics' rules were made after the poems; architecture, after houses; grammar, after language; and governments go *per hookum* and *crookum,* and then demonstrate it *per hookum.*"[1] In the same way, defiance and disobedience became in colonists' minds meritorious and legitimate acts that preserved political privileges and economic interests. Legitimate acts in turn became rights and liberties that no law could constitutionally take away from the people. Grenville was not surprised to hear John Huske proclaim in Parliament on 9 March 1764 that "smugglers of molasses instead of being infamous are called patriots in North America."[2] After all, for three months before that date colonial agents had been admitting that the trade persisted in defiance of the law and had been advising that the Treasury connive at it by lowering the duty to the level of the usual bribe. Nor was he astonished to learn in 1763 that "inhabitants of the maritime provinces," where the contraband trade centered, had "already [begun] to entertain some extraordinary opinions concerning their relation to and dependence on their Mother Country."[3] The same process, to a less extreme degree, went on in smuggling counties in England. From his experience in England, and from his knowledge of America, Grenville realized that colonists were too practiced and too committed to tax evasion to be restrained effectively by methods of enforcement that did not depend on self-interest.

Grenville used this principle as a guide for another reason as well. He sensed that new taxes would be much worse than useless dead letters if the government could not collect them. Failure to execute these laws would lead to further disobedience in America and encourage more daring claims of independence by an increasingly powerful people.[4] On the other hand, if British officials could collect the taxes, if Americans obeyed them out of self-interest, the government would have made an important start toward changing the practice and structure of politics within the empire. New taxes would therefore have to be "judiciously chosen, not only with a view to the revenue which they will produce, but for other, and . . . greater, political purposes."[5]

With such high stakes, Grenville had to be certain that even minor taxes would be paid. Success or failure in small matters might have a cumulative effect, not only on the size of the public purse, but also on the struggle for political control. For both fiscal and political reasons, Grenville kept alert for opportunities to raise without trouble even a little tax revenue. When the Treasury noticed that South Carolina planters were petitioning for the right to ship rice to foreign colonies, Grenville and his colleagues agreed to it on the proviso that exporters pay a duty of seven pence per hundredweight of rice. Because merchants who sent rice to Britain or to Europe south of Cape Finisterre already paid this duty, the Treasury could be sure that it would not inhibit trade or encourage smuggling. It would also not contribute much to the revenue. More important than any contribution, however, it would keep rice merchants and planters accustomed to paying taxes at the local customs house.[6]

Grenville saw a similar opportunity in the colonial wine trade. Both McCulloh and Ware had insisted that the Treasury could extract a revenue from this trade, and, following their advice, Grenville on 18 November 1763 ordered the customs commissioners "to prepare a clause for levying a duty on all wines imported into His Majesty's colonies in America and the West Indies."[7] By the time the clause was prepared, the Treasury had discovered that "the inhabitants of Madeira have . . . long had a kind of monopoly of the wine trade to our colonies" because colonists could legally import wine from that island directly and thus avoid the expense of shipping it through Britain. Madeira had taken "the advantages that monopolists usually take, of advancing the price and lowering the quality." The Treasury responded to this situation by proposing a tax of seven pounds per ton on those wines and by lowering the duties on wines imported through Britain to four pounds per ton, ten shillings of which would be collected in the colonies "to make the respective Custom House accounts checks upon each other." These changes, the Treasury hoped, would have the happy result of lowering the price of wine and increasing the revenue. Vintners on Madeira would be forced by the new competition to lower their prices and, in effect, pay the new tax. Merchants in Britain would benefit from their larger share of the trade.[8] The American revenue would grow; consumers of this luxury would gladly allow collection of the taxes to guarantee a supply of cheaper wines. Because colonists who drank wine were generally of the better sort, the payment of these duties would habituate society's leaders to legal transactions at the customs house. Probably for much the same reason, the Treasury also imposed light duties on two luxuries from the British West Indies, coffee and pimento. As Whately pointed out, "Those who can afford to indulge in such delicacies should contribute something to the public wants, and ease from heavier burdens the necessaries of the poor." That something would not amount to much, so the wealthy would pay the tax. Luxury taxes never yielded a great deal of revenue in Britain, but they served to remind the rich of their obligations to society. Luxury taxes would yield far less in the colonies, but the Treasury hoped that respectable men would grow accustomed to paying taxes on wines, coffee, and pimento and, ultimately, to trading legally.[9]

Taxes on luxuries and on rice were minor additions to the revenue compared with the molasses duty. They were also minor reforms when considered next to Grenville's other plans: ending drawbacks on foreign goods reexported from Britain to the colonies and imposing a stamp duty. The First Lord understood this difference very well; although he used the same basic strategy in planning his major changes, he applied it even more carefully.

Removing the Drawback on Foreign Linens

Probably because he thought Charles Jenkinson was familiar with the course of James Oswald's investigations into the linen trade and drawbacks paid in it, Grenville assigned him the job of examining the subject and making recommendations. In late December 1763, the Treasury initiated discussions of the trade with William Tod. During the next two and a half months, Jenkinson and Tod kept in touch. The Secretary and his colleagues could hardly have been surprised by Tod's advice to stop paying all drawbacks; after all, the lobbyist had been offering that suggestion for a quarter of a century. The choice of Tod, in fact, reveals the bias of the Treasury toward sweeping change. So does Grenville's failure to inform linen merchants in London or in Bristol, whom he could expect to object, about his investigation. Even Peregrine Cust, who had been a partner in a firm of linen drapers and knew something about the trade, was unaware of the First Lord's intentions.[10] Clearly, Grenville did not want to give the drawback's proponents a chance to mount a parliamentary campaign against removal before he even introduced it.

Jenkinson supplemented Tod's information with accounts from the Customs Office and the East India Company.[11] By March 1764, he recommended that the Treasury stop paying drawbacks on all foreign products and manufactures reexported to the British colonies. Grenville agreed with the suggestion. On 9 March, he told the House that "foreign goods exported to North America pay now only half the subsidy." In the future, he announced, "They shall pay the whole subsidy."[12]

If the reexport trade continued at its present volume, Grenville could expect a substantial savings for the revenue. In 1761, the Treasury paid out over £99,000 in drawbacks on all goods; in 1763, on white calicoes and foreign linens alone, the total was £70,701.[13] Grenville did not anticipate collecting these sums, however. He hoped that removing the drawback would benefit the nation in another way. "To encourage the consumption of our own produce and our own manufacturers in preference to those of other countries has been at all times an undisputed maxim of policy," Whately noted in 1765, "and for this purpose high duties and even prohibitions have been laid on foreign commodities." The "general tendency" of removing the drawback "is to extend the same principle to the American" markets. As an example, the Secretary pointed to "the foreign linens, which thereby become less merchantable for this trade than the British."[14]

There was, of course, danger that raising the price of foreign manufactures by taxing them more heavily would encourage smuggling of these goods from Europe or manufacturing of them in the colonies. Neither Jenkinson nor Whately nor, presumably, Grenville took the latter threat seriously. "As to the idea of people of the colonies becoming manufacturers themselves," scoffed Jenkinson, "I see no reason to apprehend it at present." "Whenever they can work cheaper than the manufacturers of this country, they will become so," he went on, but "this is not the case at present, nor likely to be so soon."[15] Moreover, the Treasury planned to delay that day's arrival even longer by paying bounties on colonial flax and hemp exported to Britain and Ireland. By removing the raw materials of the linen manufactory from America, Britain would add height to the barrier that incipient colonial manufacturers already faced from the high cost of labor.[16]

Smuggling concerned the men at the Treasury more. On the back of an account describing the taxes and drawbacks on linens exported to America, Jenkinson scribbled a reminder to himself of a warning he had apparently received from Richard Jackson. There was a trade from the Orkneys to Boston and to Philadelphia in foreign linens, and Jenkinson knew that this was probably an illicit commerce. In their report of 16 September 1763, the customs commissioners had observed that British ships "now frequently arrive from Holland and other foreign places . . . at Cowes and in the Orkneys." In these ports, the masters reported that their cargo was destined for "some foreign settlement, and enter[ed] only a few boxes or bales of goods . . . which they immediately ship[ped] outwards again for New York, or some other ports in the British colonies, and thus gain[ed] legal clearances for these colonies and admission thereby to our American ports." Once there, the masters unloaded the whole cargo.[17] The commissioners, however, had a plan to prevent this fraud, one that appealed to Grenville. After Parliament's passage of this legislation, he announced in the House on 9 March, "No ships shall be cleared out [*for*] North America unless [they] shall unload all [their] goods, . . . take . . . clearance out of the whole, and pay the duty for the whole."[18] To hinder this illicit trade further, the Treasury also planned to inflict a severe penalty on men who declared that their foreign goods were bound to other foreign ports, received the drawback, and then sold those goods in America. Upon detection, the drawback would be forfeited, and the exporter of the goods and the master of the ship would "forfeit double the amount of the drawback . . . and treble the value of the said goods."[19] Would merchants and masters still take this risk or the even greater one of sailing directly to the colonies with their contraband? Was the profit to be made on smuggled goods so great as to induce merchants and masters to take that gamble? Men at the Treasury doubted that they would. Tod calculated that removing the drawback would increase the price of foreign linen in American markets between 12 and 16 percent. He also pointed out that during the war, when the price of colonial exports remained at their usual level, colonists were paying between 20 and 25 percent more for foreign linens than they did in peacetime. The significance of this information was clear to Grenville. Raising the price of foreign linens by stopping the drawback would not be so onerous or unusual a burden for colonists as to encourage smugglers. Furthermore, if men did choose to run contraband textiles into America, they would be risking severe losses for what most smugglers would consider a small profit.[20] The Treasury could thus feel reasonably safe that removing the drawback would tempt neither smugglers nor manufacturers. Accordingly, Grenville went ahead with his plan.

Considerations Favoring a Colonial Stamp Tax

Almost four months before Jenkinson began consulting with Tod, Grenville directed him to start McCulloh to work on a colonial stamp tax. The virtues of such a tax were obvious to the First Lord and his assistant and probably had been so since McCulloh first suggested the tax in July 1763. Part of their enthusiasm may be explained by the Treasury's experience with English stamp duties. Between 1756 and 1762, Jenkinson discovered, stamps on various documents grossed an average of £287,307 annually. Moreover, the charges of collection, about nine and one-half pence per pound, were nominal compared to the management of many taxes. After paying these charges, the public's purse was richer by £260,647.[21] What made this tax so peculiarly attractive to planners of colonial taxation, however, was not its record of success per se but the cause of its success.

"The true idea of a stamp duty," Jenkinson observed, "is that the Crown has the monopoly of the sale of papers for certain purposes at a price fixed by law; the profits of which are to be applied to the public benefit."[22] To preserve that monopoly, the law held that unstamped papers used for those "certain purposes" had no legal force to bind parties using them. Thus, as McCulloh said, the law "in great measure would execute itself, except in a few particulars; for in all suits depending, the people settled in the colonies must for their own security comply with the directions of the law." Furthermore, "In all cases of warrants of attorney, procurations, protests, and other matters in the intercourse of business, the safety of the parties concerned would likewise enforce an obedience."[23] Americans would have to buy the stamps or place their property and persons in jeopardy. Their self-interest would force them to obey the law. Such a tax, rhapsodized Jenkinson, "is not subject to the frauds to which Customs House duties are liable, nor to the severities of excise, . . . nor is it necessary to enter any man's doors for the purpose of collecting it."[24] Grenville certainly grasped these points, for he told the House in 1764 that a stamp duty was "the least exceptionable" that Parliament could impose on the colonies "because it requires few officers and even collects itself." He also understood that this was an ideal tax to impose on a people accustomed to violating British laws and evading British taxes. A stamp tax would be almost impossible to violate: If a colonist wished to evade it, he would have to give up any thoughts of acquiring more land, participating in trade, holding office, hiring an apprentice, borrowing money, or defending himself in court. In short, everyone who wished to prosper economically or hold on to what he had would have to buy stamps.[25]

Stamp duties had other readily apparent virtues as well. They would make the enforcement of other British laws in America easier. Requiring stamps on customs clearances, bonds, bills of lading, and cockets would improve the regulation of trade and the collection of duties. If a cocket, for example, did not bear a stamp, the customs officer held in his hand prima facie evidence of attempted smuggling.[26] The only way of eluding this guard was forgery, and Grenville could justifiably believe that most smugglers would think a long time before resorting to counterfeiting. Smugglers who were successfully prosecuted lost their property. Forgers lost their lives.[27] Thus stamps would give American customs officers a more certain means to detect frauds and a more severe sanction to intimidate potential lawbreakers.

Finally, a stamp tax was also a politically judicious imposition. There were twenty-six colonies and islands in British America, each differing from others in the degree of its prosperity, in its economic interests and ambitions, and, in some cases, in its form of government. Seemingly all of these colonies were jealous of each other and endlessly alert for signs that another colony or the Mother Country was harming their interests and favoring a rival's. Grenville had himself witnessed the arguments between agents from different colonies over the distribution of the money due the provinces for their services during the war, and he had drawn the appropriate conclusions about the hostilities and suspicions between colonies.[28] To prevent "complaints of inequality," taxes imposed by Britain should affect each colony about the same in proportion to its wealth.[29] A stamp tax was probably the most equitable imposition possible. The unique characteristics of each colony could be taken into account by adding to a general law specific clauses describing and covering the special situations and the appropriate documents. Moreover, the Treasury could use this same flexibility to distribute the burden of paying stamp duties equitably between the prosperous and the poor. In the normal course of their economic activity, the industrious poor used certain documents for certain purposes. Once the Treasury determined what these documents were, Parliament could set lower rates on them and thereby lighten the burden on the poor. Documents habitually used by the well-to-do—for instance, applications for surveys of larger land grants—could be taxed more heavily. A stamp tax was the most "equal" duty that Parliament could impose, on individuals as well as colonies.[30]

The relative ease of executing a stamp tax, the small costs of collection, the ways it strengthened enforcement of other laws, the flexibility that made it the most equitable tax Parliament could impose—all these attributes disposed Grenville during 1763 to favor a colonial stamp tax. One other consideration may have weighed heavily with him as well. From several sources, Grenville had heard about the potentially dangerous ideas Americans had about the nature of their relationship with the Mother Country. The First Lord was not inclined to spend his time disputing the point in letters, pamphlets, and speeches. He was determined to settle it with successful exertions of British power. The several characteristics of a stamp tax made it the ideal choice for successfully asserting and executing British authority in an unprecedented and important way: the imposition and collection of an internal tax. In February 1765, Whately (and others) gave the stamp tax "the appellation of a *great measure* on account of the important point it establishes, the right of Parliament to lay an internal tax upon the colonies."[31] He did so, of course, after some vehement protests against that right from America. But in March 1764, well before those protests began to arrive in London, Grenville told the House that he was "convinced this country [has] the right to impose an inland tax." He added that he "love[d] the spirit of freedom and its commercial spirit, but would have neither at [in]dependence of this country." He then challenged the members, "If any man doubts the right of this country, he will take the opinion of a committee immediately." Jenkinson soon followed the First Lord with this flat assertion: "He could easily confirm the right of England to impose taxes upon North America from Acts of Parliament and resolutions of the House of Commons."[32] These statements reveal more than the confidence and preparation of the Treasury on an issue of potential debate in 1764. They also reveal that Grenville and his colleagues were as determined to establish this right in 1764 as they were later and that they regarded it as an important right to establish beyond dispute.[33] Imposing and collecting stamp duties in the colonies would, they anticipated, have that effect.

Only one consideration in 1763 might have held Grenville back from commissioning the preparation of a colonial stamp tax: a discouraging answer to the question, could the colonists pay stamp duties and still buy increasing amounts of British manufactures? Grenville, however, did not need to speculate much on that answer. He knew that the volume of Americans' commerce was steadily growing and interpreted this as a sign of economic prosperity. Moreover, McCulloh had sent along with his July 1763 letter to Jenkinson "a brief state of such taxes as are usually raised in His Majesty's old settled colonies on the continent of America, *viz.* North and South Carolina, Virginia, and Pennsylvania." Though McCulloh's enclosure has not survived, what it indicated and what his motive was for sending it are clear. He hoped to persuade Grenville that colonial taxes were so low that no reasonable parliamentary tax could materially affect the American market for manufacturers. He obviously succeeded, for in early September 1763, Jenkinson told him that Grenville wanted him and Thomas Cruwys to draft a stamp tax for the colonies.[34]

After events revealed the Stamp Act to be a disastrous mistake, Grenville occasionally tried to limit his responsibility for it. At times, he hinted that it was not originally his idea and that it "was not so much his choice as [it was] a condition imposed upon him when he succeeded Lord Bute." The first claim was true, the second false. That Grenville, who spent most of his tenure as First Lord resisting the real and imagined machinations of Bute, would faithfully execute a command from his enemy is as implausible as is the thought of Bute, who recognized his own ignorance of finance, setting such a condition. At the same time Grenville was commanding McCulloh and Cruwys to draft a bill, he was insisting to the King that His Majesty must "suffer no secret influence whatever to prevail against the advice of those to whom he trusted the management of his affairs."[35] Grenville also claimed later "that the King was particularly desirous to have [a stamp tax], and frequently called upon him to bring it on," despite Grenville's wish that it "be done . . . deliberately." There is no evidence to support Grenville's claim, even in Mrs. Grenville's diary entries during the fall and winter of 1763–1764 in which she recorded every command or suggestion relating to politics that the King made to her husband. Moreover, on 10 March 1764, Grenville noted that the King was "highly pleased with what had passed the day before in the House . . . concerning the supplies of the year." George III evidently showed no signs of displeasure when Grenville postponed consideration of the colonial stamp bill until the next session.[36] The Stamp Act was fully Grenville's responsibility from July 1763 onward.

Drafting the Stamp Bill

Even in the beginning, Grenville did not encourage a deliberate examination. Rather, he pressed McCulloh and Cruwys to make decisions and write drafts rapidly.

The two men first met on 14 September. Although they were in some sense rivals for the Treasury's attention and approval, and despite an important difference between them on how the money was to be used, they seem to have worked together efficiently. Each drew up a schedule of duties on papers he was most familiar with; on 26 October, they combined their efforts. McCulloh acquainted Cruwys with legal procedures in the colonies, and the two men examined "American and plantation laws." Apparently they were in general agreement on administrative details of distributing the stamps, collecting the duties, and inspecting the distributors' accounts. McCulloh even commiserated with Cruwys on the difficulties of this subject. When Cruwys consulted him about "the method I had for distributors to account upon giving security, . . . he told me it was a matter which Mr. Grenville had in contemplation, conceiving it to be the most difficult thing he had to encounter."[37] The two could not, however, compromise on the basic issues of methods of collection and appropriation. The Solicitor to the Stamp Office wanted the receipts from the tax to be paid into the English Exchequer. McCulloh frankly stated that he did not want the money sent to England, that it should be used "to raise a fund from the colonies to obtain a credit for securing the issuing of exchequer bills of union." Cruwys wanted the fund to be available for the Treasury to use as it saw fit. McCulloh wanted Parliament to use the bills of union "to preserve one uniform [medium] of trade and [to allow] the colonies to [bear] the expense of preserving the Crown's acquisitions, . . . keeping up the militia, . . . providing cash to purchase presents for Indians . . . [and] raising bounties to encourage people to settle in the said colonies." McCulloh added that he hoped Britain could ultimately raise by taxation each year the five hundred thousand pounds he estimated would cover these expenses; at present, though, he was "certain such an attempt would meet with the fullest opposition."[38]

McCulloh was also certain that his plan would meet with firm opposition from Cruwys. On 29 October, he appealed to Grenville for a chance to draw up his own version of a stamp bill. Grenville, who surely had a good idea of what its contents would be from McCulloh's plan in July and from conferences with him in September and October, agreed that the Treasury should consider McCulloh's scheme formally. On 8 November, McCulloh completed his draft. In the preamble, he added to the expenses that the bills of union would secure the "discharg[ing of] the salaries of His Majesty's governors and other officers abroad." Cruwys took this draft, put it into proper legal form, and presented it to the Treasury with his own on 19 November.[39]

On 14 October, Cruwys learned from McCulloh that Grenville wanted "me . . . to settle forms of a law agreeable to [McCulloh's] plan," so Grenville must have been tempted by the suggestion for securing exchequer bills with the receipts from colonial stamp duties. Perhaps the First Lord already saw the possibility of charging interest on the bills and applying it to the expenses of imperial defense, a proposal Grenville made in the House when he was no longer at the Treasury.[40] He probably agreed with McCulloh that "paper bills of credit are at present absolutely necessary as a medium in trade" in the colonies. He also saw, though, that "allowing the colonies to issue bills of currency as a tender in law among themselves . . . and the frauds committed by them . . . have often injured the trading interest of this Kingdom."[41] Virginia's currency and debtor legislation had recently infuriated British merchants and encouraged them to think about trying to petition Parliament to abolish any use of paper currency as legal tender in America. Any effort to issue a new currency, even one secured by tax collections in sterling, would probably draw opposition from the mercantile community. It might also be criticized by the Board of Trade, which had recommended and gained disallowance of Virginia's statute on insolvent debtors by the Privy Council in July 1763. Clearly, Cruwys and his superiors at the Stamp Office were already skeptical of McCulloh's idea, and Grenville could not exclude them from the drafting of this bill. Nor could he exclude the Board of Trade; indeed, Cruwys had already done research there. The element of surprise that Grenville planned to use in the case of the drawback would be denied to him here. Merchants would inevitably hear about his plan to create a new paper currency and would have in hand prepared arguments when Whitehall and Westminster discussed the bill. Nor would these be stale, twenty-five-year-old arguments in favor of a particular interest, dealers in foreign linens. They would be fresh grievances against attacks on the sanctity of property. Delivered to a House composed of property owners, they would have a considerable potential to disrupt proceedings and to amend, delay, or defeat the stamp bill.[42] After weighing the potential for parliamentary opposition against the possible benefits of exchequer bills for the empire, and perhaps recalling that the mercantile interest had had sufficient strength to defeat the plan that he and Pitt had favored in 1759 for registering seamen and limiting their service in the navy, Grenville decided against McCulloh's scheme. Probably for a similar reason, his desire to prevent a political furor in America, he rejected the proposal to use part of the money raised by the stamp duties for officials' salaries. These decisions made, the Treasury had no difficulty choosing Cruwys's draft over McCulloh's. As Thomas has observed, McCulloh's schedule of duties was "too crude and sweeping"; he did not even graduate his duties on offices and land grants according to their values.[43] The Solicitor's version promised to raise a larger revenue with less danger to British trade to America. On 22 November, the Treasury ordered him to prepare a bill based on his preliminary draft.

Thus, between 8 September and 22 November, the Treasury had had McCulloh and Cruwys convert a vaguely formulated idea into the basis of a bill to present to Parliament. Ironing out the remaining details could be left to Cruwys. Aware that the bill should be in nearly final form well before Grenville had to introduce it in the House, Cruwys set to work. On 19 January 1764, Whately told him to have the draft ready by the twenty-fifth "in order that [it] might be referred to the Lords of Trade." Five days later, the commissioners of stamps inspected his work, accepted it, and sent it to the Treasury.[44]

The Fate of the Drawback on Linens

The initial response in the House was quite favorable when Grenville recommended on 9 March imposing stamp duties and removing the drawback. Even prominent critics of the administration's colonial policy praised Grenville's efforts to raise the price of foreign goods reexported to the colonies. John Huske noted that he "would certainly have [the drawback] diminished, as it would be a bounty on our own manufactures." Sir William Baker, the major spokesman for the opposition, agreed that "it [was] proper to lay high duties upon" foreign commodities and did "not object to the addition of duty on reexportation of India goods, cambrics, etc." These same critics changed their minds, however, when Richard Glover, a London merchant, and Peregrine Cust began questioning in committee the wisdom of this plan, insofar as it "allowed no drawback on white calicoes or foreign linens."[45]

On 10 March, Glover told the House that removing the drawback on these goods would encourage smuggling from Holland or manufacturing in America. He may also have pointed out that under existing law, goods denominated "white calicoes or muslins" in fact were often foreign calicoes that had been dyed in England. Printed or dyed calicoes were more expensive and popular than the white, which were taxed at a lower rate than those printed in foreign countries. To encourage the dyeing industry, Parliament had decided to permit domestically dyed calicoes to be exported as white. Thus Glover and other linen merchants could plausibly argue that any act that harmed their trade would also harm a part of the British manufacturing interests. However plausible this thinking may have seemed to them, it did not impress the House. By a voice vote, the members approved incorporating into the colonial bill a resolution removing the drawback on all foreign goods.

Glover tried again on the fourteenth. He reasoned that consideration of the drawback's removal on its own merits might postpone the linen legislation indefinitely or kill it immediately, while leaving the drawback issue in obviously popular legislation, which was moving quickly through committee, might assure its passage. He suggested, therefore, that removal be made into a separate bill. No one deigned to comment on this idea, and Glover did not bother to make a formal motion. Grenville clearly would have his way; the drawback would be removed.[46]

Then on 16 March, Grenville agreed that the House would hear witnesses and arguments for retaining the drawback on foreign linens on the twenty-third. Because his majority was secure, Grenville had no reason not to refuse to call witnesses, and because he hoped to end the session by Easter, he must have wanted to conserve the working time of the House.[47] He probably decided to extend this courtesy because his friend Cust, who had in mind a number of people (including Whately's friend William Allen) capable of testifying to the smuggling trade from Holland and to the potential for manufacturing linen in the colonies, asked for it.[48] Grenville may also have wished to be courteous at this late date to merchants from London and Bristol. He cannot have expected to hear any unfamiliar arguments or learn any startlingly new information. Probably, too, these courtesies indicate that he was already disposed to change his recommendation on white calicoes.

On 19 March, the latest accounts of the exports of white calicoes and foreign linens to America arrived at the Treasury.[49] Jenkinson studied them, then reported to Grenville.[50] At stake was over £60,000 a year in drawbacks, about £26,000 for white calicoes, and £34,000 for the most popular foreign linen, German narrows. At stake, too, was a certain amount of damage to the dyeing interest. Grenville decided to reduce rather than abolish the drawback on white calicoes. He planned to accomplish this by formally retaining the drawback while imposing an ad valorem duty on white calicoes. Originally, he wanted this duty to be "£5 for every £100 of the true and real value of which goods according to the gross price at which they were sold," but before he presented this proposal to the House on 23 March, he lowered the rate to £4 15s. Jenkinson estimated that this tax would produce £8,667 in revenue annually. More important than that consideration, though, was the opportunity to experiment further with ad valorem taxation on foreign goods reexported to the colonies. Taxing by quantity was indeed simpler, but it did not give the Treasury the flexibility it needed to tax each piece of luxury cloth at a higher rate than cheaper, more popular goods.[51] If an ad valorem tax could be devised to cover the fine and coarse linens that were indiscriminately described as narrow Germans, "All . . . linens would then be thoroughly completely agreeable to the maxim of laying taxes in differing proportions on the consumption of the rich and on that of the poor." This way, "While the indulgences and refinements of the one are converted into beneficial branches of the public revenue, the other may with more cheerfulness contribute out of their pittance the mite they owe to the service of the state they belong to."[52]

After the witnesses against removing the drawback on foreign linens and calicoes finished on 23 March, Grenville moved his amendment. Peregrine Cust was not impressed, nor were Baker and Huske, who had reversed their position of two weeks before. They argued that the price of calicoes would still be too high, and they repeated their predictions of dire consequences if the House did not insist on retaining the drawback. The House did not insist. Indeed, many members became openly restless as Huske "prated" over the drawback. Finally, the opponents of Grenville's motion conceded its passage without calling for a division. The completeness of Grenville's victory was underscored three days later, when the House refused, nem. con., to allow a petition "against the disallowing of the drawbacks on calicoes and foreign linens" to be brought up.[53]

Still, the First Lord was willing to meet in his office with linen merchants to discuss these recent events. During the discussions, Grenville made a graceful concession. When he had made his motion on 23 March, he included a provision that would have permitted merchants who shipped white calicoes to America to delay paying the ad valorem tax until 10 September 1764, though payments of the drawback ended 1 May on other goods. Now he agreed that merchants who had purchased white calicoes on or before 25 March 1764 and shipped them to North America before 1 March 1765 would not have to pay the new tax. This provision, he probably observed, would protect merchants who bought calico while Parliament was still debating the drawback. The Treasury prepared an engrossed rider exempting such purchases, and Grenville added it to the bill at the last possible moment, just before the third reading on 30 March.[54] The reaction of the North American merchants was epitomized by the Society of Merchant Venturers in Bristol, which voted an honorary freedom of the Society to Grenville "for the ready protection he afforded and the great services he did to the trade of this city last session."[55] While merchants applauded him, the new experiment in taxation began.

Did Grenville manipulate these events deliberately toward his desired ends, removal of the drawback on most goods and the implementation of an experiment in ad valorem taxation? The initial secrecy, the bold proposal, the demonstration of the power to enact that proposal, the listening to the familiar arguments of the other side, the compromise, the concessions after victory—all hint at first glance at a scheme to achieve a necessary reform almost by stealth, while leaving the opponents of removal thankful that their experience was not worse, rather than resentful at their defeat. More likely, though, Grenville set a total removal of the drawback on all goods as soon as possible as his original goal. Then the vehemence and persistence of the merchants' protest convinced him of the political wisdom of making some concessions. Moreover, Grenville's concern about British manufacturers' competitive position in international trade surely inclined him to make a major concession on white calicoes. British dyers would clearly benefit if calicoes they printed were less heavily taxed than other foreign textiles and prints, for merchants would see their opportunity and export more to America, and consumers there would recognize a bargain and buy more. At the same time Grenville realized this, he realized that the self-interest of buyer and seller would not permit either to balk at paying a small tax on the white calicoes. Furthermore, customs officers could gauge the value of white calicoes much more precisely than they could the narrow Germans, so this trade would be an ideal opportunity to test the feasibility of that most desirable method of taxation, the ad valorem duty, on another species of textile.[56] If it worked, the ad valorem tax would be proportionately lighter on the cheaper white calicoes and thus would not inhibit sales to the poor. The First Lord was probably extracting the maximum political and fiscal advantage from a situation in which he felt compelled to compromise rather than execute a cleverly laid plot.

Events followed a strikingly similar pattern in the case of the colonial stamp duties. This time, however, Grenville was accused of plotting and carrying out an artful conspiracy. The consequences of those accusations were momentous. Moreover, though many of the arguments used against him are undeniably fantastic, others raise some interesting questions about the motives behind some of his maneuvers during 1764–1765.

Chapter VII

The Politics of Postponing the Stamp Tax
March–December 1764

After Grenville finished explaining his plans for a colonial stamp tax on 9 March 1764, John Huske and William Beckford argued that the House should delay passing any such tax until "the colonies [were] apprised of the intention of Parliament."[1] Huske put special stress on the political wisdom of a postponement. Because the colonies always wanted their "agents . . . to play for time if anything occurs in Parliament which materially affects their interest," they would regard a delay as a sign of genuine concern for their welfare. Moreover, he reminded the House, there was a precedent for notifying the colonies of business concerning them: "It [was] done in . . . Irish causes." Whether Huske had in mind sending American governors a formal proclamation from the Privy Council or a public letter from the Secretary of State, as was done in Irish affairs, or whether he was thinking of using the colonial agents to send notice to the governments in America is not entirely clear. He did, however, recommend that the information should bear this official imprimatur from the House of Commons: "This [bill should be] read two times, printed, and then sent to America for their opinions about it." This would give the colonies the "opportunity to lay . . . any objections they might have to such a bill [before] the House, by their agents" during the committee stage of debate. And, as Huske hastened to explain, he did mean *any* objections. Because American colonists were not represented in Parliament, they were unable to object to a bill in its entirety at the procedurally proper moment, its second reading. They should, therefore, "have the right to petition against the tax" during the committee stage. This was a right that Englishmen did not have at any time during the legislative process, but the special circumstances of colonists, according to Huske, should give it to them.[2]

As Grenville listened to Huske, he heard nothing he had not heard before. "Much [had] been said by agents and others from the Continent" to him about the advantages of delay.[3] Huske had spoken to him before on this subject. Richard Jackson had at first advised against levying stamp duties and then counseled a postponement. Edward Montagu, the agent for Virginia, had joined in Jackson's arguments, as did William Knox, agent for Georgia. Some private persons, such as Eliphalet Dyer and William Allen, may have lent their voices to the campaign.[4] All these men probably pointed out that a postponement would give colonists time to express their opinions on this measure to the Treasury. Some added that many Americans believed that Parliament had no right to impose an internal tax on them. No sensible Briton could agree to that, they doubtless hastened to add, yet the courtesy shown colonists by postponing this utterly unprecedented duty would impress the Americans and could be an important step toward winning their trust. Moreover, such a tax would require research that could be completed only over several months. Colonists used many unusual legal documents, for example. Without more information, the Treasury could not hope to list them all for the purposes of taxation, let alone choose equitable, bearable rates to impose on the documents. Asking Americans for more data might enable the Treasury to avoid mistakes that could hamper sales of British manufactured goods in the colonies. That same process of gathering information might also turn up a less troublesome way of raising an American revenue, one that Americans would fully approve of and gladly obey.[5]

So when Huske spoke on 9 March, Grenville was familiar with the arguments in favor of delay. Indeed, he had taken the trouble to demonstrate his knowledge of them before Huske took the floor. Grenville believed that Britain had "the right to impose an inland tax." He admitted, however, "The officers of the revenue must strike in the dark," without full information, though he thought that a stamp tax was "the best plan." He even concluded this section of his speech by noting, "He would likewise wish to follow to a certain degree the inclination of the people in North America, if they [would] agree to the end."[6] Yet Grenville did not balance this discussion by describing the arguments against delay. This seems a curious omission for a man determined to have the House resolve immediately, "It may be proper to charge certain stamp duties in the said colonies and plantations."[7] Grenville knew the objections to delaying the bill; he also knew that they were weighty ones. Why did he decline to discuss them when he introduced the resolution? Before considering that question, it is necessary to reconstruct how Grenville measured the pros and cons of a postponement. No paper or series of papers survives that describes his thoughts. Indeed, the crucial debate may have been conducted and finally resolved within his own mind as he listened to Huske and Beckford.[8] Still, his words and actions during 1764 give substantial clues to the considerations and arguments he took into account.

The Pros and Cons of Delay

While he considered delaying a stamp tax, Grenville clearly ruled out three events as unlikely results of postponement. Since he believed that Parliament had the right to levy internal taxes on the colonies and was willing on 9 March "if any man doubt[ed] the right . . . [to] take the opinion of a committee immediately," he could not imagine that colonists could convince him to the contrary in a year's time.[9] Equally unlikely was the possibility that they could persuade him of their inability to pay stamp duties. To be sure, McCulloh's description of the weight of colonial taxation was limited and dated, and the Board of Trade had been unable to find more recent information on some colonies.[10] But Grenville had seen the trade statistics, proving to his satisfaction that the colonies' economy was prospering. Nor could he think of any reason for it to cease expanding. To guard against inadvertently taxing colonists too heavily, he planned to require only that they help pay for their defense, not that they bear the whole burden. So, as he later told the colonial agents, "Objections of inability might possibly come from some colonies, but, he believed, [they] would have very little weight."[11] Finally, Grenville seriously doubted that the colonists would suggest during the year's time another type of parliamentary taxation "so proper for America in general." Indeed, "Of the several inland duties, that of the stamps was the most equal, required the fewest officers, and was attended with the least expense in the collecting of it." As said so often, it would also all but collect itself.[12] In effect, therefore, postponement would simply provide Americans a year's grace from paying stamp duties. What benefits could possibly accrue to Britain that would justify giving up a year's tax receipts?

From the standpoint of purely fiscal considerations, there might be some substantial benefits. The information available to Grenville was, he admitted, limited. Given another year, men could gather enough information about colonial legal and commercial documents to enable them to make the bill more inclusive and precise. That same information might permit the Treasury to gauge more accurately the highest rates the colonial documents could safely bear. Moreover, it might allow planners to anticipate and guard against likely methods of evasion.[13] These could be important advantages. An act based on inaccurate or insufficient knowledge might neglect sources of considerable revenue, tax too lightly, or leave gaping loopholes. Such an act might not raise as much revenue in two years as one written by better-informed men would in half the time.

Grenville probably worried less about the other extreme, a reduction in colonists' ability to buy more British manufactures, but that chance had to be kept in mind, too. Neither possibility could have comforted the First Lord much. He probably grew more uncomfortable as early March approached, and Cruwys's bill, which had arrived at the Treasury on 24 January 1764, remained at the Board of Trade while the staff there searched for "American and plantation laws . . . [to] compare with the new law." Finally, on 6 March, Cruwys was able to inspect this information. The next day, Grenville advised the House that he would discuss the budget on the ninth. He also persuaded the House to instruct the committee on ways and means to "consider . . . proper methods for raising a revenue in the British colonies." On the seventh and eighth, Cruwys spent long hours at Whately's house and the Treasury, "settling alterations to be made in [the] act and resolutions." On 10 March, the day after Grenville introduced the resolution calling for an American stamp tax, Cruwys returned to the Treasury to continue his work.[14] This hurry did not bode well for the bill's becoming an effective means of raising an American revenue.

While there might have been sound fiscal reasons for deferring implementation of the tax, the political benefits of postponement were less obvious, and Grenville could not decide to put off the bill for even a year without considering the political ramifications of delay. This bill could not be quietly set aside. Any number of people in London knew about it; people in America would find out soon enough from their agents. All would reach their own conclusions about the reasons for the delay.

The colonial agents naturally tried to put the best possible face on the American reaction to postponement. If Grenville delayed the bill and asked the colonies for their opinions on it, the agents argued, he would learn invaluable information, discover the willingness of colonists to contribute to the support of their own defense, and earn the goodwill of Americans. Whether the agents realized it or not, though, they were making these arguments to a man already dubious about the possibility of gaining colonial goodwill while beginning the process of raising money in America. Indeed, he had chosen a stamp tax as the best mode of taxing the colonists, in large part because he doubted both their willingness to contribute and their goodwill. From Grenville's standpoint, gaining the colonists' confidence and obedience would, of course, be highly desirable, but would postponing the tax while claiming he was doing so out of respect for their opinions generate goodwill in the colonies and inspire colonists to obey British laws and pay British taxes? Grenville's experience in politics inclined him to be skeptical that this would be the outcome of delay, and especially so if it appeared to

Americans that he was postponing the tax out of weakness or uncertainty. An examination of his methods of dealing with other political problems at the same time he was mulling over postponement of the stamp tax reveals Grenville's conviction: The government had to avoid at all costs any action that might give its domestic and foreign opponents the impression that it was timid or indecisive.

The politicians Grenville was most familiar with, the men in Parliament, were always alert for any signs that the King's government lacked the will or the ability to enforce support for its positions and policies. During the fall of 1763, Grenville had noted, "The great engine of our adversaries is to represent the Administration as unsettled and fluctuating." And in the aftermath of the extremely close divisions on general warrants in February 1764, he observed that the men of the ministry had "to exert their utmost care and attention in times like these to prevent disorder and confusion, and by imitating as far as they are able His Majesty's firmness and temper to put an eventual stop to the consequences that will be endeavored to be drawn from the late divisions in the House of Commons."[15]

The First Lord saw the same necessity for firmness of conduct in dealing with Britain's ancient enemy, France. Early during his administration, the French had begun testing Britain's willingness to insist on strict observance of the peace treaty. As Grenville knew, the French had been delaying the required destruction of fortifications at Dunkerque.[16] Moreover, at least one of Grenville's colleagues in the Cabinet had "long and constantly expressed" suspicions, well known to Grenville, that the French were not complying with the treaty's regulations of fishing off Newfoundland.[17] The Treasury might have been receiving reports from its spies that France's finances were in terrible shape, but the Earl of Egmont at the Admiralty had heard from a reliable source that the French "marine was resolved to be, and certainly should be, reestablished in all events by the year 1764." The moment this occurred, Egmont's informant went on, "France was resolved to wipe off the stains of that most ignominious peace to which, for a time, she was obliged to submit, but under which her glory could not suffer her to exist." The informer then outlined the French strategy: *That Newfoundland should furnish the pretext for the intended rupture.* That in the meantime all the facilities should be given, and no dissatisfaction expressed, at the projects formed either by the English, or by the French, for the settlement of the sugar islands ceded by France. That, on the contrary, all encouragement underhand should be given, because whatever should be done in that kind would be done for the benefit of France, who was resolved to repossess them soon."[18] News of this nature doubtlessly helped inspire Grenville's decision in December 1763 to increase the amount of money he had originally planned to spend for the repair of Britain's fleet.[19] This same sort of intelligence also moved the Cabinet to recommend to the King in February 1764 that five hundred more soldiers be sent to the ceded islands.[20] By mid-1764, Grenville could not help "seeing [the French] government in no disposition to fulfill the conditions on which the peace was made," a perception that verified his and other ministers' suspicions that France was eager for vengeance and would constantly test Britain's determination and power. The acts of the French, Grenville wrote Halifax, "confirm me in my former opinion of the indispensable necessity to put a stop to these unjust proceedings by firm and temperate measures before the fire is lighted in so many parts, and fed with so much fuel as to make it impossible to extinguish it."[21]

The same general rule of conduct regulated the behavior of Grenville and his colleagues in dealing with Irish affairs. In October 1763, the King's ministers in Ireland decided they could not successfully manage Ireland's Parliament if the Irish revenue was not "freed . . . from the burden of any further pensions" imposed on it by British governments for the benefit of Britons, "except when absolutely necessary."[22] This news neither surprised nor dismayed the ministry. Before the present Lord Lieutenant, the Earl of Northumberland, had left for Dublin, the King had permitted him "to declare to the principal Members of both Houses that, unless in case of great importance, or of a particular nature, which may arise, and of which His Majesty will be the best and only judge, he does not intend to grant any pension for life or years, nor places in reversion." George III also commanded the Lord Lieutenant to assure those men "that neither you yourself nor the King's servants here (as they have assured you) do intend to recommend any such."[23] But Northumberland found that private, informal reassurances would not head off trouble. He suggested another scheme. He would "permit an address from the [Irish] House of Commons on the subject, couched in the most modest terms and in the most respectful [manner] with regard to the method of redress." He would reply to this, and the House would then vote an address of thanks to the King, who in turn would formally declare his intentions. Northumberland even presumed to advise that his reply and the King's "should be in such an affectionate, conciliatory style as may add all possible grace to so material a concession on the part of the Crown."[24]

The Cabinet immediately vetoed this plan. Halifax, the responsible minister, flatly ordered Northumberland in the King's name "to discourage any such ideas." They "impl[ied] a diffidence and suspicion very derogatory to the Royal dignity"; they gave "an air of constraint and obligation to the full and voluntary grace of His Majesty"; they cast "a public reflection on the past"; and they tied "up the hands of the sovereign in a point which depends upon his good pleasure." Grenville followed this official letter with a private one to Northumberland, explaining why the Lord Lieutenant's ideas had stirred a "great uneasiness." If this voluntary concession had "the appearance of the least force and constraint," which it would if made in reply to an address, "it would [be] . . . attributed to the weakness of government and the inability of resisting this proposition, instead of the goodness of the Crown and the disinterestedness of the Lord Lieutenant, who . . . voluntarily promised . . . to restrain the exercise of this right, and to prevent for the future whatever may have been too much for the past." Pressing the King for an official expression of his intent "would be disagreeable to him, and . . . may be thought to encroach upon the ancient and established rights of the Crown." Although, observed Grenville, "This would at all times be dangerous," it would be "more particularly at present, from the temper and spirit [of opposition to government] that has prevailed both in Great Britain and Ireland." Northumberland's concession would "be an inducement to some . . . to attempt to carry it further in Ireland." Then, this advice sent, Grenville later repeated his rule of action on such occasions. "Firmness of conduct and good government," plus support for the friends of the administration, would, he promised Northumberland, triumph over "the factious claims and unreasonable pretensions of individuals."[25]

Nothing that Grenville had heard or read before March 1764 about colonial politicians, men who, after all, already had improper ideas about the imperial relationship, would have convinced him that they would respond differently than their British, French, or Irish counterparts to any real or apparent symptoms of weakness in the government. Instead, the First Lord's informants had described a people who were ready to take every advantage they could to maintain their present power. He had long since been warned by Henry McCulloh that "the colonies from their partial interests and connections will give all the opposition in their power to . . . any . . . matter which can be proposed for the general good of the subject." Grenville thus thought it likely that American colonists would respond to unqualified concessions as he would anticipate the Irish to react. Whether Grenville publicly announced a decision to delay or simply let the session pass without taking any action, the assemblies could, in his opinion, interpret the postponement in a variety of ways, all of them bad: as a sign of indecision or weakness; as an indication of Grenville's skepticism of parliamentary support for this measure or doubt of Parliament's right to impose an internal tax; as evidence of Grenville's uncertainty of the need for further taxation; or as testimony to royal officials' inability to enforce and collect a stamp tax. The colonists, therefore, would probably spend the year of postponement drumming up support, both in and out of the House, for their position. If such were the case, the delay would neither reconcile them to the tax, nor procure more information from them, nor persuade them to acknowledge Parliament's sovereignty, nor earn their goodwill. At the end of the year, Grenville would have reaped no political benefits in America from deferral, while losing whatever revenue the tax would have raised during that time.[26]

Moreover, a postponement might be politically harmful to Britain. Grenville was keenly aware that he was sailing in uncharted waters as he planned the taxation of America, an awareness that later caused him to wish publicly that "those who had gone before him had marked out a path to him that he might more easily follow."[27] Future Treasuries might have to live with any mistakes that he made in the planning and presentation of internal colonial taxes. The sensitivity of Grenville and his colleagues at this time to the possibility of creating unfortunate precedents regarding Britain's control over imperial revenues may be clearly seen in their reaction to Northumberland's suggestion for dealing with the Irish House. It was not only the appearance of weakness that disturbed Halifax and Grenville about Northumberland's scheme; it was also the chance that adherence to his proposal might tie "the hands of the sovereign in a point which depends upon his good pleasure only" and "may be thought to encroach upon the ancient and established rights of the Crown."[28] A similar potential for difficulties lurked in any postponement of the stamp tax. Delaying it and consulting the colonies during the interim risked the creation of a precedent that would require the Treasury to follow the same procedure in the future. The agents and other friends of America were already arguing that Britain's past failure to impose an internal tax forbade any attempt to do so now. Their reliance on this type of argument proved their readiness to claim as binding precedent any past actions that would benefit them in the present. Almost certainly, they would claim that status for any postponement and consultation that occurred in 1764. Huske, for example, in his discussions with Grenville, probably had advocated establishing a precedent for delay and consultation on colonial taxes; certainly he did so in the House on 9 March 1764. As will be seen, Grenville did not respond favorably to that suggestion then. Instead, he carefully avoided creating such an officially binding precedent, and his care on that occasion reveals his concern about precedent and postponement.

By themselves, these political considerations did not absolutely foreclose any possibility of delay. But if Grenville decided a year's wait was desirable for fiscal reasons, he would have to set up the announcement and execution of that delay carefully or suffer the political consequences.

Postponing the Stamp Tax

Grenville refused to consider postponing the bill during the early days of 1764. Then, on 9 March, after John Huske had spoken, the public efforts of America's supporters succeeded where their private ones had failed—or so Huske described the events of the day. Grenville stated his hope that the stamp tax "might be done with goodwill," indicating the desirability of obtaining "further information on that subject." Then he announced his willingness "that for the present session it might go no further than [the] resolution" he had just introduced.[29]

Professor Thomas believed that Grenville "changed his mind as a result of objections made during the debate"; I suspect he entered the House that evening with the intention of doing exactly as he did. He could rely on Huske's attending a Budget Day speech. He could be confident that Huske, who fancied himself an expert on American affairs, would speak. Once Huske was on his feet, the chances were good he would advocate delay, just as he had done with Grenville in private. To be more certain that he or someone else would make this suggestion, Grenville could hint—as he did in his opening speech—that "he would . . . wish to follow to a certain degree the inclination of the people of North America, if they will agree to the end."[30] But whenever Grenville made his decision, it was not the product of a sudden impulse. He had heard arguments like Huske's before and had time to consider the alternatives. He also recognized that a House discussion on a colonial stamp tax that culminated in a resolution favoring that duty would obviate many of the objectionable aspects of a postponement. Had the Treasury begun preparing a bill but delayed bringing it to the floor, Americans might have seen this as weakness or indecision. After the discussion of 9 March and the passage of the resolution, however, Grenville probably expected that no one could doubt the Treasury's determination or the House's enthusiasm. No one could doubt, either, that the House would give short shrift to American pleas of economic poverty or political inconvenience. Furthermore, no one could imagine that the House would listen to arguments that Parliament had no right to tax the colonies.

To make sure of that, Grenville had interjected the question into the debate when he introduced the resolution. When Edward Montagu wrote to Virginia on 11 April 1764, he pointed out these facts to his correspondents there. According to Montagu, the First Lord had claimed that if even one man doubted Parliament's right to impose a stamp duty, Grenville "would take the sense of the House, having heard without doors hints of this nature dropped." Grenville then, continued the agent, "called for the sense of Parliament . . . that the House might not suffer objections of that nature at a future day," and "the Members interested in the plantations expressed great surprise that a doubt of that nature could ever exist." Clearly, Montagu felt that these expressions of opinion foreclosed any possibility of a successful challenge to Parliament's right. He also drew another conclusion from the vote. "The House appeared so unanimous in opinion that America should ease the revenue of this annual expense [of defending the colonies] that I am persuaded they will not listen to any remonstrance against it."[31] In sum, Montagu had interpreted the significance of the First Lord's actions on 9 March correctly. Grenville had wanted to let colonists know that he was dealing from a position of strength, that he had postponed the bill because he chose to, not because he thought he had to. The message of 9 March was that the bill was unmistakably, inevitably on its way to becoming law, but Grenville voluntarily decided to gain more information and, as Garth interpreted it for his employers, "to show his regard to the subjects in America, by previously consulting them."[32]

Grenville also hoped that the proceedings of 9 March would send another message to America. By obtaining a resolution in favor of colonial stamp duties, the Treasury had virtually committed itself to bringing up a bill next session. As Grenville told at least two agents in February 1765, "He was bound in honor to Parliament to call for the resolution of last year, and to propose to the House the carrying into execution of a stamp duty in all America."[33] Colonists therefore could not expect that he would drop his plans for introducing an internal tax in the House, and that knowledge would help inform their responses to the postponement.[34] As Jasper Mauduit wrote to Massachusetts, the proceedings of 9 March simply indicated that the stamp duty or its equivalent "is deferred till next year; I mean the actual laying of it."[35]

There might be other benefits to postponing the stamp tax in this fashion as well. Grenville's announcement was dramatic, more characteristic of Pitt, his unpredictable brother-in-law, than of the First Lord. As Grenville knew, introducing a resolution to the committee on ways and means without the resolution resulting in legislation was contrary to usual parliamentary practice.[36] Perhaps this irregularity would underscore for the colonists' benefit his expressions of goodwill. Perhaps it would lead them to believe him when he said, "It was far from his inclination to press any measure upon any part of the dominions without giving them time to be heard, should they have objections thereto."[37] Perhaps it would persuade them that he was honestly determined to serve their best interests. If Grenville could raise their confidence in him specifically and in the British government generally, then the collection of stamp duties and other taxes would go much more smoothly. Moreover, the habit of resisting British laws, which had been constantly renewed by smugglers and assemblymen in the past, could be broken more easily in the future.

Colonial goodwill, however, remained problematic to Grenville: something to wish for, but not to be expected and relied upon. He took care not to establish the precedent of consulting colonists before the enactment of any tax. This goal was easy to attain; he simply never consulted them. The news of Grenville's decision, and the comments he made explaining it, reached America through the agents. Since he knew that they would describe the debate to their correspondents as a matter of course, he did not have to worry about Americans' finding out about it. If colonial assemblies wanted to comment on the stamp duties or suggest rates on specific documents, they could send their petitions to the Treasury or Parliament. The agents would handle these petitions, again as a matter of routine, and thus the colonists would be using the same informal channel to reply. There was nothing unusual about this procedure. Agents and assemblies acted this way on a variety of issues. There was also nothing in it that would formally commit future First Lords to confer with colonists on other new taxes; the agents and the assemblies would be acting on their own initiative, at no official bidding. One can see these aspects of Grenville's maneuver most clearly by comparing it with Huske's, which would have had the stamp bill "read two times, printed, and then sent to America for [colonial] opinion about it." Initiative in this case would lie with the House and the Treasury to send a printed bill through formal, official channels. Even if they did not, they would be conceding the right of prior consultation to the colonies. Huske, of course, wanted to establish this right and admitted so on the floor of the House. Grenville did not want to create this precedent. He omitted reasons against postponement in his opening remarks because he feared raising the question of precedent and revealing his efforts to avoid establishing one. Then he agreed to a delay without creating any formal procedure for informing the colonies.[38] Moreover, he responded negatively to a question from Jenkinson: "Should not Government appear to take some step" to gather information from the colonies relating to the documents to be stamped? Grenville voiced some "objection" to doing any such thing and stuck to his original course. Given his refusal to adopt Huske's proposal creating an official precedent binding the House of Commons, these objections must have been rooted firmly in a similar determination to avoid any act that might officially bind Whitehall. Clearly, Grenville believed that by doing nothing he could most safely take advantage of what he believed would be the most substantial benefit of the year's delay: the time to collect more information from trusted sources and to "thoroughly digest" the stamp bill.[39]

Grenville's Meeting with the Agents

Before the session ended, the Treasury returned to work on the stamp tax. On 23 and 25 March, Cruwys and Jenkinson conferred, "settl[ing] some queries and making remarks with minutes to be observed in [the] future settling [of] the bill."[40] Later that spring, Whately wrote privately to two friends in America, Jared Ingersoll and John Temple, for information. He also studied sources in Britain, for by late July he was ready to write "a long letter" to Jenkinson about the stamp act.[41] But no one at the Treasury checked privately and discreetly with the agents about what they sent to and heard from America. Even Jackson, Grenville's private secretary and the agent for Pennsylvania and Connecticut—and thus the logical candidate for such inquiries—was not pressed for news.[42] Evidently, Grenville did not want to give the slightest impression that he was taking the initiative. He was confident that the agents would communicate accurately what they saw and heard in Parliament on 9 March. On 17 May, however, when he met with the agents at their request, he discovered that his confidence was misplaced.

Between 9 March and 17 May, the agents discovered that their memories of Grenville's announcement of the postponement differed on a crucial point. Edward Montagu, the agent for Virginia, believed, "It would be as satisfactory [to Grenville] if the several provinces would among themselves, and in modes best suited to their circumstances, raise a sum adequate to the expense of their defense." Jasper Mauduit understood "Mr. Grenville [to be] willing to give the provinces their option to raise [money by a stamp tax] or some equivalent tax."[43] But Charles Garth wrote to South Carolina that Grenville had declared "it . . . far from his inclination to press any measure upon any part of the dominions without giving them time to be heard, should they have objections thereto," implying that the First Lord wanted comments only on the tax he had introduced.[44] And on 14 March, an unknown friend of America offered advice that he would not have given to his correspondent in New York had Grenville offered the colonies the right to tax themselves: "All the well-wishers to America" believed "the [stamp] tax . . . an equitable one, and the least injurious that [could] be proposed." These well-wishers, he went on, recommended that "the several assemblies should signify their assent and desire to that tax, under the present exigencies of the state, and the necessity of the case." By doing so, the colonies would "avoid every appearance of an infringement of their liberty." Moreover, while they showed their willingness to obey Parliament, they would at the same time prevent the setting of a precedent "from internal taxes being imposed without their consent, which [would] inevitably be the case . . . if they [withheld] their assent to the stamp tax."[45]

Since Garth on 4 June made a similar recommendation for similar reasons to his employers in South Carolina, he may have been one of those well-wishers. His delay in forwarding the advice may be explained by his cautiousness. Garth hoped Jamaica would repeal its stamp tax for reasons that "might possibly be preventive of the imposition of this tax." Any premature advice might cause Charleston to draft a potentially harmful petition conceding Parliament's right to impose internal taxes when there was no need to make such a concession.[46] Another "well-wisher to America" may have been Jackson. He passed along to his friend Benjamin Franklin the suggestion that "the colonies apply . . . for a stamp act." Had Jackson, who was "most averse to an internal tax [because] God knows how far such a precedent may be extended" and who had "frequently asked [men at the Treasury] what internal tax they would not lay," believed that Grenville had agreed on 9 March to the colonies' raising this money by their own taxes, he never would have forwarded his suggestion to America.[47] When these well-wishers began to compare notes with Montagu and perhaps the Mauduits, they must have been surprised and concerned, for this comparison raised important questions. Had Grenville offered to let the colonies tax themselves? Had he indicated a willingness to consider other types of parliamentary taxes? To clarify these points, and thus "to procure the best intelligence possible" for the colonists, the agents requested a meeting with Grenville.[48]

When Grenville learned about the confusion, it must have surprised him, for he thought that he had not left those questions open to doubt. James Harris, who sat by Grenville on the Treasury bench in the House and took notes on Grenville's announcement to postpone the stamp tax, did not include in his account of that speech any such offers.[49] If

Grenville had expressed a willingness to allow the colonies to raise the money themselves or encouraged them to recommend other parliamentary taxes, Harris surely would have recorded it, for such pledges would clearly affect the Treasury's planning for the next session. But even assuming that Harris was unusually negligent, it is highly unlikely Grenville made either offer on 9 March. Allowing the assemblies to raise the money, then pay it into the Exchequer, would create difficult administrative and political problems without providing compensating advantages for Britain. When the agents mentioned this possibility to him on 17 May, Grenville immediately rejected it. When he did so, he specifically referred to the possibility of some colonies refusing to contribute, an indication that he believed such a system would permit the assemblies to continue to impede or defeat British policies.[50] This weakness would have been patently obvious to a man who for several months prior to 9 March had been reading and believing descriptions of the uncontrolled assemblies in the charter governments.[51] Grenville could not have proposed that these assemblies raise the money themselves in good faith. Did he lie on 9 March? Certainly Grenville had kept private some of his thoughts about the colonies and some of his political intentions, but he had nothing to gain by outright deception on this matter. A proposal like this might suggest weakness to Americans and encourage resistance to any tax. It would absolutely foreclose any possibility, however remote, of the assemblies' agreeing to the stamp duties and providing useful information about documents and rates. Furthermore, building up colonists' hopes of continued freedom from parliamentary taxation, then dashing them, would not establish confidence in the British government. Thus, it is unlikely that Grenville made any such offer, either with an eye to deception or as an act of goodwill.[52]

It is also unlikely that the First Lord expressed on 9 March any hope that the colonies suggest other sorts of parliamentary taxes as alternatives to a stamp tax, even though his later assurances to the agents that he would listen to any such suggestions reveal that making these assurances was not unthinkable to him. Grenville announced in the House on 9 March that he thought a colonial stamp tax was "the best plan." He also told the members, according to Jenkinson, that he "waited only for further information on that subject."[53] Saying in the next breath that he was willing to consider again other parliamentary taxes would effectively deny him part of the information he hoped to receive from America, if even one of the colonies chose that option. In March, Grenville wanted to narrow the range of colonial responses, not broaden it. But to his surprise on 17 May, he discovered that some agents had either misheard him two months earlier or misinterpreted him when he said that he "would likewise wish to follow to a certain degree the inclination of the people in North America, if they will agree to the end."[54]

After Grenville received the agents on 17 May "with great openness and affability," they began the conference by thanking him "for waiving the intended bill in the last session, upon the principle of giving the colonies the opportunity of knowing the intention of government that they might be able to remit their several objections for the consideration of Parliament."[55] Then they asked for copies of the bill to send to America. Grenville replied graciously and carefully. He "assured [the agents] that his motive for deferring [the bill] sprang from a desire of showing his regard to the subjects in America, by previously consulting them on a measure that, if the principle on which [that measure] was grounded should appear fair and just in itself, he believed could have the fewest objections of any that could be proposed." Thus the First Lord avoided reference to any "principle" of conduct that might be construed as binding; he instead described the decision as motivated by a personal desire to show his regard for colonists on this particular measure. Then, having preserved his and his successors' freedom of action, he reiterated to the agents that the colonies would have to pay some money for their defense. Parliament would not listen to pleas of inability, he warned. Moreover, that money would be raised by parliamentary taxation. He had no intention of agreeing to allow the assemblies to try to raise and appropriate the money themselves. That, he told the agents, would be "attended with very many difficulties even if it could be suposed that [all the] colonies would . . . adopt such a recommendation." Any objections that Parliament did not have the power to tax would be pointless. "The sense of the House of Commons [on 9 March was] sufficiently declaratory thereof, even if there had been no precedent of a revenue from America granted to the Crown by [the] Act of Parliament . . . establishing a post office at New York."[56]

Perhaps because some agents had already suggested to their correspondents that the colonies could propose other parliamentary taxes as alternatives to a stamp tax, Grenville told the agents that he would gladly consider such suggestions. "If they could point out any system as effectual and more easy to them," Americans should propose to the Treasury that Parliament levy it instead. Grenville promised that "he was open to every proposition [of this nature] to be made from the colonies." At this moment, though, he was "still of the same mind" about the appropriateness of stamp duties as a parliamentary tax on Americans. "Of the several inland duties, [it] . . . was the most equal, required the fewest officers, and was attended with the least expense in the collecting of it."[57] In other words, Grenville believed that it was the best tax possible from the standpoint of both the taxpayer and the government. Then he observed, "When the subject had been fully considered by them upon its proper grounds and principles, and no other method should upon the whole be suggested so proper for America in general, it would be a satisfaction to him to carry it into the House with their concurrence and approbation."[58] With this gentle, if not so subtle, hint to colonists not to waste their time trying to find alternatives, but rather to try to please him, Grenville dropped the subject.

The agents had asked "to have the particular heads of the bill, without which, [Israel Mauduit] said, it would be asking the province[s] to assent to they did not know what."[59] Grenville refused, excusing himself by saying it "was not yet thoroughly digested." He also added that assemblies would not need a copy to make their decision. The bill would be similar in form and substance to the English stamp tax, which "everyone knew." Probably "the objects for the stamp duty would be as extensive" as in the English law, "but what the rate of the stamps might be, was not determined."[60] Grenville stopped here. By doing so, he left unsaid another motive for his refusal. He had no reason to commit future First Lords to the practice of sending drafts of bills affecting the colonies through the agents to the assemblies for comment. Passing Treasury papers across the Atlantic might do just that.[61]

Grenville also did not respond directly when the agents asked him two specific questions about the weight of the American stamp duties. Were the stamps "to be as high as are by law imposed in Great Britain," they wanted to know. If not, "What proportion [would they] bear?" He took refuge in the answer that the Treasury had not made those decisions. In truth, the duties Cruwys and McCulloh had suggested were lower than English ones. Moreover, Grenville's wariness of harming colonists' ability to buy more manufactured goods would have prevented him from trying to raise over two hundred thousand pounds from this tax. Still, he was too shrewd to commit himself, however informally, to any specific duties or to an arbitrary proportion that more information might prove to be too low. He listened without comment to the agents' complaint that "it seemed to us to be unreasonable that if the stamps were to be as great as in England, [that] they should be so high."[62]

After hearing this, Grenville noted that the assemblies certainly should feel free to comment on the rates of stamps for specific documents. Then, according to that careful listener Garth, the First Lord "added he should be very ready to consult with us before the meeting of

Parliament thereon, to receive any propositions we might in the meantime be instructed upon by our respective constituents with regard to these points, if our assemblies should, as he could not doubt upon a due consideration they would, transmit us instructions with their assent to the plan for levying this money in the American dominions."[63] When Garth's hopes for good results from the repeal of Jamaica's stamp tax died, he evidently remembered this statement and also recalled Grenville's saying "it would be [a] satisfaction to him to carry [the stamp bill] into the House with [the assemblies'] concurrence and approbation." Such remarks may have as well confirmed for him the wisdom of the opinion "all the well-wishers to America" had expressed in late March. In any case, he decided he could discern within the First Lord's words an opportunity for the colonies to make themselves part of any future deliberations on taxes. Grenville "had hinted," William Knox later inferred, probably after speaking with Garth, "that the colonies would now have it in their power, by agreeing to this tax, to establish a precedent for their being consulted before any tax was imposed on them by Parliament."[64] To his employers in South Carolina, Garth did not refer to any hints from Grenville but still pointed out to them "a question not altogether unworthy [of] consideration." Indeed, "Your assenting in form," he wrote, "having in the assembly considered of the nature of the tax as signified unto you to be proposed in Parliament previous to its being carried into the House may . . . establish a precedent, of being previously consulted on all occasions that a revenue bill may be thought of in which America may be affected."[65]

Clearly, Grenville did not intend to create such an opportunity. Had that been his design, he had nothing to gain by coyly hinting at it to the agents. These were, after all, the same men who had been uncertain about his intentions after he had, he thought, clearly outlined them in his speech on 9 March. Instead, he would have explicitly stated, and made clear beyond any possibility of misinterpretation, that colonial compliance with his suggestion would give the Americans a strong precedent to rely on if and when the Treasury and Parliament considered other taxes. Indeed, the agents had even given him an opportunity for doing so with their remarks at the beginning of the meeting about a principle of prior consultation. Finally, had this been his intent, he would not have communicated it only through the agents. Grenville knew that the correct channel of official communication with the colonies was through the Secretary of State for the Southern Department. In the Treasury's memorial of 4 October 1763, Grenville had asked the King to command that official to order the governors to enforce British revenue and commercial legislation. The agents, as

Benjamin Franklin realized at the time and later observed, were not "the proper canals through which requisitions were made." They had no official status. For all the assemblies officially knew, their representatives in London could be fashioning their reports out of whole cloth. Grenville's failure to take this step reveals his intention to avoid creating any precedent.[66]

But did Grenville inadvertently make this offer on 17 May? Once one separates Garth's account of the First Lord's words from the hopeful gloss that Garth and Knox put on them, it is clear that he did not. Grenville promised he would meet with the agents, if they requested the meeting, and "receive" any suggestions the assemblies might have instructed them to make for the rates of stamps on specific documents. There was nothing extraordinary in this promise. Grenville had, in effect, extended the same courtesy to the agent for Massachusetts Bay while the Treasury was setting the rate for the molasses duty. No one claimed then or later that this bound Grenville to do the same in future cases, and, indeed, he and his successors in office had no reason to feel bound to meet informally with the agents at the agents' initiative before the Treasury finished formulating taxes. All parties to these discussions regarded them as informal and irregular. All parties also knew that the Treasury decided whether or not to hold them. As he thought about the meeting of 17 May, Garth was clutching at straws, trying to salvage something of value from what he considered an unpromising situation.[67]

Another question remains. Did Grenville encourage Garth and, presumably, the other agents to grasp at this straw—in an effort to deceive the assemblies into supporting the tax in exchange for a valuable precedent? The surviving evidence does not suggest that he did so.[68] Rather, the record of Grenville's words reveals that he carefully avoided hinting at enticing prospects. As for his comment about carrying the stamp bill into Parliament with the colonial assemblies' "concurrence and approbation," the only promise in this case was one concerning his personal reaction. Grenville would be happy to have the assemblies' approval for a stamp tax, and he would express his pleasure in the House. But the promise of his pleasure on such an occasion did not include a promise of a precedent that would bind him, his successors, or the House of Commons. And Grenville certainly guarded against any comment that the agents and their constituents might construe as a precedent for prior colonial *consent* to parliamentary taxation. On 9 March in the House, he expressed his "wish to follow *to a certain degree* the inclination of the people in North America, if they will agree" to paying stamp taxes imposed by Parliament. On 17 May, he indicated to the agents he was "very ready *to consult with us* . . . [and] *to receive* any propositions . . . we might be instructed upon . . . if our assemblies should, as he could not doubt they would, transmit us instructions with their assent to the plan for levying this money in the American dominions." The italicized words reveal that the First Lord carefully promised only to listen to suggestions from America, not to agree to them, even if these suggestions were accompanied by an affirmation of Parliament's right.[69]

Indeed, probably the most significant aspect of Grenville's meeting with the agents on 17 May is that the day passed without the First Lord making a binding promise of prior consultation or consent. Huske had already predicted publicly that such concessions would be popular with Americans. Garth clearly thought, though he did not confide this insight to Grenville, that even the prospect of creating the precedent of prior consultation would be tempting to Carolinians. Had Grenville asked him or any of the agents, they no doubt would have encouraged him to make the pledge. From Huske's remarks, and from what the First Lord knew about the assemblies' hunger for independent voices, Grenville must have realized that a promise of prior consultation would be attractive to American politicians and might mute their opposition to this particular tax. Yet not only did he not take advantage of his opportunity to make that offer, but he also scrupulously avoided accidentally making it or even suggesting it: It was too high a political price to pay for the assemblies' approbation of the stamp tax. No doubt his decision was influenced by his confidence that a stamp tax would virtually collect itself, no matter what the assemblies thought or did. Offering them a substantial concession to persuade them to accede to a tax that would enforce itself anyway would be an unnecessary surrender. But beyond questions of necessity, from Grenville's standpoint it would have been shortsighted as well. The First Lord intended to establish the unquestioned power and authority of Parliament over the colonies. He could not do that if he gave the colonies the right of prior consultation on future taxes in return for the revenue gained by their approval of one particular tax.

The Official Request for Information

Grenville must have been pleased with the results of his meeting with the agents. A serious misunderstanding had been cleared up, and the assemblies had been placed in a difficult position. If they refused to take advantage of his offer to consider any suggestions that they might have for stamp duties, and instead protested on constitutional grounds, the tax would enforce itself anyway, they would stand revealed in America as helpless to prevent the tax and too obstinate to suggest changes in it, and their constitutional ideas would be discredited. If they refused to take advantage of his offer, but muted their constitutional arguments in an effort to gain weight for their petitions, the same process would occur, and Grenville could further claim that they had tacitly given up their constitutional pretensions.[70] And if the assemblies did take him up on his offer, they would have conceded the supremacy of Parliament, which was his ultimate goal. Any of these events would be desirable; all would immediately or ultimately reduce the assemblies' power within the imperial hierarchy to its proper proportions.

Jenkinson, however, was troubled by the absence of any official request from Whitehall to the colonies for information. On 1 July 1764, he wrote to Grenville, reminding him, "In the last session of Parliament, you assigned as a reason for not going on with the Stamp Act, that you waited only for further information on that subject." Then he repeated his earlier query: "This having been said, should not Government appear to take some step for that purpose?" Although Jenkinson did not mention the session with the agents on 17 May specifically, which he certainly knew about since he was at the Treasury during it, he clearly did not think that the meeting qualified as a bona fide, official request for information. Nor did he believe that Whately's letters to his friends would serve that purpose. Some official communication with colonial governments requesting information had to be made. "Without it," Jenkinson warned, "we may perhaps be accused of neglect." He re-called, "I mentioned this to you soon after the Parliament was up. I remember your objections to it; but I think the information may be procured in a manner to obviate those objections." Grenville replied with a promise to discuss that business with Jenkinson during the next week.[71]

Grenville returned to London before 12 July, and he and his assistant presumably discussed the new suggestion. On 16, 24, and 25 July, the First Lord talked with Halifax, mostly on relations with France, but also on "other business." On 11 August, Halifax sent a circular letter to all governors in America and the West Indies. After informing them officially about the House resolution on the stamp duties, he com-manded them in the King's name to send him "a list of all instruments made use of in public transactions, law proceedings, grants, con-veyances, securities of land and money . . . with proper and sufficient descriptions of the same, in order that if Parliament should think proper to pursue the intention of the . . . resolution, they may thereby be enabled to carry it into execution in the most effectual and least burden-some manner." Should the governor feel unqualified to prepare an accurate list, he should "require the assistance of the principal officer of the law within [his] government, who is the proper person to be consulted towards procuring the said information in the manner required."[72]

It is impossible to say whether this was Jenkinson's plan. It is clear, however, that Halifax's letter did obviate the major objection that Grenville would have had against an official communication with the colonial governments. Halifax excluded the assemblies from any role in the process of gathering information. "The proper person" for the governor to consult with was the attorney general, an officer who was a member of the executive branch in all colonies and in some a royal appointee. Had Halifax and Grenville wished to, they could have ordered the governor to refer the request to the assemblies. As recently as October 1763, Halifax had commanded Gov. John Penn of Pennsylvania to inform that assembly of His Majesty's displeasure at its failure to support the war effort against Pontiac, so he was accustomed to using these channels to communicate with assemblies on financial affairs relating to defense. Grenville, since at least 1746, had been aware that it was possible, and indeed desirable in some circumstances, to communicate through the governors the commands of the British government to the assemblies on the subjects of raising men and money for the imperial defense.[73] In this case, though, he and Halifax passed up the chance, doubtlessly because doing so would have created a strong precedent for similar consultations in the future. Significantly, they also did not take this opportunity to use the governors to establish with assemblymen informal contacts of the type they advised Northumberland to make with members of the Irish Parliament in order to discuss a variety of issues. Presumably even these sorts of meetings offered assemblies too much chance to claim a binding precedent.[74] By limiting the governor's consultants to the attorneys general, Grenville and his lieutenants could defend themselves against any political enemies who might charge that they had not sought information from America without risking the establishment of a highly undesirable precedent.

Halifax's letter thus protected Grenville politically and acquired additional sources of information. After it was sent, the men at the Treasury could feel secure that they had gained an extra year without making concessions that might help preserve the assemblies' pretensions and powers. Whately used the additional time effectively. He gathered and studied more information about colonial documents, consulted again with Cruwys and McCulloh on the schedule of duties, devised a long report on his reasons for suggesting specific rates, and persuaded Grenville to add specific penalty clauses to the bill rather than rely on a general clause. By the time replies to Halifax's letter began to trickle in from the colonies in early December, Whately had a rather complete plan that he could check against this new intelligence.[75] Grenville could be confident that the extra time had benefited the bill and probably the revenue as well.

Chapter VIII

Preparing and Passing the Stamp Act
December 1764–February 1765

By the end of 1764, it was clear that the assemblies would not take advantage of the opportunity Grenville gave them. The House of Representatives of Massachusetts Bay acknowledged that "Mr. Grenville [was] willing to give the provinces their option to raise [a stamp tax] or some equivalent tax, [and] desirous, as he was pleased to express himself, 'to consult the ease, the quiet and good will of the colonies.' " The Massachusetts House demanded, however, that its agent remonstrate against this measure, "if possible . . . obtain a repeal of the Sugar Act, and prevent the imposition of any further duties or taxes on the colonies." Furthermore, the House promised its agent that he would "be joined by all the other agents." To underscore their sense of the urgency of this issue, the members of the Massachusetts House flatly informed Jasper Mauduit that if Americans were taxed at pleasure without the vote of their representatives, they would be slaves: "The power of taxing . . . is the grand barrier of British liberty, which if once broken down, all is lost."[1] New York's assemblymen used the same arguments when they addressed the lieutenant governor of the colony on the impending stamp tax. After describing the "imminent ruin" of paying taxes to "a power subordinate to none, and unacquainted with their circumstances," they predicted that in such a case "nothing but extreme poverty can preserve us from the most unsupportable bondage."[2] Grenville could be sure that these important colonies, and doubtless others, too, planned to oppose the stamp duty in Parliament.

There is no record of Grenville's immediate reaction to this news. Certainly he did not express, publicly or privately, then or later, any disappointment or surprise at these responses to the postponement of the stamp tax. Indeed, his public reaction was strikingly different from that of Robert Charles, the agent from New York, who handled that assembly's address with such noticeable "delicacy" and embarrassment that Sir William Baker, in sympathy with the colonies, scouted the possibility of New York sending "somebody fit for the purpose" to argue its position in London. Charles was probably as much angered as embarrassed, for the response from New York demonstrated his employers' rejection of the "too plain truth" he had written them about the uselessness of such protests.[3] Grenville, however, did not vent any anger he might have felt at the colonial protests. Nor did he react publicly, as did members of the Board of Trade, to "the most indecent disrespect" the two assemblies showed toward Parliament's acts and resolution and to "proceedings . . . calculated to raise groundless suspicion and distrust in the minds of [His] Majesty's good subjects in the colonies, and have the strongest tendency to subvert those principles of constitutional relation and dependence upon which the colonies were originally established." Grenville presumably agreed with the Privy Council's decision on 19 December to place these papers before Parliament for its consideration.[4] In private, he, like other members of the ministry, probably took "great offense" at doctrines advanced by James Otis in support of the colonial petition.[5] Grenville's actions, however, reveal that he believed that the best course was to respond to "indecent" arguments by enacting the stamp tax with a substantial majority and by demonstrating as he did so the virtual unanimity of the House in support of Parliament's right and power to tax Americans. Moreover, he did not plan to indulge himself in any angry recriminations during this process. To the contrary: Grenville was determined that Americans would have no cause to doubt that he was a thoughtful, moderate man who still wished to consult the ease, quiet, and goodwill of the colonies.

Preparing the Stamp Act

Before making preparations for the debate in the House, however, the Treasury had to begin preparation of the resolutions Grenville would introduce. In particular, the First Lord and his colleagues needed to settle "the rates and the mode of distribution." On 6 December 1764, Whately's lengthy report started that process. In it, Whately carefully pointed out ways in which life and the law differed in the colonies, noted that "like all other duties, and like the stamp duties in England when they were new, [the colonial stamp tax] should begin low," and made several specific recommendations, both on rates and on the method of distributing the stamps. After his report, the Treasury approved his general recommendation on the weight of the taxes and his observations on the necessity of paying attention to differences between England and America, and the men of the Treasury used both to guide their deliberations on the decisions on the rates and on the drafting of the bill.[6]

Whately's work merits extensive summary and comment because it reveals how carefully he sought to balance Britain's necessity for an expanding market in America with her need for revenue. In this case, he obviously did not plan to countenance the sort of decline in economic activity that the Treasury apparently was prepared to accept as a consequence of a threepence duty on molasses. Instead, he wished to produce legislation enacting "the great object" that Grenville had announced to the House in 1764: "to reconcile the regulation of commerce with an increase of revenue." The report is revealing for another reason as well. Whately's explicit and implicit determination to avoid making certain duties "subject[s] of clamor" displays his awareness of the political as well as economic importance of imposing an equitable tax.[7]

A good example of Whately's various concerns may be found in his discussion of placing stamps on royal grants of land in America.[8] The Crown, he explained, often received no immediate or adequate benefit from grants of Crown lands in America; "a moderate duty upon these grants would be a very reasonable imposition, and produce a considerable revenue." The Treasury should be careful, he stressed, to keep the duty low, rather than try to raise a great deal of money on the grants. "The expenses of surveying, and of fees to governors and other officers . . . are already considerable"; a heavy tax might thus have the undesirable effect of inhibiting settlement and cultivation of vacant lands. There were political reasons for setting it low as well. This would be "entirely a new duty, unknown in England, which circumstance would make it a subject of clamor if it were also high." Finally, a low duty would answer two likely objections to the taxing of these grants. First, because the tax was the same no matter what the quality or value of the grant was, it would "carr[y] with it a degree of inequality." To pay the same amount for poorer land, which would not permit its owner to recoup his money as quickly as one who had a better grant, was economically unfair. Unfairness of this sort would easily become "a subject of clamor" in colonial politics, keeping colonists skeptical of Britain's ability to exercise her authority fairly. Second, paying a tax on these documents would "give some small check to the settling of uncleared lands, . . . directly contrary to the First Principles of Colonization." Furthermore, Whately added, "This last circumstance will be insisted upon as an objection to the laying of any duty at all upon these grants." Whately, however, thought neither objection should have much effect on the Treasury's deliberations. "The smallness of the duty" would minimize the economic and political dangers of inequality rather than significantly hinder the progress of settlement and cultivation. Moreover, "the greatest check . . . to cultivation" had been the continuing practice of making "extravagant grants . . . which are retained by the present proprietors" primarily for speculation. The Treasury could, by charging higher rates on larger grants, use the stamps to discourage speculators. Proportioning the tax to the amount of land in the grant, according to Whately, would make this imposition on land grants "the more equitable." Whately probably thought in 1764 what Grenville stated in 1768, that these taxes would help prevent the granting of huge blocks of land.[9] The Secretary recommended a tax of one shilling and sixpence for grants of 100 acres or under, three shillings for 100 to 200 acres, five shillings for 200 to 320 acres, and five shillings for each additional grant of 320 acres.

Whately did not overlook in his calculations special circumstances in different colonies. Imposing a standard duty on all grants of land made by the Crown, he explained to the Treasury, would create serious inequalities. The continental colonies, "in which there [was] the greatest quantity of land ungranted and which [were] consequently the poorest," would "pay the largest proportion of this tax," while the Caribbean islands, where the King had less land to grant, where the price of land was much higher due to its scarcity and intensive development, and where the people were richer, would bear a much lighter burden. To avoid politically damaging "charges of partiality" and to increase the revenue, Whately suggested that duties on land grants in the West Indies be double those on grants in North America, "which will be some balance to the disproportion in the number of grants."[10]

Then the Secretary called attention to another difficulty. Limiting these duties to grants of land made by the Crown would exempt subjects who received land from the charter and proprietary governments. One remedy might be to put an equal duty on mesne conveyances. But, Whately warned, "This supposed invasion of right would occasion much clamor and indeed it might be difficult to say whether [those colonies'] grants are . . . properly mesne conveyances." He therefore recommended that the Treasury "confound all grants and mesne conveyances together under the same duty and not . . . make that duty too high at first." Then, he concluded, "There [would not be] a pretence to say that any are exempted from such impositions as the legislature may think proper to lay upon conveyances in general."[11]

These same general concerns influenced Whately's recommendation that the Treasury keep duties on legal proceedings lower than those in England and apply them as fairly and equitably as possible to different types of documents. He pointed out that a litigious and "really poor" people would be particularly harmed and, probably, particularly angered by heavy duties. "It is therefore proper to give them some relief by putting these duties at a lower rate than . . . in England." He suggested that the stamps be rated at between one-half and three-quarters of the price paid in England, depending on the colonial court. If this were done, "The grievance would be removed and the revenue would not suffer from the tax being so moderate, as a higher duty would certainly greatly diminish the number of suits among a people actually poor."[12]

Whately did make two exceptions to "this general principle": All appeals from the verdicts of common law courts and all proceedings in admiralty courts "for seizures made of uncustomed or prohibited goods or of prizes [taken] from the enemy" should bear the English rates. Appeals were "seldom brought unless for delay and vexation or where a considerable property [was] concerned." Contests over seizures and prizes in admiralty courts also "generally relate[d] to considerable property and [had] therefore no claim to be charged with a less duty than is paid on the like proceedings in England."[13] In the Secretary's opinion, those who could pay a heavier tax without severely damaging their economic interests should pay the tax.

Whately also advised the Treasury to take two other steps to guard the economic prosperity of the colonies. Commercial conditions and practices peculiar to the colonies, he argued, required the British government to tax bonds lightly and to distinguish carefully between articles of indenture and of apprenticeship when assessing duties. Americans usually gave bonds rather than notes of hand when they lent money. This practice, they felt, made recovery easier and more certain, and they preferred it so much that they used it "for [even] the smallest sum of money borrowed." Whately argued that because the bonds were "in such common use and . . . given for such small sums, a duty of two shillings and sixpence [the tax in England] would be very heavy." To avoid disrupting a commercial custom that regulated so many transactions, Whately recommended that a tax of threepence be levied on bonds for less than ten pounds, one shilling on those between ten and twenty pounds, and one shilling and sixpence on sums greater than twenty pounds. If the English duty on the indenture of servants, a practice common in the colonies, were imposed on Americans, it would be "a grievous tax upon labor already too dear. To exempt them from all duty [would] be a proper attention to the practice of the country." At the same time, Whately recommended that the government levy on colonists the English duty on apprentices, apparently reasoning that men who entered into this type of agreement were prosperous enough to bear the tax.

Whately hoped keeping the rates low and equitable would do more than merely insure that the duties would not harm Britain's commerce with America. Selling the stamps at a low price would also serve to diminish popular anger at the tax. Whately was doubtless aware of a fact of life that Jenkinson soon afterward expressed: "A stamp duty has ever been borne with complaint."[14] They both understood the reason for the taxpayer's anguish, too. Because a stamp duty taxed documents essential to legal proceedings and commercial transactions of all sorts, because it virtually enforced itself, because "it [was] not subject to the frauds to which Customs House duties [were] liable," and because forgery of stamps was punishable by death, the odds were that the subject would have to pay the tax.[15] All eighteenth-century English subjects disliked paying taxes, and probably most of them liked to have at least a sporting chance to avoid compliance with fiscal legislation; a stamp tax gave the government an unfair advantage.[16] To minimize the inevitable complaints, Whitehall had adopted a general rule commanding that stamp duties be kept light when first imposed, then subsequently increased. There was even greater reason to follow this rule in America, where the people were not used to obeying British law or paying British duties and where the assemblies were questioning the constitutionality of taxation by Parliament. In his report, Whately was careful to remind his colleagues of this final point.

After Whately submitted his report, on 6 December, the Treasury made an important addition to the Secretary's proposals. Grenville and his colleagues decided to accept a recommendation made by both McCulloh and Cruwys to require stamps on bills of lading "signed for any kinds of goods, wares, or merchandise to be exported from [the colonies], and on cockets and clearances granted there." These stamps, the Treasury judged, should cost four pence each, a sum that should neither inhibit trade with England nor discourage the circulation of goods along the North American coast. Indeed, if these stamps inhibited smugglers, as the Treasury expected, the volume of legitimate trade would increase. As Whately noted, this duty was "put on more to prevent frauds than to procure revenue."[17]

The Treasury also deleted some proposals. Whately's friend Ingersoll apparently "gave [Whately] no peace" until the Treasury dropped "three particular things that were intended to be taxed," duties on marriage licenses, commissions for justices of the peace, and notes of hand for small sums. Ingersoll argued that taxing marriage licenses "would be odious in a new country where every encouragement ought to be given to marriage and where there [is] little portion," that taxing justices would discourage men from serving in offices not "generally . . . profitable and yet necessary for the good order and government of the people," and that taxing notes of hands would be inconvenient in America where they "were given and taken . . . very often for very small sums." All his arguments appealed to the Mother Country's interest in increasing America's population and thus improving her markets, encouraging law and order in the colonies, and doing as little as possible to harm the economic position of the poor in the colonies.[18]

Whately also told Ingersoll that he might "fairly claim the honor of having occasioned the duties [in general] being much lower than intended." The truth of this remark is impossible to gauge, however, because no records of the Treasury's discussions have survived. Indeed, the Treasury decided to impose higher rates on newspaper advertisements, cards, and licenses for retailing liquor than Whately had recommended.[19] Despite these changes, however, the Secretary could still justly estimate that colonial stamp duties averaged only two-thirds to three-quarters of comparable duties in Britain.[20] For this reason, and because Whately and his colleagues had avoided some potentially harmful taxes, the Treasury felt secure in believing that the duties would neither sap the colonies' present economic prosperity nor stunt their future growth. Moreover, because the duties were low, because they were designed to fit the special circumstances of all the colonies, because they fell on the rich more than on the poor, and because they did not depend on officers with irritating powers of search and seizure for their enforcement, the Treasury could also feel confident that the duties would prove to be less offensive to Americans than the colonists then believed. Once colonists "after due consideration discover[ed] that the taxes imposed on them . . . [were] by no means oppressive," their confidence in the British government would surely increase, thereby helping to effect an important change in the political relationship between the colonies and the Mother Country.[21]

Preparation for the Political Debate

Grenville took pains in preparing his remarks to the House similar to those taken by Whately in preparing the bill. The intelligence from Massachusetts and New York, and the objections Ingersoll made against a stamp tax in a letter (and perhaps in person as well) to Whately, reminded Grenville that two arguments would be again broached against the imposition of stamp duties.[22] The first would question its constitutionality; the second, its expediency. These were arguments that Grenville had heard earlier in 1764 from the agents and other friends of America. He had dismissed their reasoning then, and he had not since been persuaded to change his mind. Still, Grenville realized that he should explain his continued opposition both to the House and—if called upon to do it—to the agents.

As far as the House was concerned, Grenville knew very well that men of good conscience on occasion could unpredictably decide that the government was threatening subjects' rights. Although general warrants had been used for a long time, in the past year many of Grenville's firmest supporters had decided they were unconstitutional and thus should be abolished. So even though no member had objected on constitutional grounds to the proposed stamp tax on 9 March 1764, Grenville could not therefore be sure that no one would in 1765. This possibility concerned him. Not because he feared that defections on this point might defeat the tax: Grenville made no effort to insure the attendance and allegiance of every possible supporter for this debate, which he certainly would have done had he believed the issue was in doubt.[23] He had other reasons for trying to make certain that no member would oppose the tax on constitutional principles. Division within the House on the matter of Parliament's authority to levy internal taxes on colonists could only encourage more discontent and protest in America, and Grenville did not wish to prolong a pointless and irritating debate. To help cut it off, he wanted to prove to Americans that they had no hope of gaining supporters for their petitions to the House. Perhaps he also wanted to be armed with convincing arguments in case Pitt decided to fulminate against the bill. But certainly in order to guard against any defections on principle, he carefully prepared his case for the constitutionality of the stamp tax.

In particular, Grenville was concerned about the constitutional questions raised by the existence of charter and proprietary governments. He could evidently foresee false, but persuasive, arguments being made that these colonies had been given particular privileges that in their case exempted them from parliamentary taxation. To prepare himself, he "look[ed] into the charters of some of the charter governments" with an eye to discovering precisely what privileges had been granted to them. He also checked closely those sections that defined the colonies' subservience to the laws of England. Grenville concluded that even these colonies' charters, which were far more democratic than the constitutions of the royal colonies, preserved Parliament's right to tax British subjects in America. To be perfectly sure of his conclusions, he discussed them with Lord Chief Justice Mansfield on 22 December 1764. Unsurprisingly, Mansfield agreed. But the Earl did caution that taxing America would be "a striking alteration to ignorant people," and thus might be to them an "unanswerable argument *ad homines*." Mansfield advised Grenville to "employ someone to look with this view into the origin of [the colonies'] power to tax themselves and raise money" in charter, proprietary, and royal governments.[24]

Grenville assigned this task to Jenkinson, who wrote John Pownall, the Secretary to the Board of Trade, for information and advice on this and other points. Pownall promptly replied, on 26 December. From this information, and doubtless from other sources already available to him, Jenkinson concluded that "no country ever came under the dominion of the Crown of Great Britain, but that the Parliament had made laws with respect to it, [and] the distinction between laws for raising taxes and for other purposes [was] absurd." Moreover, the charters proved to him that these colonies were, "in every respect, as well with regard to the right of raising money as well as everything else, subject to the legislature of Great Britain." Jenkinson worked these conclusions into a draft of the speech that Grenville was to deliver when introducing the stamp tax.[25] Whately evidently shared in the findings of this research as well. Grenville had asked him to write a pamphlet defending the administration's colonial legislation of 1764 and asserting the right of Parliament to impose a stamp tax. By the time Whately published the pamphlet in January 1765, he had included among his arguments the blunt statements that "the charter and the proprietary governments in America [were] . . . on the same footing as the rest. . . . All who took those grants were British subjects, inhabiting British dominions, and who at the time of taking, were indisputably under the authority of Parliament. . . . Those, therefore, to whom the charters were originally given, could have no exemption granted to them, and what the father never received, the children [could not] claim as an inheritance." Indeed, Whately added, "Nor was it ever an idea that they should; even the charters themselves, so far from allowing, guard against the supposition."[26] After studying this research, hearing and digesting Jenkinson's and Whately's conclusions from it, and adapting and arranging their thoughts and arguments to suit his own sense of how to persuade the House, Grenville had much less to fear from the "unanswerable" ad hominem argument. Perhaps he even thought that unanimity in the House on the principle of Parliament's authority to tax Americans was within his grasp.

The Meeting with the Agents

Before Grenville made his speech to the House, the agents asked him to receive a delegation from them to discuss the impending stamp tax. Two considerations prompted the request. The agents who were not members of Parliament wanted an indication from the administration as to whether the House would receive petitions that questioned the right of Parliament to tax the colonists. Also, all the agents had decided that "as most of the colonies had signified their inclination to assist the Mother Country upon proper requisitions from hence . . . , that it might have a good effect to have that inclination made known to Administration."[27] To convey that information to Grenville and to get a sense of his position on the colonial petitions, they selected four of their members to meet with the First Lord: Garth and Jackson, chosen because they were members of Parliament, and Ingersoll and Benjamin Franklin, chosen because they had "lately come from America and [knew] more intimately the sentiments of the people."[28] The agents also had reason to believe that these four either had established or would soon enjoy a friendly relationship with Grenville. Jackson had been his personal secretary, Garth had been accounted by the Treasury as a "friend" in the House, Ingersoll was advising his friend Whately on the details of the bill, and Franklin served loyally as the American postmaster. In any event, the four had no trouble arranging a meeting for Saturday, 2 February.[29]

Given the tenor of the papers from Massachusetts and New York, Grenville could easily guess that the agents had nothing new to tell or offer him. Still, he was more than ready to meet with them, and not merely out of courtesy. After they asked in May 1764 to speak with him on the subject of an American revenue, Grenville must have realized that he could trust these men to report his opinions as accurately as they could to their employers. Had the agents been less conscientious, had they been content to report different versions of his 9 March speech to America, they would not have requested an interview. He had, therefore, taken the opportunity to describe to these men and through them to the assemblies, the reasons for his recommending that Parliament impose a stamp tax on the colonies. Grenville's confidence in them, moreover, had not been misplaced. The bitter reference to his desire to consult the goodwill of the colonies in the Massachusetts assembly's letter to Jasper Mauduit proved that that agent was reporting his words and demeanor accurately. In February 1765, he was confident he could rely on the conscientiousness of the agents again. This meeting was, in his opinion, a splendid chance to create a favorable impression of himself and the British government in the minds of important Americans. If these men reported to their employers that Grenville and his colleagues were concerned about the colonies' best interests, willing to listen to suggestions from America, and ready to correct errors in policy, the distrust felt by influential colonists toward Great Britain might soften. Such a change of opinion would measurably ease the enforcement of British laws in North America. So during his meeting with the delegation of agents, Grenville planned to give the impression that "no pains have been spared . . . on the part of the Minister to hear patiently, to listen attentively to the reasonings, and to determine, at least seemingly, with coolness and upon principle, upon the several measures which are resolved."[30]

Soon after the agents arrived, it became clear they had no new matters to discuss. They wasted no time before "remonstrat[ing] against the stamp bill and . . . propos[ing] in case any tax must be laid upon America, that the several colonies might be permitted to lay the tax themselves."[31] Grenville listened patiently, giving them "a full hearing." Then he responded with carefully chosen words.

He began by telling the agents that he was fully aware that the prospect of a parliamentary tax had disturbed colonists. "He took no pleasure in giving the Americans so much uneasiness as he found he did." Still, "It was the duty of his office to manage the revenue," and "he really was made to believe that considering the whole of the circumstances of the Mother Country and the colonies, the latter could and ought to pay something." He continued to believe that the stamp tax was the best way to raise the money. He was willing, however, to repeat his earlier offer: If the agents "could tell of a better, he would adopt it."

Grenville's words were as familiar to the agents as theirs had been to him. But his demeanor and his apparent sincerity impressed them beyond the mere words. Ingersoll and Jackson praised his obvious concern in letters to the colonies.[32] Franklin was so confident of Grenville's sincerity that he soon afterward presented Grenville with a plan to raise money by charging interest on currency issued in the colonies. During the meeting, all four agents were encouraged enough to urge again that Grenville advise Parliament to requisition the money from the colonial assemblies. The people were used to it, they argued. "It would at least seem to be their own act and prevent that uneasiness and jealousy which otherwise . . . would take place." Moreover, the agents asserted, the assemblies "could raise the money best by their own officers," even better, presumably, than the smoothness with which Grenville believed a stamp act would operate.[33]

Grenville listened patiently, with no intention of revising his plans. When he met the agents in 1764, he had expressed his objections to requisitions, and the agents were suggesting nothing new. The only change in the situation was that whereas in 1764 they could only predict discontent, in 1765 they could state that it already existed. To Grenville, however, the presence or absence of discontent was essentially irrelevant to the execution of a stamp act, so certain was he that it would execute itself. he may even have assumed that the major reason for the protest was precisely the colonists' realization that they could not evade paying stamp duties. As Jenkinson had said, stamp duties have "ever been borne with complaint" because they offered little chance of evasion. As he had also stated, executing any British laws "would necessarily cause great complaints among those who had long been free from any due restraint."[34] If Grenville reasoned as his colleague did, he may have interpreted these protests as indications of real fears in America that the tax would be paid, rather than as ominous warnings that it would be difficult to collect.

Nevertheless, it behooved him to listen to the agents with an air of earnest deliberation and to avoid making the sarcastic comments about "diminish[ing] the mighty powers of the little assemblies" that Jenkinson was privately making. Nor would it do to answer arguments that stressed the importance of the colonies' trade with Britain with pointed remarks about their contraband trade with Europe and observations like Jenkinson's that "they perhaps may speak more out to the people of Holland than they choose to do here."[35] Nor did Grenville plan to answer objections that "this [tax] will stop their increase" with his colleague's rule of thumb: "Their increase is of no further benefit to this country [except] as it enables them to become more useful to it."[36] Nothing would be gained by stating these truths. Indeed, much could be lost. As Whately later advised John Temple, "To men in office, nothing is of more consequence than the utmost temperance of language." Even "the least slip is made a matter of complaint, and with a little heightening is retorted upon them against the complaints they make of others, which gives the accused persons an advantage over their accusers."[37] Moreover, aside from avoiding giving Americans and their agents any further excuse for discontent and complaint, Grenville could see an opportunity in these conversations to allay some of the suspicions influential colonists would have. If he could persuade these men that he had genuinely taken their interests into account and would continue to do so, the execution of all British laws in America would surely be easier.

Early during his argument on 2 February 1765 for using requisitions, Jackson raised an issue that was clearly disturbing to his employers and other Americans. He "plainly" told Grenville that a stamp tax, "by enabling the Crown to keep up an armed force of its own in America and to pay the governors in the King's governments, and all with the Americans' own money," would "subvert . . . the assemblies *in* the colonies." Jackson continued by suggesting that colonial governors "would have no occasion, . . . for ends of their own or of the Crown, to call [the assemblies], and . . . they would never be called together in the King's government."[38] Since Grenville had no intention of using the stamp duties to defray royal officers' salaries, he had no trouble "warmly" and convincingly refuting Jackson's claim. Reported Ingersoll, "No such thing was intended nor would, he believed, take place." Soon afterward, Grenville appeared to be as good as his word. "I understand since the meeting on 2 February," Ingersoll wrote to the governor of Connecticut, "there is a clause added to the bill applying the monies that shall be raised to the protecting and defending [of] America *only*." Apparently Ingersoll was unaware that this clause would have been part of the bill anyway. A similar provision had been included in the Sugar Act, doubtless because Grenville was determined not to provide an opening for men like Halifax to use those monies to support the civil establishment and because he was afraid independents and Tories in the House might object to the Crown's being able to spend the revenues at its pleasure on objects of its own choosing. For the same reasons, he planned to include the same provision in the Stamp Act. On 2 February, he was being strictly truthful with the agents when he pledged that stamp tax revenue would help defray the costs of defending America. Significantly, Grenville did not promise that all revenue raised in America by parliamentary taxation would, or should, go to defense. On this point, as on others regarding the future, he avoided saying anything that might create a binding precedent.[39]

The First Lord also assured the agents he would not "abridge or alter" any charter governments and announced this intent in Parliament.[40] Again, he was being strictly truthful. Grenville believed that the assemblies would inevitably lose most of their improper powers as the execution of British laws improved and the collection of British taxes proceeded. A frontal attack on the charters themselves surely would rouse troublesome political opposition in America and perhaps even in Parliament. Such an uproar would undermine the quiet process that he thought would diminish the assemblies' independence once the stamp tax began to execute itself. He was willing, therefore, to commit himself publicly to allowing charter colony assemblies to exercise in their own ways the proper functions of representative bodies. That commitment would cost him nothing politically and might ease the process of shrinking the assemblies' swollen pretensions and powers by helping to gain colonists' trust.

Grenville did not allow the agents to draw him into a theoretical discussion of what the proper functions of assemblies were. Such consideration could only prolong the controversy in America. Nor did he discuss episodes of misconduct by the assemblies. Instead, he asserted that because the divisions between the colonies prevented them from providing for their common defense, Britain had to exercise her authority for the whole community's good.[41] In much the same way, when the agents advised him to adopt a policy of requisitioning the money from the assemblies, he avoided discussing the political undesirability of leaving the power to raise this revenue in the hands of colonies that were growing appreciably stronger. Rather, he called attention to the administrative difficulties such a system would create. Suppose, he hypothesized, the colonists did try to raise their own taxes for defense. "Could [you] agree upon the several proportions each colony should raise?" The agents answered, "No," hardly a surprising response to Grenville, for he had observed their wrangling over the division of the money Parliament had allocated to them for their wartime expenses. The First Lord also knew, as he immediately pointed out to the agents, that the Treasury was equally unable to devise such proportions. As he observed, the economic circumstances of individual colonies would be "constantly varying in their proportions of numbers and ability" in the future, so this problem would never be finally or satisfactorily resolved. Even if an equitable way of settling these proportions could be hit upon, "There would be no certainty that every colony would raise the sum enjoined and . . . to compel some one or two provinces to do their duty, and that perhaps for one year only, would be very inconvenient." Thus Grenville subtly reminded the agents that some of the colonies themselves had complained against those who refused to shoulder their share of the defense burden. In contrast, a stamp tax would compel all to pay, while adjusting itself to the changing prosperity and individual circumstance of each colony. "To all this," Ingersoll recalled, "the American agents answer[ed], 'Truly, Sir, we must own there is a weight in your arguments and a force in your reasonings.' " Grenville hoped that their reports to America would demonstrate the weight and force of his position to colonists as well.[42]

Grenville also tactfully skirted the question of the constitutionality of parliamentary taxation, despite his recently acquired expertise in the subject. Colonists would realize the British sentiment in favor of such a tax, and no purpose could be served by Grenville's rehearsing the arguments to the agents. Instead, he only wished for "coolness and moderation in America." Grenville then flattered the agents by apologizing to them for pointing out the obvious. "He had no need to tell [them] that resentments indecently and unbecomingly expressed on one side [of] the water would naturally produce resentments on [the] other side." Grenville then added that Americans "could not hope to get any good by a controversy with the Mother Country." On the other hand, he could promise that the House and the Treasury would always listen "to any remonstrances from the Americans with respect to this bill both before it takes effect and after, if it shall take effect, which shall be expressed in a becoming manner," which he defined, simply, "as be-comes subjects of the same common prince."[43] Colonists would not have to acknowledge formally the supremacy of Parliament; they merely had to avoid raising the question, just as Grenville had. This was, of course, not much of a concession. By failing to raise the question, colonists in effect would be conceding the right in return for the opportunity to have a voice in the adjustment of their taxes. Still, Grenville hoped that politicians in the colonies would recognize that he had not required them to give in openly to his implied threat that they would have no say in the formulation of colonial policy until they acknowledged Parliament's supremacy.

Grenville also softened in his comments to the agents his explanation of why colonists should help pay for their own defense. Jenkinson had suggested that he stress in his speech to the House that it was only just for Americans to bear part of this burden after all Britain had done for them in the past. Whately had recently made the same point in his pamphlet, and Grenville ultimately repeated it to the House.[44] With the agents, however, he suggested that they lay "aside all considerations of [the] past . . . to consider . . . the present state of things." The Mother Country was struggling under a heavy burden of debt; she stood "in need of every relief and assistance to be had." Despite these burdens, though, Britain was still willing to help the colonists "on account of the trouble with the Indians [and] . . . for general defense against other nations and the like in so extensive a country." Could not Americans help maintain this force?[45] Artfully, Grenville had shifted from a just demand to an appeal to that most natural instinct, self-preservation. Certainly, such an appeal would be more palatable to Americans. American politicians would also find it helpful in explaining to their constituents a reluctant acquiesence to the Stamp Act.

The weight of the planned taxes also concerned the agents and their correspondents in America. Grenville assured them it would be light. He told the agents that he would "be glad to find that the stamp duty . . . should amount to £40 or 50,000" a year. If this turned out to be too heavy, the Treasury would "certainly lessen it." Moreover, he had other news to cheer Americans: The money collected from all parliamentary duties would remain in America. Furthermore, he told the agents, because the total collections would probably amount to only one hundred thousand pounds a year, Britain would still have to send annually some two hundred thousand pounds to support the troops, money that would "be spent in America."[46] The agents did not know that Grenville had told his colleagues at the Treasury on 4 December 1764 that he anticipated stamp duties to yield by themselves one hundred thousand pounds a year.[47] For obvious reasons, Grenville lowered his estimate when discussing it with the four agents on 2 February. Transmitting the higher figure to the colonists would only alarm them, and perhaps without cause, for it could prove to be optimistic. A lower estimate would create less apprehension and perhaps reconcile people to the tax more quickly.

The agents again admitted to the First Lord that his arguments had merit. They also conceded that the colonies should help pay for their own defense and should not "dispute the power of the Parliament." Nevertheless, they told him, "We are rather silenced than convinced." What concerned them was the precedent being established, a precedent other ministers could misuse in the future: "We feel in our bosoms that it will be forever inconvenient, 'twill forever be dangerous to America, that [the colonies] should be taxed by the authority of a British Parliament." The reason for their fears was the "great distance" between America and Britain, a separation that created a "general want of mutual knowledge and acquaintance with each other" and a "want of connection and personal friendships." Americans, they reminded Grenville, had no one with "anything to hope or fear from" them in Parliament. As a result, they said, "We fear a foundation will be laid for mutual jealousy and ill will, and that your resentments being kindled, you will be apt to lay upon us more and more, even to a degree that will be truly grievous." And, concluded the agents, "It will be hard under the circumstances, very hard, to convince you that you wrong us," leading all to "unknown and very unhappy consequences."[48]

Here were the suspicions and fears that Grenville most wanted to allay. He did not try to do so with an argument he would use in the House, that very few Englishmen were directly represented in the House. Rather, he replied, "Suppose your observations are entirely just, and, indeed, we must own there are inconveniences attending this matter." Even conceding this, however, did not change the basic problem facing Britain and America: The Mother Country was so overwhelmed with her fiscal and commercial crises that her ability to defend the empire was considerably weakened. "What then is to be done?" Grenville asked, to ameliorate these inconveniences. For many reasons, granting the colonies representation in Parliament was not the answer. Since none of the colonies had asked for this, no doubt they too recognized the dubious benefit of spending considerable sums to send a few men without connections, friendships, or knowledge of other members of Parliament. Should nothing be done then? Should the Mother Country continue to pay all the expenses of defense herself and let the colonies "do just what they please to do?" Britain could not afford to do this. Should Britain simply admit that North America is now a "distinct Kingdom?" Some day the two might separate, but even colonists would not say America was "ripe for that event yet." The two still mutually benefited from the connection, a fact the British knew as well as the colonists. Grenville assured the agents that men in London "do not choose to predict, nor yet to hasten the time of this supposed period, and think it would be to our mutual disadvantage for us to attempt a separation."

These questions, Grenville hoped, would inescapably lead the agents and the politically sophisticated in America toward the conclusion that any taxes imposed by Parliament would be tempered by the members' consciousness that unwise or unjust legislation would harm their own interests and might lead toward a separation injurious to the Mother Country. "Instead of predicting the worst," he advised the agents, "let us . . . hope that mutual interests as well as duty will keep us on both sides within the bounds of justice." Self-interest would keep Britain from intentionally overburdening her colonies. If she did so accidentally, the colonies merely had to call attention to their grievances in a decent way and that same self-interest would surely compel correction of the error. At this point in the discussion, Grenville reminded the agents that they had always enjoyed "an easy access" to him. For his part, he had found "with pleasure that America is not destitute of persons who, at the same time they have the tenderest regard for their interests, are well able to represent to us their affairs." In the future, "If they do it with integrity and candor, they will be sure to meet with our fullest confidence." In effect, Grenville was pointing out to the agents that their meetings demonstrated that the two sides could discuss their differences fairly and freely, with respect and concern for each other's opinions and interests, in an atmosphere that would be favorable to the correction of honest mistakes. He was also making the same point to their employers in America. The colonies had good relations with the Treasury through their agents. If they nurtured that relationship carefully, they could be sure of having powerful friends at court. "Let mutual confidence, and mutual uprightness of intention take place," Grenville concluded, "and no considerable ills can follow."[49] He did not add that Britain, not the colonies, would ultimately determine what was in America's best interest.

Grenville did not expect immediate results from his conversation with the agents. He must have anticipated that they would encourage opposition to the bill in the House, because he assured them, "The House will hear all [their] objections."[50] Still, he could justifiably hope to reap some benefits from his contacts. To the best of his ability, he had avoided saying anything that would assist enemies of British authority in America. Moreover, he had signaled to reasonable men in the colonies that he, too, was reasonable on the subject of taxation and had no ulterior motives of drastic political reform. He had also given these temperate men arguments they could use against any political opponents. He may have felt that as his comments became more widely known through the give-and-take of debate in the colonies, they would have the same result that he hoped similar private assurances about pensions would have on members of the Irish House. "It seems reasonable to suppose that it will have all the good effect which is intended by it in removing jealousies, quieting the minds of the people, and enabling those who are well disposed towards the King's government to answer the arguments of opposition."[51] Finally, Grenville had indicated to colonists that they could communicate with him through the agents and shown that he would listen to complaints voiced through that channel. He could be optimistic that more and more colonists would use that channel, too. Time would pass, the stamp tax would execute itself, people would realize they could afford it, and politicians would be less and less reluctant to make bargains with the British government through their agents.

Grenville's Speech

In his discussions with the agents, Grenville had tried to impress upon them, and thus their employers, that he understood and would make some allowances for the special nature of the colonists' situation. In his discussion of the stamp tax in Parliament, however, he planned to discuss this new tax in the context of the members' experiences in governing Britain. He hoped this would prevent any members from deciding America posed constitutional problems that required especially delicate handling and would cause them to believe, as Grenville did, that colonial problems could be dealt with comfortably within the boundaries of their political experience and the British Constitution. Indeed, he intended to insist that America would become a unique problem only if Parliament did not impose the stamp tax and did create, thereby, a precedent for special treatment.

Grenville had begun preparing for this debate on 10 January 1765, when the King opened Parliament. On that day, George III expressed his confidence in Parliament's "wisdom and firmness in promoting that obedience to the laws, and respect to the legislative authority of this Kingdom, which is essentially necessary for the safety of the whole; and in establishing such regulations as may best connect and strengthen every part of my dominions, for their mutual benefit and support." In their address of thanks for the speech, the members of the House replied nem. con., "We will proceed . . . with that temper and firmness, which will best conciliate and insure due submission to the laws, and reverence to the legislative authority, of Great Britain." That process began in earnest on 6 February. That day, in a "pretty lengthy speech," Grenville "in a very able and," Ingersoll thought, "a very candid manner . . . opened the nature of the tax, urged the necessity of it, [and] endeavored to obviate all objections to it."[52] He "proposed taxing America from public motive[s]." Indeed, "Private considerations of his own choice," Grenville went on, "would have prevented him if they had been consulted." Grenville's investments in sugar lands on Barbados and Jamaica had not been generally known in the House; this reference served to inform them that, contrary to the Americans' arguments that members would not be taxing themselves, the First Lord and some others in his audience would have to pay this tax.[53]

Grenville then brought up the subject that friends of America had been talking about privately: This tax was a new and different exercise of Parliament's power. Grenville agreed that it was new, and he "wish[ed] those who had gone before him had marked out a path to him which he might more easily follow." Had that been the case, "His conduct would then have been less liable to misconstruction." With this introduction, he moved smoothly into a review of his reasons for delaying the present proposal for a year. He did so, he reminded the House, "to gain all possible information, and to give Americans an opportunity of conveying information to this House, whose ears are always open to receive knowledge and to act to it." He then added, "The officers of the revenue have done their duty in gaining all possible knowledge of the subject." Grenville evidently did not dwell on the colonists' refusal to take advantage of this opportunity, leaving the members to draw their own conclusions about which party had been more than fair and which had been foolishly obstinate.[54] Thus Grenville was putting potential supporters of America on the defensive by forcing them to explain this failure, while at the same time making no harsh comments that could be reported to the colonies.

Grenville went on to recall that in 1764 he had been ready to determine immediately if Parliament had the right to tax the colonies, if any member doubted that it did. This reminded his audience that no one had objected then and placed the burden of explaining last year's silence on anyone who objected now. Grenville then commented that he "wished now to avoid that question if possible, because . . . no person [could] doubt it." Nevertheless, he felt obliged to discuss the matter on this occasion.

At this point, Grenville began to acquaint the House with the fruits of the Treasury's recent investigation of this matter. His intent was to foreclose, not to begin, debate, to silence potential opponents with his command of detail and cogency of argument, and to leave them literally speechless. The colonies based their arguments on "the general right of mankind not to be taxed but by their representatives." Grenville immediately pointed out that this argument "goes to all laws in general." Colonists could not, consistent with logic or experience, claim to be bound by commercial regulations and exempt from taxes; they were either totally independent or totally dependent. Granting colonists this exemption would, in essence, be setting them free from the laws of trade and navigation. Moreover, the First Lord went on, the "general right" Americans were claiming was not shared by Britons: "The Parliament virtually represents the whole Kingdom, not actually. [The] great trading towns, the merchants of London, and the East India Company are not represented." Indeed, Grenville observed, "Not a twentieth part of the people are actually represented."[55] The inference he wanted his audience to draw is clear. Colonists had no right to treatment that differed from Englishmen's. Their claim of a "general right" was in fact a claim of special privilege, one that would put them beyond the control of Parliament.

Furthermore, the special privilege was one that they could not claim: "All colonies are subject to the dominion of the Mother Country, whether they are a colony of the freest or the most absolute government." And, aside from this legitimate general principle, British colonies also could not claim any exemption from parliamentary taxation on the basis of their charters. Such an exemption was beyond the power of the Crown to grant, even if a king had done so, and "in fact the Crown [had] not done it." Then Grenville revealed that he knew the charters well enough to anticipate and refute arguments from them before an opponent brought such issues up. What about the Maryland charter of 1633, which promised exemption from duties? That applied only to "those duties which the Crown then thought it had the right to impose; all subsequent duties on tobacco [were] so many taxes imposed on Maryland." Did not the Pennsylvania charter of 1680 forbid the Crown to impose taxes? To be sure, it did, "but the right of Parliament [was] saved in express words." What about the nearly independent governments of Connecticut and Rhode Island? In their charters, "There [were] these words: 'according to the course of other corporations within our Kingdom of England'; corporations are not exempted from tax in England, so they ought not to have any exemption." As for the royal governments, no powers or exemptions were given them further than making "general laws according to the custom of England"; these colonies could not legitimately claim that their charters exempted them from parliamentary taxation.

Moreover, all the colonies had been taxed by Parliament in the past. Using Pownall's research on this point and Jenkinson's observations on it, Grenville emphasized that 25 Car. 2 imposed duties "upon the plantations to be levied and collected within the plantations." These customs had been paid and collected since that time. The Post Office Act "impose[d] an internal tax upon North America." Molasses was first taxed in 1733. And the Sugar Act "passed the last session of Parliament . . . imposed a tax upon many articles."

Grenville closed this section of his speech by observing that even if these precedents did not exist, and even if the charters did contain exemptions, the stamp tax would still be constitutional. The declaration of 7 & 8 Will. 2 that "all laws, by-laws, usage and custom in the plantations repugnant to this Act or to any other law in this Kingdom are illegal and void" would have justified taxing the colonies in 1765. The First Lord also referred to what he regarded as a case analogous to America's, the controversy over William Molyneaux's pamphlet in the Irish and English Parliaments during William's reign. "The Parliament here attacked that pamphlet's doctrine and its account" and "declared . . . that such proceedings would prove fatal not only to England, but to Ireland itself." This reference had unmistakable connotations to Grenville's audience. Molyneaux's pamphlet, *Case of Ireland,* argued for Ireland's legislative autonomy; Parliament's firm and successful rejection of its arguments in theory and practice had helped insure Britain's domination over Ireland. The First Lord's argument by analogy was also unmistakable. If Parliament would be equally firm in rejecting the assemblies' arguments in favor of their legislative autonomy, the outcome would be equally beneficial for the British empire.[56] Finally, having prepared the House to regard any arguments against his proposal as "strange language," Grenville moved on to consider "the propriety and expediency of laying this tax."

According to Jackson and Ingersoll, Grenville's crushing rebuttal of the colonial position was not delivered angrily or in a spirit of bitterness toward America. Grenville spoke "of the colonies in general in terms of great kindness and regard." He may have criticized their interpretation of their charters, but he also "in particular [told] the House there was no intention to abridge or alter any of their charters."[57] Though he had referred to "the strange language he [had] met with in conversation and public writings on this subject," he warned the members "not to suffer themselves to be influenced by any resentments which might be kindled from anything they might have heard," an allusion, Ingersoll believed, "to the New York and Boston assemblies' speeches and votes." Moreover, Grenville magnanimously excused these excesses to the House: "This was a matter of revenue, which was of all things most interesting to the subject."[58] Even in the midst of his attack on their doctrines, the sort of attack he had not made during his meeting with the agents, Grenville did not forget the usefulness of appearing moderate and thoughtful before his unseen but—he hoped—attentive audience across the Atlantic.

By the time his opponents spoke on the expediency of the stamp tax, Grenville hoped that the House would have already dismissed their arguments. Well aware that most members were unfamiliar with America, he dramatized the prosperity of the colonies by comparing the cost of their civil establishments and the amount of their indebtedness with Great Britain's. The Treasury had gathered the relevant statistics, probably with an eye more to their political use than to checking the ability of the colonies to pay a tax. These accounts revealed that "the whole of North America, consist[ing] perhaps of 16 or 1,700,000 inhabitants, pays only about £64,000 a year for its establishment." Furthermore, "The debt of North America . . . amounted to £848,000"; those debts had amounted "to about £2,000,000; . . . [and] the great part of [them] will be discharged in a few years." Grenville stated scrupulously that he did not know the cost of government in North Carolina and Maryland; he noted that he had no account of Pennsylvania's indebtedness; he made the caveat that "he [spoke] this only from the best information he [had] been able to receive." But he also knew that these qualifications would not matter with the House; the contrast between Britain and America was so stark that it would stick in the members' minds.

Americans' motive for objecting to taxation, Grenville suggested, was a simple and understandable one. Like Britons, they did not want to pay taxes. "The western country," Grenville observed to the House, "desires an exemption from cider, the northern from a duty on beer." Yet "the true way to relieve all is to make all contribute their proper share." In justice, Americans should contribute, too. Grenville explained the great increase in the navy's expenses by noting that they were "incurred in a great measure for the service of North America." As for the army and its importance to the colonies, Grenville reminded the House, "We have expended so much on the support and defense of North America; we have given them so great . . . security after they were before in continual wars." To be sure, the French had been "removed," but Great Britain continued "employing her troops" against other enemies. No military man thought the numbers of those troops too great for the job; indeed, "Many military men [believed them] to be not sufficient." The House probably would see the obvious conclusion to this, though Grenville still intended to call attention to it. "The money for these expenses must be raised somewhere, [though] contributors will be displeased."

From conversations with the agents, Grenville could be certain of two arguments: Americans would object that a parliamentary tax would "produce disturbance and discontent and prevent improvement among the colonies"; Americans would recommend that the House permit the colonies to tax themselves. It seemed wisest to him to raise these objections himself and discredit them before an opponent discoursed on them. The easiest way to discredit them, he decided, was to discuss them in terms that would be familiar to the House. Would this particular tax cause disturbance and discontent? Grenville answered with his own question: "When will the time come when enforcing a tax will not give discontent, if this tax does produce it after what we have done and suffered for America?" Experienced politicians surely would recognize that this was the most opportune time to tax Americans, while their gratitude should be fresh. If they objected at this moment, they would object even more after memories faded. Indeed, they would probably claim later that the House decision against a stamp tax in 1765 established a precedent. "If we reject this proposition now," Grenville predicted, "we shall declare that we ought not to tax the colonies. And we need not declare after a year's time that we ought not, for then we cannot."[59] He was not proposing this tax in order to cause disturbances in the colonies: "He [had] no motive, he [could] have no motive, for taxing a colony, but that of doing his duty." But the possibility of causing some discontent could not deter the House now. If the members refused to act on their resolution of 1764, they would, in effect, be giving up any hope of taxing America in the years ahead.

If the House made this decision, the members should not try to excuse themselves by imagining that colonial assemblies could and would tax their constituents for the support of a British army. Asked Grenville, "How can so many colonies fix the proportion which they shall pay themselves?" He then brought home the difficulties and dangers of attempting this by making an analogy with England. Suppose "each county was to do this in England; [suppose] we were to assess the sum and let them tax themselves. What danger [would] arise from this." Moreover, in the case of America, the danger would not be purely administrative and fiscal in nature. It would be political as well, for "while [the colonies] remain dependent, they must be subject" to Parliament. Allowing them to tax themselves would weaken this dependence. In the past, "They have in many instances encroached and claimed powers and privileges inconsistent with their situation as colonies." Grenville did not speculate on the consequences of enhancing the powers of those assemblies. The members would presumably be doing that themselves, and the First Lord did not want observers to communicate to America any of his statements as extreme. Instead, he made this suggestive observation, "If [colonists] are not subject to this burden of tax, they are not entitled to the privilege of Englishmen." He could safely assume that his English audience would understand this to mean as well that they would not be dependent on Britain.

Grenville then discussed the propriety of imposing a stamp tax in this particular case. It would arouse less economic discontent than almost any other tax. It would not touch the necessities of the poor but would "take in a great degree its proportion from the riches of the people. As in lawsuits and commercial contracts, it increases in proportion to the riches." Moreover, it did not require a "great number of officers, [or] . . . unconstitutional authority in great boards" for colonists to complain about. Indeed, he told the House, "He [had] inquired [of] North America whether they objected to this particular species of tax, and . . . not heard one gentleman propose any other," which indicated that it was the most acceptable of any taxes Parliament might impose.[60] Finally, he assured his audience that the special nature of the tax itself would reduce the seriousness of any discontent or disturbance that might arise. "The tax in a great degree executes itself, as the instruments not stamped are null and void, and no person will trust that, especially as the case may be brought by appeal to this country." The tax would be collected, no matter what was said by its opponents in Britain or America.

Grenville ended his speech artfully, with a reference that tied together all that had gone before and appealed to his audience's practical ideology of government. The stamp tax, he concluded, "is founded on that great maxim, that protection is due from the governor, and support and obedience on the part of the governed."[61] This statement succinctly summed up the ideal and reality of hierarchical eighteenth-century Britain. Clearly, Grenville expected his reference to have a powerful impact on his listeners and outweigh in their minds any theorizing that an opponent might do about the status and rights of colonies.

Passage of the Stamp Tax

The debates on the bill after Grenville's speech went as the First Lord had hoped. The House remained unmoved by arguments from merchants that the colonists could not bear the tax and by criticisms from

William Beckford of Grenville's constitutional arguments. The impassioned declaration by Isaac Barré describing Americans as "a people jealous of their liberties . . . who will vindicate them, if ever they should be violated," momentarily stunned the House, but Barré himself had already weakened its impact by admitting earlier in the debate that if America was to be taxed, he "approve[d] that kind of tax as being the most equal and produc[tive]."[62] When Beckford tried to delay the bill with a procedural motion, the ministry prevailed, 245 to 50. Moreover, Grenville had not merely won by a crushing majority. As Whately later noted, the debate proved that "not a single Member of Parliament . . . will dispute" the right of Parliament to tax the colonies, for "the expediency only was debated."[63] Sadly, Ingersoll wrote home to Connecticut, "Perhaps [there] may be some further debate upon the subject, but to no purpose I am very sure, as to the stopping or preventing the Act [from] taking place."[64]

Despite the vote on 6 February, the agents persisted in their plans to convince the House to hear petitions against the tax on its second reading. It is unlikely that they believed that these petitions, if read in the House, would persuade members to change their minds about the stamp tax. Rather, they hoped that if the House agreed to hear the petitions, "A precedent would have been established that would have prevented any future attempt to tax America, until at least the public in America had been apprised thereof."[65] To help accomplish this goal, Edward Montagu drafted a petition that not only asked that the House take Virginians' "unhappy circumstances into consideration" and permit their assembly to continue "in the possession of the rights and privileges they had so long and uninterruptedly enjoyed," but also prayed that the House would hear counsel representing the assembly "against the bill that might be intended to charge stamps or any other duties on the colony of Virginia." His strategy was clear. If the House heard both petition and counsel, the precedent of notification before taxation would have been firmly established, for the House would have acknowledged that either colonists themselves or counsel that they had hired and instructed had the right to appear *in person* against proposed taxes. The distance between London and America guaranteed that colonists would need a year's warning to exercise this right properly. Moreover, by inserting the phrase "or any other duties" in his petition, Montagu was apparently trying to establish this precedent in cases of customs duties as well as internal taxation. Garth did not make this attempt so explicitly, but his basic strategy was the same. He carefully drew up a "decent" petition, imploring the House not to "approve of any bill that might be offered charging stamp duties in the province of

Carolina." Then he found in London three Carolinians willing to sign it. There were only three signatures on the document, he later explained, because he reserved other Carolinians to appear and give evidence against the bill, should that opportunity arise. Other agents simply planned to establish the precedent by introducing petitions drawn up in America.[66]

The first petition discussed on 15 February was not, however, one of these. Perhaps by arrangement, Rose Fuller initiated the day's debates by bringing up a petition from "several persons trading to, and interested in, the island of Jamaica."[67] In support of this petition, Sir William Meredith made what he and the agents hoped would be a telling argument. Grenville in 1764, Sir William asserted, had in effect conceded the colonists' right to petition against this bill. The purpose of the postponement, he continued, had been to give the colonists time to petition Parliament if they chose to do so. Grenville immediately and flatly denied Meredith's assertion. During the debate on 6 February, he had described the postponement as designed "to gain all possible information, and to give Americans an opportunity of conveying information to this House, whose ears are always open to receive information and to act on it." Now he repeated this point, then specifically elaborated on what he had not intended to be the result of his decision in 1764. He had postponed the bill, he claimed, "to give time for information, not for opposition."[68] He then reminded the House that hearing petitions against tax bills prior to their passage was contrary to the practice of Parliament and refreshed the members' memories further by having the clerk read the order of 8 March 1732. He and his supporters followed this with the argument that colonists, like Britons, could always petition for the repeal of a tax "after that tax [was] laid, and experience had of its effects," but that Americans neither needed nor could claim any exemption from the rules of the House. Moreover, some of the government's spokesmen added, London merchants, not colonists, had signed this petition, and Englishmen certainly could not claim this exemption. The arguments that "strongly objected to" receiving the petition so obviously found a receptive audience that Fuller withdrew his petition from consideration.[69]

Despite this development, the agents and their allies introduced their petitions, even though they were now clearly bereft of what they hoped would be a persuasive argument, that the postponement was intended to extend the opportunity to petition to the colonists. Meredith presented Montagu's petition, and his description of its contents touched off "a pretty warm debate."[70] Charles Yorke claimed that the petition questioned Parliament's right to tax Americans, and therefore the

House could not receive it.[71] This point seemed persuasive and conclusive to the House. As Whately later remarked, the House could not accept the petitions because doing so "would have been an admission that the right was questionable, which we [could not] admit."[72] And Jackson explained the agents' failure by noting that "the House would not suffer its power to be questioned, . . . its constitutional right."[73] Interestingly, there is no record that Grenville himself made such constitutional arguments against the petitions. He may have remained silent during these debates, thus confining himself to his earlier points about the aim of the postponement and the practice of Parliament. If so, perhaps his reticence may be explained by his desire to appear cool and moderate and by his wish to agitate constitutional arguments as little as possible, for he certainly agreed with Yorke and Whately insofar as the constitutional issue was concerned.[74] Indeed, apparently so did Fuller, who spoke against receiving Montagu's petition.[75] The House refused to receive the petition by "a great majority." Garth's "decent" petition and one from the Connecticut government, presented by Richard Jackson, met the same fate.[76] By the end of the day, the agents had nothing to show for their efforts to create a useful precedent, while Grenville had once more preserved Britain's freedom of action.

The agents soon had to use the same weapon that had already failed them. During the committee stage on the bill, the Treasury added a clause stipulating that suits involving violations of the stamp tax might be tried in an admiralty court at the discretion of the plaintiff. Yorke, whom Grenville had asked to look over the bill, objected to this, arguing that since "the stamp duties have nothing of a maritime or commercial nature, the precedent may, in argument, be extended far, to other future taxes upon the colonies." Yorke evidently did not understand that this probably helped persuade Grenville to add the clause. The agents chose not to call attention to this fact. Instead, they objected on two different grounds. First, it "infring[ed] on English liberty by taking away trials by jury." Second, it was highly inconvenient "to take people from one end of America almost to the other." Grenville saw the justice of the second objection and planned to increase the number of admiralty courts in America. As for the first, speakers for the Treasury bluntly replied, "There is no safety in trusting the breach of revenue laws to a jury of the country where the offence is committed." Indeed, "Even in England," they continued, authorities "never can obtain verdicts where smuggling is practiced and therefore always bring the causes up for trial to London."[77] As usual, Grenville's practice of explaining problems in America by referring to problems in England prevailed. As usual, the agents did not get what they wanted, only what

Grenville wished them to have. Their only consolation was their success in making some minor alterations in the bill during committee debates on 19 and 21 February.[78]

Grenville's parliamentary campaign came to a triumphant close on 27 February, when the bill was passed without a division. He had successfully convinced the House of the propriety and expediency of the measure, and he had gained the overwhelming expression of sentiment on its constitutionality that he had desired. The success of his efforts to persuade Americans of his goodwill and concern for their interests remained to be seen, of course. He did not plan, however, to rest his hopes of molding the opinion of influential Americans to suit his purposes merely on the agents' reports on his meeting with them and on parliamentary debates. He had other plans as well, plans whose success he believed would help solidify and guarantee Britain's control over North America.

Chapter IX

Dispensing Places "of Emolument and of Influence" December 1764–July 1765

After his victory in Parliament, Grenville was openly magnanimous to the colonies. With them, as with the linen merchants, he made a point of drawing attention to his willingness to make concessions after the demonstration of his power to enact what he chose. Colonists and their agents had strongly argued that paying tax revenues into the English exchequer would cause a serious shortage of specie in America and precipitate a sharp drop in their purchases from Britain. Grenville suspected this was true and certainly wished to avoid depressing a trade he believed was crucial to Britain.[1] Moreover, since he had become First Lord, he had been trying to reform the system of paying troops in America. At present, the Treasury had to contract annually with private merchants for the shipment of a hundred thousand pounds. The profit these money contractors made irritated him, as did the percentage of specie shipped that the Treasury had to pay to the captain of the vessel carrying it and to the commanding officer of the fleet in America.[2] Thus, for economic and fiscal reasons, it seemed necessary to keep the revenue collected by stamp distributors and customs officers in the colonies.

Grenville tried to make a political virtue of these necessities by declaring his intention to keep tax money in America in order to benefit the colonies. After the King signed the Stamp Act, Whately and Jenkinson began devising an appropriate procedure. Work went slowly, and Grenville felt compelled to remind Whately that failure to make provisions for keeping the taxes in the colonies would "occasion great clamor" and "give just cause of complaint as being contrary to what was publicly declared upon the subject." Finally, by early July the Secretaries had settled on a plan that satisfied them and enabled Grenville to hope Britain would benefit politically from his apparent concession to colonial desires.[3]

In another effort to make certain that Americans believed he thought of them only with benevolence, Grenville evidently convinced Secretary of State Halifax, the officer responsible for the colonies, to let the session pass without presenting the proceedings of the assemblies of

Massachusetts Bay and New York to the Commons and the Lords, even though the Privy Council had on 19 December 1764 determined them to be "worthy [of] the consideration of Parliament."[4] As Charles Lloyd, Grenville's private secretary, later explained, the First Lord was well aware that the Houses of Parliament could not have responded to a formal submission of these papers in any way other than "votes of censure and severity towards the offenders." Enacting a stamp tax was sufficient for Grenville's (and Britain's) purposes. "In lenity to the colonies," continued Lloyd, "any severer animadversion on their conduct was spared." Though his assistant did not explain further, Grenville's leniency was likely not without ulterior motives. Forebearing to punish the assemblies would not impair execution of the tax, and "impos[ing] and . . . secur[ing] the collection of the tax would be," in and of itself, an "effectual vindication of [Parliament's] right."[5] On the other hand, parliamentary censure would gratuitously continue the war of words over colonial rights, retard the acceptance of Parliament's authority, and hinder the development of trust in the British government. As far as Grenville was concerned, the proper course of action was clear. Accordingly, his only reference to the two assemblies' votes and proceedings on 6 February was his advice that the members "not suffer themselves to be influenced by any resentments which might have been kindled from anything they had heard out of doors" and, indeed, excuse any excesses by remembering "that this was a matter of revenue, which was of all things the most interesting to the subject."[6] Halifax either agreed with Grenville's decision or found himself with no choice but to withhold the papers after Grenville made these remarks.[7]

Grenville had another opportunity to display publicly his regard for the colonies, with the appointment of men to administer the tax in America. He knew how important it was to select men who would do their duty strictly and fairly. He also knew that if he could choose men who were also acceptable to colonists, he would have helped to allay Americans' suspicions and apprehensions about parliamentary taxes. These considerations remained foremost in his and his colleagues' minds as they thought about the best way of filling the positions created by the Stamp Act.

The Decision to Employ Americans

When Whately delivered his report to the Treasury on 6 December 1764, he remarked that "the greatest difficulty attending the act" would be insuring an efficient distribution of the stamps. Enforcement would not be a problem—but only if the proper types and quantities of stamps were available in all areas of the colonies and at the times they were needed. To insure that this would occur, Whately believed, "It will be better in most places to appoint two joint head distributors, if it can be made worth their while, that they may be checks upon each other, and that in case of death, there may be no failure in the business of the office." One of the two, he suggested, should be the secretary to the colony's council, "who is always a considerable person and an officer of government"; the other, "an eminent merchant or planter." These men would themselves handle distribution of stamps in colonial capitals. They would supply stamps to clerks of county courts for towns the clerks lived in, to customs officers for the seaports, and to clerks of circuit courts "for the business of the counties [they] . . . pass through." With this system, Whately predicted, "The inhabited parts of the country may be sufficiently supplied." If any areas remained uncovered by these provisions, he went on, "Underdistributors must be appointed by the head distributors, but these will be but few." The Secretary also planned to assist the distributors by permitting them to give a large discount to private persons who bought stamps in bulk with the intention of selling them themselves. For their troubles, head distributors would receive 7.5 percent of the money they collected. Soon after hearing Whately's proposal, the Treasury approved it.[8]

Thus, Grenville and his colleagues decided against appointing English distributors and sending them to America. The previous winter, Henry McCulloh and Benjamin Barons, an Englishman who had been in the customs service in America, had applied for positions that might have been created in 1764, had Parliament then passed the stamp tax, so this alternative had been brought to the Treasury's attention.[9] Grenville rejected this option, however. Whately later explained Grenville's motives by telling the agents that the First Lord wanted "to make the execution of the act as little inconvenient and disagreeable to the Americans as possible." Grenville also wanted to do justice to the colonists, "for, as they were to pay the tax, he thought strangers should not have the emoluments."[10] He mentioned to Ingersoll that Americans had informed him they were poor, "unable to bear such tax; others told him [they] were well able." So Grenville had decided to let Americans "take the business in [their] own hands, [to] see how and where it pinches, and [to] let us know it; in which case it [should] be eased."[11]

These statements reveal a mixture of political and economic motives. Grenville clearly expected that his refusal to let "strangers . . . have the emoluments" from the tax would generate goodwill in America toward him and toward the British government. English distributors would doubtless rouse the same sort of ire in American assemblies as English pensioners did in the Irish Parliament. To foster more goodwill in Ireland, the ministry was trying to cut back on the number of pensioners. For much the same reason, Grenville was determined not to give Americans this grievance. Moreover, he probably expected Americans to recognize that distributors whose economic interests immediately depended upon continued prosperity in the colonies would be more sensitive to "how and where [the tax] pinches" and more likely to "let us know it" than would be English strangers whose economic interests in America solely depended upon selling more stamps. Furthermore, English officials would be more inclined to tell the Treasury, as other Englishmen had done, that Americans were "well able" to pay the duties.

Whether Americans recognized the truth of this latter motive or not, Grenville and Whately certainly appreciated its validity. Aside from considerations of political goodwill, both men were fully aware, well before 6 December, that many of the forms and procedures for doing legal and economic business in the colonies were different from those in England. Because of their experience in using these forms and procedures, Americans would be less likely to misunderstand the purpose of a document and charge colonists too much. When Ingersoll deliberated accepting the distributorship in Connecticut, both personal friends and friends of America argued that he "should be able to assist . . . with the construction and application of the Act better than a stranger not acquainted with [American] methods of transacting." Whately, who had an abiding interest in American life, who was personally close to Ingersoll, and who had worked with him on the stamp bill, was doubtlessly one of those friends.[12] This advantage of American distributors had crossed Whately's mind before 6 December, as he wrestled with the unfamiliar documents of the colonies. In his report, Whately was clearly concerned with the possibilities that distributors would give taxpayers inefficient service, subject them to unmerited prosecutions for nonpayment, or extort unjustifiably heavy settlements from them for penalties they owed.[13] All men were susceptible to temptation, but if Americans were the distributors, self-interest in maintaining their position in local politics and society would help deter them from inefficiency and injustice. Americans would be less likely than English distributors to take steps, by omission or commission, to injure colonists economically, thus causing political clamor and diminishing the ability of colonists to buy more British goods.

To insure that the colonial distributors would fulfill these purposes, Whately carefully chose candidates for the distributorships: the secretary to the council, "always a *considerable* person," and an "*eminent* merchant or planter."[14] The words that I have italicized reveal Whately's desire to appoint men whom their fellow colonists recognized as occupying important stations in the political and economic life of their colonies. The respect colonists felt for these men's reputation and power would assist the administration of the tax. The concern that the distributors would feel to maintain their status would encourage them to administer the tax as justly and equitably as they could and to waste no time informing England of any overly burdensome duties. Furthermore, as Whately knew, the negligence and corruption of the customs officers in the past had had the unhappy effect of teaching colonists to regard and to treat even the most important British acts of trade as being of small value.[15] Reforming the customs officers would end "that licentiousness"; administering the stamp tax successfully would aid in restoring colonists' respect for the laws and authority of Great Britain. The Treasury would thus fulfill what Whately termed one of "the principal objects of a British minister's care," the "cement[ing] and perfect[ing of] the necessary connection between [colonies] and the Mother Country."[16] The involvement of eminent Americans in the administration of the tax would help Britain attain this desirable end in another way as well. These men would, through their service to the Crown, be demonstrating their personal acquiescence in this exercise of Parliament's power. Such an example from men whom colonists respected might soothe popular fears about Britain's motives for taxing Americans, relieve apprehensions about the weight of those taxes and the possibility of a harsh execution of them, and thus hasten popular acceptance of Parliament's sovereignty.

After accepting Whately's recommendation that the Treasury name only eminent Americans as the distributors, Grenville apparently never wavered from that decision. After 6 December, the men at the Treasury assumed that colonists would administer the tax and, in fact, concentrated on finding means to realize optimal benefits from such appointments. Indeed, Grenville had every reason to adhere to his decision. Employing Americans would not negatively affect the collection of a tax that executed itself; that policy would help in routine administration and in the speedy adjustment of burdensome rates; and it might improve feelings in the colonies toward Whitehall and Westminster. But the First Lord evidently soon discovered that he would have to modify Whately's suggestion that the secretary to the council and an eminent merchant or planter be named to distribute the stamps in each colony.

The Decision to Give the Agents the Patronage

At some time before March 1765, Grenville decided that the Treasury should appoint only one distributor per colony. Unquestionably, considerations of administrative economy strongly influenced Grenville's change of opinion. One of the principal attractions of a stamp tax to Grenville was that "few officers" with high salaries were required to administer it. Whately's plan would negate that advantage by reserving 15 percent of the gross revenues for each colony to the two distributors, thus making the colonial tax substantially more expensive to collect than English stamp duties.[17] Given the Mother Country's need for revenue, and given his confidence that the tax would not depend on the presence of officials for its execution, the First Lord doubtlessly felt compelled to gamble that one distributor could handle the business of an entire colony.

If only one man would be appointed, however, should he be the secretary to the council or an eminent merchant or planter? According to Ingersoll, the Treasury decided "to have the secretaries of the respective colonies be the distributors . . . and the governors and councils a kind of Board of Commissioners to superintend the whole." Ingersoll's relationship with Whately and the time he spent at the Treasury make it reasonable to assume that the Treasury at the very least considered this alternative and probably adopted it temporarily. But, as Ingersoll noted, "This plan was departed from, for what reason I never knew."[18] Instead, at some time in early March 1765, Grenville summoned Barlow Trecothick, a prominent American merchant who had directed mercantile opposition to the Stamp Act. When Trecothick arrived, he discovered that Grenville "desired him to name a person, some friend in whom he could confide, for the office of [stamp] distributor of the province of New York."[19] About the same time, Whately asked the colonial agents to meet with him because "Mr. Grenville was desirous to make the execution of the Act as little inconvenient and disagreeable to the Americans as possible, and therefore did not think of sending stamp officers from hence." Grenville "wished to have discreet and reputable persons appointed in each province from among the inhabitants, such as would be acceptable to them." Whately thus asked the agents to nominate men for their "respective colonies, informing [the agents], that Mr. Grenville would be obliged to [them] for pointing out to him honest and responsible men, and would pay great regard to [the] nominations."[20]

Clearly, Grenville had not decided against appointing any colonial secretary, for one of the first warrants the Treasury issued was in the name of Andrew Oliver, secretary of Massachusetts Bay. The most probable explanation for this decision is that the First Lord wanted to name in each colony the most "discreet and reputable persons" that he could, those who were the most acceptable to the inhabitants. The distributor might be a secretary, an assemblyman, or a person without office. So long as he was unquestionably a man of stature in the colony, he would serve the First Lord's purposes. In the case of Oliver, for example, Whately told John Temple that the Treasury could not have chosen a better person: "I have always heard a great character of him, and I was glad that the office was given to so very respectable a person."[21]

Grenville could safely assume that the agents and other friends of America would know the identities of similarly outstanding men in the other colonies and would not hesitate to recommend them to the Treasury. Opportunities to make the First Lord of the Treasury feel "obliged to [one] for pointing out to him honest and responsible men" did not occur everyday, and particularly not to men who had recently opposed him on a major measure. Moreover, as Trecothick aptly observed to Grenville, that he included them in the appointment process was "a honor done" them, a sign of his respect for their judgment.[22] Thus flattered by Grenville's confidence in them and tempted by the prospect of having the First Lord in their debt, the agents would nominate for the distributorships men who met his criteria.

Grenville and Whately made those criteria clear in their meetings with Trecothick and the agents. Grenville wanted Trecothick to name a friend he could confide in. Grenville could be reasonably sure that the merchant would nominate someone he had done business with and trusted enough to extend credit to. Such a man was not likely to be obscure in New York's mercantile community. Nor was the nominee likely to be poor; Trecothick understood that the distributors would have to post a sizable bond to guarantee performance of duty.[23] Whately was more explicit, plainly telling the agents that Grenville wanted men whose reputation would make them acceptable choices to their fellow inhabitants. Moreover, these men should possess the ideal traits of administrators: honesty; responsibility; and the ability to be discreet, that is, to be judicious, prudent, circumspect, and cautious in their dealing with others.[24] Interestingly, the Treasury proposed no political test for nominees. Grenville did not discuss the matter at all with Trecothick. Whately, by offering distributorships to Ingersoll and Franklin, who "had given all [possible] opposition" to the Stamp Act, indicated to the agents that the Treasury was not concerned by the opinion their nominees previously held about the tax.[25] All Grenville and his colleagues expected was that the men named by the agents would fulfill the criteria outlined.

Grenville's reasons for choosing the most prominent colonists, rather than restricting himself to colonial secretaries, were similar to those that convinced him in the first place that Americans should be named to the positions. The more prominent the Americans, the more completely Grenville would realize the political, economic, and administrative advantages of choosing a colonist. As for a nominee's position on the Stamp Act, Grenville probably concluded that he would not likely find a prominent American who had supported it. Moreover, by choosing men whose opinions and stature in their colonies were similar to Ingersoll's and Franklin's, Grenville would be taking a step, he thought, toward some of his basic political goals.

During the agents' 2 February meeting with Grenville, Jackson had outlined in some detail the "uneasiness and jealousy" that colonists felt about parliamentary taxation and its future application. Grenville had observed in response, "Let mutual confidence and mutual uprightness of intention take place, and no considerable ills can follow."[26] Appointing prominent colonists—men with substantial interests to defend and with the experience and knowledge of colonial conditions necessary to defend others' interests as well—would assist in relieving fears and building confidence. Indeed, according to one observer, a major reason Zachariah Hood, who was appointed stamp distributor for Maryland, so impressed the "court-cringing politicians" in London was that he grasped this fact: "He is supposed to have wisely considered that if his country must be *stamped,* the blow would be easier borne from a native, than a foreigner, who might not be acquainted with their manners and institutions."[27] If the newly appointed distributors had opposed the stamp tax before its passage, thus proving that they shared other colonists' concern for the future and desire to avoid taxation, despite their service to Britain, their presence as distributors would soothe their fellow Americans. In sum, by appointing the most prominent colonists—irrespective of previous opinion or political office—Grenville could be more certain that he was creating a situation in which mutual confidence could develop more quickly.

Moreover, the First Lord could hope that he was demonstrating the uprightness of his intentions toward the colonies. Grenville had assured the agents on 2 February that he and his successors would certainly lighten any taxes that were too heavy. He had also told them that Americans would always find "an easy access" to the Treasury, stating, "We on our part find with pleasure that America is not destitute of persons who, at the same time that they have the tenderest regard for their interests, are well able to represent to us their affairs." Then he had promised, "If they do it with integrity and candor, [they would] be sure to meet with [the government's] fullest confidence."[28] By offering appointments to Ingersoll and Franklin, and to others of commensurate repute who had opposed the stamp tax in their own colonies, Grenville was showing colonists that the confidence he had expressed in such men was not merely a gesture. He was also demonstrating that the assurances he had given—to listen carefully to complaints from America and to act when colonists pointed out burdensome duties—were not lightly made.

Furthermore, Grenville and Whately described in the most disinterested terms the Treasury's motives in naming eminent colonists. During his 2 February meeting with the agents, Grenville had openly hoped "that mutual interest as well as duty will keep us on both sides within the bounds of justice." But during discussions with Trecothick and the agents, Grenville and Whately did not describe or allude to economic and administrative benefits Britain would gain by the appointment of Americans. Instead, Grenville and Whately declared that their "motives . . . were those of convenience to the colonies," explaining that these appointments would "make the execution of the Act as little inconvenient and disagreeable to the Americans as possible." Grenville, therefore, "did not think of sending stamp officers" from Britain.[29] By remaining silent about the Mother Country's interest in revising overly burdensome duties before they could either seriously harm Americans' ability to purchase British goods or foster more political disaffection, Grenville and Whately were encouraging colonists to regard the Treasury's decision as Trecothick did, "as a favor that [Grenville was] willing to put the principal offices into the hands of the Americans." If Americans read remarks like these from the agents and reached the same conclusion, and if they too took the dispensation of the distributorships as "something conceded, conferred, or done out of special grace or goodwill, [as] an act of exceptional kindness, as opposed to one of duty or justice," they would interpret these appointments as proof of London's unforced regard for them and concern for their prosperity.[30] Such an interpretation could not help but improve Americans' trust in the British government and hasten the day when they fully accepted parliamentary sovereignty.

Preparing to Execute the Stamp Act

The agents responded to Grenville's request for names as he wished. "By [his] plausible and apparently candid declaration," Franklin later recalled, "we were drawn in to nominate." Ingersoll decided to take the post for himself. Franklin, however, declined the Treasury's offer, naming instead his friend and political ally, John Hughes of

Philadelphia.[31] Soon, more nominations arrived at the Treasury for approval, and warrants were issued.[32] Careers and lives hung in the balance as these men made their choices, though they were totally unaware of and, indeed, unprepared for the significance of their decisions.

On at least one occasion, Grenville had to choose between two men. In late 1764, Richard Henry Lee, a prominent Virginia politician, had applied for the distributorship of that colony. Edward Montagu, Virginia's agent, proposed that the Treasury name Col. George Mercer, a planter and land speculator who was then in Britain. In support of his candidate, Montagu shrewdly reminded Grenville that in July 1763, when Mercer announced he was going to England on private business, "The general assembly . . . , approving of his conduct while in their service, were pleased to recommend him to their Sovereign in the most genteel terms, and also desired their agent to assist him as far as might be in his power." Montagu also informed Grenville that Mercer "was a Member of the general assembly, and had great interest" in Virginia. These testimonials, especially the one from the House of Burgesses, proved to be effective. During the summer of 1765, Montagu "attribute[d] Colonel Mercer's appointment . . . to [the assembly's] recommendation," calling Grenville's approval "a compliment" to the colonial legislature.[33] Mercer, upon his subsequent resignation, told his enraged countrymen that his commission "was solely obtained by the general recommendation of their representatives in general assembly."[34] The source of information for both Montagu and Mercer was clearly the First Lord, for on 24 February 1766, Grenville told the House that he had appointed some stamp distributors "at the recommendation of the assemblies, as Colonel Mercer by that of Virginia."[35]

Grenville gave the job to Mercer, judging that in a contest between two reputable men, the more reputable was the one distinguished by endorsement of the local legislature. This should not have been an unreasonable assumption on his part. Moreover, by acting upon resolutions of colonial assemblies, Grenville would give them an impression of himself as a moderate, reasonable man who respected their opinions and had no designs on their legitimate powers. Finally, Grenville could expect that the sight of a man whom the assembly had honored executing an act it had opposed might hasten the acceptance of parliamentary sovereignty by the people and their representatives. For these reasons, Mercer was a better man for the job than Lee.

Grenville claimed in Parliament that he had appointed other distributors because they, too, had been nominated by their assemblies. He did not mention who these men were, and any independent evidence on these appointments has disappeared, if it ever existed. Perhaps he interpreted the Connecticut assembly's decision to make Ingersoll a special agent to assist Richard Jackson in opposing the stamp tax as a recommendation for preferment.[36] In any case, Grenville must have had some basis for making this remark on 24 February 1766, for he was leaving himself open to challenge for further information on this point. No one from the Rockingham administration questioned his version of events, however.

Throughout April and May 1765 the names presented by the agents and other friends of America permitted Grenville, as Whately noted on 10 May, "to direct his choice throughout to the most proper choices." The Secretary reported to John Temple that Grenville "except in the new colonies, . . . has confined himself to colonists, and those of the most respectable people in their several provinces."[37] As time passed, though, the Treasury no longer could apply its criteria so strictly, though it delayed as much as it could, according to Charles Lloyd, in an effort to secure "persons of the best credit" in all the established colonies. With 1 November fast approaching, however, the Treasury needed to have someone to distribute the stamps in Maryland, North Carolina, and South Carolina.[38] On 13 June, the Treasury issued a warrant for the appointment of Zachariah Hood, an Annapolis merchant who was in London buying for his store, as distributor in Maryland. News of Hood's appointment startled the colony's governor, who said, "Everybody seems to be surprised how the person . . . named could make interest to be nominated." Hood and his friends, who first recommended him to Grenville, may have in fact inflated his standing in the province. An observer with connections in Maryland who communicated the news of his appointment to America sarcastically wrote that Hood, "late a sojourning merchant of the city of Annapolis," had become "at present Z[achariah] H[ood], Esq., at St. James." But the same source also observed that Hood had received the distributorship "for his many eminent services to his King and country during the late war"; Hood later recalled, before he resigned his place, that he returned from London expecting "the most agreeable and endearing reception," in part because of "some considerable service that he had done or designed his country." So Grenville probably had some reason to believe that Hood would soon become, if he was not already, a person of eminence and considerable repute in the colony. Perhaps he was further encouraged toward this conclusion by Hood's success in gaining the support of Cecelius Calvert.[39] Hood was also a native American, with sufficient property to travel to London and obtain credit there. Finally, a distributor had to be found for Maryland. Hood came close enough to meeting Grenville's criteria for the office to merit appointment.

On 9 July, Dr. William Houston was named by Grenville and his colleagues as North Carolina's distributor. Little is known of the circumstances of this appointment, which came as a distinct and unpleasant surprise to Houston himself when he learned of it on 16 November. On that occasion, Houston complained, "There was too much of the Star Chamber made use of [in North Carolina], in condemning him unheard; especially as he had never solicited the office; nor had he [previously] heard he was appointed stamp officer." One of Henry McCulloh's business agents, Houston probably owed his nomination to McCulloh, who could vouch for his birth, residence, property, reputation, and, indeed, existence.[40]

Also on 9 July, the Treasury issued a warrant for Caleb Lloyd as the distributor for South Carolina. Lloyd's appointment had been delayed for some time, despite a recommendation from J. E. Colleton, an M.P. and a member of the powerful Colleton family of England, Barbados, and South Carolina, and by Robert Nugent, another M.P. Both Colleton and Nugent were staunch supporters of Grenville in the House, and they were probably seconded by Charles Garth, who owed Colleton several favors and must have consulted with him when Grenville asked the agents to nominate the distributors.[41] Still, these men could not move Grenville easily, for Lloyd had one major deficiency as a candidate. He had not been born in America, and, as Jenkinson explained to Nugent, Grenville had decided that, whenever possible, no one would become a distributor "unless he was a native of the colonies and a man of property."[42] On 9 July, however, Grenville finally yielded, probably to the pressure of time and to anticipation of the King ending his ministry, for Grenville did not trust his most likely successors to handle the distributorships properly.[43] He must have consoled himself for this deviation from his policy by thinking that people in the colony would identify Lloyd with the Colletons of Carolina.

A few days earlier, on 5 July, the Treasury had approved a report from the stamp commissioners, dated 27 April 1765, on the establishment of administrative machinery in America and in London for the collection of the American duties. The explanation for the slowness of this response, so unlike the speed with which the Treasury responded to the customs comissioners' reports during 1763, is not readily apparent. Whately had observed in May that parliamentary business was engrossing the Treasury's attention, and, after Parliament adjourned for the summer, Grenville's worsening relations with George III consumed much of the First Lord's time and energy.[44] Still, Grenville had faced a much stronger opposition in Parliament during 1763–1764 when relations with the King had been touchy as well. The problems in the spring and early summer of 1765 must then be regarded as only partial excuses. Perhaps the Treasury looked upon these steps as pro forma matters, despite the insistence of the stamp commissioners that they were not. Two of the decisions Grenville and his colleagues approved, however, merit attention.

The first of these was the First Lord's decision to accept the stamp commissioners' advice that governors should not be granted the privilege of naming a temporary replacement for any distributor who died in office. If such an event occurred, the governor instead was to inform the commissioners in London. They would either appoint someone immediately or authorize the governor to name a temporary distributor until they made the permanent appointment.[45] At first glance, this seems to promise awkward moments: How could stamps be distributed without a distributor? The commissioners, ever solicitous of the King's revenue from stamp duties, obviously thought that the greater evil would be the appointment of a man who could not raise the proper securities for the performance of his duty and could be tempted to dip into the King's purse. This possibility would disturb Grenville, too. Moreover, the First Lord probably wanted to be certain that the most socially and politically respectable men in the colonies served as distributors. The best way to insure this was to keep even temporary appointments out of governors' hands.

Also on 5 July, Grenville decided to accept, at least in part, the stamp commissioners' recommendation that American stamp distributors be allowed a higher percentage of the gross collections in their colonies than their English counterparts. The commissioners had argued that if the Treasury did not offer "at least" 8 percent of the gross, no one "fit to be a distributor" would take the job. This advice doubtless sprang not from any knowledge the commissioners had of America, but from their own difficulties in keeping English stamp distributors from resigning.[46] This recommendation probably evoked skepticism at the Treasury. Two months earlier, Whately had been confident that distributors in the colonies would discover their positions "both as a place of emolument and of influence, as the appointment of the underdistributors [would] be left to them . . . entirely."[47] He expressed no fear then that eminent men would regard 7.5 percent as too small a salary for themselves and their appointees. Indeed, he had no reason to fear this. Ingersoll had estimated that the produce of the tax in Connecticut would be somewhere between £2,000 and £3,439 10s. a year, and he had not scorned having between £150 and £258 in sterling each year as a reward for his work.[48] Nor was Colonel Mercer deterred by 7.5 percent of the £12,000 he expected to collect annually in Virginia.[49] Certainly the prospect of receiving 7.5 percent of the gross receipts in New Hampshire and Maryland did not keep two Americans in London, George Meserve and Zachariah Hood, from actively soliciting and eagerly accepting their appointments.[50] Still, Grenville must have reasoned that the benefits of having the most eminent colonists possible as the stamp masters were not worth risking for the sake of half a percentage point. He therefore agreed to 8 percent. The commissioners may have hoped that he would agree to an even higher figure; their use of the words *at least* hints in that direction, but Grenville did not respond. He was confident that 8 percent would attract the colonists he wanted.

Consequences of the Distributorships for the Internal Politics of the Colonies

Whately's observation on one of the distributors' benefits, "the appointment of the underdistributors [being] left to them . . . entirely," raises a final question. The Secretary and his chief were certainly familiar with the use of patronage to win and hold support for the ministry in Britain. Indeed, as Sir Lewis Namier has observed, Grenville was "extremely sensitive to anything connected with office patronage." The reason for this sensitivity is not hard to find: Grenville believed he had to control as much patronage as he could to maintain his own power in the House and in the Cabinet.[51] In the case of the distributors, he did agree that the distributors would have the sole power of naming their assistants. Moreover, he agreed to give them an allowance for postage and one for the transportation of stamps and money, steps that would increase distributors' profits.[52] Is it possible that Grenville and Whately though that giving the distributors these advantages would ultimately generate more political support for Britain in the colonies? If so, how?

Whately brought up the subject of distributors' patronage during a discussion of benefits that might attract reputable colonists. Obviously, if a politician had jobs he could fill, he had an advantage over those who had no places to give and his influence in local politics would increase. Thus the office would be personally advantageous to distributors. Whately surely did not expect that the distributors would have a great many offices at their disposal, however. In December 1764, he had observed that the distributors would have to appoint only a few assistants. He must have revised that figure upward when the Treasury decided to appoint only one distributor per colony, or else he would not have been so certain that all the distributors would have to appoint underdistributors. Nevertheless, the Treasury probably still believed, as Grenville declared to the House on 6 February 1765, that one of the beauties of a stamp tax was that it required "no great number of offices" to administer.[53] Enough officers would have to be appointed to make the place politically useful to the distributors, but surely not so many as to create an army of placemen under their control.

Whately did not speculate on the advantages the Mother Country might reap from the distributors' dispensation of their patronage. If the thought had occurred to anyone at the Treasury that the patronage of this tax might create a large pro-British faction merely out of the dispensation of offices, they would have dismissed it immediately as fantastic. There would be too few places at the distributors' disposal for that to occur. Nevertheless, American underdistributors in the colonies would serve as local examples of Grenville's determination that strangers would not enjoy the profits of the tax and that its administration should be as convenient to the colonists as possible. The lesser officials, like the distributors, would serve as indisputable evidence of British goodwill, even in the most remote parts of some colonies. Moreover, to the more ambitious in those areas, the sight of these officials would remind them of the benefits one might gain by currying favor with an official involved in the administration of a British tax—a reminder that could be useful to British governments. It is difficult to imagine that this thought did not occur to Grenville and Whately, who saw every day at the Treasury fresh examples of how the hope of appointment affected men's political behavior. Indeed, William Knox, who became close to Grenville after 1765, claimed in his account of the Grenville ministry, "The principle upon which the [stamp] duties were laid, and the consequences that would have followed from them, had the most direct and certain tendency to impede the colonies in their progress to independence." Specifically, Knox observed, "The collection of duties would occasion a considerable increase in the number of persons holding offices under the Crown, and deriving their appointments from British interest, and would be a severe check upon the propagation of antimonarchical principles within the colonies, and upon illicit connections with foreign countries."[54]

Grenville, however, probably did not plan to depend solely on the temptations of office to make the benefits of cooperation plain to Americans. He must also have counted on the distributors to help him accomplish that goal as they successfully suggested revisions in the rates. On 2 February, Grenville had told Ingersoll, Garth, Jackson, and Franklin that "resentments indecently and unbecomingly expressed [by colonists] would naturally produce resentments" among the British.

Grenville assured the agents, however, that the Treasury and Parliament were "open to any remonstrances" against the stamp tax, but only if they were made "in a becoming manner."[55] One of these agents became a distributor; another named a close friend; and the other two doubt-lessly made recommendations. All understood Grenville's point and communicated it to America.[56] Colonists could thus expect to be heard only if they at least implicitly acknowledged the power and right of Parliament to tax colonists. But if they did so, they had reason to be optimistic about the results. Franklin was explicit in his advice to John Hughes, the new distributor for Pennsylvania: "Your undertaking to execute [the Act] may make you unpopular for a time, but your acting with coolness and steadiness, and with every circumstance in your power of favor to the people, will by degrees reconcile them." More-over, he continued, "A firm loyalty to the Crown and faithful adherence to the government of this nation, which it is the safety as well as honor of the colonies to be connected with, will always be the wisest course for you and I to take, whatever may be the madness of the populace or their blind leaders, who can only bring themselves and [their] country into trouble, and draw on greater burdens by acts of rebellious tendency."[57] Grenville surely never saw this letter, but its contents would not have surprised him. He had not commented on colonial petitions to instruct Franklin and the others on this point. Rather, Grenville aimed at the audience in America, for he could be certain that the agents would pass along this advice. He could also be certain that the distributors, who had already demonstrated their acquiescence to Parliament's right by accepting their jobs, would take this advice and succeed in easing the colonists' burdens by convincing the home government that the two countries' mutual interests were harmed.

Grenville had already indicated to Franklin that duties on newspaper advertisements and some other items might be altered in the next parliamentary session.[58] This success, coupled with other changes sug-gested by the distributors, would provide colonists with an obvious contrast between the British response to "becoming" critiques of the stamp tax and those of colonial demagogues. The demagogues would stand revealed as powerless to prevent the enactment of the stamp tax, powerless to stop its execution, and powerless to effect necessary changes in it. Either they would admit their impotence and revise their views, or they would lose political popularity to the men who could bring about necessary changes.

Before leaving office in July 1765, Grenville had reason to believe that this process had already begun in Massachusetts, a troublesome colony. In April, the Treasury learned that the Massachusetts assembly had selected Jackson to be the colony's agent.[59] The election of Gov. Francis Bernard's business agent and Grenville's private secretary must have been received at the Treasury as a decision in favor of moderation and reconciliation. Jackson's nomination had to be particularly heartening, coming as it did from an assembly that during the previous year had sent to London letters reeking of sedition. Then, in mid-June, Jenkinson received a personal letter, dated 3 May, from Benjamin Hallowell, who reported, "Most people [in Boston] realize that they have done themselves harm by their disrespectful behavior." Hallowell went on, "The writers and stirrers up of the great opposition to the legislative power of Great Britain are heartily sorry for their conduct." Delighted by this news, Jenkinson gave a copy of the letter to Grenville, remarking how the letter showed "that our firmness here [had gotten] the better of the obstinacy of the colonies, and that all there [would] end well." Grenville's response was guarded. Still, the news must have encouraged him, for the lesson Boston's politicians were already taking to heart could only become plainer as time passed: The distributors and other colonial moderates could accomplish more for America than demagogues ever would.[60]

Chapter X

Thoughts and Hopes about Future American Revenue
March–July 1765

Soon after the House approved the stamp tax, Richard Jackson wrote to Connecticut that he saw no reason to fear that the tax would ever be "multiplied or augmented."[1] His wish may have been father to that prediction, because *ever* is a long time. Nevertheless, his assessment of the immediate future was evidently accurate. No document in the official papers at the Treasury or in the personal papers of Grenville and Jenkinson indicates that the First Lord planned to investigate other sources of colonial revenue during the summer of 1765. Had he expressed such a wish verbally, surely Whately, who had planned the stamp tax, would have heard of it. But Whately informed John Temple in June that he knew of no such schemes. Then the Secretary predicted that although "to explain and enforce the [present tax] laws may be the business of some future [parliamentary] session, . . . I do not expect to see more taxes, for the purposes of revenue at least, for some time." Parliament might impose some duties to regulate trade, but these, according to Whately, would be "small, occasional, and advantageous to the country that pays them."[2]

Whately did not go on to explain why the Treasury had no intentions of imposing more taxes on Americans in the immediate future. He did, however, make it clear that Grenville and his colleagues were not pausing because they believed the present taxes would defray the entire expenses of defending the colonies. Whately doubted that Britain would realize more than one hundred thousand pounds a year from the existing legislation, forcing the Mother Country to send at least two hundred thousand pounds more each year to America. It is possible that Whately deliberately understated the Treasury's true expectations in order to soothe Temple's apprehensions about the impact of the tax on trade, but other evidence suggests that men at the Treasury privately assumed Britain would have to send substantial sums to America. When preparing arguments for the stamp tax, Jenkinson had estimated that Britain would send about two hundred thousand pounds to the colonies. Perhaps drawing on this calculation, Grenville had told the agents on 2 February that he guessed the annual produce of all the taxes would be around one hundred thousand pounds, requiring "a balance of more than £200,000 sent over every year from England to be spent in America."[3] The First Lord apparently believed that the stamp tax alone would raise one hundred thousand pounds, but even if it did, and even if the most sanguine estimate of receipts from the molasses duty proved true, Britain would still have to provide between one hundred thousand and one hundred fifty thousand pounds a year to the colonies.[4] He could be certain, therefore, that collections from American taxes would fall well short of expenses. Why, then, did Grenville not consider other ways of raising money there?

Surely, one major reason was the Treasury's determination to avoid inadvertently taxing the colonies too heavily, thereby reducing their economic expansion, which would in turn diminish their ability to buy more and more British goods. Moreover, taxes that were too heavy would provide colonists with legitimate political grievances, which would erase from their memories all the efforts Grenville had made to increase their trust in the Mother Country. Avoiding the economic and political consequences of excessive taxation had been the goal of the Treasury for some time. As Whately had mentioned to Temple in November 1764, "Those who are at present in Administration are anxious for the prosperity of the colonies and highly sensible of their importance." He also predicted, "All that is to be aimed at [by the present and proposed taxes] seems to be to raise as much as the colonies can without grievance supply towards relieving the Mother Country of part of her annual expense."[5] Events bore out this prediction. Whately himself was careful to remind his colleagues of these aims when he advised them to keep stamp duties on legal proceedings in the colonies lower than the duties on corresponding documents in English courts because "the people[in America] really are poor and the multiplicity of their suits is the consequence of their poverty." He then concluded, "It is therefore proper to give them some relief by putting these duties at a lower rate."[6] Grenville and the others evidently agreed, even though some of them clearly felt that the poor in America were not the equivalent of the desperate, propertyless English poor. Jenkinson, for example, conceded that individuals in the colonies were poor, "if it is meant thereby that they have debts." But to him, this indebtedness was a sign "of a country that is rising into wealth, to apply all its cash for the purchase of stock and to exert all its credit for that purpose." "Though they are not therefore rich in money," he reasoned, "they are rich in stock, which are real riches, and the proper object of taxation." Still, Jenkinson emphatically stated, "They certainly ought never to be taxed as high as this country."[7] Grenville concurred with his two assistants. Like Jenkinson, he was skeptical of arguments that emphasized the poverty of the colonies. When the agents told him on 2 February 1765 that Americans were poorer than Britons, he replied that "measuring this point" was difficult. Furthermore, he added, "However opulent some in these Kingdoms are, [it is] well known the many can but live." But the First Lord followed this rebuke by telling the agents that the colonies would probably pay only one hundred thousand of the at least three hundred thousand pounds needed annually to maintain the army in America. "Is this too much?" he asked. "We think it is not, but if on trial we find it is, we will certainly lessen it."[8] Given the determination of the men at the Treasury to avoid burdening the colonies too heavily, it would have been a pointless exercise for them to look for new taxes before they could judge the impact of the present legislation.

Moreover, Grenville hoped that revenue from the stamp taxes would increase as the colonies grew in numbers and wealth, thus obviating the necessity of imposing entirely new duties for some time. He had confidently asserted in the House that Americans "have increased under former taxes, and they will flourish under these."[9] If so, more people would be buying commodities that were either taxed directly, like foreign linens, coffee, and wine, or taxed indirectly, like rum. Whately, in his pamphlet praising the American taxes of 1764, had spelled out the implications of this process: "Duties so low, and now first laid, will not at present contribute largely to the exigencies of the public, . . . but on the other hand, they will be an improving revenue, because they are laid upon numerous articles of general consumption among an increasing people, and if not productive of a great fund immediately, will be at least a wide foundation for a considerable future revenue."[10] In Grenville's opinion, a stamp tax should produce the same results. He had told the agents that such a tax would "always keep pace" with the colonies' "constant increase" and their "constantly varying . . . numbers and ability."[11] To be sure, Grenville was emphasizing in this conversation the equity of a stamp tax, which would not fall with equal weight on all colonies. There can be little doubt, though, that he was fully aware that greater numbers of prospering people would inevitably be involved in more lawsuits, more contracts, more land grants, and so on, and would thus buy more stamps. As he announced to the House, "The stamp tax takes in a great degree its proportion from the riches of the people. As in lawsuits and commercial contracts, it increases in proportion to the riches."[12] Grenville, therefore, could legitimately hope that as the colonies increased, the receipts from the stamp tax and other duties would increase apace, so that Americans would come closer and closer to paying for their own defense. Such an increase in revenue would be relatively painless economically, because it depended on a growth of population and wealth, not upon additional burdens on individuals. Moreover, it would be relatively painless politically. There would be no new taxes that could renew popular clamor against Britain. Any necessary changes would be adjustments to the present system, executed, as Whately said, "to explain or enforce the laws."[13] So Grenville's hopes that Britain would not need major revenue legislation for some years, in addition to his wariness of taxing colonists too heavily, kept him from thinking seriously about and planning for additional taxes. As far as he was concerned, in the foreseeable future the Treasury should be content to enforce and collect the newly established duties.

Criteria for Amending the Tax Laws

Whately also told Temple in June 1765 that some changes might be necessary in the recently passed legislation to clarify its meaning or strengthen its enforcement. The men at the Treasury probably understood that the bill was imperfect. Ingersoll, whose "thorough knowledge of the business" of distributing stamps Whately admired, questioned some of the wording of the Stamp Act because of possible misinterpretations.[14] The Attorney-General, Sir Fletcher Norton, also had serious reservations about some language in the act. In Norton's opinion, the law could create difficulties for the Crown in recovering money owed it, and the Attorney-General therefore asked Thomas Cruwys to remember that opinion and to remind him of it during the next session.[15] Grenville and his colleagues had been apprised by Benjamin Franklin that they had inadvertently failed to change the duty on newspaper advertisements from two shillings to one shilling. The Treasury gave Franklin reason to believe that the advertisement duty might be lowered during the next parliamentary session along "with some other amendments which it is supposed the bill may be found then to want, as it is now."[16] Finally, the Treasury could not have known at the time what tactics the ingenious American smugglers would adopt to evade payment of the various duties imposed on colonial trade in 1764. "Inconsiderable as [these duties] are," Whately had written in early 1765, "the payment of them will be often avoided by frauds and subtleties, which no penetration can foresee, and experience only can discover and prevent."[17] Once these tricks of the illicit trade had become apparent, they would have to be countered.

At the same time that Grenville and his colleagues accepted the inevitability of some alterations in the revenue legislation, they steeled themselves against amending the laws too quickly, not wishing to change the act because of incomplete or biased evidence. In early January 1765, Joseph Harrison, the collector at New Haven, had a brief conversation with the First Lord, who "made some general inquiries about the late Act of Parliament, and the sentiments of the people in America about it." As the conversation proceeded, Harrison discovered that Grenville "did not like to hear that there should be any surmise of [the Sugar Act] not being likely to produce the sum expected."[18] The initial collections from those duties, which were quite low, did not dismay the men at the Treasury, for Jenkinson's informant at Boston had relayed to the Treasury the news that Bostonians "had laid in great stores of goods previous to the commencement of" the Act, which would "prevent the receipt of any considerable sums for some times." Jenkinson believed that collections would "gradually improve," and he surely took pleasure in pointing out that the smallness of the collections and the stability of the price of molasses at Boston proved to his satisfaction that the duty was not oppressive and that the French, "not the people of the colonies who purchase" molasses, "would be forced to pay the duty."[19] About the same time, Whately publicly declared that he could foresee no ill consequences in the colonies from the payment of threepence.[20] Grenville must have reached similar conclusions. He could not otherwise have countenanced Whately's publication of these opinions. Grenville certainly made no plans to lower the duty during the parliamentary session of 1765, nor did he change his mind in the months that followed. Whatever his confidence might have been in the ultimate success of the duty, however, whenever Grenville discussed his intentions with friends of America, he emphasized merely that he wanted to give threepence a fair trial. When Barlow Trecothick complained to him about it, Grenville simply replied, "It would be absurd to rescind an Act before [becoming] acquainted with its operation."[21] When Ingersoll lobbied against the duty, he met with the same response. "Many things have been said about the molasses duty," he reported to a merchant in Newport, "but after all they don't intend to repeal or alter the present Act without at least trying it." Ingersoll solaced himself and his friend with the belief that the British "think they must [lower the duty] by and by," a conclusion he probably reached as a result of the Treasury's emphasis on giving it a trial and of the assurances that men there constantly gave that a duty would be reduced once it was seen to be harmful.[22] By stressing that he wanted to see how the duty operated, rather than discoursing on his confidence in it, Grenville had left himself a graceful avenue of retreat if the need for one arose. He had also avoided giving any impression of himself as an obstinate, overconfident minister, unwilling to pay attention to evidence that contradicted his original policies.

Furthermore, Grenville was making an important point to both agents and interested merchants. The Treasury was unwilling to make major revisions in colonial tax legislation solely on the basis of uncorroborated, ex parte testimony. As Whately remarked appropos of the molasses tax, "Something more than mere apprehensions and general assertions are necessary to condemn a tax which appears so proper on so many accounts." The Secretary went on, "Unless experience should prove that [the tax] is attended with bad consequences, or stronger objections can be made to it than have come to my knowledge, I cannot join in foreboding evils that I do not foresee."[23] Before the Treasury would amend any taxes, the men there would have to have reliable proof that the duties were either unenforceable or harmful at their present rates. Actual experience for a reasonable period of time was the best way to obtain such proof. To be sure, the opinions of colonists and other interested parties were not unwelcome at the Treasury. Indeed, Grenville, Whately, and Jenkinson had unofficially solicited these opinions in the past and doubtlessly intended to continue that practice in the future.[24] But without evidence based upon the experience of attempting to pay or collect taxes, no group could assume that its opinion would prevail.

Once the colonists, their agents, and their allies grasped this last point, they would be less likely to fall prey to grandiose expectations of influence—and the resultant disappointment. From the Treasury's standpoint, a more realistic attitude would reduce the chance of political outrage and charges of bad faith directed against Whitehall. Also, Grenville and his colleagues could reasonably expect that they would learn to make the strongest possible case for their suggestions. Clearly, one reason Franklin could be given "some expectations" for the lowering of the stamp duty on newspaper advertisements was that information from other sources had already convinced Whately in December 1764 and Grenville in February 1765 that a two shilling tax would be too heavy.[25] If the colonial distributors made equally impressive arguments against rates on other documents, and buttressed them with actual experience, they could expect an equally favorable hearing. It was this sort of care that Grenville was calling for when he assured the agents that Americans "well able to represent . . . their affairs . . . with integrity and candor" would receive the Treasury's fullest confidence.[26] Britain as well as the colonies would benefit, for the home government would have in its hands reliable proof that a specific tax was harmful or ineffectual and could take quick steps to correct it.

Insisting on proof based on experience in the enforcement and collection of a tax also protected Britain's colonial revenue. As Whately had remarked to Temple, he did not wholly credit all the objections made by colonists to the threepence duty on molasses because he knew that Americans were "inclined to object to all taxes."[27] Grenville had already reached similar conclusions. On 17 May 1764, he told the agents that he "doubted not but that the colonies would wish . . . to have no tax at all." Americans wanted an exemption from taxation for the same self-interested reasons that "the western country [in England] desires an exemption from [the] cider [tax], the northern country, from a duty on beer," and the landed interest from the four shilling land tax. "The true way to relieve all," the First Lord observed, "is to make all contribute their proper share."[28] If the Treasury started giving full credit to colonists' ex parte petitions, Americans would pay less than their proper share for protecting the empire.

Moreover, permitting the colonists and sympathizers to get their way on these matters would have serious political consequences as well. Americans and their merchant allies would, in essence, control revenue legislation affecting the colonies if the Treasury and Parliament followed colonists' suggestions without examining them in the light of experience. Indeed, the power and authority of the British government would be placed at the service of a part of the empire, rather than that part being required to contribute to the welfare of the whole. Grenville expressed his opinion of this situation most pungently in 1766, when he attacked the Rockingham ministry for "the overbearing delegation of administration to a club of North American merchants at the King's Arms Tavern, who he hoped would never be suffered to give law to Great Britain."[29] Needless to say, he was consciously exaggerating the case in 1766 for his political purposes at that time. Still, his insistence in 1765 that the Treasury would require reliable evidence before it altered American taxes bespeaks his determination then as well as later that no colonists or "club" of merchants would ever get the privilege "to give law to Great Britain." For if they were conceded this privilege by omission or commission, much of the political good he believed he had accomplished with the colonial taxes of 1764–1765 would be negated.

The Necessity of Enforcing the Colonial Taxes

To make certain that Britain gained these political advantages and enhanced the revenue, it was essential for the Treasury to monitor closely the performance of customs officers and stamp distributors. Grenville and his colleagues were aware that British laws "had been executed for some time in a most negligent and shameful manner." They were also well aware that "the negligence of the officers of the Crown" had not only diminished the Mother Country's commerce with the colonies, and reduced the revenue from them, but had had adverse political effects as well. Colonists who had been free from due restraints on their trade and from payment of taxes were "very unwilling to be made again subject to them"; instead, they were ready to question British authority when the government resumed its effort to enforce duties.[30] If the Treasury was negligent in insisting that the officers of the revenue maintain accurate records, make frequent reports, and explain the reasons for any lack of success, then there was reason to believe that the same process could occur again.

So Grenville and his colleagues continued to observe closely the enforcement of the legislation of 1764 during April, May, and June 1765. As a result of their attention to reports and their determination to halt corruption and negligence in the customs service, they provided officers in Rhode Island, Maryland, and Pennsylvania with visible proof of the Treasury's concern over enforcement of the law.[31] Less concern was visible over the operation of the Stamp Act in America, however, because its execution would not begin until 1 November. It is highly unlikely, though, that Whately would have forgotten his earlier worry that the effective distribution of stamps throughout the colonies would be the greatest difficulty attending the tax, nor would he have neglected to examine the reports on this procedure, from both distributors and other colonists.[32] Franklin believed, moreover, "We [Americans] may another year hope for an allowance of a person to strike the stamps at Philadelphia on all paper for newspapers and almanacs." This step, by moving from London the printing of stamps, would facilitate the supply and distribution of stamped paper.[33] That such a measure was contemplated at the Treasury reveals a concern over the smooth functioning of the law. Finally, Thomas Cruwys noted the Attorney-General's fear that the Crown would have difficulty recovering money owed the distributors by private individuals and the underdistributors, indicating that stamp commissioners, law officers, and the Treasury would all carefully observe the mechanics of collecting money for the stamps.[34]

Attention paid by the Treasury to the execution of the new taxes was not merely inspired by a desire to reverse the trends in law enforcement of the past years. Without doubt, it was also inspired by the thought that the Mother Country should not miss taking full advantage of a golden and fleeting opportunity. Grenville and his colleagues had devised taxes that they believed would be enforced by the colonists' self-interest, if the officers responsible were alert, efficient, and honest. The colonists' customers, Grenville was confident, would pay the molasses duty. As for the stamp tax, as John Dickinson later wrote, "The makers of that Act knew full well, that the confusions that would arise from the disuse of [legal papers], would COMPELL the colonies to use the stamped paper, and therefore to pay the taxes imposed. For this reason, the Stamp Act was said to be a law THAT WOULD EXECUTE ITSELF."[35] Grenville himself could not have expressed it better. In sum, these new taxes, if administered efficiently, would guarantee that Britain would raise a revenue in the colonies.

Producing an American revenue was, of course, "a great and necessary measure." So was "establish[ing] the right of Parliament to impose" taxes, payment of which would, in effect, make colonists acknowledge the right of Parliament and, thus, establish it.[36] Moreover, Grenville had made certain that Parliament's authority to tax would not be qualified. Even though he had felt obliged in 1764 to postpone the stamp tax for a year, he had skillfully avoided giving the colonists any precedent that they could cite in any future claims of prior consultation on taxation. And, while making it clear to Americans that the Treasury would welcome suggestions for changes in colonial taxes, Grenville had also made it clear that these suggestions would not be successful unless they implicitly conceded Parliament's authority and had the support of evidence based on experience with a tax. In sum, if the present taxes were not defeated by inept or corrupt administration, colonists could not resist paying them and would soon discover that to amend tax laws they would have to frame their petitions in the way Grenville required. Thus, the collection of the molasses and stamp duties would gradually and effectively establish the supremacy of Parliament.

This prospect clearly was not a pleasant one to many colonists. They understood that the present taxes could signal an end to the independence of action they had enjoyed for several years, and they were disturbed enough to voice disapproval of those taxes in America and Britain. Grenville responded to their outcries with carefully chosen, moderate, encouraging words. He did not bluntly state his ultimate political goals to them any more than he had flatly declared to Bute and the King the advantages he expected to gain by becoming Secretary of State in May 1762, and for the same reasons. Such bluntness would have increased apprehension and retarded the realization of his political purposes. With the Americans and their friends, Grenville had tried to soothe misgivings and reconcile them to accepting the collection of the revenue and the supremacy of Parliament by encouraging them to believe that they would always have "an easy access" to the powerful and that the powerful would always do their best to serve the best interests of Mother Country and colonies alike.[37] The consultations with the agents, the solicitation of American opinion, the amendments to the stamp tax in committee, the appointment of colonists as distributors, and the decision to keep the revenue in America were all intended, in part, to demonstrate the sincerity of Grenville's words. From the response of the agents and of Trecothick, there was good reason to believe that Grenville's words and actions had impressed them.[38] Impressing them further was the willingness of Grenville and his colleagues during February, March, and April 1765 to be "attentive to such applications as the American agents [had] lately made to them on several occasions" and to act on them by altering the Sugar Act, by placing bounties on various types of colonial lumber, and by adopting many of the colonists' suggestions for amending the administration's bill concerning the quartering of soldiers in America. One "considerable merchant in London," who was familiar with the negotiations on these matters, wrote to a friend in Connecticut during April, "We are fully persuaded that the present Administration is as reasonable and upright as any we are likely to see." Indeed, he continued, "I am convinced more is to be obtained from them for America by fair, candid, private representations, than by public opposition."[39] There is no record of anyone's ever having made precisely these statements directly to Grenville. Still, the eagerness and hopefulness with which the agents and merchants adopted the tactics described in this letter, and their gratitude and pleasure at their successes, made it obvious that they were convinced of the efficacy of approaching him with "fair, candid, private representations" and of the inutility of confronting him with "public opposition." Grenville could reasonably expect that they would pass on their conclusions about the best way of dealing with Whitehall when they described their victories in letters to their correspondents and employers in America. He could also hope that influential colonists would reach similar conclusions and that the colonies as a whole would accept their proper place in the empire—both with greater speed and cheerfulness than could have been expected in 1763. In mid-June 1765, as Grenville read Hallowell's letter of 3 May 1765 from Boston, that hope must have seemed close to a reality.[40]

But if the taxes were slackly administered, if the British government gave colonists the impression that it was willing once more to tolerate widespread evasion of the laws, then the favorable opportunity to establish the supremacy of Parliament would be wasted. Indeed, it might be lost forever. Since his first days at the Treasury, Grenville had been keenly aware that the colonies' "vast increase in territory and population makes the proper regulation of their trade of immediate necessity lest the continuance and extent of the dangerous evils above mentioned may render all attempts to remedy them hereafter infinitely more difficult, if not utterly impracticable."[41] Failure to take full advantage of the situation that he and his colleagues had worked so hard to create would leave a rapidly growing people the chance to eschew acknowledging Parliament's sovereignty and to mature in numbers and power without forming the habit of obeying British laws and paying British taxes. But let the taxes be successfully collected, let the outrage of colonists die as they realized that the burden was not excessive and that they could make suggestions to the Treasury, and the disparities between a people "continually increasing in numbers and in strength" and another people who "perhaps have come . . . to [their] full growth" would become sources of wealth, not events to be feared.[42] So Grenville was determined to see that the officers of the revenue smoothly and competently administered and collected the taxes Parliament had imposed during 1764–1765.

Significances of Grenville's Dismissal

The odds against the government taking full advantage of its opportunity, however, lengthened almost immediately. By May 1765, the King had tired of Grenville for a combination of political and personal reasons. George III had come to resent Grenville's tireless efforts to keep civil list expenditures within the annual amount allotted to them of £800,000, and the more so because the First Lord accompanied those efforts with lengthy lectures in the Closet on the need for royal economies. To Grenville's face, the King merely "seemed disinclined to lessen any part of what he appropriated to his own use"; but within his own heart, the anger and frustration George III felt at what he later sarcastically termed Grenville's "hobbyhorse, the reduction of expenses," grew rapidly and ominously.[43] Equally infuriating, as far as the King was concerned, was Grenville's obsession with controlling as much of the patronage of the Court as he could, even though some of these places were well beyond the normal purview of the Treasury and the usual domain of the Leader of the House. "No office fell vacant in any department," the King later recalled, "that Mr. Grenville did not declare he could [no longer] serve if the man he recommended did not succeed."[44] To Grenville, of course, civil list expenditures and Court patronage were legitimate concerns of his office. George III did not deny this in principle, but he certainly objected to Grenville's peculiar methods of dealing with those concerns.[45] Fed up with Grenville's methods, the King tried to open negotiations with Pitt, failed, and then suffered the full vengeance of Grenville and his colleagues, who used the King's extremity to force him to break promises he had made in 1763 to Bute's brother and Henry Fox. Then, as had happened in October 1762, Grenville suffered the consequences of underestimating the lengths to which desperation could drive men. By 6 July, Grenville told his brother, "It is generally understood that . . . Lord Rockingham is to be First Lord of the Treasury." The general understanding was correct. On 10 July 1765, the King dismissed Grenville, and Rockingham duly became First Lord.[46]

The appointment of this "puerile and *anile* administration" was fraught with ominous significance for Grenville.[47] As he indicated to George III during their final meeting as minister and monarch, he understood "that the plan of [the King's] new Administration was a total subversion of every act of the former." The Rockinghams had opposed the Stamp Act. Moreover, their pedigree could be traced to Newcastle's administrations, which had featured a colonial policy that Rockingham's secretary later apotheosized as "salutary neglect." To Grenville, reinstatement of such a policy would be anything but salutary. Not only would it deprive Britain of a colonial revenue, but it would also squander a unique political opportunity. Grenville, therefore, on 10 July appealed to the King and served warning to his successors.

He began by reminding the King of his royal approval of "the regulations concerning the colonies." Then "he besought His Majesty, as he valued his own safety, not to suffer anyone to advise him to separate or draw the line between his British and American dominions, [for] . . . his colonies were the richest jewel of his Crown."[48] Grenville promised the King that he would oppose in the House any attempts to repeal legislation passed during his administration or to cast doubt on Parliament's right to tax the colonies. Finally, he advised George III, "If any man ventured to defeat the regulations laid down for the colonies by a slackness in the execution, [the King] should look upon him as a criminal and the betrayer of his country."[49] Out of office as well as in, Grenville was determined to do all he could to achieve that "great and necessary measure," to insure that the American colonies would help pay for their defense and subordinate themselves to Britain politically.

Chapter XI

"The Author of all the Troubles in America"
August–December 1765

Less than a month after Grenville left the Treasury, copies of the resolutions passed by the Virginia House of Burgesses in May 1765 arrived in London. Whately dutifully forwarded them to his former chief. As Grenville read them, he noted that they "declar[ed] the Parliament of Great Britain enemies of their country" and argued that "the sole right of imposing taxes is in themselves." Clearly, these were "dangerous and desperate doctrines," of such seriousness that the new ministers would have to execute his legislation.[1]

The Virginia resolves, according to Whately, could not "escape the notice of Parliament." Indeed, they were so extreme that even though "it may not suit the system of the present ministers to produce them, . . . that may not hinder their being called for" from the floor by members unconnected with the government. Grenville concurred in this judgment. The resolutions were indeed, he replied to Whately, "of too extravagant a nature to escape notice and exceed any notions which I could entertain of that extravagance."[2] The Rockinghams would have to face this matter, whether by their own choice or by their certain knowledge that the House would demand some action—a prospect that delighted Grenville. "I am curious," he cheerfully wrote to Robert Nugent, "to know what answer our new ministry will give to them, . . . [because] some of those respectable personages seemed to be of the same opinion last year."[3] He was certain that any plans the present ministry might have laid to undo his labors of the past two years had been themselves undone, ironically, by the very colonial extremists whom the new ministers had encouraged by opposing the stamp tax. Examination of the Virginia resolves would maintain the unanimity he had achieved earlier in the year on constitutional issues and would create unity on the Stamp Act itself. "I cannot believe," Grenville flatly predicted, "that these newfangled and desperate doctrines . . . will find advocates to support them in council or in Parliament when the fatal consequences of them come to be seriously weighed and considered." In the face of such a unanimous desire to defend and assert Parliament's supremacy, no ministers would dare be lax in enforcing the new trade regulations or in collecting the molasses and stamp duties. Indeed,

Grenville expected that "in council" the ministers would share fully in this desire and thus would execute his policies with the vigor of personal conviction as well as that of political compulsion.[4]

Grenville must have also been pleased as he contemplated the other ways by which the colonial extremists had injured themselves. The demagogues had called attention to themselves in America as well as in England. Colonists would have no difficulty recalling the violence of the demagogues' rhetoric as self-interest compelled the payment of the stamp tax. Furthermore, Americans would not have any difficulty noticing the stark contrast between the hot words and the ultimate result. The impotence of the demogogues to force changes in British policy could not be missed, nor could the determination of the Mother Country, stiffened by their wild protests. Moreover, after British response to the Virginia resolves, colonial extremists would have no shadow of a claim that their position had support in Parliament. Instead, it would be so clear that their extremism had cost them the only friends they had that they could not even tempt their fellow Americans with the forlorn hope that someday their arguments would command a majority in the House. "Certainly," Grenville observed happily to Nugent, the Rockinghams were "the properest persons that could be chosen to put an end to such dangerous and desperate doctrines."[5]

In August 1765, then, Grenville believed that the House of Burgesses had removed the only obstacle that might have hindered collection of the stamp duties and other colonial taxes. His confidence in this outcome remained unqualified into October. Then letters began to arrive from America. Riots had occurred in Boston and Newport during August. Other letters passed along the news that "the assembly of deputies from the several provinces, in order to appeal jointly for a repeal of the Act, [would meet] in New York." When Whately commented on these letters, he said to Grenville, "The rage of the people seems not to be confined to the Stamp Act." Moreover, he continued, "The officers of the customs are also the object of it." Then Whately called Grenville's attention to the logical conclusion of that attack: "If that should be avowed, then the clear point is, whether the Parliament has a right to impose any taxes at all there." Yet even this intelligence and Whately's inferences from it probably did not immediately weaken Grenville's confidence. After his description of events in America, the former Secretary assured Grenville, "The language of the ministry is, I am told, resolute, and they have certainly written to Governor Bernard, directing him to enforce the execution of the law vigorously." Whately did add that he believed that the administration was "undetermined about the measure to be taken and the mode of proceeding if the tumult continues."[6] This thought, however, probably did not disturb him or Grenville very much at that time. If rioting continued after 1 November, the date the Stamp Act was to go into effect, colonial ports and courts would be closed for want of stamps. The resultant anarchy and confusion would convince all responsible colonists, and doubtless many who were behaving irresponsibly, of the necessity of submitting and paying the tax. Indeed, anticipation of such horrors would probably cool tempers and settle the disorder before 1 November.[7] Comforted by that vision, pleased by the prospect for vindication of the stamp tax, Whately predicted on 25 October that the riots and rhetoric in America "will prove only a popular cry of the day, not attended with any consequences."[8]

Grenville soon discovered otherwise. A few days after Whately sent that letter, Nugent informed Grenville that Rockingham was encouraging merchants and manufacturers in Bristol, Liverpool, and Lancashire to send petitions to the Treasury, criticizing use of the navy to attack smuggling into America. Grenville immediately responded by asking his friends to oppose all petitions that would "cast . . . some reflections upon the late ministry and particularly upon your humble servant."[9] Grenville next received word of Rockingham's intentions from Whately, who had been sifting through reports from America and absorbing snatches of gossip. "I have some reason to believe what you will hardly expect: . . . you will be told that the appointment of natives to be distributors was improper, and the [use of] smuggling cutters, especially in America, [is] to be decried."[10] The likelihood that the Rockinghams, even as they enforced the Stamp Act, might try to undermine two policies that Grenville deemed crucial to the operation of the revenue laws and, consequently, to the political subordination of America, compelled the former First Lord to attack the new ministers openly. Grenville decided that they would have to be pressed, and pressed hard, when Parliament opened on 17 December, to take strong measures against American rioters. He and other members of his administration began to coordinate plans for the upcoming session. By 27 November, Grenville had heard a more disturbing report, "from one who [seemed] most likely to know": The Rockinghams were "resolved (if possible) to repeal the American tax."[11] Without doubt, these reports, the steadily worsening news from the colonies, and the growing certainty that the Stamp Act had not executed itself on 1 November strengthened Grenville's determination to protect his colonial program by conducting an aggressive parliamentary campaign against the ministry's prudence and courage and against the Americans' loyalty.

When Parliament met, Grenville offered an amendment to the

Address to the King, declaring the colonies to be in rebellion and comparing that rebellion to the Jacobite rising in Scotland in 1745. He justified the amendment's necessity by sarcastically referring to the ministry's address, "as if it [were] drawn by the captain of the mob."[12] To his surprise, however, his arguments fell on deaf ears. The House's obvious lack of enthusiasm for the motion obliged him to withdraw it. The address then passed nem. con. Undaunted, Grenville returned to the attack three days later, moving that the House adjourn only until 7 January, rather than the fourteenth as the ministry wished. During debate on his motion (which was ultimately defeated, 77 to 35), Sir William Baker angrily "treat[ed] Grenville as the author of all the troubles in America."[13] Thus were exposed early the emotions and the arguments that underlaid much of the great debate on the Stamp Act in 1766. Although no one could know at the time, thus too were foreshadowed Grenville's ultimate defeat and the accusation that would dog him for the rest of his life and into the historiography of his age.

Grenville's Excuses

Grenville answered Baker with the same excuse that many historians have made for him, throwing "the blame from himself on the Parliament."[14] This retort rang false to his contemporaries in the House. Although they rarely admitted it so openly, they knew as well as Ingersoll did that "in modern times, convincing the minister is convincing the House . . . , especially in matters of revenue."[15] They also knew that this maxim was particularly appropriate in the case of Grenville and American taxation. After all, Grenville had persuaded the House in 1763 to delay lowering the molasses duty, even though a majority had favored an immediate revision of the tax. The former First Lord had also abruptly postponed in 1764 an obviously popular proposal, the imposition of stamp duties on colonists, and had no difficulty in convincing the House to go no further than a resolution of intent. That same year, he had substantially altered in committee the House's original vote to remove the drawback on foreign goods reexported to the colonies and easily won House approval for his changes. For him to claim that he had merely followed the House's wishes on American taxation was blatantly preposterous. Indeed, such a claim was so obvious a reversal of the truth that he rarely repeated it in later debates.

In fact, he usually took the opposite tack, praising his own role in the genesis of the Stamp Act. He "wish[ed]," he told the House in 1766, that "the Stamp Act had more faults than it did." Then it would appear "to be repealed rather from a yielding to reason than to violence."[16]

Grenville freely confessed that he had not foreseen that violence. There was no question in his own mind that he had misjudged the extremists' power to mobilize an effective resistance to the stamp tax. But he insisted that his was an understandable, unavoidable error. As he told the House, "He had himself very good reason to believe the Americans would submit to the tax." After all, "The principal person in the colonies adopted the office of distributor. Mr. Franklin recommended his friend Hughes to that employment." Would Franklin have done that, asked Grenville, "if it had been expected that the distributor would have been torn in pieces?"[17] Obviously the answer was no. The implication of this reasoning was clear. If the agents, who knew America well, and Franklin and Ingersoll, who had just arrived in London from that country, could not predict violent resistance to the Stamp Act, then Grenville could hardly be expected to have foreseen and guarded against it.

Most modern historians have been struck by the plausibility of this excuse and have endorsed it without much question.[18] Still, despite the obvious sensibility of this explanation for the First Lord's mistake, it is worth a closer look. Grenville was certainly familiar enough with riots in England. He knew how dangerous hungry men could be; indeed, his administration had been forced to take extraordinary measures to prevent food shortages in England during 1764–1765.[19] Grenville also understood that unscrupulous, self-interested men could raise mobs to serve their personal goals. John Wilkes's success at winning the verbal and physical support of the London mob in 1763 surely kept that knowledge fresh in Grenville's mind.[20] And he was certainly aware that organized assaults upon royal officials were no novelty in Britain or America. Reports from the cider country indicated that excisemen dared inspect presses only during the day, for "were they to visit in the night, they surely would be murdered."[21] Smugglers in Britain regularly battled with vessels of both the customs service and the navy.[22] In America, such attacks occurred frequently enough for Grenville to recommend to the King that the military in America be instructed to help protect "the officers of the revenue from the violence of any desperate or lawless persons who shall attempt to resist the due execution of the laws in the same manner as is practiced in England."[23] So Grenville understood the potentially destructive impact of hunger and the terror of famine and starvation on men, and he had practical experience with demagogues' and lawbreakers' use of mob violence against authority. Yet neither his knowledge nor his experience deterred him in the case of the Stamp Act. The reasons they did not illuminate the causes of his great mistake.

The Increasing Potential for Popular Disturbances in America

In Grenville's experience, the danger of riots increased dramatically when the poor were uncertain that they could afford or find food. This uncertainty could arise from the availability and the price of victuals; it could arise from an inability to find employment; or it could arise from a combination of these factors. Such a situation had existed in March 1763, when mobs of sailors recently discharged from the navy committed "divers outrages in many parts of [London] to the danger of the property and even lives of His Majesty's subjects." Egremont and the King were forced to take the unpopular step of ordering troops to be ready to assist the magistrates "in order to prevent the mischiefs which might happen from such a dangerous body of desperate men, in case of the least delay in putting a stop thereto."[24] But the conditions that made the sailors dangerous did not exist in America; of that, Grenville was certain. The official statistics that indicated a phenomenal growth in commerce to and from the colonies amply proved to his satisfaction that the colonies were prospering. Moreover, these statistics did not include Americans' lucrative clandestine commerce with the West Indies and Europe. The illegal trade with Europe alone had burgeoned from McCulloh and Ware's estimate in 1763 of four hundred thousand to five hundred thousand pounds per year to Grenville's own calculation in 1765 of "considerably more than five hundred thousand pounds."[25] Legal and illegal trade of this volume strongly implied that farmers were finding markets for their crops, laboring people were finding jobs, and artisans and merchants were finding customers. In sum, colonists were employed. And, given the high cost of labor in the colonies, a working man there was earning a good wage or making a good profit.[26]

Of course, poor harvests could drive the price of food beyond the reach of even these men. Also, a heavy public indebtedness, and the weight of the taxes necessary to pay interest and retire principal, could force producers of food and sellers of goods to raise their prices to a level appropriate to a time of natural scarcity. As Grenville observed during the English food shortages of 1766, "I don't see how provisions can be low while taxes are so high, or how men can buy [corn] *dear* and sell *cheap*" to the poor.[27] But these conditions did not exist in America either. No one from the colonies had complained to Grenville of an actual or imminent famine. Rather, the agents and the assemblies had stressed that the colonies could feed themselves even if forced by British taxes to undergo a difficult conversion to manufacturing.[28] Artificial scarcity was equally unlikely. The public indebtedness of all the colonies was only around eight hundred thousand pounds, and the annual cost of civil government for all of them was merely forty thousand pounds a year.[29] Barring an agricultural catastrophe, prices of provisions would remain well within the budget of the poor colonists. To Grenville's mind, then, the fear of unemployment, the specter of famine, and the terror of starvation that in Britain had the potential to erupt in public convulsions were absent in the colonies. In England, "A mob [was] easily formed out of [unemployed men], and . . . other discontented spirits." Although such men could not "overset government, . . . [they could] give a very great deal of disagreeable trouble."[30] In America, Grenville thought, this was nothing more than a remote possibility.

Recently, however, scholars have determined from careful examination of tax lists, inventories, and like documents that the economic situation in Boston, New York, and Philadelphia was not as sound as Grenville believed it to be.[31] Clearly, the widening and deepening poverty in American cities did not compare with the desperate circumstances of the poor in London. But just as clearly, the poorer among the King's subjects in America were disturbed by the drift toward a society similar to England's, frankly described by Grenville as one in which some enjoyed opulent wealth but "the many can but just live," and were not inclined to acquiesce in any further drifting.[32] The poorer colonists judged, and judged correctly, that collection of the stamp duties would increase their financial burdens and widen the gap between rich and poor. They were prepared to resist such a measure, even if resistance required desperate action.

Grenville, however, had received no hint of this poverty from either the agents or the assemblies. To be sure, the agents did argue that the colonies were poor and could not afford to pay the stamp tax. But desperate riots were not the consequences they had predicted for collection of the molasses duty, and presumably the stamp tax as well. Instead, they stoutly insisted that the tax would force the colonies to start manufacturing for themselves and confidently predicted success.[33] Privately and publicly, Grenville and his colleagues scoffed at such notions. The cost of labor was too high in America to permit the development of much manufacturing. Moreover, Grenville believed he could delay the day that the cost of labor would drop by judicious use of bounties to encourage agriculture.[34] Finally, the argument that colonists could survive such an abrupt change indicated that Americans believed they could endure even serious slumps in trade without critical economic or social difficulties. Grenville saw no reason not to share their confidence. He also saw no reason to suspect that demagogues could draw upon the resentments of a desperate crowd to oppose the stamp tax. Thus, though he was told that the stamp tax "would produce disturbance and discontent and prevent improvement among the colonies," he did not hesitate imposing it.[35]

Changes in Colonial Politics

Not only was Grenville unaware of the seriousness of urban poverty in America, but he was also kept ignorant of significant developments in the theory and practice of politics there. During the eighteenth century, a variety of shocks—some as obvious as war, some as subtle as religious revivals—had changed the old system of deferential politics. By the 1760s, politicians of all persuasions felt obliged to appeal to and to manipulate the voters through pamphlets, speeches, and even machine-like organizations.[36] In the course of ever-intensifying struggles for popular support, the participants became increasingly aware that theirs was not merely a personal contest, but also one between two competing doctrines. The gentry, wealthy and conservative, stressed "the necessity of an indivisible body politic or attempted to confine the mass of people by assigning them a share of power within a 'balance' system."[37] In essence, they were insisting that they were best qualified to govern in the interests of all the people because of their economic and social status. The populace could be trusted with a limited voice in the selection of its leaders, but should have little say beyond that. The gentry's opponents, who styled themselves "popular" leaders, charac-terized these arguments as clever lies, designed to prevent the people from recognizing how the wealthy used government to serve them-selves rather than to preserve and protect the community. In Boston, dramatizing this insight was peculiarly easy for the popular leaders. The most prominent conservative, Thomas Hutchinson, who had tried to thwart the popular will throughout his career, held four lucrative and powerful offices.[38] Moreover, according to popular leaders, the gen-try's rapacity was such that even excesses like Hutchinson's would not satisfy them. To gain more, they would try to remove every popular check on them. Their real aim, therefore, was not limiting the people's voice in government. It was removing it entirely. James Otis did not doubt that "the worst enemies of the charter governments are not to be found in England. ... A set of men in America, without honor or love to their country, have been long grasping at powers which they think unattainable while those charters stand in the way." Everyone in Boston knew that Otis was referring to Hutchinson and his allies.[39] To help defeat Hutchinson's schemes, Otis and men like him in other colonies were groping toward a theory that justified what they already practiced, interest-group politics.

Ingersoll and Franklin were both familiar with the new politics, Ingersoll as a conservative and Franklin as the friend of Philadelphia's artisans. Interestingly, both men were willing to adopt the other side's vocabulary when it suited their purposes. Ingersoll suggested to Whately that taxing Americans would be "like burning a barn to roast an egg"; he also warned that any parliamentary tax "would go down with the people like chopped hay." These homely metaphors, so dear to popular politicians, had no effect at the Treasury.[40] Franklin arrived in England fresh from a defeat at the polls, a disaster he attributed in part to "the wretched rabble brought to swear themselves entitled to vote" by his opponents.[41] But evidently neither man shared his knowledge with Grenville about the ways popular leaders analyzed words and actions in politics. Nor did either man point out to the First Lord that many politicians in America had much experience and at least occasional success in communicating their fears of ulterior conservative motives and goals to the people. Did Ingersoll and Franklin realize that Grenville's tactic of speaking moderately and soothingly about his concern for the colonists, while pursuing a policy designed to reduce the powers of the popular assemblies, corresponded closely to the tactics of colonial conservatives? Perhaps they did not, though in retrospect the similarity is clear. Whether they did or not, however, they certainly missed the significance of that congruence.

From the beginning of the Stamp Act crisis, popular leaders had dismissed Grenville's efforts to speak of the colonists "in terms of great kindness and regard, and in particular [assuring them] there was no intention to abridge or alter any of their charters" as either insignificant or deliberately deceptive.[42] They kept their attention focused on his purpose—raising a revenue in the colonies by parliamentary taxation—and on the implications of that taxation. The threepence duty on molasses increased the "apprehensions" of the committee that drafted in May 1764 the instructions for Boston's representatives: "These unexpected proceedings may be preparatory to new taxations on us." Furthermore, "If our trade may be taxed, why not our lands? Why not the produce of our lands and everything we possess or make use of?" The end of Parliamentary taxation was clear: "This we apprehend annihilates our charter right to govern and tax ourselves."[43] Grenville's efforts to dispel suspicion with moderate language actually increased it. The Massachusetts House of Representatives viewed the delay of the stamp tax as an effort to tempt the colonies into acquiescing in the raising of an American revenue; Pennsylvania assemblymen claimed that Grenville had not used "the proper canals" to communicate his request for information.[44] And James Otis, while conceding that Grenville had "more than once" declared his intention of consulting the "ease, the quiet, and goodwill of the colonies," sarcastically observed, " 'Tis possible he may have erred in his kind intentions . . . , and taken away our fish, and given us a stone."[45]

Moreover, well before Grenville made any decision on the appointment of distributors, the town of Boston had instructed its representatives in May 1764 to "preserve that independence in the House of Representatives which characterizes a free people." To do so, it was "particularly" necessary to require that "the seats of such gentlemen as shall accept of posts of profit from the Crown or governor while they are members of the House shall be vacated, . . . till their constituents shall have the opportunity of reelecting them, if they please, or of returning others in their room."[46] Clearly, the popular leaders believed that colonial placemen would not defend colonial rights againt a minister bent on destroying them.[47] Rather, they would assist him in his efforts. When men like Otis and Samuel Adams realized during the summer of 1765 that the Treasury planned to increase substantially and noticeably the number of Americans who owed part of their economic livelihood and political influence to Whitehall, they had no doubts about what Grenville expected to gain from these appointments. And had they doubted his intentions before, they could not any longer once they learned the identity of the distributor for Massachusetts, Andrew Oliver, Hutchinson's brother-in-law. In their opinion, Grenville had thrown the decisive weight of the British government onto the scales of political conflict in America, and he had done so on the side of a faction already committed to limiting popular liberties.[48] This act signaled to Adams and men like him that the most desperate form of resistance was both appropriate and necessary. They predicted—accurately, as the surviving evidence shows—that many other colonists would be willing to help distribute stamps and thus help subvert colonial liberties.[49] They also recognized that they could not passively resist the stamp tax for another reason: It would virtually execute itself. Grenville's careful choice of a stamp tax had the unanticipated effect of removing any possibility of a devisive debate among popular leaders about the best form of resistance. There was only one choice. Either they roused the people to physical resistance, or they submitted. The decision was easy. Because their practical experiences and their political ideology enabled them to see beneath Grenville's reassuring words an attempt to destroy the powers of the colonial assemblies, they could not accept the consequences of yielding.

Ironically, then, Grenville's moderate language and appointment of American distributors contributed to the popular leaders' fears of a universal conspiracy against liberty and strengthened their resolve to resist the stamp tax.[50] Some questions linger: Were their suspicions accurate? Was Grenville consciously trying to deceive colonists about his political purposes? Without question, Grenville did not discuss his maneuvers to avoid establishing a precedent for prior consultation with colonists on issues of parliamentary taxation. In his meetings with the agents, he did try to avoid disputes over constitutional issues. He did not detail the excesses of the assemblies in public, nor did he openly discuss concerns he might have felt about their political ideology. Moreover, he did not call the agents' attention to the fact that a stamp tax would execute itself, though he did point this out in the House. His reticence on these matters had the effect of obscuring somewhat his convictions about the seriousness of the political situation in the colonies and about the necessity of establishing parliamentary supremacy. There can be no doubt that he was trying to do precisely that. Yet his motives for doing so probably were inspired not by a desire to deceive, but rather by a wish to foreclose a divisive and, he believed, an ultimately pointless debate. Grenville was sure that the molasses and stamp duties would collect themselves, confirming in the process Parliament's right to raise a revenue in America when and how it chose. Continuing to raise and debate that issue could only retard the development of goodwill between the Mother Country and the colonies, so Grenville avoided discussion of some of his actions and thoughts.

Still, even if the popular leaders in the colonies saw deceit and conspiracy where there was none, they accurately perceived Grenville's political goal and were rationally apprehensive of it.[51] Grenville wanted the power of Parliament to be uncircumscribed and unchallenged, of that they were certain. Indeed, the men who had personally felt the full force of Grenville's persuasiveness were both aware of and concerned about this prospect. Ingersoll claimed, "No man sees in a stronger light than I do the dangerous tendency of admitting for a principle that the Parliament of Great Britain may tax us *ad libitum;* I view it as a gulf ready to devour." Grenville could not relieve these fears, because he could do so only by giving binding pledges that would limit Parliament's power. So he tried to make these apprehensions bearable by convincing colonists of his own moderation and concern for their interests and, by implication, of the moderation and concern of those who would follow him as First Lord. He succeeded with Ingersoll, who believed Grenville when he remarked, "We trust we shall never burden you unreasonably," and pointed out, "You find and I trust always will find an easy access to those who from their office have the principal conduct of revenue laws." The popular leaders in America, however, were unimpressed by Grenville's claim to moderation and certainly did not share his trust in the moderation of future First Lords and the reasonableness of Parliament in the years ahead. Indeed, asserted Charles Thomson, a popular leader who was a close friend of Franklin's and who understood from him that the motives behind American taxation were more political than fiscal, "When taxes are laid merely to *'settle the point of independence,'* and when the quantity of the tax depends on the caprice of those who have the superiority," the men doing the taxing "will doubtless lay it heavier to bring down the spirits or weaken the power of those who claim independence" and thus leave Americans with no incentive to work or save. What impressed all these men, not just Thomson, was that they had no assurance that Parliament would not, say, tax their land and use the money for purposes other than defense. As Lord North, who had served at the Treasury during 1763– 1765, later observed in Parliament, the colonists truly did not have any such assurance. "In point of right," North noted, "there is no difference [between internal and external taxes]; in point of operation, there certainly is: external might not go further, internal might." Thus, he concluded, Americans were understandably concerned in 1765 that they might not have "the perpetual enjoyment of their assemblies."[52] Given the popular leaders' knowledge of Parliament's constant search for new sources of revenue in England and their notions about the ways the Treasury dominated politics there with patronage, the Americans' concerns were utterly rational and their suspicions of the motives behind Grenville's words and actions completely understandable.

Aids to Resistance

Grenville not only strengthened colonists' resolve to resist, but he also unwittingly assisted the popular leaders' cause. The First Lord's insistence on keeping the molasses duty at threepence irritated merchants who normally would have inclined toward conservatism. His acquiescence in the act that placed harsh restrictions on colonial currency alienated an even broader segment of the population. His commitment to requiring coastal vessels to take out cockets describing their cargoes infuriated those merchants, masters, and planters who were involved in the intracolonial trade.[53] All these groups had petitioned against the administration's policies during 1764–1765. None had received any satisfaction. Moreover, their frustration must have been increased by their knowledge that customs officers in the colonies objected as strenuously to these policies as they did. It is hard to believe that men like John Temple, Benjamin Hallowell, and Joseph Harrison hid their opinion that threepence was too high a duty on molasses from the merchants they consorted with in New England.[54] And when masters swore at the documents they had to complete to obtain cockets, customs officers probably responded to these oaths by complaining about the intricate records Grenville was requiring them to keep on ships, their destinations, and the details of their cargoes.[55] If Grenville did not listen either to people in trade or to the officers assigned to regulate it, how could he be convinced of imperfections in the system? Of what value was such a minister's assurances that Britain's self-interest would prevent Parliament from overburdening the colonies? In a situation such as this, popular disturbances might serve a useful purpose by calling attention to the depth of discontent with administrative policies.

The same sorts of frustrations must have built up rapidly in conservative circles over the impending stamp tax. Grenville had been apprised of the widespread opposition on political and economic grounds to this tax, but he had disregarded it. Furthermore, the First Lord had convinced the House that it should not even receive the moderate petition from Massachusetts Bay against the Stamp Act. His explanation for this, preserving the practice of the House, was to conservatives both inappropriate, considering the special circumstances of the case, and dangerous, because it appeared to leave colonists with no way to voice opposition to a tax prior to an unsuccessful or burdensome execution of it.[56] Finally, some merchants in Boston may well have heard about Temple and Hallowell's doubts about the wisdom of a stamp tax.[57] Again, the logic of the situation pointed toward the one remaining form of protest. In the past, conservative elements in the colonies had either openly directed or tacitly supported riots in critical situations. By late 1765, they were prepared to do the same.

Popular leaders were soon aware that Grenville's policies had given them the chance to practice coalition politics. Accordingly, when they learned the identity of the distributors, they took steps to isolate those unfortunates from their normal allies in politics and from others in their social class. Pointed references to the "mean mercenary hirelings or parricides among ourselves, who for a little filthy lucre would at any time betray every right, liberty, and privilege of their fellow subjects" began to appear in the press.[58] In this fashion, popular politicians adopted the language of conservatives, and stood forth as the defenders of the interests of a united body politic. Such a tactic might have aroused the suspicions of the people these popular leaders usually appealed to, except that Grenville and the agents had frequently chosen as distributors traditional antagonists of the people, like Andrew Oliver in Massachusetts, or representatives of the gentry. The attack on old foes thus allayed, at least for a time, popular suspicions. When normal tensions did return, and the different groups in the coalition against the Stamp Act began to remember their attitudes toward each other, the popular leaders found themselves in the advantageous position of being mediators between the conservative classes and the crowd, a position they would skillfully maintain and manipulate throughout the revolutionary period.

Grenville also inadvertently handed popular leaders some potent weapons they could attack the distributors with. The wisdom of hindsight makes it incredible that the First Lord could not guess that demagogues in the colonies might accuse the distributors of conniving at the stamp tax for their own gain. He had certainly felt that American smugglers were capable of making similar charges to serve their own purposes. In early 1765, he had refused to name John Temple's brother collector of the customs at Salem because he believed people would accuse Temple of forcing out the popular John Cockle to make room for his relative. This might, as Whately explained, "expose [Temple] to reflections which, however unjust, might rather diminish than increase your authority, and might at this juncture be prejudicial both to you and the service."[59] Perhaps Grenville was confident that colonists would know that the distributors had not favored the tax, and thus demagogues would not dare make these charges. Perhaps he believed that if the charges were made, they would be so palpably false that they would discredit the accusers rather than the accused. Whatever the reason, the First Lord certainly overlooked or underestimated the extent to which conspiracy against the people for personal gain had become a familiar and almost unquestioned way for Americans to explain certain men's political behavior.

Grenville, moreover, evidently did not anticipate, or else shrugged off, the political impact of charges that the distributors had betrayed their country's liberties. Certain that self-interest would compel colonists to pay the tax, he probably was equally certain that Americans would recognize that these men were in fact the most effective protectors of their interests. As Ingersoll recalled later, when men assumed in England that the colonists would have to submit to the stamp tax, friends of his, among them probably Whately, had argued that he would "be able to assist [the colonists] with the construction and application of the Act better than a stranger not acquainted with

[American] methods of transacting." For this reason, Ingersoll believed, "Upon my honor I thought I should be blamed if I did not accept the appointment."[60] Grenville and his colleagues must have made similar assumptions about colonial reactions. If they thought at all about accusations that might be hurled at the distributors, the men at the Treasury doubtlessly believed that these charges would soon be revealed as mischievous and false.

Exposing distributors to verbal and written abuse was, however, the least injurious consequence of Grenville's decision to name native colonists to these places. By doing so, he was inadvertently "giving the colonists a lever by which to pry [the distributors] loose from their positions." As Edmund and Helen Morgan observed, "If [they] had been Englishmen, strangers to the country, with no property or interests invested in it, they could have withstood the pressure of the populace much longer."[61] Moreover, the forced resignations were only the immediate results of Grenville's decision, not the most important ones ultimately. Having once convinced colonists that a conspiracy involving fellow Americans had existed, the popular leaders had less trouble convincing them in the years after 1765 that it still existed. Having once demonstrated their power to punish the domestic enemies of the people, they could more easily intimidate into silence those who doubted the accuracy of their analysis and encourage into resistance those who were timid. Having once proved their power over the crowd, they could plausibly tell conservatives that only they could restrain its excesses. And having once proved themselves as the people's friends, they could continue to expect the benefit of the doubt from the crowd. No patriot leader ever described the events of 1766–1776 as predetermined, and none executed political maneuvers during that period with unquestioning confidence in the outcome. In retrospect, however, it is clear that in the politics of resistance and revolution, success begat success.

"The Author of all the Troubles"

In retrospect, it is also clear that Grenville was closer to being "the author of all the troubles in America" than many historians have believed. Yet he was not the sort of author that Sir William Baker described. Grenville did not overlook obvious signs of potential trouble in the colonies, nor did he hide them from the House.[62] Rather, it was Grenville's perception that Britain would have difficulties governing the colonies in the future that inspired him to attempt reforms that would both extract a revenue from America and help establish the colonies' political subordination. Ironically, it was his success at devising and executing such reforms that brought on disaster. Grenville carefully left colonial demagogues and smugglers only one avenue of resistance, an avenue he was confident they would be unable or unwilling to take. Unaware of the details of recent political and economic developments in the colonies, he did not realize that he had forced into a corner men who were both able and willing to take desperate measures. In an earlier America, his schemes probably would have succeeded. Even in 1765, the enticement of the underdistributorships attracted applications from men who subsequently supported the cause of American liberty. In October of that year, William Samuel Johnson represented Connecticut at the Stamp Act Congress. Four months earlier, though, he had written Ingersoll, "Since we are doomed to stamps and slavery, and must submit, we hear with pleasure that your gentle hand will fit on our chains and shackles, who I know will make them set easy as possible." This flattery was followed by an offer to help Ingersoll put the chains on Johnson's neighbors at Stratford.[63] Johnson, like Ingersoll and Grenville, had not realized that a desperate struggle was about to begin. When it came, he chose the side moving toward rebellion. Yet Johnson's apostasy should not obscure the possibility that concessions on some other matters might have fatally divided the coalition against the Stamp Act. William Smith of New York advised in May 1765 that the stamp tax should be followed "by the redress of the grievances of the provinces in all other respects." This would, Smith said, "sweeten the late impalatable draught, and art may prevent the evils which force must inevitably bring on."[64] But Grenville always found persuasive fiscal and political reasons to avoid making such concessions and thus remained inflexible on these points.

Unsurprisingly, after the King removed him from office, Grenville immediately used what influence he had against concessions to colonial demands. In early 1766, it was essential to him that "every gentleman of worth and honor [attend Parliament] in a crisis which will probably decide on the future happiness and welfare of the Kingdom much more than any other thing which I have ever seen" and that all resist yielding to American protests "upon this great occasion when the sovereignty and very being of this Kingdom is at stake." The particular gentleman of worth and honor to whom Grenville was writing, John Hamilton, did attend Parliament and did vote against repeal of the Stamp Act.[65] The majority who sat in the House, however, remained unpersuaded by the former First Lord's arguments, to the surprise of Grenville and his followers, even though several supporters of repeal conceded that some cogent points had been made on Grenville's side.[66] When it became apparent that the House would not vote to enforce the Stamp Act,

Jenkinson, at Grenville's behest, tried to avert repeal by moving an amendment to substitute *explain and amend* for *repeal*. What specific amendments the two men had in mind are unknown. Benjamin Franklin believed they "meant to reduce it to a stamp on cards and dice only, and that merely to keep up the claim of right."[67] If Franklin was correct, Grenville clearly was willing to sacrifice a revenue for the right, because Whately had long before warned him that "no duty is so open to frauds" in England as that on cards and that "frauds may be more easily committed in the colonies."[68] Indeed, Henry Seymour Conway, who evidently was privy to the same information that Franklin was, made sure that all the members understood this, sarcastically saying *before* Jenkinson offered his amendment, "If the tax is confined to cards and dice, the object will indeed be a small one."[69] This point did not trouble Grenville and his followers. As Jenkinson explained, Parliament may "have asserted our right," but "a right which is never properly exercised is no right at all, and yet this seems to be the doctrine of many of those who have joined in the assertion of it."[70] Grenville and his friends wished to preserve that right effectually, so much so that two of them told an American, "They would cheerfully vote for a repeal next year if the Americans would tamely submit to the Act." Another of Grenville's friends informed the House that he would be satisfied if the members "cut down the Stamp Act not merely to a frigate but even to a single plank . . . [so long as] some vestige remains of our power and authority over America."[71] The arguments were to no avail: The House rejected Jenkinson's motion and voted for repeal by a substantial majority.[72]

Debates in Parliament during the years following repeal saw the same pattern repeat itself. Grenville would make cogent arguments, predict dire consequences, fulminate against the current administration's policies (usually its lack of policies), and occasionally make concrete proposals, such as his suggestion of a test act that would require American officials and assemblymen to swear to Parliament's sovereignty before they took office. The House would listen, more often attentively than not, for Grenville became during the late 1760s "the ablest man of business in the House of Commons, and, though not popular, of great authority there from his spirit, knowledge, and gravity of character."[73] Then the members would reject his proposals and support the administration. Toward the end of the decade, Grenville became sufficiently fatalistic about his situation to suggest to the House, "Let us follow the advice of the poet: laugh when we must, be candid when we can, and vindicate the measures of every administration."[74] Finally, he devoted himself to complaining about the lack of any plan for America, without suggesting any of his own. When Lord North, his former colleague at the Treasury, replied with a cutting allusion to men who called for a plan without having any themselves, Grenville snapped back that it was North's duty to propose a plan, not his, and, besides, he had received no encouragement to form one.[75] He returned to this theme shortly before his death, in one of his last comments on "the question of America (which has come every year before the House, neither for our honor or entertainment)." On 26 April 1770, Grenville reminded the House, "I have ever said, I wish to see a plan and a system," adding, "I framed a plan. I framed a system."[76] He did not live to see the ultimate results of that plan and that system.

At the high tide of early 1765, Grenville could not see disaster ahead. At that time, Whately flatly asserted, "No period of our history can within the same compass boast of so many measures with regard to the colonies founded upon knowledge, formed with judgment, and executed with vigor, as has distinguished the beginning of His Majesty's reign."[77] Obviously Grenville hoped, probably he expected, that his tenure at the Treasury would be remembered in this way. Indeed, as he reflected on his administration, soon after his dismissal, he reminded Robert Nugent, "We have often fought and may I add conquered together." He then added, "I have the best reason to think that no crime except that of success which is common to me and my friends has ever been imputed to us."[78] He was soon to discover otherwise. The most favorable epitaph for his approach to colonial policy, therefore—and indeed the most just one—is not Whately's, but Lord Hervey's observation on another spectacular failure in eighteenth-century British political history, Walpole's plans for reforming the excise taxes in 1733. After surveying the contemporary criticism of Walpole's decision, Hervey remarked, "Those . . . who accuse Sir Robert Walpole of want of penetration in not foreseeing the difficulties into which this scheme would lead him, are of that class (and a numerous one it is) who imagine that every event is so little casual, that whatever is, could not have been otherwise; and of course, with equal folly, impute all success to prudence, and all disappointments to indiscretion."[79]

Appendix A

Henry McCulloh's "General Thoughts"

Without question, the author of "General thoughts with respect to such regulations as are humbly conceived to be necessary in America and in the islands in the West Indies lately ceded to us by France" was Henry McCulloh. The proposal of issuing exchequer bills of union that would be secured by duties collected in America was uniquely his. He made a similar suggestion to Halifax in 1751 and 1755, to Grenville in October 1763, and to Rockingham in 1765. No one else ever broached this particular plan to a minister during this period.[1]

Precisely dating "General thoughts" is more difficult. The reference in its title to territories "lately ceded to us by France" reveals that he wrote the paper after George III and Louis XV signed the definitive treaty of peace on 10 February 1763.[2] McCulloh's suggestion that Parliament should lower the molasses duty from sixpence to a lower figure proves that he wrote "General thoughts" before 4 April 1764, when George III approved the American Revenue Act of 1764, which reduced the duty to threepence. The only other clue in the document to its date is McCulloh's use of *lately* in the title, which implies he was writing soon after the formal cessions. How soon, however, is uncertain. In eighteenth-century usage, *lately* could cover a period of several months.[3]

Fortunately, a memorandum from McCulloh to Jenkinson titled "Remarks with respect to the collectors of the customs in North America" has survived.[4] It suggests that Grenville received "General thoughts" in July 1763, at or about the same time that he received McCulloh's drafts of bills creating exchequer bills of union and levying stamp taxes on Americans.[5] McCulloh followed his usual practice and failed to date "Remarks." Still, establishing the date of composition for "Remarks" is relatively easy, if one keeps in mind that from July until mid-November 1763, McCulloh was in regular, personal contact with Jenkinson and other officials at Whitehall.[6]

On 14 July, the Treasury asked the customs commissioners for a list of all their officers serving in the colonies. That same day, Grenville and his colleagues ordered the commissioners to comment within a week on the questions Jenkinson had asked them on 21 May. There is no explicitly stated connection between these orders and "Remarks," but it seems unlikely that McCulloh would have expended his time making pointed comments on how much money collectors in the colonies made, how they performed their duties, and whether they were in residence, had he not known that the Treasury wanted this sort of information as soon as possible. He compiled the information, wrote "Remarks," and sent it to Jenkinson as quickly as he could. Doubtlessly, he hoped to win the Treasury's favor by supplying the men there with the desired information before the commissioners bestirred themselves, for he tacked on to the end of "Remarks" a request that "Mr. McCulloh hopes . . . to be appointed Collector of Philadelphia or any other collection now executed by deputy, which [he conceives] is contrary to law."

In this case, though, haste made waste. In his memorandum, McCulloh had observed that "Mr. Kennedy is Collector of New York, worth upwards of £600 *per annum*. He has resided there for several years, but has not regularly transmitted his accounts." At that moment, McCulloh was unaware that Kennedy would never mend his ways; he had died on 14 June 1763. By 30 July, that news had reached England. On that day, Sir Gilbert Elliot wrote to Jenkinson and reminded him that both Newcastle and Bute had promised that Kennedy's successor would be Andrew Elliot, Sir Gilbert's brother.[7] Between his contacts with Jenkinson, his personal attendance at Whitehall, and his sources at the customs house, who had told him New York's accounts arrived irregularly, McCulloh must have heard about Kennedy's death as soon as Elliot did. Had he known about this vacancy when he wrote "Remarks," McCulloh, who hoped to be appointed to "any . . . collection now executed by deputy," would have asked for New York. But by late July, "Remarks" was already in Jenkinson's hands.

This is of paramount importance in dating "General thoughts." When McCulloh asked for a job in "Remarks," he noted,

> If any regulations are made with respect to coast cockets in America, the appointment of an officer as supervisor and comptroller of the entries and coast cockets in the charter governments might be a good and effectual means of obstructing that trade. And Mr. McCulloh humbly apprehends that from the knowledge and experience he has had in business he could (if appointed in that character) be of great use to the Crown and to the public.

This passage reveals that during July some officials were considering whether to use cockets to regulate the coasting trade in North America. As was discussed above, it is highly unlikely that this idea originated either with the customs commissioners or at the Treasury. No unofficial adviser of the Treasury proposed this scheme other than McCulloh. It is therefore probable that the Treasury was at that time considering his proposal. Moreover, a comparison of "General thoughts" with "Remarks" reveals that "General thoughts" was out of its author's hands when he began "Remarks."

McCulloh devoted part of "General thoughts" to a description of the offices he thought should be created to execute his suggestions. New officers, he pointed out, would be needed to administer the bills of union, and a Treasury Remembrancer would be helpful in sending all revenue accounts to Britain. In "Remarks," he again stressed the usefulness of a Treasury Remembrancer and, in addition, recommended the creation of a supervisor of coastal cockets in the charter colonies. If McCulloh had realized that such an office might be helpful to the public and lucrative to himself before he sent "General thoughts" to the Treasury, he would have added this recommendation to the paper. Certainly no considerations of style or construction would have deterred him from attaching an appendix making such a recommendation to "General thoughts": That paper is organized in a ramshackle, haphazard fashion. Moreover, the section concerning the new offices was near the end, so he could have inserted his addition without much recopying. More important, by the time he wrote "Remarks," McCulloh had come to believe that a supervisor of coastal cockets would make more money than any collectorship, for he told Jenkinson that he would rather be named supervisor than collector of any port in North America. His avarice would have overcome any reluctance to tamper with the structure of "General thoughts." The position of supervisor was an afterthought of McCulloh's, a recognition that he might profit directly from his scheme, which occurred to him while the First Lord of the Treasury was studying "General thoughts."

One mystery seemingly remains. If McCulloh was so eager to be made a supervisor of coastal cockets in the charter colonies, why did he not strengthen his petition with a reminder that he had suggested the adoption of that plan? Does this omission indicate that the original idea was not his? When answering these questions, one should remember that McCulloh asked on 12 December 1763 to be appointed, "if a stamp duty take place, . . . supervisor and comptroller of the [stamp] distributors' accounts" without mentioning that he had made the original suggestion to impose stamp duties on colonists and then worked at Grenville's request for months on drafts of a bill.[8] McCulloh's modesty in this case probably stemmed from a reluctance to ask for office as a reward for advice until he could be certain that the Treasury would act upon his suggestions. The phrasing of his 12 December 1763 letter—"*if* a stamp duty takes place"—indicates that he was not then fully confident that such a tax would ever be enacted. Basing his claim for office on personal virtues, on "great application," and "knowledge and experience . . . in business" seemed safer. When he did convince himself that his proposal was going to bear fruit, McCulloh was not backward about claiming a share of the harvest as a reward for sowing the seed. "As I apprehend a stamp duty is to take place in America," he then wrote Grenville, "I most humbly hope Your Honor will be pleased to appoint me inspector and surveyor and comptroller of the stamp duties in Virginia, and such other colonies as may be put under the view of the said officer." He reminded the First Lord, "I have had some share in planning out . . . this affair and most humbly hope that I shall have the honor of having some share in the execution of the plan."[9]

Initially, McCulloh was as uncertain about the fate of his proposed regulations of the American coastal trade as he was about the stamp duties. His language in "Remarks" exposes his doubts in July 1763: "*If* any regulations are made with respect to coast cockets in America," he wanted to be supervisor in the charter colonies, but "*if* no such regulations are made," he would accept with pleasure an appointment as a collector of the customs. Yet when the commissioners advised the Treasury on 16 September to adopt McCulloh's plan to use cockets to "prevent . . . the circulation of smuggled commodities in the British colonies, or from thence to Great Britain," McCulloh never renewed his written petition to be made supervisor. He may well have scouted this possibility verbally during his meetings on the stamp tax with Grenville and Jenkinson in October. If he did so, he quickly discovered that the First Lord had no intention of creating such an office. Grenville hoped to avoid enlarging the customs service in America. One of the chief attractions of McCulloh's scheme to him was no doubt the hope that it would enable Britain to check illicit trade without forcing the Crown to appoint more officers and pay more salaries. As a result, the inventor of the plan did not benefit directly from it.

General thoughts with respect to such
Regulations as are humbly Conceived
to be necessary in America and in the Islands in
the West Indies lately ceded to us by France[10]

The regulating the Trade of America so as to prevent the Clandestine Importation into the Charter Government of Goods and Merchandize of different kinds which are afterwards shipp'd from thence Coastways to all his Majesties other Colonies, is, as is humbly conceived, the first great Object to be taken into Consideration.

Before the late war the French introduced into Cape Breton Great quantities of East India Piece goods as also Tea Coffee and Chocolate and many of their home Manufactures as Cambricks Coarse Linnens, woolen Stockings, and several other Species of Goods.

The Dutch likewise often sent Sloops or small vessells to Newfoundland or at least to the Banks where the fishery was Carried on, with various goods, which they disposed of to the Masters of Ships belonging to Rhode Island and to the other Charter Governments which goods after being landed were again Shipp'd Coastways to his Majesties other Colonies.

I acknowledge that it will be difficult if not Impossible to prevent the people of Rhode Island etc. from Carrying on a Clandestine Trade with the french and Dutch so far as it relates to their own Consumption, but such regulations may be made as shall prevent from Shipping Contraband Goods Coastways to his Majesties Southern Colonies, in which Goods Clandestinly purchased from the French and Dutch are principally Consumed.

Therefore, what I would humbly offer to the Consideration of the Administration is, that by a Law Enacted by the Parliament of Great Britain for that purpose all merchants or Traders shall be Obliged to report at the Custom houses in the respective Colonies the different Species or Qualities and Quantities of Goods imported from Great Britain, and that when such Goods are Shipp'd from One Colony to another it shall be Expressly mentioned in the Cockets which are made out by the Collectors, what part or proportion of the said Goods so imported from Great Britain are Shipp'd Coastways by them. This is the method taken at the Customhouses in Great Britain to prevent frauds in Debenture Goods; but in America it is Absolutely necessary for the preventing of Smuggling that all goods whatsoever should be Subjected to this regulation.

And if the Cockits are defective in their particular and do not shew that the Goods Shipped Coastways have been imported from Great Britain or from such other places as are allowed of by Law, the said Goods shall be liable to be Seized and Condemned According to the usual form.

The Amount of the Goods clandestinly imported into America have been, by men Acquainted with the Trade Computed at upwards of Five hundred thousand Pounds Sterling per Annum. But if the Coasting Vessels there were put under the regulations above proposed, no great Quantity of prohibited goods could be Carried to the Southern Colonies, In which the far greater part of the said Goods are at present Consumed.

The people in the Charter Governments likewise import Considerable quantities of French Sugar and Molasses for which they Seldom pay any duty, Yet after they have made Rum from this French Molasses They Ship it Coastways, as if they had regularly Paid the Duty. Previous, therefore, to their Shipping any Rum or Sugar etc. Coastways to the Southern Colonys they ought to be Obliged to take out Cockets, and to prove to the Satisfaction of the Collector, That they had paid the Duties at Importation. This would have a good Effect in preventing the said Clandestine Trade.

And provided the duty upon French Molasses was reduced from 6d. to a penny per Gallon it would bring a Revenue to the Crown of Upwards of £12,000 Sterling per Annum, the present high duty being the great motive for the Contraband Trade.

His Majesties Subjects in America and in the west Indies are Intitled to import wine for their own use from Madeira the Western Islands and the Canaries only but if liberty were granted them to import Wines from Portugal Spain and Italy also Duty of four pounds per Ton would I apprehend, raise on the Continent of America and in the West Indies a very considerable Revenue.

But in this Case also, when these wines are Shipp'd Coastways there ought to be proper care taken to regulate the Cockets; which will always be Effectual means of Obstructing, if not preventing all Clandestine Trade.

There are many other Commodities imported into America which may be made liable to a Duty but the people settled there, Especially in the Charter Governments, have always given great Opposition to any Act of this nature passed here; and as they Conceive very wrong notions of their privileges it is humbly Submitted, whether it may not be for the Service of the Crown, and of the Publick, not to make too Sudden a change in their Course of Commerce. But in all Events the regulating their Coast Cockets is Absolutely necessary, as it will Obstruct their Clandestine Trade and Consequently increase the Exportation of our home Manufactures and other goods usually Shipp'd from this Kingdom and may also be the means of raising a Fund for the use of America.

The want of a fund Applicable to the use of America produced many and fatal Effects before the Commencement of the late war and the Establishing a new fund in America will be found Absolutely necessary for the relief of the Mother Country. The Settlement of new Colonies even with the Utmost Economy will be Attended with great Expence. If a fund be created for the use of the Plantations and if there are not such Bills of Credit introduced for a medium in Trade as shall Equally pass Current in all the Colonies on the Continent of America for the same

Value the Public I humbly Conceive will not receive any Considerable Advantage therefrom, as Bills of Credit now in Use in One Colony will not pass current in another.

For Instance, the Old Bills of Currency which still remain in Rhode Island and Connecticut, will not pass in New York or Pensilvania, but at a very high discount even to near half the Nominal Value of the Bill nor will the Bills of Credit in North Carolina pass in Virginia for less value than 35£ percent discount so that this course of Business, if the Dutys paid into the hands of the Collectors of the respective Colonies were to be brought into one fund and Applied to the Charge of the New Colonies to be Settled in Louisiana or to any other use that the Administration should think proper there would be a loss of more than one third of the whole value in bringing it into Sterling. The necessity therefore of Introducing one Uniform currency or medium of trade in all the Colonies, is self-evident. It will be said that all the Dutys may be paid in Sterling money; but this cannot be done without repealing all those Laws which have been made for Introducing paper Bills of Credit.

The Governments in the respective Colonies have always pleaded necessity for Issuing their Bills of Currency; and that they could not Carry on their Trade and Commerce without them; but the Method they took in Introducing them was unjust and fraudulent as they never Allowed any Interest upon the Bills.

Now if it is thought Agreeable to the Wisdom of the Administration not only to create a Fund for the use of America, but also to Introduce Bills or Cash Notes (which may be Entituled the Bills of Union) to pass as a Medium in Trade in all the Colonies on the Continent of North America and to Carry an Interest of 4 percent (which Interest might be paid from the duties on merchandize imported there) such Bills would in all respects be of much more Service to the Public and to the Trading Interest than the Bills of Currency which the Colonies Issue for themselves. For as was above observed, the Colonies do not allow Interest upon the paper Bills of Credit which they Issue and from that cause and from often Issuing too many of them, They have greatly depreciated their value, to the loss of the British Merchants trading there.

But if Bills of Union are Introduced at 4£ percent Interest and that under the Sanction of Parliament They pass as a Medium in Trade—it cannot be thought that they will alter in their value or be depreciated in the manner that the Bills in the Colonies have formerly been.

Another great advantage to the Public, and what will prove of Infinite Service in Relief to the Mother Country, is, That as the Government may be put to great Expence in the Settlement of new Colonies, in the regulating and keeping up a Militia, and in making presents to the Indian nations, a fund should be raised from the Duties on wine, Rum, Sugar, Molasses, etc.—which at a moderate Computation will Amount to upwards of Thirty thousand pounds Sterling per Annum. Our Government could Issue in Bills of Union upwards of five hundred thousand pounds Sterling on the Credit of this Fund, which would Enable the Administration here to take many great and Commendable Steps for the General wellbeing and Settlement of Our Colonies without putting this Kingdom to any Considerable Expence. These funds might even be afterwards Enlarged in relief of the mother Country.

The Colonies from their partial Interests and Connections, will give all the Opposition in their power to this or any other matter which can be proposed for the General Good of the Subject. But if paper Bills of Credit are at present Absolutely necessary as a Medium in Trade, the issuing of Bills of union under the Sanction of parliament will as is above Observed be of infintely more Service to the Public and to the Trading Interest Than that of allowing the Colonies to Issue Bills of Currency as a Tender in Law amongst themselves. By which and the frauds Committed by them, They have often injured the Trading Interest of this Kingdom.

Some new regulations with respect to the Indian Trade, and the keeping up a friendly Correspondence with them is absolutely necessary, but this is a Matter of so mixed and complicated a nature, that the more it is Considered, the more difficulties will Occur in forming or planning any Law here, for the General direction of this Trade. But, as I humbly Conceived if each of the Colonies were by Law Authorized to nominate a Commissioner to Attend to Indian Affairs, and that such persons so named by the respective Colonies were directed to meet once or oftener in every year at a proper place to be Appointed for that purpose and that the said Commissioners or a Majority of them were impowered to regulate the said Trade, and that the regulations made by them were to have the force of a Law with respect to the Traders, I humbly Conceive many happy Consequences would follow, and a friendly Correspondence be Constantly kept up with the Indians, but in all Cases whatsoever the Regulations made by the Commissioners should not be binding, nor Continue in force longer than until His Majesties pleasure should be known thereupon.

It may be further proper to Observe, that if this Course is pursued the Colonies may be Easily brought to Contribute to the charge which will necessarily Attend the keeping up a Correspondence with the Indians. But on the other hand, if the Course of the Indian Trade is regulated by a Law made here, it will throw the whole of the Expence upon the

Crown, as the colonies will not readily Contribute to any matter wherein they have not some share of the direction.

If the above regulation take place, it will be very proper and necessary to appoint a Treasurers Remembrancer, who ought to reside in America and whose duty and Office should be to bring all the General Accounts of the Revenue there into one view, and Afterwards transmitt them here to the Right Honourable the Lords Commissioners of his Majesties Treasury.

And if Bills of Union are Introduced in America it will be also proper to Appoint a Clerk of the Checks, and that he have the Types and a Counterpart of the Checks along with him, in Order to distinguish false from true Bills.

The Course of the Auditors, Receivers, and Accountants proceedings in America ought to be Carefully examined, as there are many Openings left for Encroachments both upon the Crown and on the Subject. How far the Auditor's patent Intitles him to any direction or Management of the finances in the new Colonies, is Submitted.

With respect to the Islands lately ceded to us in the West Indies, I shall only pray leave to Observe, that if Dominica is made a free Port, and that small dutys are paid upon the Introduction of Rum, Sugar and Molasses, and such other Goods as may be permitted to enter there, a Considerable Revenue for the use of America may be raised thereupon and that it may be the means of Enlarging our Trade and Navigation.

If it is thought proper to lay any of the above matters before Our Representatives in Parliament, They will require to be put into a different dress.

Nathaniel Ware

I have described the career of Nathaniel Ware and the impact of his opinions and investigations upon Grenville at greater length elsewhere.[1] Still, it seems appropriate here to discuss briefly Ware's fate after he turned in his 22 August 1763 report to the Treasury.

No document describing Grenville's response to Ware's letter has survived. Probably none ever existed, for the First Lord's usual way of dealing with reports was to read them, digest their contents, and file them away without notation or comment. And there is no sign Grenville ever gave Ware another assignment after he completed his inquiries into the molasses trade. That is not surprising: There was no other colonial business pending that Ware's particular expertise could assist with, and thus his usefulness as adviser and investigator was at an end. Moreover, the reward that he received for his services took him out of the ambit of colonial policy and, indeed, out of London.

Grenville did not exempt Ware from the Treasury order of 25 July 1763. It would have been surprising had he done so, for he was besieged by petitions for exemptions by men with strong political connections, and any exceptions might have overturned the whole policy.[2] So as the end of 1763 approached, Ware was finally confronted with the decision he had evaded for years. He would have to return to Boston or lose his place. He could not bring himself to return. On 3 January 1764, the customs commissioners informed the Treasury that he had been disciplined, presumably for his failure to go to America. Eight weeks later, the Treasury signed the warrant of Benjamin Hallowell as comptroller at Boston, "in the room of Nathaniel Ware, resigned."[3]

But Ware's story does have a happy ending. Although the mechanics of the exchange are unclear, probably through Grenville's intervention and with the concurrence of Halifax, who controlled appointments to the office in question, he was made British counsul at Málaga. It was a job ideally suited for a man with a knowledge of trade and commercial regulations, and a location perfectly chosen for someone who suffered in cold weather. Ware did not enjoy his good fortune for long; he died at Málaga in 1767.[4] Still, he did have the pleasure of living his last years in a post both profitable and important and in a place with a warm climate, far from the New England winters and the vengeful colleagues and colonists he had tried so hard and for so long to escape. That he succeeded in escaping was due in part to the following letter.

22 Aug 1763[5]

Sir

I find upon Enquiry that ye Importation of foreign Molasses into America has increased greatly during the War to the Amount, it is sayd, of Sixty thousand Hogsheads annually: five times the quantity I had mentioned upon another occassion, when, without the least view to a Tax, any random guess, which I took care should be within the Truth, was sufficient for my Purpose.

However the above conjecture as to quantity being too vague to depend upon, I have endeavoured to ascertain the Number of distilleries at present on that continent; & I find in Nova-Scotia 2—in New-Hampshire 1—in Massachusetts-Bay 64—in Rode-Island & Connecticut upwards of 40—in New-York & the Jerseys 4—in Pennsylvania 6—(those of ye Southward are many but too inconsiderable to be mentioned)—in ye whole 117 distilleries working off, at a medium between 100 and 550 Hogsheads each, 38625 Hogsheads Molasses annually.

When the great & universal consumption of Rum amongst these People in their Fisheries, Navigation, Seamen, Laborers, the Indian Supply, the Exportation to NfoLand, guinea, & sometimes even to Ireland are considered, the above quantity, besides ye usual Importation from our own Islands for use of the better Sort of People only, seems not to exceed what may be supposed necessary.

But beside what goes to the [?] there is a farther consumption of Molasses in Beer & in their Food, thro' out all that continent, to the amount of five thousd Hogsheads more than is sayd to be imported from all the British Islands, so that, if our calculations be Just, the foreign only must exceed 43625 Hds.

There has always been a considerable Charge attending the Importation; first, about one peny Sterl. to the officer for Connivance, then a provincial Impost in, I believe, all the Colonies: & in 1758 the Massachusetts-Bay, a People of all others the most concerned in this Article, ventured to raise a former Excise on the Home consumption of Rum from 4 to 8 pence currency, that is, from 3 pence to 6 pence sterl. p^r gallon. this Excise, after one years Experience, was continued for the next; & afterwards renewed for two years more.

The old duty therefore of 6 pence sterl. on foreign Molasses may very well be exacted, provided all those provincial Impositions are taken off. otherwise that Trade must totally fail.

Now should this last be the Intention, beside the difficulty of forcing a whole People to a Sudden Change of an article of so universal a consumption, it must ruin the Provinces more immediatly concerned, & greatly distress the others. for where shall they all find a market for their Lumber? at present any of them could probably supply all ye Wst Indies.

did the Molasses or Rum of our own Islands, or any other article of their Produce lye on Hand, even at a much higher Price than in any of the foreign Islands; or were not ours abundantly supplyd with Lumber, or whatever else ye continent affords, it were indeed something: but this is so far from being the case that Lumber does not in the West Indies pay the carryage thither; the Profit is made in ye Return & as to the Price of their Produce, that of Molasses the article under consideration is in our Islands from 8 to 9 pence sterl. per gallon; in the other Islands from three half pence to four pence half peny, which difference in the prime cost establishes the certainty of ye payment of the old duty on the Importation; provided, as above, all provincial Impositions are taken off.

But we contribute by this Trade to the support of the colonies of a rival Power. true, but at the same time they become thereby dependent upon us. & in case of a Rupture what use may not be made of such an advantage?

The British Molasses imported is sayd not to exceed, at present, 15 thousand Hogsheads. should a high duty be layd on the foreign only, that quantity will probably be doubled by collusion of the People in our Islands. this it seems is no more than has formerly been practiced.

Was the duty to extend to molasses only, the foreign Islands would manufacture theirs into Rum for ye use of ye continent, as in part they do already; or, which would be much ye same in the end, our own Islands would do it for them.

Should the proposed duty fall short of Expectation, (and there must, I fear, after all be a large deduction for Frauds, under the Term Leakage) there are other articles pointed out by their own assemblys which may be brought in aid. Such are—a Tonage on shipping—a duty on Sugars—an excise on Wine, Lemons, Oranges, & Limes, which may the more reasonably be adopted by Government as those Provinces are now rid of all Expense in garrisoning their Frontiers etc. I am

S^r,

22th August   with profound respect.
    1763   Your most obdt
                        & most devoted
                        humble servt
                        Nath: Ware

P.S.

as ye foregoing Information could be collected only from ye People of that country, who are extremely cautious of giving any Light into their own affairs, the various shifts & pretenses I was obliged to make use of in my Enquiry has occasioned this delay. I likewise proposed adding an account of all Impositions on Molasses and Rum thro'out the several Provinces, but applying to the Board of Trade was disappointed: either they had not those Laws, or knew not where readily to come at them, or perhaps did not think proper to give every one access to them, without a particular order.

Charles Jenkinson's Memorandum

The author of this memorandum was almost certainly Charles Jenkinson. He was the only politician at Whitehall during this period who believed that as soon as the price of labor fell in America, colonists would begin manufacturing for themselves, and no British legislation could prevent them from doing so. As he told Benjamin Hallowell on 12 January 1765, "As to the idea of [Americans] becoming manufacturers themselves, I see no reason to apprehend it at present." He continued, "Whenever they can work cheaper than the manufacturers of this country, they will become so of course."[1] So the presence of this comment in the memorandum, "it may be believed that [the colonies] will certainly engage in [manufacturing] as soon as they can, and nothing prevents them but their inability," strongly suggests that Jenkinson wrote it.

There is another clue that points toward Jenkinson. Of the men at the Treasury, he was the bluntest in private assessments of the purpose and proper functions of colonies. "The increase of our colonies," he wrote on 18 January 1765, "is certainly what we wish, but they must increase in such a way as will keep them useful to the Mother Country."[2] In the memorandum, this same sentiment was expressed with even greater bluntness. "It will also be said that this [tax] will stop their increase, but their increase is of no further benefit to this country than as it enables them to become useful to it." The choice of language and the tone of this remark are distinctively Jenkinson's.

When did Jenkinson write the memorandum? Charles R. Ritcheson has argued that it was written sometime before October 1764 and has claimed that its purpose was to convince Grenville that a colonial stamp tax was both constitutional and expedient, and thus to insure continuation of work on it during the remainder of 1764.[3] Two references in the paper indicate that Ritcheson erred. Jenkinson noted in it that "we *last year* laid a tax on foreign manufactures with a view to giving a preference to our own" in American markets (my emphasis). This could only be a reference to the alterations in the drawbacks in the Sugar Act of 1764. Jenkinson also observed that "no new tax . . . has been laid upon the colonies [since 25 Car. 2] except the post office duties and those of . . . 6 Geo. 2, which were not executed until *last year*" (my emphasis again). This comment clearly referred to the Treasury's determination to collect the molasses duty after the threepence rate went into effect after 29 September 1764. That duty was not regarded as new at the Treasury; indeed, the legal description of the Sugar Act called it "an act . . . for continuing, amending, and making perpetual" 6 Geo. 2.[4] These references to "last year" are proof that Jenkinson wrote the memorandum in 1765, not 1764.

Why did he write it? Clearly, Ritcheson's explanation is not persuasive. If Jenkinson composed it in 1765, he was writing after the Treasury had decided on 6 December 1764 to adopt Whately's plan for a stamp tax. It is unlikely, therefore, that the purpose of the memorandum was persuading Grenville to go ahead with that measure. The more likely explanation for Jenkinson's efforts is that this was part of the preparation for the parliamentary debate. There is one other possibility. This paper and Ryder's notes on the speech Grenville made on 6 February 1765 are strikingly similar not only in arguments and evidence cited, but even in some instances in phrasing: Is it possible that it was Jenkinson's record of that speech? Perhaps so, but I doubt it. Jenkinson was no novice at abstracting speeches in the House. In fact, he was quite good at it. None of his notes on other debates are as elliptical as parts of this paper are or as disorganized as the paper is as a whole. Moreover, Ryder's account reveals that Grenville used a different organizational framework than the one in this paper. In all probability, Jenkinson was drafting arguments that Grenville could use to explain and justify his decision to propose a colonial stamp tax to the House. As is frequently the case with authors as they write early drafts, he jotted down thoughts as they occurred to him. Grenville then used them as the basis of his carefully constructed speech introducing the stamp tax on 6 February 1765.

The Right of Taxing the Colonies not merely an Act of Power but a Constitutional Act of Legislation founded upon Principle and justified by Precedent.[5]

The Principle is that all who are intitled to Protection ought equally to bear the Burthen of It, and that They who have the Management of that Protection can be the only Judges of what the Burthen should be.

This acknowledged with respect to the general Powers of Legislation if it were doubted it could be shewn that no Country ever came under the Dominion of the Crown of Great Britain but that the Parliament had made Laws with respect to It. The Distinction between Laws for raising Taxes and for other Purposes absurd.

Property a less sacred Right than Liberty; Property the Creature of Society, and therefore more the Object of the Laws of Society.

Mr. Locke evidently mistook the Declarations of Parliament in favor of the Rights of Parliament to levy Taxes in Opposition of the Claims of the Crown for Declaration in favor of the People at large.

The Statute de Tallagio non concedendo says, that no Tallage or Aid shall be laid or levied by the King or his Heirs in this Realm without the good will & Assent of the Archbishops, Bishops, Earls, Barons, Knights, Burgesses and other the Freemen of the Commonality of this Realm, & the Petition of Right the 3^d of Charles the 1st, reciting this, and the other old Statutes on this Subject, declares that no Man hereafter be compelled to make or yield any Gift, Loan, Benevolence, Tax or such like Charge without common Consent by Act of Parliament: The Facts that gave Rise to this Petition sufficiently shew that it was made in Opposition to the Power claimed by the Crown and no other.

The Bill of Rights at the Revolution declares that the levying Money for, or to, the Use of the Crown by Pretence of Prerogative without Grant of Parliament for longer Time, or in other manner than the same is or shall be granted is "illegal." The Recital to this Instrument clearly expresses that the illegal Acts of Parliament gave Occasion to this Declaration.

The Idea of the Legislature of this Country is not a compleat Representation.

Upon this Principle it is the Doctrine of Parliament that every Member after he is chosen is no longer to be considered as the Representative of any particular Place but as one of the Representatives of the Dominions of the Crown of Great Britain at large.

If the Consent of all the People was necessary to impose a Tax many of the Richest Towns in England would have an equal Right with the Colonies to complain, but the Legislature of Great Britain have frequently exercised the Right of Taxing the Colonies.

By the 25 of Charles the Second.

By the Post Office Act the 9th of Queen Anne.

By the 2d of Geo. 2d. The Greenwich Hospital Act.

By the 6 of Geo 2d. The Sugar Act.

These were all considered as Taxes in the Mode of passing thro' Parliament; the Revenues arising from Them appropriated and applied as other Revenues etc. No Difference between Internal & External Taxes.

The Post Office Act, an Internal Tax.

The 19th Sect. *Posts to cross Ferries gratis,* a Proof of this.

Their Charters also shew that They are in every respect as well with regard to the Right of raising Money as every thing also subject to the Legislature of Great Britain.

The Expediency of This Act is evident; 1st from the Distresses of the Mother Country; 2dly from the Abilities of the Colonies.

Since the 25th of Charles the 2d. more than Four additional Subsidies have been imposed on this Country, and an Immense Number of Internal Taxes, and yet no new Tax has since that Time been laid upon the Colonies except the Post Office Duties and Those of the 6 of Geo. 2d. which were not executed 'till last Year.

The People of this Country amounting to about 8 Million, pay annually near £10,000,000 a Year in Taxes, that is about 25 Shillings a Head.

The People of the Colonies pay in taxes for the Expence of Their Establishments, but £150,000 per Annum; and if you consider Them as 1,800,000 of People it is at the Rate of 1s. & 8d. per Head; and if you consider the Continental Colonies alone They pay not more than 9 Pence per head.

The Common Tax in Rhode Island & Connecticut for the Expence of Their Establishment is but 2 d. in the £; but it is said the Colonies are in Debt.

The Debt of the Colonies at the End of the War amounted but to £2,097,000 of this They have already discharged £1,409,000 & there remains to be discharged but £688,000 for which Provision is made, so that the Whole will be discharged in 1769, except in the Case of New Jersey only.

From whence it is clear that the Colonies are not in Debt, and it evident from the Expeditious manner in which They have been able to discharge the Debt contracted by the War that They are able to Contribute to the Publick Burthen and have great Resources within Them.

But it may be said that the Individuals are poor, if it is meant thereby that they have Debts, it may in One Sense be true; It is the Nature of a Country that is rising into Wealth to apply all Its Cash for the Purchase of Stock, and to exert all its Credit for that Purpose, though They are not therefore rich in Money, They are rich in Stock, which are real Riches, and the proper Object of Taxation, but They want Money, This is a Consequence of the Former, but any Taxes that have hitherto been proposed will not draw any Money from Them. I believe the most sanguine Person does not expect that this Tax with what has hitherto been proposed will produce the Third Part of what must be annually sent from Great Britain to maintain the Establishments there, and not even so much as the difference between the present Military Establishment there, and that of the last Peace.

It may further be said that by imposing Taxes upon the Colonies, We shall drive Them into Manufactures This can only be true if We should impose Taxes on Manufactures and thereby make Them dearer to Them, but there is not any one Tax upon British Manufactures that are sent to the Colonies; There are Bounties given to many, and though We last Year laid a Tax on Foreign Manufactures with a View to give a Preference to Our Own, and indeed it was high time considering how much the Price of Labor is increased in this Country by the additional Load of Taxes laid upon It yet the present Tax and every other internal Tax can have no Place in this Objection as it will tend rather to increase the Price of Labor in the Colonies and diminish instead of increase Their Abilities to intermeddle with Manufactures, and as to any Threat the Colonies may fling out, that disgusted with the Proceedings of the Mother Country, They will on that Account engage in Manufactures it may be believed that They will certainly engage in Them as soon as They can and nothing prevents them but Their Inability.

It will also be said that This will stop their Increase, but Their Increase is of no further Benefit to This Country than as it enables Them to become more useful to It; Upon this Principle You ought never to tax Your Colonies; All the Advantage You have hitherto derived from Them has been commercial: It is Time to endeavor now to derive Revenue from Them likewise. They certainly ought never to be taxed so high as this Country, but That is no Reason They ought never to be taxed at all.

But it said that by this Measure You will render Their Assemblies useless; the Purport of This Objection is, that the Parliament of Great Britain ought not to exercise its full Constitutional Powers, and not to exercise Them when a proper Occasion offers, is in fact to resign Them, least You should interfere with, and diminish, the mighty Powers of the little Assembles of any One of Your Colonies; but the truth is, that the present Law does not interfere with the Powers that any of the Assemblies ever have exercised or perhaps ever can exercise: It provides for their general Defence, the Charge of which has always hitherto been borne by Great Britain, and We are going now to exercise a Power which We always had, which We have already frequently exercised, and the Discretion We use should rather be a matter of Comfort to the Colonies as it clearly points out, that where Necessity does not call upon Us, where Their own Assemblies can sufficiently answer the Purpose, We do not mean to exercise it: But if it had affected the Power of These little Legislatures I will never suppose that the immediate Protection of the Parliament of Great Britain is not more valuable, more conducive to the Security of Their Liberty and Their Propertys, than the Protection of Their own Legislatures; I speak the Language of Parliament. In the Address presented to King William against Mr. Molyneaux's Book, and the Procedings had in the Irish Parliament for that purpose; It was declared by Parliament that such Proceedings would prove fatal not only to England but to Ireland itself.

A Stamp Duty has ever been born with Complaint; It is not Subject to the Frauds to which Custom House Duties are liable, nor to the Severities of Excise. It is not a Burthen upon Trade, nor is it necessary to enter any Man's Doors for the Purpose of collecting It. The true Idea of the Tax is that the Crown has the Monopoly of the Sale of Paper for certain Purposes at a Price fixed by Law; the Profits of which are to be applied to the Publick Benefit, and there is a particular Propriety in this Tax with respect to the Colonies, for the Colonies need not and perhaps ought not to be supplied with Paper but from Great Britain; Parliament grants to the Crown the exclusive Right of selling it, and authorizes it to fix the Price.

The 25th of Charles the 2d.: certainly a Money Bill.

The Post Office Bill was certainly a Money Bill. The Resolutions voted in the Committee of Ways and Means; The Money to be produced by These appropriated to the Publick Service, and for carrying on the War against France; The Bill much controverted, the present Objection never taken.

The 6th of George 2d. certainly a Money Bill; It was voted in a Committee, and the House rejected a Petition against it in Consideration that it was a Money Bill.

Notes

Notes to Introduction

1. Sir Lewis Namier, *England in the Age of the American Revolution*, p. 41. Namier's image is so apt as a description of the thrust of the historical literature that Jack P. Greene used it in the title of his excellent historiographical essay "The Plunge of Lemmings: A Consideration of Recent Writings on British Politics and the American Revolution."

2. Ian R. Christie and Benjamin W. Labaree, *Empire or Independence, 1760–1776: A British-American Dialogue on the Coming of the American Revolution*, p. 26. For a similar conclusion, see P. D. G. Thomas, *British Politics and the Stamp Act Crisis: The First Phase of the American Revolution, 1763–1767*, p. 112.

3. When the Rockingham ministry lowered the duty to one penny and extended it to cover foreign and British molasses, the tax yielded over eighty thousand pounds between 1768 and 1772. It was by far the most effective means of taxing Americans devised during the Revolutionary period. See Thomas, *British Politics*, p. 271.

4. Benjamin Franklin to Joseph Galloway, 11 October 1766, *Franklin Papers*, 13:449. Throughout the text and notes, I have changed the spelling, capitalization, and punctuation of direct quotations when it was necessary to do so to conform with modern usages. All words in italics in a quotation were italicized in the original version, except where I identify italicized passages as my own. For an excellent study of the currency issue, see Joseph Ernst, *Money and Politics in America, 1755–1775: A Study in the Currency Act of 1764 and the Political Economy of Revolution*.

5. For a stimulating discussion of counterfactual hypotheses, see John M. Murrin, "The French and Indian War, the American Revolution, and the Counterfactual Hypothesis: Reflections on Lawrence Henry Gipson and John Shy."

6. Grenville's speech, 9 March 1764, *Ryder Diary*, p. 234.

7. "Plan of forts and garrisons proposed for the security of North America and the establishment of commerce with the Indians" [1763], George Grenville Papers relating to the Peace of Paris, HEHL, STG Box 12. Other copies may be found in the Shelburne Papers, WLCL, Shelburne 57:267–286 and in the Egremont Papers, PRO, P.R.O. 30/47/22, bundle 2, fols. 84–87. Its presence in these three files strongly suggests that it was taken seriously at Whitehall.

8. The Treasury to the King, 4 October 1763, PRO, T. 1/430, fol. 332; and *Regulations*, p. 94.

9. Jared Ingersoll to Gov. Thomas Fitch of Connecticut, 11 February 1765, *Ingersoll Papers*, p. 309.

10. See Richard Jackson to Fitch, 9 February 1765, *Fitch Papers*, p. 317. In an apparent reference to Whately's pamphlet, Benjamin Franklin described it as written "under [the] direction of the ministry, with a view to make us Americans easy; which shows some tenderness for us." Franklin to John Ross, 14 February 1765, *Franklin Papers*, 12:67.

11. Ingersoll to Fitch, 11 February 1765, *Ingersoll Papers*, p. 312.

12. Douglas Hay, "Property, Authority, and the Criminal Law," in Douglas Hay et al., eds., *Albion's Fatal Tree: Crime and Society in Eighteenth-Century England*, p. 51; and Grenville to William Knox, 28 July 1768, George Grenville Letterbooks, HEHL, ST 7, ii. Grenville was discussing the political situation in the colonies after the Stamp Act

crisis, but his remarks about the foundation of government are clearly references to general principles he believed applied to government at all times. For another reference to principles of government, see his remark to the House on 19 April 1769, "No government can be carried on without the will of the governed," in Cavendish Diaries, BL, Egerton MSS. 219, fol. 308. Similar statements about the power of opinion may be found in the remarks of many of his contemporaries. When Charles Lloyd, Grenville's secretary, closed his pamphlet *A defense of the majority in the House of Commons, on the question relating to general warrants,* he referred pointedly and proudly to his belief that the ministry's actions deserved the confidence and good opinion of the people (p. 66). And the anonymous compiler of *British liberties, or the free-born subject's inheritance* (London, 1766), approvingly quoted Sir William Temple's observation that *"opinion* is the true ground and foundation of all government, and that which subjects *power* to *authority.* For *power* arising from *strength* is always in those that are *governed,* who are *many;* but *authority* arising from *opinion* is in those that *govern* who are *few.* . . . *Authority* arises from the opinion of *wisdom, goodness,* and *valor* in the person who possess it" (pp. lxi–lxii).

13. *Regulations,* p. 88.

14. Ibid., p. 90.

15. The Treasury to the King, 4 October 1763, PRO, T. 1/430, fol. 332.

16. Whately to John Temple, 12 June 1765, *Bowdoin-Temple Papers,* p. 60.

17. For discussions of Newcastle's views on American taxation, with extensive quotations from the relevant documents in his papers, see Thomas, *British Politics,* pp. 52–53, 58–60, 85–86; and Sir Lewis Namier and John Brooke, *Charles Townshend,* pp. 114–19.

18. Romney Sedgwick, the editor of the King's correspondence with Bute, concluded that the few surviving letters between the two after March 1763 "are clearly the remains of a much more voluminous and politically compromising correspondence" that the two men destroyed. Thus, a collection that might have offered invaluable insights into the formulation of American taxation has been lost forever. *Bute Letters,* lxv–lxvi.

19. To the extent that scholars have speculated on Grenville's motives, opinion seems divided between those who insist that his foremost motive always was raising a revenue and those who believe that after December 1764, when petitions against the stamp tax from Massachusetts and New York arrived in London, the assertion of Parliament's constitutional supremacy became a major motive as well. For an example of the former opinion, see Christie and Labaree, *Empire or Independence,* pp. 51–52; for examples of the latter, see Thomas, *British Politics,* pp. 86, 113; Edmund S. Morgan and Helen M. Morgan, *The Stamp Act Crisis: Prologue to Revolution,* pp. 87, 97–98; and Jack M. Sosin, *Agents and Merchants: British Colonial Policy and the Origins of the American Revolution 1763–1775,* p. 65.

20. Sketch of Grenville by Thomas Pitt, Jr., in Namier and Brooke, *House of Commons,* 2:539. For similar comments on Grenville's character, see Edmund Burke's speech, 19 April 1774, *Parliamentary History,* 17:1239.

21. The men who doubted Grenville's honesty most while he was First Lord of the Treasury were members of his own family, who nursed bitter memories of his refusal to resign his place in October 1761 when his brother, Earl Temple, and his brother-in-law, William Pitt, left office. For example, see James Grenville to Pitt, 3 February 1764, *Correspondence of William Pitt, Earl of Chatham,* ed. W. S. Taylor and J. D. Pringle, 2:285. Few of Grenville's other contemporaries shared this opinion.

22. Charles Jenkinson to Grenville, 7 April 1759 and 29 December 1759, *Grenville Papers*, 1:291, 335.

23. Thomas Pitt, Jr., in Namier and Brooke, *House of Commons*, 2:539. Other members of Parliament also noted this characteristic of Grenville's on occasion. For example, see Lord George Sackville to General Irwin, 16 November 1761, Historical Manuscripts Commission, *Report on the Manuscripts of Mrs. Stopford-Sackville*, 1:87; and Nathaniel Ryder's comments on Grenville's speech, 24 March 1767, *Ryder Diary*, p. 336. Examples of Grenville's caution abound in his private and public correspondence, particularly in matters of appointment. For examples, see Grenville to Lord Barrington, 6 March 1765, and Grenville to the Duke of Marlborough, 15 December and 31 December 1764, George Grenville Letterbooks, HEHL, ST 7, ii.

24. Ryder's note, 4 March 1766, *Ryder Diary*, p. 319.

25. Namier and Brooke, *House of Commons*, 2:539; and Horace Walpole to Lord Hereford, 11 March 1764, in *Walpole's Correspondence*, 38:341. Repetitiousness characterized his conversations with "men of business" as well as his speeches. See William Knox, *Extra Official State Papers. Addressed to the Right Honourable Lord Rawdon . . .*, 2:34–35; Franklin to Joseph Galloway, 11 October, 1766 *Franklin Papers*, 13:449; and John Brooke, *King George III*, pp. 107–8.

26. Perhaps an example of a reporter taking advantage of Grenville's repetitiousness may be found by comparing Ryder's notes of Grenville's remarks on 9 March 1764 with Grenville's recollection of those remarks on 14 January 1766. Ryder recorded Grenville as merely saying, "If any man doubts the right of this country [to impose an inland duty], he will take the opinion of a committee immediately." Grenville remembered, "When I proposed to tax America, I asked the House, if any gentleman would object to the right; I repeatedly asked it, and no man would attempt to deny it." *Ryder Diary*, p. 235; *Parliamentary History*, 16:102.

27. Jackson to Jenkinson, 18 September 1763 and 7 January 1764, *Jenkinson Papers*, pp. 191–92, and Liverpool Papers, BL, Add. MSS. 38202, fol. 12.

28. Garth to South Carolina, 5 July 1764, in Edmund S. Morgan, ed., *Prologue to Revolution: Sources and Documents on the Stamp Act Crisis, 1764–1766*, p. 17. Garth was listed among the "friends of government" absent from the House during the debate on general warrants in Jenkinson's notes, [18 February 1764], Liverpool Papers, BL, Add. MSS. 38337, fol. 192.

29. For the two men's friendship, see Whately to Ingersoll, [Spring 1764], and Ingersoll to Whately, 6 July 1764, *Ingersoll Papers*, pp. 292, 295. For Ingersoll's discussions of the stamp tax, see Ingersoll to Whately, 28 January 1765, Ingersoll to Fitch, 11 February 1765, and Whately to Temple, [February 1765], PRO, T. 1/433, fol. 410, *Ingersoll Papers*, p. 314, and *Bowdoin-Temple Papers*, p. 51. For Grenville's opinion of Ingersoll, see Whately to Temple, 10 May 1765, *Bowdoin-Temple Papers*, p. 52.

30. Jenkinson's letters to Grenville during the late 1750s testify to his care in writing pamphlets and public papers. These letters may be found in *Grenville Papers*, vol. 1. See especially Jenkinson to Grenville, 24 May 1760, 11 October 1760, and 18 June 1761, *Grenville Papers*, 1:341–43, 353–54, and 367–68. Nathaniel Wraxall made this striking observation about Jenkinson's speaking style in the House during the 1770s: "He used to remind me of a man crossing a torrent on stones; and so carefully did he place his foot at every step, as never once to wet his shoe." James Harris made similar observations about Jenkinson's strengths and weaknesses as a speaker in 1766. See Nathaniel Wraxall, *Historical Memoirs of My Own Time*, 1:538–39; and Harris Diary, 21 February 1766, quoted in Namier and Brooke, *House of Commons*, 2:676.

31. For Jenkinson's sharing of research, see Chapter VIII. On occasions, Jenkinson

also shared drafts of pamphlets. Compare the two unfinished drafts of replies to David Hartley's pamphlet *The Budget* in Liverpool Papers, BL, Add. MSS. 38338, fols. 1–6, 178–191, with [Thomas Whately], *Remarks on "The Budget"; or, a candid examination of the facts and arguments offered to the public in that pamphlet.*

32. The word *proper* was the King's. See the King to Bute, [mid-March 1763], *Bute Letters,* p. 202.

Notes to Chapter I
The Background of Colonial Taxation

1. Richard Rigby to the Duke of Bedford, 16 September 1762, in Sir Lewis Namier and John Brooke, *Charles Townshend,* p. 73. For Bedford's mission to France, see Z. E. Rashed, *The Peace of Paris 1763,* pp. 159–200.

2. Townshend to Newcastle, 13 September 1754, Namier and Brooke, *Charles Townshend,* pp. 38–40.

3. The King to Bute, [mid-March 1763], *Bute Letters,* p. 202.

4. For information about all these men, see the appropriate entries in Namier and Brooke, *House of Commons.* For some interesting contemporary comments on the members of the Treasury Board, see Henry Fox to Bute, 11 March 1763, quoted in Earl of Ilchester, *Henry Fox, First Lord Holland: His Family and Relations,* 2:228–29. For examples of papers on taxation that may be found in North's and Jenkinson's files, see North Papers, Bodleian Library, MSS. North, b. 6, fols. 297–303; and Liverpool Papers, BL, Add. MSS. 38334, fols. 217–18, 223–24, 297–301. For Martin's comments on an American stamp tax, see Martin to Newcastle, 26 February 1759, Newcastle Papers, BL, Add. MSS. 32888, fol. 252. The paper Martin enclosed in his letter may have been the draft of a bill Henry McCulloh sent to the Earl of Halifax in 1755, which may be found in Newcastle's papers, in Add. MSS. 33030, fols. 334–35.

5. Newcastle to the Earl of Hardwicke, *Hardwicke Correspondence,* 3:426.

6. For accounts of the relationship between Grenville and Bute during 1760–1762, see Lewis M. Wiggin, *The Faction of Cousins: A Political Account of the Grenvilles, 1733–1763,* pp. 231–96; and Sir Lewis Namier, *England in the Age of the American Revolution,* pp. 283–418. For evidence of Bute's wariness about Grenville, see the King to Bute, 23 December 1762 and 6 January 1763, *Bute Letters,* pp. 176, 182.

7. Jenkinson's notes, 4 March 1763, Namier and Brooke, *Charles Townshend,* p. 91.

8. The King to Bute, [mid-March 1763], *Bute Letters,* p. 202.

9. For Egremont's consulting with Halifax, see the King to Bute, [mid-March ? 1763], *Bute Letters,* p. 202. I suspect Sedgwick misdated this letter. In it, the King mentioned rumors about the necessity of Egremont's sending a letter to the Board of Trade for its advice on the settlement of the new acquisitions. These rumors had reached the Board of Trade by mid-February. See John Pownall to Egremont, 15 February 1763, Egremont Papers, PRO, P.R.O. 30/47/14, fol. 234.

10. The King to Bute, 13 January and [mid-March ? 1763], *Bute Letters,* pp. 184, 202–3. For an account of the procedure Egremont ultimately used, see Jack M. Sosin, *Whitehall and the Wilderness: The Middle West in British Colonial Policy, 1760–1775,* pp. 57–60.

11. Rigby to Bedford, 16 February 1763, *Bute Letters,* p. 188.

12. Note that when Lord North could not find out the particulars of Rigby's mission to Paris in 1762, he wrote his father, "The members of the Cabinet keep their secret so well that I conclude they are pretty well agreed among themselves." North to the Earl of Guilford, [Fall 1762], Bodleian Library, MSS. North, d. 23, fol. 183.

13. The King to Bute, June 1757, *Bute Letters*, p. 6.

14. For the King's speech, see *Parliamentary History*, 15:984. Bute freely confessed his ignorance of the details of finance to both Grenville and Charles Yorke. See "Narrative," [soon after 11 October 1762], *Grenville Papers*, 1:484–85; and "Conversation with Lord Bute," 9 April 1763, *Hardwicke Correspondence*, 3:387. I have inferred Bute's basic ideas about finance and commerce and his beliefs about their relationship from his long political connection with George Bubb Dodington, who constantly was pressing his ideas on these subjects and recommendations for policy on Bute. For these ideas, see Dodington to Lord Talbot, 4 October 1760, *Dodington Journal*, pp. 389–96; for a full explication of them, see John L. Bullion, "Honor, Trade, and Empire: Grenville's Treasury and 'the American Question,' 1763–1765," (Ph.D. diss.), pp. 158–62. Documents describing the relationship between Bute and Dodington may be found in *Dodington Journal*, pp. 397–442; and Historical Manuscripts Commission, *Eyre Matcham MSS. Various MSS.*, 6:47–54. George III and Bute valued Dodington's friendship, political support, and advice enough for the King to elevate him to the English peerage as Baron Melcombe on 6 April 1761. This was a significant sign of the King's approval of him, for George III was very reluctant to create new peers. See Bute to Egremont, n.d., PRO, P.R.O. 30/47/29, bundle 3.

15. See arguments against raising the beer tax in *The Gentleman's Magazine*, 33 (June 1763): 271. Grenville later recalled with pride his "having undertaken the defense of the laborer and manufacturer, by [my] opposition to the tax on strong beer," in his pamphlet, *A reply to a letter addressed to the Right Honorable George Grenville, etc. In which the truth of the facts is examined, and the propriety of the motto fully considered*, p. 7. For an account of Grenville's talks with Pitt in 1761, see Wiggin, *Faction of Cousins*, p. 235.

16. "Mr. G. G. on the supplies for the army," [9 December 1761], Liverpool Papers, BL, Add. MSS. 38334, fol. 46. See also "Mr. G. G. on the Address," [14 November 1761], ibid., fol. 42.

17. Oswald's speech, [November–December 1761], Namier and Brooke, *House of Commons*, 3:238.

18. Bute to Grenville, [10 December 1761], *Grenville Papers*, 1:418. For Townshend's speech on 9 December, see Liverpool Papers, BL, Add. MSS. 38334, fols. 19–22. Townshend did not deny then that the war was adversely affecting Britain's financial status and her economy, but he argued that "neither our agriculture, our commerce, or our marine have suffered like those of France by the German war" and added that neither the nation's credit nor her treasure was yet exhausted. For his change of heart, see the King to Bute, 18 December 1762, *Bute Letters*, p. 74.

19. Townshend's speech, 25 January 1762, Walpole, *Memoirs of George III*, 1:105.

20. Newcastle to Hardwicke, 25 February 1762, *Hardwicke Correspondence*, 3:344.

21. See Namier, *England in the Age of the American Revolution*, pp. 312–26. For Oswald's involvement, see Namier and Brooke, *House of Commons*, 3:238.

22. Jenkinson, "Observations on the money faculties of the state in 1762," [Summer 1762], Liverpool Papers, BL, Add. MSS. 38334, fols. 233–38.

23. Bute to Egremont, 26 July 1762, *Bute Letters*, p. 127; and the King to Bute, 26 July 1762, ibid., p. 126.

24. Grenville to Jenkinson, 28 June 1761, *Jenkinson Papers*, p. 10; and Grenville's "Narrative," [after 11 October 1762], *Grenville Papers*, 1:450.

25. For Grenville's account of this episode, see his two "Narratives," [after 11 October 1762], ibid., 1:449–53, 482–85. A summary of contemporary reaction to his demotion may be found in Wiggin, *Faction of Cousins*, pp. 273–76; a lucid narrative of the event and its aftermath is in Namier, *England in the Age of the American Revolution*,

pp. 345–403. Neither historian, nor any contemporary, called attention to the fact that Grenville was trying to seize control of the negotiations. As Egremont wrote Bedford, however, if the preliminaries were not agreed on by the time Parliament met, "supplies must be asked, provision made, and money raised for carrying on the war, which would create an impossibility of going on with the same terms of negotiations." Egremont to Bedford, 16 September 1762, HEHL, STG Box 16(17). For Bute's awareness of this, see the King to Bute, 24 October 1762, *Bute Letters*, p. 151. Bute publicly "impute[d] only timidity to Mr. Grenville" and explained that his removal as Leader was due to his fear of defending the treaty against Pitt. Horace Walpole to Sir Horace Mann, 28 October 1762, *Walpole's Correspondence*, 6:91–92.

26. See 9 December 1762, *Commons Journals*, 29:393.

27. John Bindley to Jenkinson, 12 April 1763, *Jenkinson Papers*, p. 141; Bute to Fox, 30 November 1762, Holland House Papers, BL, Add. MSS. 51379, fol. 115; the King's speech, 25 November 1762, *Commons Journals*, 29:354.

28. [Thomas Whately], *Considerations on the trade and finances of this Kingdom and on the measures of administration, with respect to those great national objects since the conclusion of the peace*, pp. 3–4, 11. Whately's opinions on the impact of taxation on the economy were shared by Grenville and by the other Secretary to the Treasury during Grenville's administration, Charles Jenkinson. For Grenville's appreciation of the effect of taxation on food prices for the poor, see his letter to Augustus Hervey, 26 September 1766, George Grenville Letterbooks, HEHL, ST 7, ii. For Jenkinson's reference to "how much the price of labor is increased in this country by the additional load of taxes laid upon it," see Appendix C. Hence it is not surprising that John Almon judged Whately's pamphlet to be a "defense of Mr. Grenville's system of finance, and of the principal measures of his Administration, in which there is a good deal of useful information." [John Almon], *Biographical, Literary, and Political Anecdotes, of several of the most eminent persons of the present age, never before printed*, 2:104. There are other indications as well that men at Whitehall during 1762–1763 were concerned about taxation's effect on future trade. For arguments similar to Whately's, see *The sentiments of an impartial Member of Parliament, upon the two following questions, 1. Whether Great Britain ought to be desirous of a peace in the present situation of her affairs? 2. What sort of a peace Great Britain has reason to expect?*, pp. 1–7, 19–23. William Knox later made the same arguments Whately did about the effects of taxation on trade, noted that the Grenville administration had recognized them, and praised what Grenville had begun to do toward dealing with them. See *The present state of the nation: particularly with respect to its trade, finances, etc. Addressed to the King and both Houses of Parliament*, pp. 16–18, 29–36. Grenville himself privately praised Knox for the "temper and force . . . [and] knowledge and precision" of most of the major arguments. For an excellent discussion of this pamphlet and its preparation and public reception, see Leland J. Bellot, *William Knox: The Life and Thought of an Eighteenth-Century Imperialist*, pp. 84–95. Knox had previously described the effects of heavy taxation on Britain's economy in a paper he sent to Grenville during the fall of 1763. See ibid., pp. 55–57; for a copy of the paper itself, see WLCL, Knox Papers, 9:4. Finally, see also Junius to the *Public Advertiser*, 21 January 1769, in [Philip Francis], *The Letters of Junius*, ed. John Cannon, p. 29, and the thoughtful "Note on Authorship" in the same book, pp. 539–72.

29. *Commons Journals*, 29:354; and the King to Bute, 6 January 1763, *Bute Letters*, p. 181. For the interest of the King in this, see ibid., p. 135; for the interest of Cabinet members, see ibid., pp. 174–95. For evidence of Grenville's attachment to economy in managing the navy's affairs, see Wiggin, *Faction of Cousins*, pp. 225–26.

30. Bute to Sir John Phillips, 23 February 1763, Bute Papers, BL, Add. MSS. 36797,

fol. 34; "Estimate . . . for the service in North America," [February–March 1763], Egremont Papers, PRO, P.R.O. 30/47/24, bundle 3, fol. 33; and Jenkinson to Bute, 4 March 1763, in P. D. G. Thomas, "New Light on the Commons Debate of 1763 on the American Army," p. 111. For an excellent overall account of decisions on the army in America, see John Shy, *Toward Lexington: The Role of the British Army in the Coming of the American Revolution,* pp. 45–83.

31. "Abstract of His Majesty's Ships," [before November 1762], Liverpool Papers, BL, Add. MSS. 38335, fols. 280–82.

32. Several papers relating to this concern may be found in the George Grenville Papers, HEHL, STG Box 16. See also Hardwicke to Newcastle, 22 January 1763, Newcastle Papers, BL, Add. MSS. 32946, fols. 159–62b; and the King to Bute, 8 November 1762, *Bute Letters,* p. 160.

33. Burke to Charles O'Hara, 30 December 1762, *Burke Correspondence,* 1:161; and Yorke to the King, 17 December 1762, George Grenville Papers, HEHL, STG Box 17(18). See also Shy, *Toward Lexington,* pp. 73–74.

34. These quotations are taken from the two best sources for the substantive arguments of the government on 9 December 1762. The Earl of Shelburne moved the approval of the preliminaries in the House of Lords. His notes for his speech are in the Shelburne Papers, WLCL, Shelburne 165:309–28; they have been published in *The American Revolution, 1763–1783: A Bicentennial Collection,* ed. Richard B. Morris, pp. 12–16. Shelburne's lack of knowledge about commerce or the colonies at this time, his close association with Fox, and the ministry's choice of him to begin debate are facts that convincingly argue that his speech was an official statement on the articles. The second source is "The principal arguments . . . offered in favor of the treaty," *Parliamentary History,* 15:1271–72. These arguments are not extracted from notes made in the House that day. Instead, the editors of *Parliamentary History* took them verbatim from the account in the *Annual Register,* where they were described as the replies to arguments against the treaty "by the best writers" favoring it. *Annual Register* 5 (1762): 59–60. Nevertheless, the close congruence of Shelburne's speech with these arguments, plus the strong probability that Shelburne's speech represented the official position of the ministry, suggests strongly that arguments very similar to "The principal arguments" were made in the House.

35. Grenville's notes on the preliminaries, made during November–December 1762, emphasized this point. George Grenville Papers, HEHL, STG Box 17(35). For similar arguments, see Jenkinson's report on the articles' advantages for Britain, [November–December 1762], Liverpool Papers, BL, Add. MSS. 38336, fols. 29–30.

36. Shelburne used these statistics in his speech. Custom House Accounts, Shelburne Papers, WLCL, Shelburne 111:258–60, 262–64, 278–79, 345. These accounts were presented to the House on 7 December 1762, *Commons Journals,* 29:392. For Grenville's suspicions about American smuggling while he served as First Lord of the Admiralty, 1762–1763, see Burke, 19 April 1774, *Parliamentary History,* 17:1240.

37. See the relevant documents in PRO, C.O. 5/62–63; and "Extracts of letters between Amherst and Pitt," [October 1760–October 1761], Egremont Papers, PRO, P.R.O. 30/47/14, fols. 203–4.

38. H. Grenville to Grenville, 27 September 1751, George Grenville Papers, HEHL, STG Box 25(37).

39. Dodington to Talbot, 4 October 1760, *Dodington Journal,* p. 391.

40. Treasury minutes, 14 January 1763, PRO, T. 29/35, fol. 14; and 17 March 1763, *Commons Journals,* 29:572.

41. See the discussion of this document in Shy, *Toward Lexington,* pp. 66–67; and

idem, *A People Numerous and Armed: Reflections on the Military Struggle for American Independence,* pp. 267–68.

42. Thomas noted this disagreement within the Grenville administration. Perhaps it first surfaced as Bute's ministry considered taxing the colonies. P. D. G. Thomas, *British Politics and the Stamp Act Crisis: The First Phase of the American Revolution, 1763–1767,* pp. 35–36.

43. The King to Bute, [mid-March 1763], *Bute Letters,* p. 202; and Egremont to the Board of Trade, 5 May 1763, in Thomas, *British Politics,* p. 40. For indications Egremont was working on this matter in February, see Pownall to Egremont, 15 February 1763, and "draft of a letter to the Board of Trade," endorsed February 1763, Egremont Papers, PRO, P.R.O. 30/47/14, bundle 1, fol. 234, and P.R.O. 30/47/22, bundle 2, fols. 37–42.

Notes to Chapter II
A Cautious Beginning

1. Namier and Brooke, *House of Commons,* 3:398; and Sir Lewis Namier and John Brooke, *Charles Townshend,* pp. 84–87.

2. 28 January 1763, *Commons Journals,* 29:417.

3. For an account of these difficulties, see Hardwicke to Newcastle, 22 January 1763, *Hardwicke Correspondence,* 3:452–53. The two Secretaries and Mansfield quickly turned to American affairs after 10 February. The King to Bute, [mid-March ? 1763], *Bute Letters,* pp. 202–3; and Pownall to Egremont, 15 February 1763, Egremont Papers, PRO. P.R.O. 30/47/14, bundle 1, fol. 234.

4. Newcastle to Hardwicke, 4 September 1762, *Hardwicke Correspondence,* 3:414; the King to Bute, 11 October 1762, *Bute Letters,* p. 145. The impact of Fox's optimism and drive on George III may be seen by comparing accounts of two interviews the King had with Charles Townshend, the King to Bute, [early October 1762], and 10 November 1762, ibid., pp. 142, 161; and by reading contemporary opinion on Fox's influence in *Annual Register,* 5 (1762): 62.

5. Fox to Bute, January 1762, and Shelburne, "Memorandum on the events of 1762," *Shelburne Correspondence,* 1:139–41.

6. Bute to Thomas Worsley, 28 November 1762, Bute Papers, BL, Add. MSS. 36797, fol. 24; and "Conversation with Lord Bute," 9 April 1763, *Hardwicke Correspondence,* 3:387.

7. Egremont to the Board of Trade, 5 May 1763, Shelburne Papers, WLCL, 99:283–90; and the King to Bute, [mid-March 1763] *Bute Letters,* p. 202. I am not aware of any other contemporary paper describing criteria an American tax should meet, but I have found an illuminating report on the advisability of laying an additional duty on exports of coal that lists customary considerations in planning new taxes. Among these is the assumption that the consumer would try to avoid the tax by either finding other suppliers or ceasing to buy those goods. Other questions than those drafting new customs legislation generally asked were "what effect might (or is it probable?) an additional duty have on the particular trade, or any other, and also on the revenue?" and "what is that duty which would be most likely to increase the revenue without hurting any trade, or any individual?" Robert Weston to Jenkinson, 3 March 1765, Liverpool Papers, BL, Add. MSS. 38339, fols. 77–82. For another example of Weston's careful advice, see Add. MSS. 38204, fols. 112–13.

8. Cecilius Calvert to Horatio Sharpe, 19 January 1760, in John Shy, *Toward*

Lexington: The Role of the British Army in the Coming of the American Revolution, p. 45; and Lord Kinnoul to Newcastle, 16 December 1762, Newcastle Papers, BL, Add. MSS. 32945, fol. 376.

9. "Mems. Definitive Treaty, plan of the army," 19 February 1763, Newcastle Papers, BL, Add. MSS. 32947, fols. 46–48b; and Rigby to Bedford, 23 February 1763, in P. D. G. Thomas, *British Politics and the Stamp Act Crisis: The First Phase of the American Revolution, 1763–1767,* p. 38.

10. Betty Kemp, *Sir Francis Dashwood: An Eighteenth-Century Independent,* pp. 184–87; and "Explanation of the several branches of His Majesty's revenues arising in the plantations at the King's free disposal," [1762–1763], North Papers, Bodleian Library, MSS. North, b. 6, fols. 297–303.

11. Jeremiah Dyson to Customs Commissioners, 16 February 1763, PRO, T. 11/27, fol. 128; Martin to William Wood, 4 March 1763, ibid.; and Treasury minutes, 15 March 1763, ibid., T. 29/35, fols. 26–27.

12. For Oswald's longstanding interest in the linen trade and linen manufactory, see Romney Sedgwick, *The History of Parliament: The House of Commons, 1715–1754,* 2 vols. (Oxford, 1970), 2:325; and Namier and Brooke, *House of Commons,* 3:238.

13. "Arguments . . . in favor of the Treaty." [9 December 1762], *Parliamentary History,* 15:1272.

14. Robert Yeates to Jenkinson, 19 December 1763, *Jenkinson Papers,* p. 245; and "Conversation with Lord Bute," 9 April 1763, *Hardwicke Correspondence,* 3:387.

15. Martin to Customs Commissioners, 31 January 1763, PRO, T. 11/27, fol. 128.

16. "Conversation with Lord Bute," 9 April 1763, *Hardwicke Correspondence,* 3:387; and Shelburne, "Memorandum on the events of 1762," *Shelburne Correspondence,* 1:141.

17. For the provenance of the proposal, see Yeates to Jenkinson, 19 December 1763, *Jenkinson Papers,* p. 245. Touchet ended his life a bankrupt, and his papers have evidently disappeared. Namier and Brooke, *House of Commons,* 3:533–36. The loss of these papers and the vague references to the proposal as a tax on linen, particularly Russian linens, have caused historians to overlook the possibility that part of Oswald's scheme involved the modification of the drawback on foreign linens reexported to the colonies. The chief evidence suggesting that this alteration was part of the plan is Oswald's past advocacy of this cause of domestic linen manufacturers, the letter from Martin to the customs commissioners on 31 January, and the involvement of Tod, who in 1764 lobbied hard with Jenkinson and Grenville for total abolition of the drawback. Tod to Jenkinson, 13 March 1764, Liverpool Papers, BL, Add. MSS. 38202, fol. 156.

18. Oswald's speech, 24 February 1766, *Ryder Diary,* p. 310.

19. Tod told Jenkinson on 13 March 1764 that the basic arguments for and against removing the drawback had not changed in twenty-five years and recommended that he study a pamphlet written then for some idea of the debate. I have followed his advice and assumed that Oswald knew about and agreed with the arguments on smuggling in *A letter from a merchant who has left off trade to a Member of Parliament in which the case of the British and Irish manufacture of linen, threads, and tapes, is fairly stated, and all the objections against the encouragement proposed to be given to that manufacture fully answered,* pp. 69–75.

20. Sir William Musgrave to William Eden, 10 March 1783, Auckland Papers, BL, Add. MSS. 34419, fol. 120. Oswald was probably familiar with the approximate value of the drawback, for Tod certainly was. See also "Account of the amount of drawbacks," 15 April 1763, PRO, T. 1/430, fols. 326–28.

21. Martin to Wood, 4 March 1763, PRO, T. 11/27, fol. 128.

22. For the taxes on cider and wines, see 8 March 1763, *Commons Journals*, 29:535. On 9 March, the House received accounts of the stamp duties on insurance policies and bills of lading, a sign the administration was planning to suggest a change in the duties. Ibid., p. 536. See also Kemp, *Dashwood*, pp. 84–85.

23. Grenville to Walpole, 8 September 1763, *Grenville Papers*, 2:114; and Martin to Wood, 4 March 1763, PRO, T. 11/27, fol. 128.

24. "Mems. Definitive Treaty, a plan of the army," 19 February 1763, Newcastle Papers, BL, Add. MSS. 32947, fols. 46–48b.

25. Rigby to Bedford, 23 February 1763, in Thomas, *British Politics*, p. 38. The identities of Rigby's informants are unknown.

26. Jenkinson to Bute, 4 March 1763, in P. D. G. Thomas, "New Light on the Commons Debate of 1763 on the American Army," pp. 111–12. This report found its way into North's papers, which may indicate that Grenville's Treasury wanted to keep an accurate record of what Ellis said on 4 March 1763. For a later example of Jenkinson's alertness to pledges, see Jenkinson to Grenville, 2 July 1764, *Grenville Papers*, 2:373. Sir Roger Newdigate recorded Ellis's statement in words similar to Jenkinson's, but he also added this ambiguous entry to his notes on the speech: "Next year America to pay itself." Did Ellis make what Sir Roger took to be a pledge that the government would impose and collect taxes on Americans during 1764? Did Sir Roger believe that the Secretary at War indicated that these taxes would pay the entire expenses of the army in America? The reference in his diary is too vague to answer either question. It is clear, however, that no one in the Grenville Treasury referred in 1764 to any pledge made in 1763, so this reference probably is Sir Roger's personal interpretation of the significance of Ellis's remarks. See Newdigate Diary, 4 March 1763, in Thomas, "New Light on the Commons Debate of 1763," pp. 111–12. For the identities of the other members who took notes on this debate, see Thomas, *British Politics*, p. 39.

27. Shy, *Toward Lexington*, pp. 74–78.

28. Jenkinson to Bute, 4 March 1763; Thomas, "New Light on the Commons Debate of 1763," p. 111; and Walpole, *Memoirs of George III*, 1:195. As Thomas noted, Beckford's statement seems astounding when one recalls his opposition to American taxation during and after the Stamp Act crisis. His suggestion may indeed have been inaccurately reported. Yet Jenkinson was ordinarily a meticulous reporter of debates in the House, and his accounts of other members' speeches on 4 March are in essential agreement with the report of James West and the notes of Sir Roger Newdigate on those speeches. Moreover, there is reason to believe that Beckford had been friendly toward proposals of American taxation in the past. On 4 June 1754, he wrote to the Duke of Bedford, "By the desire of a very worthy gentleman, Mr. Henry McCulloh, I have sent a small treatise to [your] house, and will do myself the honor some day or other of paying my respects to you with the said gentleman." *Correspondence of John, Fourth Duke of Bedford, Selected from the Originals at Woburn Abbey*, ed. Lord John Russell, 2:150. For examples of the treatises McCulloh wrote for ministers during the 1750s, see two McCulloh letters to the Earl of Halifax, 10 December 1751, BL, Add. MSS. 11514, fols. 93–94, and [1755], ibid., 33030, fols. 334–35; and McCulloh to the Board of Trade, [1757], ibid., 32974, fols. 310–13. In all these, McCulloh suggested imposing a variety of regulations and taxes on colonists, including stamp taxes. Almost certainly the paper Beckford forwarded to Bedford, who had been interested in the colonies since the aborted Canadian expedition of 1746–1747, was of a similar nature. That Beckford agreed to introduce McCulloh to Bedford strongly implies that at that time he approved of those proposals. Finally, there is evidence that

Beckford also approved of the Grenville administration's initial efforts to raise a revenue in America. On 9 March 1764, he told the House, "Mr. Grenville's plan was good." He later supported that legislation during the debates on it in committee. In 1765, he again expressed his approval of the ministry's efforts to raise a revenue by taxing foreign molasses at threepence per gallon. See Thomas, *British Politics,* pp. 55–58; Beckford's speech, 6 February 1765, *Ryder Diary,* pp. 256–57. For these reasons, it is likely that Jenkinson's notes on Beckford's comments on 4 March 1763 were accurate.

29. James West to Newcastle, [4 March 1763], Newcastle Papers, BL, Add. MSS. 32947, fols. 265–69b; and Jenkinson to Bute, 4 March 1763, Thomas, "New Light on the Commons Debate of 1763," p. 111.

30. Newcastle to Hardwicke, 3 March 1763, Add. MSS. 32947, fols. 163–65b; and Shy, *Toward Lexington,* pp. 78–79.

31. Walpole, *Memoirs of George III,* 1:197–98; see also Fox to Bute, 11 March 1763, Earl of Ilchester, *Henry Fox, First Lord Holland, His Family and Relations,* 2:228. In her book on Dashwood, Professor Kemp has proved that he was a highly competent Chancellor in every area but the presentation of the budget to the House.

32. Kemp, *Dashwood,* pp. 84–87; Lawrence Henry Gipson, *The British Empire before the American Revolution,* 10:184–88; and "Conversation with Lord Bute," 9 April 1763, *Hardwicke Correspondence,* 3:387.

33. Bute to Fox, 2 March 1763, Ilchester, *Fox,* 2:225, and Newcastle to the Duke of Devonshire, 5 March 1763, *Bute Letters,* p. 197.

34. 9 March 1763, *Commons Journals,* 29:537.

35. For the membership of this committee, which also included Samuel Martin and Sir John Turner from the Treasury and "all the merchants of the House," see 17 December 1762, ibid., 29:402. I gauged Jenkinson's probable reaction to the Molasses Act from his arguments on the dependence of the French West Indies in November–December 1762 and from a paper in Jenkinson's files, "A state of the present branches of the customs in America, with hints for their improvement," [early 1763], Liverpool Papers, BL, Add. MSS. 38334, fols. 223–24, which makes the same sort of assumptions described above in the text.

36. Treasury minutes, 25 March 1763, PRO, T. 29/35, fols. 26–27. The law officers answered that the King could dispose of this revenue as he pleased. Law Officers to Treasury, 9 June 1763, Liverpool Papers, BL, Add. MSS. 38335, fol. 103.

37. Fox to [Shelburne?], 17 March 1763, Namier and Brooke, *Charles Townshend,* p. 93; see also the discussion of Townshend's negotiation in ibid., pp. 84–88, especially the comment Rigby made on 16 February 1763.

38. John Bindley, "Queries and Answers relative to North America," [n.d.], Townshend (Charles) Papers, WLCL, Box 8, bundle 34. Bindley's tentative suggestion about the use of naval vessels reveals that the paper was written before 24 March 1763, when the Treasury obtained leave to bring in a bill to allow the employment of the navy for customs enforcement. From 1761 through 1764, Bindley served on the Excise Board, as Secretary and as Commissioner, and habitually sent suggestions for improving the revenue to officials. He and Townshend were close friends at this time, and he probably did this research at Townshend's request. Namier and Brooke, *House of Commons,* 2:90–91.

39. For the date, see Thomas, *British Politics,* p. 39.

40. Grenville to Walpole, 8 September 1763, *Grenville Papers,* 2:114. Grenville did not identify who made these complaints, or when, but it is likely they arose in debates over the molasses duty.

41. 30 March 1763, Harris Diary, in Namier and Brooke, *Charles Townshend,* p. 92.

42. 19 March 1763, *Commons Journals,* 29:597.

43. The King to Bute, [mid-March 1763], *Bute Letters,* p. 202.

44. The use of procedural maneuvers to avoid embarrassing confrontations on delicate issues was common during the eighteenth century. Using procedure against Townshend would have particularly pleased Fox, who was determined to "drive Charles Townshend from the Board of Trade" by indirect means, in this case by making Shelburne Secretary of State. Fox to [Shelburne?], 17 March 1763, Namier and Brooke, *Charles Townshend,* p. 92. For an excellent discussion of House procedures, see P. D. G. Thomas, *The House of Commons in the Eighteenth Century;* for a description of the tactic used to kill Townshend's bill, see ibid., pp. 50–51.

45. Jasper Mauduit to Andrew Oliver, 23 March 1763, Namier and Brooke, *Charles Townshend,* p. 92. In the text and notes, references to Mauduit are to Jasper, not to his brother Israel, who assisted him in the performance of his duties as agent for Massachusetts. When I describe Israel's activities, or quote him, I refer to Israel Mauduit.

46. 19 March, 24 March, 26 March, 28 March 1763, *Commons Journals,* 29:597, 606, 614, 617.

47. See Thomas, *House of Commons,* p. 50.

48. 30 March 1763, Harris Diary, Namier and Brooke, *Charles Townshend,* p. 92.

49. 24 March 1763, *Commons Journals,* 29:609. On 30 March, the House postponed discussion of the amended Molasses Act, took up the discussion of the bill extending the powers of the navy, and then immediately returned to the Molasses Act. This arrangement of debates suggests that the government was using its bill to justify postponing Townshend's. Ibid., pp. 622–23.

50. Grenville to Walpole, 8 September 1763, *Grenville Papers,* 2:114. Grenville did not specify who made this argument, but it would have answered Townshend's demand for an immediate reduction of the duty.

51. 30 March 1763, *Commons Journals,* 29:623.

52. Oswald to Bute, 13 April 1763, Namier and Brooke, *Charles Townshend,* p. 96. The context of Oswald's remark and his references to the Board of Trade and the Secretary of State make it clear that he was referring to decisions on the governance and development of the new acquisitions. Oswald's opinion that the parliamentary opposition would concentrate on the arrangements made for the new territories was shared by the Earl of Sandwich, who began serving as Secretary of State for the Northern Department after Egremont's death. See Sandwich to [Fox], 16 September 1763, in Earl of Ilchester, ed., *Letters to Henry Fox, Lord Holland with a few addressed to his brother Stephen, Earl of Ilchester,* p. 181.

Notes to Chapter III
"The Particular Habits of His Life"

1. 5 March 1770, *Parliamentary History,* 16:870.

2. Ian R. Christie and Benjamin W. Labaree, *Empire or Independence, 1760–1776: A British-American Dialogue on the Coming of the American Revolution,* p. 26; P. D. G. Thomas, *British Politics and the Stamp Act Crisis: The First Phase of the American Revolution, 1763–1767,* p. 112; Thomas R. Barrow, *Trade and Empire: The British Customs Service in Colonial America, 1660–1775,* pp. 174–75.

3. Christie and Labaree, *Empire or Independence,* p. 26; Thomas, *British Politics,* p. 112; Barrow, *Trade and Empire,* p. 174.

4. Bute to Bedford, 2 April 1763, Bute Papers, BL, Add. MSS. 36797, fols. 36–38.

5. See "Narrative," [after 9 November 1761], *Grenville Papers,* 1:409–11. Grenville gave a similar narration of events to the Earl of Hardwicke before Hardwicke's letter to Newcastle of 17 October 1761, which lends credence to this story. Even more credence is lent to it by the fact that James Grenville did not resign his office until 12 October. Had Temple immediately expressed a desire that his brothers resign, no doubt James would have resigned earlier. See Lewis M. Wiggin, *The Faction of Cousins: A Political Account of the Grenvilles, 1733–1763,* p. 255; and James Grenville to Bute, 12 October 1761, *Grenville Papers,* 1:394.

6. "Heads of Lord Bute's Letter," 13 October 1761, *Grenville Papers,* 1:395. For the arguments Grenville made against accepting the job of Leader, see ibid., p. 396 and "Narrative," [after 9 November 1761], ibid., p. 412.

7. Newcastle to Grenville, [7 October 1761], ibid., pp. 393–94. In the "Narrative" he wrote after 9 November 1761, Grenville indicated that he had "made a stand against this proposition" until Bute had obviated his objections in a letter on 13 October. The Newcastle letter is strong evidence to the contrary, as are Grenville's notes on Bute's 13 October letter. Historians should handle the various "narratives" Grenville wrote during this period with great care, especially when he describes his own motives. For reasons given in the text above, Grenville was intent on justifying his actions to his immediate family in these "narratives" and therefore deleted all traces of his own ambitiousness.

8. See Wiggin, *Faction of Cousins,* p. 255, and "Narrative," [after 9 November 1761], *Grenville Papers,* 1:414.

9. See "Narrative," 12 April 1762, *Grenville Papers,* 1:427–29, for this quotation and for the details of Temple's control over the family estates in Buckinghamshire.

10. See, for example, the reactions of Horace Walpole and the King to rumors about Temple's possible reaction and to the family's behavior toward Grenville. Walpole, *Memoirs of George III,* 1:65; "Heads of Lord Bute's Letter," 13 October 1761, *Grenville Papers,* 1:395.

11. "Narrative," [after 9 November 1761], *Grenville Papers,* 1:412; "Heads of Lord Bute's Letter," 13 October 1761, ibid., p. 396.

12. "Narrative," [after 9 November 1761], ibid., p. 412; and "Heads of Lord Bute's Letter," 13 October 1761, ibid., p. 395.

13. Ibid., p. 395.

14. Bute was being remarkably frank when he insisted that Grenville's serving as Leader was essential to this ministry. To Newcastle on 26 September 1761, he stated the same thought even more strongly. Sir Lewis Namier, *England in the Age of the American Revolution,* p. 294. See also the King to Bute, [27 September, 1761], *Bute Letters,* p. 64; and Newcastle to Bedford, 6 October 1761, *Correspondence of John, Fourth Duke of Bedford, Selected from the Originals at Woburn Abbey,* ed. Lord John Russell, 3:49.

15. "Heads of Lord Bute's Letter," 13 October 1761, *Grenville Papers,* 1:396. Namier pointed out that in Bute's letter this passage reads, "From the minute you are there, your honor, my honor, your disgrace, my disgrace is his, to all intents and purposes," and Namier concluded that Grenville "was already subconsciously cutting out Bute as a superior intervening between himself and the King." Namier and Brooke, *House of Commons,* 2:538–39.

16. Newcastle to Grenville, [13 October 1761], and [7 October 1761], *Grenville Papers,* 2:397, 393–94.

17. Newcastle to Devonshire, 31 October 1761, in Namier and Brooke, *House of Commons,* 2:539; and "Narrative," [after 9 November 1761], *Grenville Papers,* 1:415.

18. By late October, Grenville was sufficiently sure of his position to begin asking for jobs for his friends. See Newcastle to Bedford, 29 October 1761, *Correspondence of John, Fourth Duke of Bedford*, 3:67. Grenville justified these requests to Newcastle by referring to his concern about the "want of marks of credit and power" from the throne and the administration, and cited this as one of "his real objections to the taking of the lead of the House of Commons upon him." Newcastle to Devonshire, 31 October 1761, in Sir Lewis Namier, *England in the Age of the American Revolution*, p. 301. For a perceptive discussion of the events of late October, see Wiggin, *Faction of Cousins*, pp. 252–53.

19. This was Mrs. Grenville's opinion, but she probably shared it with her husband, who discussed his most intimate political confidences with her. Mrs. Grenville's Diary, 19 November 1763, *Grenville Papers*, 2:244.

20. For a narrative of these vacillations, see Namier, *England in the Age of the American Revolution*, pp. 302–26.

21. The King to Bute, two letters, both mid-May 1762, *Bute Letters*, pp. 104–5.

22. The King to Bute, 19 May 1762, ibid., p. 109.

23. Bute to Grenville, 22 May 1762, and "Narrative," [after March 1763], *Grenville Papers*, 1:447, 450.

24. Henry Fox, "Memoir," [after 3 August 1762], *Lennox Letters*, p. 69; and Bute to Egremont, 26 July 1762, in *Bute Letters*, p. 127.

25. Grenville's notes on the Cabinet meeting of 26 July 1762, George Grenville Papers, HEHL, STG Box 14(43).

26. Bute to Fox, 4 October 1762, in Earl of Ilchester, ed., *Henry Fox, First Lord Holland, His family and Relations*, 2:189–90.

27. The King to Bute, 11 October 1762, *Bute Letters*, p. 145.

28. "Narrative," [soon after 11 October 1762], *Grenville Papers*, 1:484–85.

29. The King to Bute, ca. 4 April 1763, *Bute Letters*, pp. 209–10, and 11 April 1763, ibid., p. 217.

30. Grenville to Bute, 25 March 1763, *Grenville Papers*, 2:33–40; the King to Bute, 25 March 1763, *Bute Letters*, p. 205.

31. At this time, Bute intended that Charles Townshend would become First Lord of the Admiralty. Perhaps Grenville wanted Pitt there to keep an eye on Townshend.

32. The King to Bute, 27 April 1763, *Bute Letters*, p. 230; and Namier and Brooke, *House of Commons*, 2:540.

33. Grenville's speech, 5 March 1770, Cavendish Diaries, BL, Egerton MSS. 221, fol. 34. Grenville made a similar statement on 26 April 1770, ibid., fol. 25.

34. The King's speech, 19 April 1763, *Commons Journals*, 29:666; for Grenville's authorship, see the King to Bute, 16 April 1763, *Bute Letters*, p. 225.

35. The quotation is from Treasury to the King, 4 October 1763. This memorial is not ony a comprehensive summary of Grenville's acts to strengthen the American customs service, but also a revealing glimpse of his attitude toward smugglers. It is conveniently reprinted in *EHD*, 9:638.

36. Excise Commissioners to Treasury, 13 May 1763, PRO, T. 1/426, fols. 337–38.

37. "Observations on the hints to prevent smuggling," [n.d.], Liverpool Papers, BL, Add. MSS. 38339, fols. 138–39. My understanding of smuggling in Britain has been much improved by reading Cal Winslow, "Sussex Smugglers," in Douglas Hay et al., eds., *Albion's Fatal Tree: Crime and Society in Eighteenth-Century England*, pp. 119–66; and Hoh-Cheung Mui and Lorna H. Mui, "Smuggling and the British Tea Trade before 1784," pp. 44–73.

38. For a narrative, see Lawrence Henry Gipson, *The British Empire before the American Revolution*, 10:187–94; for the proposed amendment, see 23 March 1763,

Commons Journals, 29:604; for some negotiations that fell through due to public pressure on the members, see Grenville to William Dowdeswell, 17 November 1763, George Grenville Letterbooks, HEHL, ST 7, ii, and [unknown] to Grenville, 18 December 1763, George Grenville Papers, HEHL, STG Box 23(51).

39. Excise Commissioners to the Treasury, 22 April 1763, PRO, T. 1/426, fols. 213–14.

40. 9 March 1764, *Ryder Diary,* pp. 233–34 Grenville was anticipating a common argument. A year later, an attorney for the Duke of Atholl asked, "Has the Isle of Man, or have the high taxes, which the necessities of government have laid on trade, been the cause of this great evil [smuggling]?" 13 February 1765, *Parliamentary History,* 16:32.

41. "Stations for frigates, sloops, and cutters, round Great Britain and Ireland," [1763], George Grenville Papers, HEHL, STG Box 18(33).

42. "Account of tea cleared of the East India Company from 5 April 1753 to 5 April 1763 for home consumption, Ireland, and America," PRO, T. 1/426, fols. 213–14; Jenkinson to the Customs Commissioners, 19 September 1763, ibid., T. 27/28, 428; Wood to Jenkinson, 9 January 1764, *Jenkinson Papers,* p. 252; and 9 March 1764, *Ryder Diary,* p. 234.

43. Wood to Jenkinson, 9 January 1764, *Jenkinson Papers,* p. 245.

44. For examples of cooperation between the Treasury and the Admiralty, see Phillip Stephens to Thomas Whately, 27 September 1763, 29 November 1763, and 23 April 1764, PRO, T. 1/424, fols. 142, 150, 194. For the request to the Secretary of State, see Treasury Minutes, 18 July 1764, ibid., T. 29/36, fols. 14–16. For Mortimer, who was vice-consul at Ostend, see William Mortimer to the Treasury, [after 26 July 1764], George Grenville Papers, HEHL, STG Box 20(8).

45. The Treasury to the King, 4 October 1763, in *EHD,* 9:638.

46. "List of Customs Officers," [1763], Liverpool Papers, BL, Add. MSS. 38334, fol. 216. Despite the awareness of politics that the existence of such a list reveals, this paper still has written on it, "Mem. Inquire by letter to the Customs what officers of the customs do their duty personally, what by deputy?"

47. Grenville to General John Lambton and Sir Thomas Clavering, 4 October 1764, George Grenville Letterbooks, HEHL, ST 7, ii. Grenville was promising that he would insure a fair inquiry into allegations against Lambton's brother, the collector at Sunderland.

48. Whately to Customs Commissioners, 11 February 1764, PRO, T. 11/27, fol. 188; Treasury minutes, 14 April 1764, PRO, T. 29/35, fol. 182; Treasury minutes, 25 June 1764, PRO, T. 29/35, fol. 233; Treasury minutes, 23 October 1764, PRO, T. 29/36, fols. 56–57; John Robinson to Jenkinson, 13 August 1764, *Jenkinson Papers,* pp. 315–16; M. Henniker to Jenkinson, 18 September 1764, Liverpool Papers, BL, Add. MSS. 38203, fol. 156; Treasury minutes, 24 October 1764, PRO, T. 29/36, fol. 57; and for the dismissals during 1764, see PRO, T. 11/27, fols. 223–25. For an indication of how widely known Grenville's reputation for insisting that customs officers do their duty was, see Walpole to Henry Seymour Conway, 6 April 1766, *Walpole's Correspondence,* 39:62.

49. Bindley to Jenkinson, [after 5 January 1765], Liverpool Papers, BL, Add. MSS. 38204, fol. 7.

50. Grenville to Jenkinson, 22 August 1764, *Jenkinson Papers,* pp. 323–25.

51. Claudius Amyrand to Jenkinson, 27 July 1764, Liverpool Papers, BL, Add. MSS. 38203, fol. 49; and Jenkinson to J. S. Mackenzie, 14 August 1764, *Jenkinson Papers,* p. 317.

52. Treasury minutes, 26 June 1764, and 19 July 1764, PRO, T. 29/36, fols. 1, 16–17.

53. For a brief description of this, see Gipson, *The British Empire before the American Revolution*, 10:194–98.

54. Treasury minutes, 25 July 1764, and 10 May 1764, PRO, T. 29/36, fols. 24–25 and ibid., T. 29/35, fols. 192–93.

55. 13 February 1765, *Parliamentary History*, 16:31–32.

56. The Receiver General to the Customs Commissioners, 12 October 1764, George Grenville Papers, HEHL, STG Box 20(5). For the agreement with Atholl, see Gipson, *The British Empire before the American Revolution*, 10:197–98.

57. Burke's speech, 19 April 1774, *Parliamentary History*, 17:1239.

58. Ibid., p. 1240.

59. Burke's speech, 19 April 1774, Parliamentary Diaries of Matthew Brickdale, Book IX, Bristol University Library, Bristol, England, microfilm copy in the Library of Congress.

60. Burke's speech, 19 April 1774, *Parliamentary History*, 17:1239–40.

61. The quotation is from Alexander Wedderburne's speech, 19 April 1774, Brickdale Diaries, Book IX. Wedderburne had been a loyal follower of Grenville during the 1760s and made his remarks in defense of Grenville against Burke's criticism.

62. Grenville to Thomas Grenville, 13 May 1745, *Grenville Papers*, 1:35. For his comments on naval strategy, see another letter to his brother Thomas, 10 October 1745, ibid., p. 44. During his stay at the Admiralty, Grenville worked ceaselessly to further his brother's career in the navy. In the case of the yard at Kinsale, reform served not only the nation's interest but his family's as well.

63. Grenville to Thomas Grenville, 28 December 1745, ibid., pp. 48–49.

64. See Grenville to Bedford, 24 October, 29 November 1746, *Correspondence of John, Fourth Duke of Bedford*, ed. Lord John Russell, 1:182, 196; and Bedford to Grenville, 11 November, 24 November 1746, *Grenville Papers*, 1:54–55.

65. Much of Grenville's frustration with his colleagues stemmed from their constant refusal to fulfill a promise they had made to him that Thomas Grenville would have a separate command. See Grenville to Thomas Grenville, 2 April 1747, *Grenville Papers*, 1:58–60. For his efforts to get an appointment to the Treasury, see Grenville, "Narrative," 12 April 1762, ibid., pp. 425–26.

66. Ibid., p. 427.

67. Grenville's speech, 9 March 1764, *Ryder Diaries*, p. 234. For the best description of Pelham's accomplishment, see P. G. M. Dickson, *The Financial Revolution in England: A Study in the Development of Public Credit, 1688–1756*, pp. 228–43.

68. The information in this paragraph is from Stephen F. Gradish, "Wages and Manning: The Navy Act of 1758." The quotations are from ibid., pp. 48, 46. Grenville was so proud of this act that he held it in his hand when he sat for his official portrait as First Lord of the Admiralty.

69. See Gradish, "Wages and Manning," pp. 63–65.

70. Wiggin, *Faction of Cousins*, pp. 225–26.

71. Grenville to the Earl of Egmont, 16 April 1764, *Grenville Papers*, 2:294.

Notes to Chapter IV
"The First Great Object"

1. Grenville's notes on the Cabinet meeting, 26 July 1762, George Grenville Papers, HEHL, STG Box 14(43), Bedford to Egremont, 15 September 1762, ibid., Box 16(16); "Alterations in the last *projet*," [September 1762], Liverpool Papers, BL, Add. MSS. 38336, fol., 284. There are several references to smuggling in the West Indies and

to corrupt customs officers in Henry Grenville's correspondence with his brother. See, for example, H. Grenville to Grenville, 9 July 1751, George Grenville Papers, HEHL, STG Box 25(31).

2. Grenville's draft of a letter to Bedford, October 1762, ibid., Box 17(6); and Cabinet minutes, 25 October 1762, ibid., Box 14(43).

3. "Preliminary articles of peace," 29 November 1762, *Commons Journals*, 29:365.

4. The Admiralty to Egremont, 21 March 1763, PRO, S.P. 42/64, 150/17.

5. The Board of Trade to the King, 15 March 1763, and 21 March 1763; instructions given to the commander-in-chief of the convoy to Newfoundland, [29 March 1763], George Grenville Papers, HEHL, STG Box 17(28–30).

6. See the Treasury's announcement on 24 March 1763, *Commons Journals*, 29:609. For the orders, see Admiralty to Egremont, 27 May 1763, PRO, S.P. 42/64, 150/33a; for the Cabinet meeting, see Cabinet minutes, 2 June 1763, Egremont Papers, PRO, P.R.O. 30/47/21.

7. Grenville to the Earl of Bath, 30 April 1763, George Grenville Letterbooks, HEHL, ST 7, i. See also Grenville to Humphrey Morice, 20 April 1763, ibid. Grenville had to deal with these men carefully and honestly, because they were potential supporters of his administration in the House.

8. Jenkinson to Customs Commissioners, 21 May 1763, PRO, T. 11/27, fol. 136.

9. Jenkinson to Customs Commissioners, 14 July 1763, ibid., fol. 146. In the margin of the copybook opposite this letter, a clerk noted "CC, to hasten their report relating to the revenue in America." For a copy of the report, see Customs Commissioners to Treasury, 21 July 1763, ibid., 1/426, fols. 269–73. Grenville had a copy in his files, too. George Grenville Papers, HEHL, STG Box 13(5). This copy is incorrectly dated 1764.

10. The documents are described in an editorial note in *Grenville Papers*, 2:373–74. McCulloh mentioned that he had submitted similar proposals to Halifax in 1755; copies of these may be found in McCulloh to Halifax, [1755], Newcastle Papers, BL, Add. MSS. 33030, fols. 334–35.

11. [McCulloh], "General thoughts," [June–July 1763], George Grenville Papers, HEHL, STG Box 12(28). A copy of this paper, with an explanation of my reasons for attributing it to McCulloh and dating it as I have, may be found in Appendix A. For an excellent account of McCulloh's career, see Charles G. Sellers, Jr., "Private Profits and British Colonial Policy: The Speculations of Henry McCulloh." Thomas Barrow cogently argued that suppressing the clandestine trade was a major concern of Grenville's Treasury, both in *Trade and Empire: The British Customs Service in Colonial America, 1660–1775*, pp. 164–80, and in "The Background to the Grenville Program, 1757–1763." Barrow did not, however, notice the contributions of McCulloh and Nathaniel Ware and thus overestimated the significance of the customs commissioners' reports.

12. Nathaniel Ware to [Grenville?], 22 August 1763, George Grenville Papers, HEHL, STG Box 12(14). For a copy of this letter, see Appendix B. In this letter, Ware felt constrained to explain his delay in procuring intelligence about the clandestine trade in molasses. This reveals that Ware had spent what seemed to him a considerable amount of time since his last contact with the Treasury and perhaps indicates that he had heard some hints of impatience from that quarter. Grenville had, after all, lost his patience with the customs commissioners after seven weeks. Because of this comment about delay, it seems reasonable to conclude that Ware's initial contact with the Treasury came during July, if not earlier. It is also reasonable to conclude that Ware stressed during this first contact the dangers posed by the colonies' clandestine trade to Britain's political and commercial control of America, rather than pointing out ways of raising a colonial revenue. In his 22 August 1763 letter, Ware referred to an estimate he

had made of the annual volume of molasses smuggled into America "upon another occasion, when, without the least view to a tax, any random guess, which I took care to be within the truth, was sufficient for my purpose." For the dates of Ware's various leaves, see "Copy of the list of officers in the plantations . . . absent from their duty," 8 March 1763, Liverpool Papers, BL, Add. MSS. 38334, fol. 37. One reason historians have not noticed Ware's role in the planning of Grenville's American program has been their mistaken belief that he was in America. See, for example, Barrow, *Trade and Empire*, p. 176.

13. Ware to Newcastle, 16 June 1758, Newcastle Papers, BL, Add. MSS. 32881, fol. 81. See also Ware to [H. B. Legge?], 28 January 1758, PRO, T. 1/384, no. 144.

14. Ware to Bute, 6 July 1762, Bute Papers in the possession of the Marquess of Bute, Isle of Bute, Scotland.

15. Ibid.

16. [Ware], "Observations on the British Colonies on the continent of America," [n.d.], *MHSC*, 1st ser., 1 (1792): 66–84. In *Toward Lexington: The Role of the British Army in the Coming of the American Revolution*, p. 63n., John Shy asserted that this paper was one of those sent by Paine Wingate to Jeremy Belknap on 23 October 1775, and he therefore concluded that Ware was the grandfather of Col. Mesech Weare, a revolutionary leader in New Hampshire during the 1770s and 1780s. Weare's grandfather, however, died during the 1730s. Moreover, this paper was not given to the Massachusetts Historical Society by Belknap, but by Edward Davis in 1791. See *Proceedings of the Massachusetts Historical Society* 1 (1839): 26. Shy also speculated that the report, which is addressed "To the Right Honorable the Earl of ———," was perhaps written to Bute. But in his letter to Bute on 6 July 1762, Ware noted that he "had presumed to offer some imperfect observations on the present state of the Northern colonies" to Halifax. This probably referred to a copy of the "Observations" published in *MHSC*. Furthermore, in his introduction to "Observations," Ware referred to "your lordship's distinguished attention to whatever relates to the British colonies." Halifax was well-known in London during the 1750s for his interest in the American colonies and for the vigor with which he executed his duties as President of the Board of Trade. Bute had no such reputation. Ware to Bute, 6 July 1762, Bute Papers, Scotland; [Ware], "Observations," p. 67.

17. It is unclear whether Almon was referring to Ware's ideas or not. Still, a "naval officer" was a provincial customs official in many colonies, and Ware did recommend in "Observations" that the Crown pay the salaries of colonial governors and other executive officers, a part of the scheme by the gentleman from Boston that Almon found particularly sinister. Almon's recollection may indicate that Ware's ideas were taken seriously before Grenville came to office. See [John Almon] *Biographical, Literary, and Political Anecdotes of several of the most eminent persons of the present age, never before printed*, 2:81.

18. "Observations" was clearly written before November 1762. Even if one does not accept it as the report Ware referred to in his 6 July 1762 letter to Bute, the text of "Observations" makes it apparent that Barrow erred when in *Trade and Empire*, p. 176, he said that the comptroller composed it in 1763. In "Observations," Ware advised that Britain should keep Guadeloupe and return Canada to the French when peace was concluded. A man who wanted an English place from the Bute administration would hardly have made this argument after the publication of the preliminaries in November 1762. Furthermore, if he had been so foolhardy, he would have referred to the decision to keep Canada as a mistake.

19. Ware to Bute, [1762], North Papers, Bodleian Library, a. 6, fol. 238. The

archivist for the papers on the possession of the Marquess of Bute, Catherine Armet, in a private communication on 5 February 1981, pointed out that the endorsement on Ware to Bute, 6 July 1762, was in the handwriting of Charles Jenkinson. I am indebted to Miss Armet for her kind assistance and her observations on this point.

20. All quotations from McCulloh in this section may be found in Appendix A. See also [Ware], "Observations," p. 80.

21. Ibid., p. 79. While Ware was serving as comptroller at Boston, the collector there, Sir Henry Frankland, publicly called attention to the continuing "illicit trade between Holland and other parts of Europe and the neighboring colonies; and [to the] great quantities of European and Asiatic goods . . . clandestinely brought from thence into this port, by land as well as sea." He also stated his determination "to use [his] utmost endeavors to prevent the carrying on a trade so prejudicial to our Mother Country and detrimental to the fair trader." *Boston Post-Boy,* 19 February 1753. Small quantities of these goods were occasionally seized during Ware's sojourn in Boston. Ibid., 3 September 1750, 14 October 1751, 25 March 1754, and 9 September 1754. Thus Ware's comments on the clandestine trade were probably the results of knowledge he gained as an officer.

22. [Ware], "Observations," p. 80.

23. 9 March 1764, *Ryder Diary,* p. 234; and Grenville to Lord Botetourt, 3 November 1765, HEHL, George Grenville Letterbooks, ST 7, ii. Indeed, his later estimate set the volume of the trade at "considerably more than £500,000 a year."

24. 12 December 1753, *Parliamentary History,* 10:168. Ware himself was keenly aware of the opprobrium attached to informers and tried to protect himself against that judgment. See his disclaimers of personal vindictiveness and hopes for reward in his letter to Bute, 6 July 1762, Bute Papers, Scotland.

25. [Thomas Whately], *Considerations on the trade and finances of this Kingdom, and on the measures of administration with respect to those great national objects since the conclusion of the peace,* pp. 65–66.

26. "Arguments . . . in favor of the Treaty," [December 1762], *Parliamentary History,* 15:1272.

27. [Whately], *Considerations,* p. 11.

28. [Whately], *Considerations,* p. 53. See also *Regulations,* pp. 90–92.

29. Grenville's speech, 9 March 1764, *Ryder Diary,* p. 234.

30. See "General thoughts," in Appendix A; and [Ware], "Observations," pp. 80–83.

31. Customs Commissioners to the Treasury, 10 May 1759, and 21 July 1763, PRO, T. 1/392, fols. 38–39, and T. 1/426, fols. 269–73. The quotation is from the 1763 report. For the Treasury's decision to look up the 1759 report, see Jenkinson to Customs Commissioners, 25 July 1763, ibid., T. 11/27, fol. 147.

32. For the usual procedures of eighteenth-century Treasuries, see Elizabeth E. Hoon, *The Organization of the English Customs System, 1696–1768,* pp. 45–61. For a description of Grenville's concern about ignorance at the Treasury over customs procedures and papers, see C. Amyrand to Jenkinson, 17 July 1764, Liverpool Papers, BL, Add. MSS. 38203, fol. 49.

33. Jenkinson to Customs Commissioners, 25 July 1763, PRO, T. 11/27, fol. 147.

34. Jenkinson to Customs Commissioners, 1 August 1763, ibid., fol. 137. Emphasis added. The entries in this minute book are occasionally out of order.

35. Jackson to Jenkinson, 18 September 1763, Liverpool Papers, BL, Add. MSS. 38201, fol. 114. For the commissioners' report of 16 September and their instructions, see John Fremantle to Jenkinson, 16 September 1763, and Customs Commissioners to the Treasury, 16 September 1763, PRO, T. 11/27, fol. 161.

36. Treasury minutes, 21 September 1763, PRO, T. 29/35, fol. 82; and Thomas Whately to Customs Commissioners, 23 September 1763 (two letters), ibid., 11/27, fols. 154–55, 160.

37. "Instructions to American officers," 3 November 1763, ibid., T. 1/426, fol. 459.

38. Customs Commissioners to the Treasury, 28 September 1763, ibid., fols. 314–15. For Hulton's activities in Germany and Grenville's approval of them, see Henry Hulton to the Treasury, 23 August 1763, ibid., fol. 280, and Hulton to [?], October 1763, Hulton Letterbook, Manchester College, Oxford.

39. Warrant for Henry Hulton as Plantation Clerk, 29 October 1763, PRO, T. 11/27, fol. 174. For Hulton's ambitiousness, see Freemantle to Charles Lloyd, 27 March 1764, George Grenville Papers, HEHL, STG Box 196(15).

40. See Treasury minutes, 28 September 1763, PRO, T. 29/35, fol. 85; and the Treasury to the King, 4 October 1763, in *EHD*, 9:637–39. For the action of other departments, see Board of Trade minutes, 10 and 22 October 1763, *JCTP*, January 1759 to December 1763, pp. 389–90; Thomas Gage to Halifax, 9 December 1763, *Gage Papers*, 1:2; and Carl Ubbelohde, *The Vice-Admiralty Courts and the American Revolution*, pp. 47–50.

41. For Ware's involvement, beginning before 22 August, see Appendix B; for McCulloh's, which began at least by 8 September, see P. D. G. Thomas, *British Politics and the Stamp Act Crisis: The First Phase of the American Revolution, 1763–1767*, pp. 70–71.

42. Temple to Whately, 10 September 1764, and Whately to Temple, 5 November 1764, *Bowdoin-Temple Papers*, pp. 24–28; and 9 March 1764, *Ryder diary*, p. 234.

43. "General thoughts," Appendix A; Ware, "Observations," pp. 74–75; Treasury to the King, 4 October 1763, *EHD*, 9:638.

44. Whately to Customs Commissioners, 10 November 1763, PRO, T. 11/27, fol. 161.

45. 9 March 1764, *Ryder Diary*, p. 235.

46. Treasury minutes, 21 November 1763, and 9 January 1764, PRO, T. 29/35, fols. 107, 124. Grenville cannot have been heartened, either, by accounts of a quarrel between naval officers and customs officers in Boston. Treasury minutes, 9 January 1764, and 2 February 1764, ibid., fols. 126, 146. For Grenville's determination to keep the navy's budget as low as possible, see Grenville to Egmont, 16 April 1764, George Grenville Letterbooks, HEHL, ST 7, i.

47. 9 March 1764, *Ryder Diary*, p. 235. This statement is similar to one made by McCulloh in his 1755 paper, that a stamp tax "executes itself, since no man will receive a security without its being stamped, when he knows it will be void thereby." McCulloh to Halifax, [1755], Newcastle Papers, BL, Add. MSS. 33030, fols. 334–35. For the activities of McCulloh during September and October 1763, see Thomas, *British Politics*, pp. 70–71.

48. 9 March 1764, *Ryder Diary*, p. 234.

49. Thomas, *British Politics*, p. 40.

50. Wood to Jenkinson, 10 January 1764, *Jenkinson Papers*, p. 254.

51. Hulton to [?], December 1763, Hulton Letterbook, Manchester College, Oxford.

Notes to Chapter V
Taxing Molasses

1. For the characteristics of customs commissioners, see Sir Lewis Namier, *The Structure of Politics at the Accession of George III*, p. 21; and W. R. Ward, "Some

Eighteenth Century Civil Servants: The English Revenue Commissioners, 1754–98," pp. 27–35.

2. Customs Commissioners to the Treasury, 21 July 1763, 10 May 1759, PRO, T. 1/426, fol. 269, and 1/392, fol. 38. Other historians who have written on the origins of the molasses duty of 1764 have failed to notice the indirect recommendation in the 21 July report. For example, see Allen S. Johnson, "The Passage of the Sugar Act," pp. 509–10.

3. Customs Commissioners to the Treasury, 16 September 1763, PRO, T. 1/426, fol. 289.

4. Customs Commissioners to the Treasury, 21 July 1763, ibid., fol. 269.

5. Customs Commissioners to the Treasury, 16 September 1763, ibid., fol. 289.

6. 9 March 1764, *Ryder Diary*, p. 234; and 22 March 1764, Harris Diary, quoted in P. D. G. Thomas, *British Politics and the Stamp Act Crisis: The First Phase of the American Revolution, 1763–1767*, p. 58.

7. Jenkinson to Benjamin Hallowell, the comptroller of the customs at Boston, 12 January 1765, *Jenkinson Papers*, pp. 346–47; and *Regulations*, pp. 84–85.

8. [Ware], "Observations on the British Colonies on the continent of America," [n.d.], *MHSC*, 1st ser. 1 (1792): 83.

9. See below and Appendix B for a discussion of the solutions Ware did propose.

10. Ware to Newcastle, 26 June 1758, Newcastle Papers, BL, Add. MSS. 32881, fol. 82; Ware to [Legge ?], 28 January 1758, PRO, T. 1/384, no. 144; and Ware to Bute, [1762], North Papers, Bodleian Library, a. 6, fol. 238. For Ware's comment about his apprehensions, see Ware to Bute, 6 July 1762, Bute Papers, Scotland. For the Treasury's orders, see Jenkinson to Customs Commissioners, 25 July 1763, PRO, T. 11/27, fol. 147.

11. Fremantle reported to Jenkinson on 11 August that he had notified all absent customs officers to set out for America by 31 August or face the consequences. Ware must have immediately applied for an exemption, for Grenville observed on 8 September that every absent officer had asked to be exempted from the order. PRO, T. 1/426, fol. 274; and *Grenville Papers*, 2:114.

12. Appendix B. Some of Ware's warnings and recommendations may have been based as much on his experiences in Boston as on his investigations in London. For instance, he himself had seized some smuggled French molasses and rum. *Boston Post-Boy*, 26 January 1750/1. Moreover, he had been in Boston when some merchants of that port had publicly complained about the "great quantities of French rum . . . of late . . . illegally imported into this province" and warned "that a number of gentlemen are determined to put a stop to such trade, by openly discovering such rum in order to its being seized." Ibid., 29 October 1750. Finally, he may have already been on duty when Sir Henry Frankland seized 190 chests of lemons. Ibid., 4 June 1750.

13. Appendix A.

14. 6 January 1764, Mrs. Grenville's Diary, *Grenville Papers*, 2:481. Allen S. Johnson believed that Grenville did contemplate paying civil officers' salaries out of the receipts from parliamentary taxes during February 1764. His argument, however, has been effectively challenged by Jack M. Sosin. See Johnson, "The Passage of the Sugar Act," p. 512; Jack M. Sosin, *Whitehall and the Wilderness: The Middle West in British Colonial Policy, 1760–1775*, p. 80n.; and my discussion below.

15. The Treasury was sufficiently concerned about the French entering into the distilling of rum to insert into the Sugar Act a clause forbidding its importation into any British colony in America. 4 Geo. 3, c. 15, sec. 18, in *Statutes at Large*, 26:39–40.

16. Jackson to Jenkinson, 18 September 1763, *Jenkinson Papers*, pp. 191–92.

17. Appendixes A and B.

18. "An estimate of tea, sugar, and molasses, illegally imported into the continent of North America in one year," [December 1763], Liverpool Papers, BL, Add. MSS. 38335, fol. 243. The approximate date of this paper may be determined by noting that it cites the figures for the legal trade in tea from 1 January through 17 November 1763. It generally took the customs house in London about a month to compile the latest totals of trade. For example, the figures for the period 1 January–31 December 1763 became available on 31 January 1764. See ibid., 38337, fol. 150.

19. For this estimate, and his eagerness to help the Treasury, see Jackson to Benjamin Franklin, 12 November 1763, and 27 December 1763, *Franklin Papers*, 10:371, 413. For his recommendation of Eliphalet Dyer to Jenkinson, see Jackson to Jenkinson, 7 January 1764, Liverpool Papers, BL, Add. MSS. 38205, fol. 7. Dyer obviously impressed men at the Treasury, for he was appointed collector of the customs at New London on 31 May 1764. See "Appointments to North America," PRO, T. 11/27, fol. 224.

20. See *Regulations*, p. 80, and [Whately], *Considerations on the trade and finances of this Kingdom, and on the measures of administration with respect to those great national objects since the conclusion of the peace*, pp. 99–100.

21. Appendix B.

22. The figures Ware used (see Appendix B) are confusing. I am unclear how he reached his conclusion that the distilleries used 38,625 hogsheads, and his references to the total consumption of British molasses are unclear. Still, that he concluded that the volume of the contraband trade was below the level at which rumor had placed it is beyond question. McCulloh guessed that if foreign molasses were taxed at one penny per gallon, the revenue would gain twelve thousand pounds annually. Assuming that a hogshead equalled one hundred gallons, this figure indicates a trade of 43,200 hogsheads a year. See Appendixes A and B.

23. "An Estimate," [December 1763], Liverpool Papers, BL, Add. MSS. 38335, fol. 243; and "Calculation concerning the molasses duty," [1763–1764] PRO, T. 1/434, fol. 272. Johnson identified this latter paper as Whately's work. Johnson, "The Passage of the Sugar Act," p. 511. For Grenville's conclusion, see his speech, 9 March 1764, *Ryder Diary*, p. 234.

24. Grenville's speech, 30 April 1766, Harris Diary, in Thomas, *British Politics*, p. 49; and Jasper Mauduit to Massachusetts, 30 December 1763, *MHSC*, 1st ser. 6 (1800): 193.

25. H. Grenville to Grenville, 26 October 1759, discusses the state of Grenville's investments in Barbados. George Grenville Papers, HEHL, STG Box 22(16). Merrill Jensen noticed the importance of sugar exportations to the West Indians during 1763–1764 in *The Founding of a Nation: A History of the American Revolution, 1763–1776*, pp. 174–79. Failure to grasp this significance marred an otherwise perceptive account of the Sugar Act by Jack M. Sosin, *Agents and Merchants: British Colonial Policy and the Origins of the American Revolution, 1763–1775*, pp. 81–82.

26. See Thomas's discussion of Fuller's and Beckford's roles, in *British Politics*, pp. 55–60. In 1766, Fuller supported lowering the molasses duty to one penny in the hope it would raise more revenue than the higher duty. Ibid., p. 270.

27. For an interpretation that the Treasury seriously considered four pence and for Grenville's comments on the futility of petitions for repeal, see Jasper Mauduit to Massachusetts, 30 December 1763, *MHSC*, 1st ser. 6 (1800): 193. See also Jackson to Franklin, 12 November 1763, *Franklin Papers*, 10:371.

28. Mauduit to Massachusetts, 30 December 1763, *MHSC*, 1st ser. 6 (1800): 193.

29. Jackson to Franklin, 12 November 1763, *Franklin Papers*, 10:371.

30. *Regulations*, p. 80.

31. "An estimate," [December 1763], Liverpool Papers, BL, Add. MSS. 38335, fol. 243.

32. The quotation is from *Regulations*, p. 80.

33. [Whately], *Considerations*, p. 99. In their letters to America, Mauduit and Jackson expressed a willingness to go along with twopence, and Whately's account in *Considerations* makes it clear they did not hide this opinion from the Treasury. Mauduit to Massachusetts, 30 December 1763, *MHSC*, 1st ser. 6 (1800): 193; Jackson to Franklin, 12 November 1763, *Franklin Papers*, 10:371.

34. "An estimate," [December 1763], Liverpool Papers, BL, Add. MSS. 38335, fol. 243.

35. Mauduit to Massachusetts, 30 December 1763, *MHSC*, 1st ser. 6 (1800): 193.

36. Ibid., 11 February 1764, pp. 194–95. For the petition, see Mauduit et al. to the Treasury [n.d., read 27 February 1764], PRO, T. 1/430, fols. 204–5.

37. Mauduit to Massachusetts, 11 February 1764, *MHSC*, 1st ser. 6 (1800): 195.

38. See n. 15 above.

39. For the language from the petition, see PRO, T. 1/430, fol. 204. The notice Grenville and his colleagues took of certain arguments in it may be seen in the Treasury minutes, 17 February 1764, ibid., T. 29/35, fol. 160.

40. 30 April 1766, Harris Diary, in Thomas, *British Politics*, p. 49. This version of events was also published by Whately in 1766, and no one challenged his account, either. *Considerations*, p. 99.

41. [Whately], *Considerations*, p. 99. I suspect Whately's comment is a fuller version of Grenville's sentiments than Ryder's notes on his speech, 9 March 1764, *Ryder Diary*, p. 234.

42. West India Merchants to the Treasury, 18 February 1763, PRO, T. 1/424, fol. 115. For Grenville's attitude toward Cust, see Namier and Brooke, *House of Commons*, 2:292.

43. The author of "An estimate" wanted to set the duty at thirty shillings, as did Sir George Amyrand, one of Grenville's financial advisers. Grenville rejected this as too tempting to smugglers. Liverpool Papers, BL, Add. MSS. 38335, fol. 243; and 22 March 1764, Harris Diary, in Thomas, *British Politics*, p. 57.

44. Grenville to Lord Northumberland, 26 February 1764, *Additional Grenville Papers*, p. 94. Mauduit noted in his 11 February 1764 letter that it would be impossible to oppose colonial taxation effectively; surely Grenville reached much the same conclusion. *MHSC*, 1st ser. 6 (1800): 194.

45. Sir Lewis Namier and John Brooke cite this opinion of Horace Walpole's as an accurate judgment in *Charles Townshend*, p. 121.

46. Mauduit to Massachusetts, 11 February 1764, *MHSC*, 1st ser. 6 (1800): 194–95.

47. [Whately], "Calculations concerning the molasses duty," [1763–1764], PRO, T. 1/434, fol. 272. Whately concluded that setting the duty at threepence would reduce the total volume of the trade from 80,000 to 62,222 hogsheads per year. I have assumed that twopence would not reduce the volume and thus calculated its highest possible produce. In this document, Whately did not do this, but instead calculated the produce of a one penny duty. For the reference to the Scottish stamp duties, see "State of the revenue arising from stamps," [1764] Liverpool Papers, Add. MSS. 38338, fols. 125–71.

48. Ryder did not take notes on Grenville's discussion of the Guinea trade, but from

Cust's reference, it is clear that his remarks were similar to Whately's analysis in *Regulations,* pp. 86–87. Whately's comments also reveal the Treasury's confidence on this question: "As to the trade upon the coast of Guinea, this is no longer a matter of speculation." Ibid., p. 82. For Cust's remarks, see 9 March 1764, *Ryder Diary,* p. 236. For Cust's status in the House as an expert on British interests in Africa, see Namier and Brooke, *House of Commons,* 2:292.

49. William Mutter to the African Committee, 10 January 1764, PRO, C.O. 388/51, no folio number. Because Cust was also involved in the rum trade from the British West Indies to England, he would fit the description of the "West-India gentlemen" Mauduit said had been at the Treasury in January–February 1764.

50. Perhaps this news encouraged the Treasury to assume confidently that American merchants could pass the duty on to other consumers of their rum as well. *Regulations,* pp. 81–87.

51. Ibid., p. 80. I have changed the order of these observations in the text.

52. A letter from London, 24 March 1764, in the *New York Mercury,* 4 June 1764.

53. Grenville had learned that customs collections in 1763 exceeded those in 1762 by £391,186. Wood to Jenkinson, 9 January 1764, Liverpool Papers, BL, Add. MSS. 38202, fol. 18. He therefore concluded that "stationing ships has been of service" in increasing receipts. Grenville's speech, 9 March 1764, *Ryder Diary,* p. 234.

54. Jenkinson to Hallowell, 12 January 1765, *Jenkinson Papers,* p. 346.

55. 4 Geo. 3, c. 15, preamble, *Statutes at Large,* 26:33.

56. 6 January 1764, Mrs. Grenville's Diary, *Grenville Papers,* 2:481.

57. For Thomas's comment, see *British Politics,* p. 36. For examples of Grenville's arguments to the agents, see Garth to South Carolina, 5 June 1764, in Edmund S. Morgan, ed., *Prologue to Revolution: Sources and Documents on the Stamp Act Crisis, 1764–1766,* p. 28; Ingersoll to Fitch, 6 March 1765, in Jared Ingersoll, *Mr. Ingersoll's Letters Relating to the Stamp Act,* pp. 25–26. For Grenville's disavowal of any intention to use the money for purposes other than defense, see Ingersoll to Fitch, 11 February 1765, *Ingersoll Papers,* p. 313. For Jenkinson's comment, see Appendix C. For a discussion of it, see Chapter VIII, n. 27.

58. Johnson, "The Passage of the Sugar Act," p. 512. Johnson also cited as proof of this intention that the Treasury considered the cost of the civil establishments in the colonies on 23 January 1764. But as Sosin pointed out, the only colonies under consideration that day were Georgia and the Floridas, which were so small that Britain had to support their establishments. *Whitehall and the Wilderness,* p. 80n.

59. The argument that the plan was abandoned because Grenville realized after 11 February the molasses duty would not cover the army's expenses is Johnson's, in "The Passage of the Sugar Act," p. 512. For various estimates of the produce of the duty, see Appendix A, [1763]; Appendix B, 22 August 1763; "An estimate," [December 1763], Liverpool Papers, BL, Add. MSS. 38335, fol. 243; and "Calculations," [1763–1764], PRO, T. 1/434, fol. 272. Grenville surely knew that duty would fall well short before February. Johnson did not consider estimates from a stamp duty. For these, see editorial note, 5 July 1763, *Grenville Papers,* 2:374; and Israel Mauduit's "Account of a Conference between Mr. Grenville and Several Agents," [n.d.], *Jenkinson Papers,* p. 307.

60. Mauduit to Massachusetts, 7 April 1764, in Lawrence Henry Gipson, *The British Empire before the American Revolution,* 10:231.

61. Ibid.

62. Townshend to Newcastle, 23 March 1764, in Thomas, *British Politics,* p. 59. Thomas's discussion of the passage of the duty through the House is excellent. Ibid., pp. 52–60.

63. 9 March 1764, *Ryder Diary*, p. 236; and the description of the debate on 22 March in Thomas, *British Politics*, pp. 57–58.

64. [Whately], "Calculations," [1763–1764], PRO, T. 1/434, fol. 272.

65. Whately, "Whately's plan," [6 December 1764], printed in E. Hughes, "The English Stamp Duties, 1664–1764," pp. 264, 260.

66. For the produce of the sixpence duty from 1758 through 1762, see Liverpool Papers, BL, Add. MSS. 38334, fol. 241.

67. Jenkinson to R. Wolters, 18 January 1765, *Jenkinson Papers*, p. 348.

68. *Regulations*, pp. 81–82.

69. In his petition to the Treasury against the imposition of a threepence duty, Mauduit observed that the principal merchants of Massachusetts claimed that the trade could not bear a tax of more than one penny per gallon. Mauduit himself admitted that he would accept twopence "silently," which indicated that he did not agree. There was no reason, however, for Grenville to assume that the smugglers of Massachusetts would also be silent, especially since they had asked for one penny. Jasper Mauduit's petition, [read 27 February 1764], PRO, T. 1/430, fol. 204.

70. *Regulations*, p. 80.

71. The quotation is from Whately to Temple, 8 November 1764, *Bowdoin-Temple Papers*, p. 37.

72. The molasses duty went into effect on 29 September 1764. See the orders of the Treasury regarding the islands, in Jenkinson to Customs Commissioners, 20 October 1764, and Whately to Customs Commissioners, 25 October 1764, PRO, T. 11/27, fol. 236.

73. *Regulations*, p. 100.

74. Ibid., p. 87.

Notes to Chapter VI
New Sources of Revenue

1. Sir George Savile to [? Acklom], [August 1768], WLCL, Miscellaneous Collections (1765–1773).

2. 9 March 1764, *Ryder Diary*, p. 236.

3. "Plan of Forts," [1763], George Grenville Papers, HEHL, George Grenville Papers relating to the Peace of Paris, STG Box 12; McCulloh made the same point in "General thoughts," Appendix A.

4. Grenville first publicly noted the urgent need for effective collection of taxes in the Treasury's memorial to the King, 4 October 1763, in *EHD*, 9:638. For an example of his using this type of reasoning to oppose efforts to repeal the Stamp Act, see his second speech of the day, 7 February 1766, *Ryder Diary*, p. 288.

5. *Regulations*, p. 86. Whately was boasting, of course, that the ministry's taxes had been judiciously chosen, but his boasts still reveal the Treasury's twin goals.

6. The merchants themselves suggested that this duty be imposed in their petition to the House of Commons, 16 March 1764, *Commons Journals*, 29:959, so Grenville could be reasonably certain the duty would be paid. William Knox estimated that this duty and an identical one on rice shipped to Madeira and the African islands would yield between fifteen hundred and two thousand pounds a year. Parliament decided not to permit direct shipment of rice to the African islands, so Grenville could expect the collection to be substantially less. 24 March 1763, ibid., p. 605.

7. See Appendixes A and B; and Whately to the Customs Commissioners, 18 November 1763, PRO, T. 11/27, fol. 161.

8. For the quotations, see *Regulations*, pp. 74–75; for a good description of the tax, see Ian R. Christie and Benjamin W. Labaree, *Empire or Independence, 1760–1776: A British-American Dialogue on the Coming of the American Revolution*, pp. 37–38.

9. *Regulations*, pp. 75–76. For an idea of the relatively low yield of luxury taxes compared to the land tax, see "Ways and Means for 1765," *Parliamentary History*, 16:63–75.

10. Yeates to Jenkinson, 29 December 1763, *Jenkinson Papers*, p. 245; and Tod to Jenkinson, 13 March 1764, Liverpool Papers, BL, Add. MSS. 38202, fol. 156. Ten days before Yeates contacted Tod, the Treasury indicated interest in the drawbacks by obtaining an order from the House of Commons for accounts of all tea, china, calicoes, and other East India goods exported to America since 1753, broken down by years, with the drawbacks paid on each type of goods itemized. 19 December 1763, *Commons Journals*, 29:710. The customs commissioners evidently were not consulted on this matter. Indeed, in their 16 September 1763 report, they assumed the drawback would continue to be paid. PRO, T. 1/430, fol. 289. Nor was the Board of Trade consulted. I have deduced Cust's ignorance and Grenville's secrecy from the apparent lack of merchant opposition to abolishing the drawback until after 9 March, when Grenville introduced it. After 9 March, Cust and Richard Glover organized a vigorous, persistent protest in London, Bristol, and Wiltshire that was not discouraged by several defeats in the House of Commons. Had these men known of the plans beforehand, surely they would have tried to persuade Grenville not to introduce the measures. For evidence of their activities after 9 March, see the discussion later in Chapter VI; Tod to Jenkinson, 13 March 1764; Resolution of the Society of Merchant Venturers of the City of Bristol, 13 March 1764, in W. E. Minchinton, ed., *Politics and the Port of Bristol in the Eighteenth Century: The Petitions of the Society of Merchant Venturers, 1698–1803*, p. xx; and 20, 22, and 26 March 1764, *Commons Journals*, 29:968, 979, 986. It is instructive to compare the absence of signs of concern about the drawback before 9 March with interested people's advance knowledge of and reaction to the plans to introduce a colonial stamp tax. See, for example, Benjamin Barons to Jenkinson, 6 February 1764, Liverpool Papers, BL, Add. MSS. 38202, fols. 83–84.

11. See the various accounts on the exports of foreign linens in Liverpool Papers, BL, Add. MSS. 38202, fol. 157; 38204, fol. 96; and 38337, fols. 87–89, 219.

12. 9 March 1764, *Ryder Diary*, p. 235; and the resolutions of the committee of ways and means, 10 March 1764, *Commons Journals*, 29:935.

13. "Account of the amount of drawbacks upon each article of foreign goods," 15 April 1763, copy in PRO, T. 1/430, fols. 326–28; and "Account of drawbacks upon white calicoes and foreign linens," 19 March 1764, Liverpool Papers, BL, Add. MSS. 38337, fol. 222.

14. *Regulations*, pp. 58, 60. Jenkinson noted in early 1765, "We last year laid [a] tax on foreign manufactures with a view to give preference to our own." See Appendix C. For an argument that abolishing the drawback was chiefly intended to be "an indirect tax on America," see Franklin B. Wickwire, *British Subministers and Colonial America, 1763–1783*, pp. 119–21.

15. Jenkinson to Hallowell, 12 January 1765, *Jenkinson Papers*, p. 346. See also *Regulations*, pp. 61–67.

16. *Regulations*, pp. 68–69. For the popularity of this bounty with agents and merchants, see P. D. G. Thomas, *British Politics and the Stamp Act Crisis: The First Phase of the American Revolution, 1763–1767*, p. 67.

17. Customs Commissioners to the Treasury, 16 September 1763, PRO, T. 1/430, fol. 289.

18. 9 March 1764, *Ryder Diary*, p. 236. The italics are mine, to call attention to the misstatement in the published version of the diary that "no ship shall be cleared out *of* North America."

19. 4 Geo. 3, c. 25, sec. 16, *Statutes at Large*, 26:39.

20. Tod to Jenkinson, 13 March 1764, BL, Add. MSS. 38202, fol. 156. For the estimate of the increase in price of British linens and the argument that the profit would seem too small to smugglers, see *A letter from a merchant who has left off trade to a member of Parliament in which the case of British and Irish manufacture of linen, threads, and tapes, is fairly stated, and all objections against the encouragement proposed to be given to that manufacture fully answered*, pp. 69–75, the pamphlet Tod recommended that Jenkinson read in 1764.

21. "State of the revenue arising from stamps," [1764], Liverpool Papers, BL, Add. MSS. 38338, fols. 125–71.

22. Appendix C. Jenkinson's thoughts on a colonial stamp duty were doubtless about the same in 1763, for he advocated enacting one then, just as he did in 1765.

23. Henry McCulloh, "General thoughts . . . with respect to the late American stamp duty bill," [1765], Rockingham Papers, Sheffield Central Library, Wentworth Wode-house Muniments, R. 65 - 6. McCulloh made a similar statement in the paper he submitted to Halifax in 1755, Newcastle Papers, BL, Add. MSS. 33030, fols. 334–35. He surely made the same general remarks to Grenville in 1763.

24. Appendix C.

25. 9 March 1764, *Ryder Diary*, p. 235. Indeed, Grenville was so confident in 1763–1764 that the tax would enforce itself that he rejected Thomas Cruwys's sugges-tion on 21 January 1764 that the bill include several penal clauses rather than just "the general clause of penalties." [Cruyws], "The American Stamp Office Law Bill," 29 October 1765, Hardwicke Papers, BL, Add. MSS. 35911, fol. 21. Indeed, many colonists also believed that a stamp tax would virtually execute itself, and for the same reasons. See, for example, these comments made in a pamphlet written by three members of the Connecticut assembly and printed by the assembly's command. "It must be supposed that the people in America will buy and sell their lands; nay, in a multitude of instances, they will not know how to subsist without such dispositions. They will also be necessitated to give and take obligations, and to use paper for various other purposes, or there will be of course so great a stagnation of business as almost to bring on a dissolution of their civil and political existence. [The stamps] will be found as necessary as the use of agriculture itself. . . . Indeed the supposition of the necessity and the certain use of the articles to be charged can be the only foundation to render a revenue arising therefrom worthy of notice, as otherwise the effect will be altogether precarious." [Jared Ingersoll, Ebeneezer Silliman, and George Wyllys], *Reasons why the British colonies in America should not be charged with internal taxes by authority of Parlia-ment, humbly offered for consideration, in behalf of the colony of Connecticut*, reprinted in *The Public Records of the Colony of Connecticut*, ed. Charles J. Hoadley, 12:662. For a description of items generally taxed by stamp duties in Britain, see E. Hughes, "The English Stamp Duties, 1664–1764." Several historians have written useful accounts of the preparation of the Stamp Act, including Thomas, *British Politics*, pp. 69–84; Lawrence Henry Gipson, *The British Empire before the American Revolution*, 10:246–70; Edmund S. Morgan, "The Postponement of the Stamp Act"; Charles R. Ritcheson, "The Preparation of the Stamp Act"; and Jack M. Sosin, *Agents and Merchants: British Colonial Policy and the Origins of the American Revolution, 1763–1775*, pp. 49–54. Curiously, none of them ever emphasized the point that it would virtually collect itself, which Grenville singled out as being of paramount importance in his decision.

26. Whately to Temple, [February 1765], *Bowdoin-Temple Papers,* p. 50.

27. For an intriguing discussion of the treatment of forgery in eighteenth-century English law, see Douglas Hay, "Property, Authority, and the Criminal Law," in Douglas Hay et al., eds., *Albion's Fatal Tree: Crime and Society in Eighteenth-Century England,* pp. 38n., 59–60. Men at the Treasury were either unaware of or shrugged off other difficulties stamp officers had had in executing this tax in England. For those difficulties, see Hughes, "English Stamp Duties," pp. 246–50.

28. Treasury minutes, 29 July 1763, PRO, T. 1/430, fol. 336.

29. Thomas Whately, "Copy of Mr. Secretary Whately's general plan for an American bill," [6 December 1764], Hardwicke Papers, BL, Add. MSS. 35910, fol. 313. Hughes published part of this plan as an appendix to "English Stamp Duties," pp. 259–64. This consideration, that a colonial tax would have to be "as general an imposition as can be devised," made stamp duties "seem preferable" to Whately "to a tax upon Negroes, which would affect the Southern much more than the Northern colonies, though [that] tax would be more easily collected and less liable to evasion." Whately evidently was referring to an import tax on slaves coming into America and obviously assumed that masters and merchants would be reluctant to land slaves on isolated coasts, could not conceal their cargoes easily, and thus would not be tempted to smuggle. Whately to Ingersoll, [Spring 1764], *Ingersoll Papers,* p. 294.

30. For an extended discussion of how the Treasury designed the stamp duties to insure their equality, see John L. Bullion, "Honor, Trade, and Empire: Grenville's Treasury and 'the American Question,' 1763–1765," pp. 264–65, 269–80.

31. Whately to Temple, [February 1765], Whately-Temple Letterbook, HEHL, STG Box 13(6). The printed version of this letter in the *Bowdoin-Temple Papers* does not italicize *"great measure."*

32. Speeches of Grenville and Jenkinson, 9 March 1764, *Ryder Diary,* pp. 235, 236. The diarist's notes of Grenville's speech had the First Lord saying "dependence of this country"; "independence" makes more sense in the context of the statement. Ryder made two other errors in the transcription of this speech; see ibid., 235n., and n. 18 above.

33. For the argument that the Treasury did not become interested in the issue of British sovereignty until 1765, see Thomas, *British Politics,* p. 86.

34. See the description of this document in *Grenville Papers,* 2:374. For Jenkinson's act in September 1763, see [Cruwys], "The American Stamp Office Law Bill," 29 October 1765, Hardwicke Papers, BL, Add. MSS. 35911, fol. 18. There has been some scholarly controversy over whether Cruwys was McCulloh's collaborator. For a list of the most relevant accounts, see Thomas, *British Politics,* p. 72. See also McCulloh's statement that he assisted Cruwys, in ibid., p. 83.

35. Sir George Colebrooke recorded the gossip about Grenville's accusation of Bute. His comments are quoted in Cornelius P. Forster, O.P., *The Uncontrolled Chancellor: Charles Townshend and his American Policy,* p. 31n. Walpole must have heard a similar story, for in 1775 he wrote, "Grenville . . . adopted from Lord Bute a plan of taxation formed by Jenkinson." Walpole, *Memoirs of George III,* 3:24n. Perhaps it was based on a garbled version of Jenkinson's role in dealing with McCulloh during the summer and fall of 1763; perhaps, too, this story rested on the erroneous assumption that Jenkinson continued to follow Bute's orders and do his business even after he began to work with Grenville. For Grenville's comment to the King, see 29 August and 8 September 1763, Mrs. Grenville's Diary, *Grenville Papers,* 2:201, 205.

36. Forster, *Uncontrolled Chancellor,* p. 31n. Writing in 1815, Nathaniel Wraxall recorded a somewhat similar account. Wraxall, *Historical Memoirs of My Own Time,*

1:486–87. There is no evidence from the period 1763–1765 that supports this version of events. For the King's response to Grenville's speech of 9 March 1764, which implies that George III did not object to the postponement of the Stamp Act, see Mrs. Grenville's Diary, 10 March 1764, *Grenville Papers*, 2:495. Grenville's papers during 1765–1770 do not contain any accounts of the Stamp Act that are anywhere close to the version of events that Colebrooke and Wraxall heard, and in his speeches to the House, Grenville was never reluctant to claim the Stamp Act as his own. He did on occasion note in Parliament that he proposed the stamp tax "in consequence of the repeated wish of almost all sorts and conditions of men" and that "His Majesty, ever desirous to divide the burdens among the people equally, wished to see them divided equally in this instance," but such statements do not confirm the story of a royal command. See Grenville's speech, 5 March 1770, Cavendish Diaries, BL, Egerton MS. 221, fol. 34.

37. [Cruwys], "American Stamp Office Law Bill," 29 October 1765, Hardwicke Papers, BL, Add. MSS. 35911, fol. 18.

38. Cruwys, Minutes of a conference with McCulloh, 12 October 1763, Bute Papers, BL, Add. MSS. 36226, fols. 357–60.

39. Thomas, *British Politics*, pp. 71–72.

40. [Cruwys], "American Stamp Office Law Bill," 29 October 1765, Hardwicke Papers, BL, Add. MSS. 35822, fol. 19. For Grenville's later proposal, see Thomas, *British Politics*, pp. 352–53.

41. Appendix A.

42. See the description of the discontent of British merchants in Gipson, *The British Empire before the American Revolution*, 10:172–73.

43. Thomas, *British Politics*, p. 83.

44. [Cruwys], "American Stamp Office Law Bill," 29 October 1765, Hardwicke Papers, BL, Add. MSS. 35811, fol. 21.

45. 9 March 1764, *Ryder Diary*, pp. 236, 238; and the resolution of the Society of Merchant Venturers, 13 March 1764, in Minchinton, ed., *Politics and the Port of Bristol*, p. xx.

46. For a brief description of the speakers in these debates and their views, see Thomas, *British Politics*, pp. 55–59. I have fleshed out the account of Glover and Cust's arguments by referring to descriptions of earlier arguments against removing the drawback, since Tod told Jenkinson on 13 March 1764 that nothing new had been said in these debates. Liverpool Papers, BL, Add. MSS. 38202, fol. 156. For the point about "white calicoes," see *Regulations*, p. 72.

47. On calling witnesses, see P. D. G. Thomas, *The House of Commons in the Eighteenth Century*, pp. 20–24; for Grenville's eagerness to end the session by Easter, see Grenville to Northumberland, 10 March 1764, *Additional Grenville Papers*, p. 100.

48. 20 and 23 March 1764, *Commons Journals*, 29:968, 979.

49. Fremantle to Jenkinson, 19 March 1764, Liverpool Papers, BL, Add. MSS. 38202, fol. 175. Copies of the accounts may be found in ibid., Add. MSS. 38337, fols. 220–24.

50. [Jenkinson], report on accounts, [after 19 March 1764], ibid., Add. MSS. 38338, fol. 192.

51. See [Jenkinson], "Draft clause relating to the drawback on muslin and white calicoes," [23 March 1764], ibid., Add. MSS. 38337, fol. 291, for the proposal to tax them at five pounds. For a description of Grenville's statement to the House on 23 March, see Thomas, *British Politics*, p. 59. This description gives the incorrect impression that Grenville extended ad valorem duties to other linens as well.

52. *Regulations*, p. 73.

53. Ibid. For James Harris's acidulous description of Huske's speech on 23 March, see Namier and Brooke, *House of Commons,* 2:660; for the House's action, see 26 March 1764, *Commons Journals,* 29:986.

54. 4 Geo. 3, c. 25, sec. 15, *Statutes at Large,* 26:39; 30 March 1764, *Commons Journals,* 29:1015.

55. Minchinton, ed., *Politics and the Port of Bristol,* p. 191n. See also Grenville to Samuel Smith, 24 April 1764, George Grenville Letterbooks, HEHL, ST 7, i. For an account of these debates from the perspective of the North American merchants, see *New York Mercury,* 4 June 1764, and *Boston Post-Boy,* 11 June 1764.

56. For the difficulties of dealing with German narrows, see *Regulations,* p. 73.

Notes to Chapter VII
Postponing the Stamp Tax

1. Garth to South Carolina, 17 April 1764, Namier and Brooke, *House of Commons,* 2:660.

2. 9 March 1764, *Ryder Diary,* p. 237. For an excellent description of the stages of legislation, see P. D. G. Thomas, *The House of Commons in the Eighteenth Century,* pp. 45–64. From Huske's emphasis on the colonists not being represented in the House, on printing the bill, and on the right of petition, it is clear he was suggesting a way to include Americans in the legislative process of the House on all bills of interest to them.

3. Dyer to Ingersoll, 4 April 1764, *Ingersoll Papers,* p. 291.

4. For a discussion of the people who may have counseled delay, see Fred J. Ericson, "The Contemporary British Opposition to the Stamp Act." See also Jackson to Franklin, 11 August 1764, *Franklin Papers,* 11:313–14; Huske to Committee of Merchants at Boston, 17 August 1764, in *Boston Gazette,* 29 October 1764; and Edward Montagu, agent for Virginia, to Virginia, 11 April 1764, in *Virginia Gazette* (Purdie and Dixon), 3 October 1766.

5. One can get an idea of their probable arguments in Ryder's notes on Grenville's speech, 9 March 1764, *Ryder Diary,* p. 235. Grenville made these remarks before Beckford and Huske spoke, a further indication that he had been listening to the agents and Huske talk about postponing the bill before 9 March. See also Jenkinson to Grenville, 1 July 1764, *Grenville Papers,* 2:373, for Jenkinson's recollection of the First Lord's statements about the necessity for more information as the cause for postponement.

6. 9 March 1764, *Ryder Diary,* p. 235.

7. 10 March 1764, *Commons Journals,* 29:930.

8. Thomas believed that Grenville made his decision on the night of 9 March as he listened to the debate. I suspect he made his mind up before he came to the House that night. See P. D. G. Thomas, *British Politics and the Stamp Act Crisis: The First Phase of the American Revolution, 1763–1767,* p. 74, and my discussion later in this chapter.

9. 9 March 1764, *Ryder Diary,* p. 235. I have inferred the basic considerations in Grenville's mind as he considered postponement from his speech on 9 March and from his comments to the agents on 17 May. With the exception of one crucial subject, which I shall discuss later in this chapter, there was no reason for Grenville to avoid discussing his thoughts on either occasion.

10. Cruwys's "law bill" reveals that the Board of Trade had collected only extracts from American and plantation laws for his inspection by 6 March, even though the Board had had the bill since 25 January. "American Stamp Office Law Bill," 29 October

1765, Hardwicke Papers, BL, Add. MSS. 35911, fols. 20–21. McCulloh's information must have been dated. In 1763, he provided Grenville with some figures on expenses of government in North Carolina, but in 1765 the First Lord complained of not being "able to get at the figures for that colony." Cf. *Grenville Papers*, 2:374, with Grenville's speech, 6 February 1765, *Ryder Diary*, p. 255.

11. Garth to South Carolina, 5 June 1764, in Edmund S. Morgan, "The Postponement of the Stamp Act," p. 361.

12. Ibid., and Mauduit to Massachusetts, 26 May 1764, in ibid., p. 359. See also Grenville's speech, 9 March 1764, *Ryder Diary*, p. 235.

13. I have inferred these considerations from Whately to Temple, 8 June and 14 August 1764, *Bowdoin-Temple Papers*, pp. 18–23; and Whately to Ingersoll, [Spring 1764], in Jared Ingersoll, *Mr. Ingersoll's Letters Relating to the Stamp Act*, pp. 1–5. All these are obvious areas where more information from the colonies would be helpful.

14. For the instruction to the committee, see 7 March 1764, *Commons Journals*, 29:918. For Cruwys's activities, see his "American Stamp Office Law Bill," 29 October 1765, Hardwicke Papers, BL, Add. MSS. 35911, fols. 21–22.

15. Grenville to Lord Lichfield, 1 October 1763, and Grenville to Northumberland, 26 February 1764, *Additional Grenville Papers*, pp. 47, 94.

16. See Cabinet minutes, 23 February 1764, ibid., p. 321.

17. Egmont to Grenville, 3 December 1763, *Grenville Papers*, 2:173.

18. For the reports of the spies, see Derek Jarrett, *The Begetters of Revolution: England's Involvement with France, 1759–1789*, pp. 47–49. For fears of the French, see Egmont to Grenville, 3 December 1763, *Grenville Papers*, 2:172–73; and Welbore Ellis's justification on 4 March 1763 for keeping a large army in America, in P. D. G. Thomas, "New Light on the Commons Debate of 1763 on the American Army," p. 111.

19. Egmont noted on 3 December 1763 that Grenville had decided to budget £150,000 for the repairs of the fleet rather than the £100,000 he had initially settled on. According to Egmont, this was still insufficient. On 5 December, the Navy Board presented an estimate of £256,739 for repairs. Ultimately, the House allocated £200,000. Egmont to Grenville, 3 December 1763, *Grenville Papers*, 2:174–75; *Commons Journals*, 5 December 1763 and 19 January 1764, 29:691, 720

20. Cabinet minutes, 9 February 1764, *Additional Grenville Papers*, p. 320.

21. Mrs. Grenville's Diary, 18 July 1764, *Grenville Papers*, 2:507; and Grenville to Halifax, 9 August 1764, ibid., pp. 422–23. See also Grenville to Sandwich, 16 July 1764, Sandwich to Grenville, 8 August 1764, and Halifax to Grenville, 8 August 1764, ibid., pp. 390–92, 417–22.

22. Northumberland to Grenville, 20 October 1763, *Additional Grenville Papers*, p. 56. For the background to this crisis, see W. E. H. Lecky, *A History of Ireland in the Eighteenth Century*, 2:70–73.

23. Halifax to Northumberland, 22 October 1763, *Additional Grenville Papers*, p. 57.

24. Northumberland to Grenville, 20 October 1763, ibid., p. 56.

25. Halifax to Northumberland, 22 October 1763, ibid., p. 57; and Grenville to Northumberland, 28 October and 26 November 1763, *Grenville Papers*, 2:146–50, 167.

26. For McCulloh's warning, see Appendix A. Huske's account of Grenville's announcement on 9 March 1764 of the postponement portrayed the First Lord as openly skeptical about the effect of a year's delay upon colonial opinions about Parliament's right to tax and as reluctant to agree to it. Moreover, Huske claimed that Grenville, "being irritated, declared his intention of convincing the colonies next

session that they [were] subject to an inland tax." Huske to Merchants Committee, 14 August 1764, *Boston Gazette,* 29 October 1764. But Huske's version of this speech is anomalous in three crucial respects. All other commentators stressed Grenville's readiness to delay the tax and his good temper, and no other commentator noted any statement by Grenville indicating that during the next session he would show the colonists they were subject to an inland tax or that he would have to do so.

27. 6 February 1765, *Ryder Diary,* p. 254.

28. Halifax to Northumberland, 22 October 1762, *Additional Grenville Papers,* p. 57; and Grenville to Northumberland, 28 October 1763, *Grenville Papers,* 2:148.

29. 9 March 1764, Harris Diary, in Thomas, *British Politics,* p. 74; Jenkinson to Grenville, 2 July 1764, *Grenville Papers,* 2:373; Huske to Merchants Committee, 14 August 1764, in *Boston Gazette,* 29 October 1764.

30. Thomas, *British Politics,* p. 74. For Huske's reputation, see Namier and Brooke, *House of Commons,* 2:660. For Grenville's remarks, see 9 March 1764, *Ryder Diary,* p. 235.

31. Montagu to Virginia, 11 April 1764, printed in *Virginia Gazette* (Purdie and Dixon), 3 October 1766. Ingersoll similarly interpreted the significance of the parliamentary resolution. "This vote I understand was taken in order . . . to let the colonies know that the Parliament thought they had the authority to lay such a tax." He also understood the vote to be a signal that Parliament was determined to raise a revenue in America. Ingersoll to Connecticut Assembly, 18 September 1765, *Ingersoll Papers,* p. 335. For an opinion that introducing a resolution and having the House approve it was "a needless formality for a mere declaration of future intent," see Thomas, *British Politics,* p. 74. But if Grenville had felt this was a formality, he could have withdrawn the resolution, for the House did not vote on it until after he agreed to the postponement. The more likely explanation is that he planned that this vote would be, as he told the agents on 17 May, "sufficiently declaratory" of "the sense of the House of Commons." Garth to South Carolina, 5 June 1764, in Morgan, "Postponement," p. 361.

32. Ibid., p. 360.

33. Garth to South Carolina, 8 February 1765, in Sir Lewis Namier, "Charles Garth and His Connections," pp. 649–50; and Ingersoll to Connecticut, 19 September 1765, Ingersoll, *Ingersoll's Letters,* p. 30. Grenville was as good as his word. See 6 February 1765, *Commons Journals,* 30:90.

34. See Jasper Mauduit to Massachusetts, 13 March 1764, in Morgan, "Postponement," p. 357; and Conway's speech, 15 February 1765, in Edmund S. Morgan, ed., *Prologue to Revolution: Sources and Documents on the Stamp Act Crisis, 1764–1766,* p. 34.

35. Mauduit to Massachusetts, 13 March 1764, in Morgan, "Postponement," p. 357.

36. Thomas, *British Politics,* p. 74. Evidently there were no contemporary objections to Grenville's tactics.

37. Garth to South Carolina, 17 April 1764, in Namier and Brooke, *House of Commons,* 2:660.

38. Ritcheson has concluded that Grenville did want to establish a precedent for colonial consent prior to taxation by Parliament, but "unfortunately . . . allowed his position to become ambiguous." See "The Preparation of the Stamp Act," pp. 553–54. If this were the case, why did the First Lord fail to use his 17 May 1764 meeting with the agents to make his position clear and continue his efforts to create the precedent? Jack M. Sosin has argued that Huske "suggested the procedure" of consulting the assemblies through their agents. *Agents and Merchants: British Colonial Policy and the Origins of the American Revolution, 1763–1775,* pp. 50, 53n., 54n. He cited as evidence a letter from

Cecilius Calvert to Horatio Sharpe, 3 April 1764, William H. Browne, ed., *Archives of Maryland* 14:144, which described a speech made by "Hurst," who argued the colonies "ought to have first notice thereof, giving them opportunity to lay before any objections they might have to such a bill to the House, by their agents." This account, however, does not describe Huske's procedure in detail. When one compares Huske's plan as Ryder recorded it with what actually occurred, there can be no doubt that Grenville did not adopt this suggestion. Thomas has argued in *British Politics*, p. 74, that "Huske's suggestion was adopted in principle." To the contrary: The principle of Huske's proposal was the establishment of a formal, official procedure integrating the colonies into the legislative process of the House. And, as Thomas himself noted, Grenville took no official steps in this matter then or later. See ibid., pp. 76–77.

39. Jenkinson to Grenville, 1 July 1764, *Grenville Papers*, 2:373. The phrase "thoroughly digest" is Grenville's. Garth to South Carolina, 5 June 1764, in Morgan, "Postponement," p. 360.

40. [Cruwys], "American Stamp Office Law Bill," 29 October 1765, Hardwicke Papers, BL, Add. MSS. 35911, fol. 22.

41. Whately to Ingersoll, [Spring 1764], *Ingersoll Papers*, p. 292; Whately to Temple, 8 June 1764, *Bowdoin-Temple Papers*, pp. 18–21; and Whately to Jenkinson, 31 July [1764], Liverpool Papers, BL, Add. MSS. 38197, fols. 259–60. Both of the correspondences were instigated at Grenville's behest. Whately apologized to Ingersoll for not answering his letter with "a date so old that I dare not acknowledge it" until he needed information about stamp duties. The volume at HEHL, George Grenville Papers, STG Box 13(6), that contains the Whately-Temple correspondence in manuscript has a contemporary notation on its cover that Whately wrote at Grenville's express command.

42. Jackson to Ingersoll, 22 March 1766, Ingersoll, *Ingersoll's Letters*, p. 43.

43. Montagu to Virginia, 11 April 1764, and Jasper Mauduit to Massachusetts, 13 March 1764, quoted in Morgan, "Postponement," pp. 357–58. Mauduit's comment is unclear. "Some equivalent tax" could refer to colonial or parliamentary taxes, and in Massachusetts the former interpretation was adopted. Possibly Ingersoll also claimed that Grenville on 9 March offered the colonies the chance to raise the money themselves. On 18 September 1765, Ingersoll wrote to the Connecticut assembly, stating that one purpose of this vote was to declare the right to impose a stamp tax and another was "to give the colonies an opportunity to agree upon some other plan among themselves that should save the need of [Parliament's] taking such a measure." This last statement is ambiguous: Was Ingersoll referring to the colonies' having an opportunity to suggest alternative parliamentary taxes on colonial commerce, or was he claiming that the colonies were being given the option of raising the money by votes in their assemblies? In assessing his meaning, historians should remember that Whately made it clear to Ingersoll in the letter he wrote during the spring of 1764 that the Treasury's offer was limited to other parliamentary taxes. Ingersoll's reply to this letter reveals that he understood Whately perfectly. If Ingersoll was claiming on 18 September 1765 that the colonies had had the opportunity of raising the money themselves, he was probably doing so disingenuously. At that time, he was defending his conduct in England during December 1764 to April 1765, and he may have been trying to take the offensive by asserting that colonists had missed the chance to avoid the stamp tax by agreeing to tax themselves. Ingersoll to Connecticut Assembly, 18 September 1765; Whately to Ingersoll, [Spring 1764]; Ingersoll to Whately, 6 July 1764, *Ingersoll Papers*, pp. 335, 294–95, and 298–300.

44. Garth to South Carolina, 17 April 1764, in Namier and Brooke, *House of Commons,* 2:660.

45. "A letter from London," 24 March 1764, *New York Mercury,* 4 June 1764. For other copies of this letter, see *Pennsylvania Gazette,* 7 June 1764, and *Maryland Gazette,* 14 June 1764. Since the author credited William Allen, Chief Justice of Pennsylvania, with persuading Grenville to postpone the tax, he probably expressed Allen's views and perhaps the opinion of Jackson, Pennsylvania's agent, as well. For Jackson, see also n. 47 below. I agree with Paul Langford's assessment that letters in colonial newspapers from anonymous correspondents in London "were and are more important than the routine information taken from the London newspapers," in part because they accurately reveal colonists' reactions to British policies. See his essay "British Correspondence in the Colonial Press, 1763–1775: A Study in Anglo-American Misunderstanding before the American Revolution," in Bernard Bailyn and John B. Hench, eds., *The Press and the American Revolution,* pp. 276–78.

46. Garth to South Carolina, 5 June 1764, in Namier, "Charles Garth and His Connections," p. 648. Garth's recommendation is quoted later in the chapter. Because his reference to its genesis is unclear, it is possible that he reached this opinion after the 17 May meeting with Grenville. Also, by 5 June he had discovered that there was no chance that the Jamaican stamp tax would be repealed in time to dissuade the House from going on with the stamp tax.

47. For the comments about internal taxation, see Jackson to Franklin, 26 January 1764, *Franklin Papers,* 11:35; for his suggestion, see Franklin to Jackson, 25 June 1764, ibid., p. 236. Jackson's letter to Franklin on 10 March has been lost, and pages are missing from his 13 April letter, so the only surviving evidence of his suggestion is Franklin's reference to "what [Jackson said] of the colonies' applying for a stamp act." This reference leaves unclear what the colonies were applying for, a stamp tax imposed by Parliament or one levied by colonial institutions. The editors of the *Franklin Papers* have assumed that Jackson first broached this suggestion on 10 March, immediately after Grenville's speech, and argued that Franklin's response makes it "probable that Jackson had given him to understand that the colonies were to be allowed some method, perhaps by stamp duties, of raising the required funds through their own legislation." I do not agree with either their assumption or their argument. In Franklin's lengthy reply to the 10 March letter on 1 June, he merely thanked Jackson for deferring the stamp tax, then went on to a detailed discussion of other matters. His first response to the 13 April letter was a brief note written on 18 June, in which he promised to "answer it fully . . . in about ten days." In a long letter on 25 June, he discussed, among other matters, what Jackson had said about the colonies' applying for a stamp tax. If one believes Jackson made his suggestion in his 10 March letter, one must explain why Franklin failed to refer to it when he mentioned the postponement of the stamp tax on 1 June, and then belatedly decided to devote a full paragraph to it on 25 June. I can think of no explanation for such a failure other than inattention or negligence, and it is unlikely that Franklin, who wrote on 1 June that he hoped the stamp tax "will never take place," would have been either inattentive or negligent in dealing with a proposal that might have affected the enactment of that tax. Moreover, if one assumes that Jackson passed along his suggestion to Franklin on 10 March, one must explain why he did not make the same suggestion to Governor Fitch when he wrote to Fitch on 10 March. That letter has not survived, but the official response of the Connecticut government, a pamphlet written by Jared Ingersoll, Ebeneezer Silliman, and George Wyllys, and titled *Reasons why the British colonies in America should not be charged with internal taxes by*

authority of Parliament, humbly offered for consideration, in behalf of the colony of Connecticut, has. That pamphlet does not mention any suggestion transmitted by Jackson. Nor does it contain any passages indicating that the Connecticut government had been given the opportunity to comment on the advisability of assenting to a stamp tax in advance. And certainly that government was not offered the chance to respond to any suggestion that the colonies might be permitted to tax themselves. If it had that chance, surely it would not have suggested parliamentary taxes on the importation of Negroes and on the fur trade as possible alternatives to a stamp tax. There is no apparent reason to believe Jackson would give different advice on this issue to the two colonies that employed him. For these reasons, I believe Jackson made his suggestion in his 13 April letter. When he made it, was he simply communicating a proposal Grenville made during his speech on 9 March? I doubt this was the case. It is improbable that a man as conscientious and as opposed to the stamp tax as Jackson was would have neglected to include in his 10 March letter any proposal made by Grenville, whether that proposal was an outright offer permitting the colonies to tax themselves or a straightforward suggestion encouraging them to apply to Parliament for a stamp tax. In either case, Jackson surely would have included the news in his account of the postponement, in order to guarantee that the Pennsylvania assembly would have the maximum amount of time to consider and to respond to Grenville's proposal. So Jackson's suggestion in his 13 April letter must have been inspired by some source other than Grenville's speech on 9 March. Finally, what was the nature of Jackson's suggestion? Franklin's response to it makes it probable Jackson was not suggesting the colonies apply for a stamp tax levied by themselves. Franklin began by dismissing the advice. In his opinion, there was "not only no likelihood that they will generally agree in such an application [for a stamp tax], but even that any one colony will propose it to the others." Then he observed, "Though if a gross sum were generally required of all the colonies, and [if] they were left to settle the mode of raising it at some general congress, I think it not unlikely that instead of setting quotas, they would fall on some such general tax, as a stamp act." Put another way, Franklin was explaining to Jackson conditions under which the colonies would be favorably disposed toward a general stamp tax. One of those conditions involved the question of who would impose the tax. Franklin clearly believed that it would have to be a colonial institution. Jackson's proposal evidently did not give the colonists the opportunity to impose a stamp tax themselves, or else Franklin would not have dismissed the plan so abruptly and so confidently. Given Franklin's certainty that Jackson's plan would be unacceptable to all, and given Jackson's probable familiarity with the advice given by "all the well-wishers," it is not likely that the editors' interpretation of Franklin's reference is correct. Rather, it is probable that Jackson suggested to Franklin that the colonies ask Parliament to impose a stamp tax, thus creating a plausible precedent for prior consultation before Parliament imposed other taxes on America. For references in this note, see Franklin to Jackson, 1, 18, and 25 June 1764, *Franklin Papers,* 11:214–20, 229, 234–40; Jackson to Franklin, 13 April 1764, ibid., pp. 175–77; editorial notes, ibid., pp. 236–37n.; and, for material relating to Jackson to Fitch, 10 March 1764, see *Public Records of the Colony of Connecticut,* ed. Charles J. Hoadley, 12:256, 299, 651–71. Morgan also believes that "Franklin's reply [on 25 June] indicates that Jackson had said something about the colonies assenting in advance to a stamp act." I do not, however, share Morgan's suspicion that Grenville may have suggested this course of action to Jackson sometime after 9 March and before 17 May. Nor do I agree with his argument that Grenville was willing to offer the colonies a chance to establish a precedent of prior consultation before parliamentary taxation. Morgan, "Postponement," pp. 363–64n.

48. Garth to South Carolina, 5 June 1764, in Morgan, "Postponement," p. 360. My interpretation of the reasons for the request for an audience follows the reasoning and argument of Thomas, *British Politics,* pp. 72–75.

49. Ibid., p. 73–74.

50. Garth to South Carolina, 5 June 1764, in Morgan, "Postponement," pp. 360–61.

51. For example, see Appendix A.

52. Morgan has argued that Grenville did offer to let the colonies tax themselves, then changed his mind before 17 May. See "Postponement," pp. 355–59, 363–65. Thomas, however, has pointed out that James Harris, sitting with Grenville on the Treasury Bench, did not record any such promise in his diary. This was the sort of pledge that Harris would have noticed, since it would affect the Treasury's future work on the bills. Garth, whose conscientiousness and carefulness are beyond dispute, also noted no such concession. Only the agents, who sat in galleries where it was hard to hear debates and who were not permitted to take notes, believed Grenville had made the offer. Thomas therefore concluded that Grenville did not make this statement. For his reasons, and for the reasons I describe in Chapter VII, I believe Thomas is correct. Thomas, *British Politics,* pp. 72–74.

53. Grenville's speech, 9 March 1764, *Ryder Diary,* p. 235; and Jenkinson to Grenville, 2 July 1764, *Grenville Papers,* 2:373.

54. Grenville's speech, 9 March 1764, *Ryder Diary,* p. 235. I suspect this statement was a source of the confusion. Grenville made it after he noted that the stamp tax was "the best plan." Perhaps he believed that "the end" clearly referred to a stamp tax, and his comment on following "to a certain degree [their] inclination" clearly referred to information and specific recommendations they might supply about such a tax. See again Thomas's cogent point about the disadvantages agents worked under. *British Politics,* p. 73.

55. The first quotation is from William Knox, *The claim of the colonies to an exemption from internal taxes imposed by authority of Parliament examined in a letter from a gentleman in London to his friend in America,* p. 32, also quoted in Morgan, "Postponement," p. 362. Knox was not present on 17 May, so I have quoted sparingly from his account, which is apparently based on conversations he had with Garth. Moreover, his account was in part a defense of Grenville, another reason to handle it cautiously. The only extant letters from participants are Jasper Mauduit's (from his brother Israel's account) and Garth's in ibid., pp. 357–61. The other quotation is from Garth to South Carolina, 5 June 1764, ibid., p. 360.

56. Morgan, "Postponement," p. 360.

57. Ibid., p. 361; and Mauduit to Massachusetts, 26 May 1764, in ibid., p. 359. Knox had a more elaborate version of Grenville's remarks about the officers. He asserted that Grenville "particularly" recommended the "mode of collecting it . . . which did not require any number of officers vested with extraordinary powers of entering houses, or in any respect served to extend a sort of influence which he never wished to increase." Ibid., p. 362.

58. Garth to South Carolina, 5 June 1764, ibid., p. 361.

59. Mauduit to Massachusetts, 26 May 1764, ibid., p. 359.

60. Ibid., p. 360; and Garth to South Carolina, 5 June 1764, ibid., p. 361.

61. Morgan implied that Grenville's refusal to send the draft bill was another sign he was trying to make it as difficult as possible for the colonies to propose alternatives. Ibid., pp. 369–70. He did not consider the possibility that Grenville wished to avoid setting any sort of precedent.

62. Garth to South Carolina, 5 June 1764, ibid., p. 361. For Cruwys's draft bill, see Bute Papers, BL, Add. MSS. 36226, fols. 353–56; for McCulloh's, see Hardwicke Papers, ibid., 35910, fols. 136–39; for a list of British stamp duties, see ibid., fols. 138–59.

63. Garth to South Carolina, 5 June 1764, in Morgan, "Postponement," p. 361.

64. Ibid., and Knox, *The claim of the colonies,* in ibid., p. 362. Knox's pamphlet was probably the source for this note in the *Annual Register:* "[Grenville] hint[ed] withal, that [the agents'] principals would now have it in their power, by agreeing to this tax, to establish a precedent for their being consulted (by the ministry, we suppose), before any tax was imposed on them by Parliament." *Annual Register* 8 (1765): 33.

65. Garth to South Carolina, 5 June 1764, quoted in Thomas, *British Politics,* p. 76. Knox wrote in 1765 that Grenville "recommended it to the agents to represent it properly to their several colonies, and to advise their respective councils and assemblies to take it under their consideration and if, upon deliberation a stamp duty appeared to them an eligible tax, to authorize their agents to declare their approbation of it, which, being signified to Parliament next year, when the tax came to be imposed, would afford a forcible argument for the like proceeding in all such cases." *The claim of the colonies,* in Morgan, "Postponement," p. 362. If Grenville had made that statement on 17 May, no doubt Garth would have been more explicit in his letter to South Carolina.

66. For Grenville's request to the King on 4 October 1763, see PRO, T. 1/430, fol. 434. For an indication that Jenkinson did not regard Grenville's talks with the agents as an official request for information that would satisfy possible critics, see Jenkinson to Grenville, 2 July 1764, *Grenville Papers,* 2:373. See also Franklin to William Pulteney, 12 March 1778, in Morgan, "Postponement," pp. 390–91; and a comment that "it has been said the Stamp Act was put off a year that the colonies might have notice to object and give their reasons against it, . . . [but] Massachusetts never had a line about it from one of the public offices." *Boston Gazette,* 20 January 1766.

67. Garth was not the only one who clung to this sort of hope. See n. 45 on Jackson, and "A letter from London," 24 March 1764, *New York Mercury,* 4 June 1764, in which "all the well-wishers to America" were described as having this opinion.

68. I made the opposite argument in John L. Bullion, "Honor, Trade, and Empire: Grenville's Treasury and 'the American Question,' 1763–1765," pp. 369–70. I no longer believe that interpretation is justified.

69. Grenville's speech, 9 March 1764, *Ryder Diary,* p. 235; and Garth to South Carolina, 5 June 1764, in Morgan, "Postponement," p. 361; italics mine in both cases. In reading these reports, one should recall what Thomas Pitt, Jr., observed of Grenville's "wariness never to suffer himself to be drawn beyond the line he had prescribed to himself." See Namier and Brooke, *House of Commons,* 2:539.

70. Members of the Committee of Correspondence of the Massachusetts House of Representatives were particularly alert to the danger of tacitly conceding rights. Committee to Franklin, 25 June 1764, *Franklin Papers,* 11:242–43.

71. Jenkinson to Grenville, 1 July 1764, *Grenville Papers,* 2:373; and Lloyd to Jenkinson, 3 July 1764, *Jenkinson Papers,* p. 307. Thomas interpreted Jenkinson's letter as an effort to persuade him to begin collecting information from America. That process had already begun, with Whately's letters to Ingersoll and Temple, as Jenkinson doubtless knew. The key word in understanding this letter is the word *"appear."* The Treasury had to make the request for political reasons, to satisfy potential critics as well as to gain what additional information it could. Thomas also argued that the delay was not inspired by a need for more information, citing the fact that the final act in 1765 was not much different from Cruwys's in 1764. But this does not take into account that the Treasury could not be sure in 1764 that the bill was so well drawn. The men there could

be more confident after reviewing the results of Whately's work, which indicated that the original bill basically was drafted properly and imposed no excessive taxes. Thomas, *British Politics,* pp. 79–80.

72. Mrs. Grenville's Diary, 26 June, 12 July, and 16 July 1764, *Grenville Papers,* 2:504–6; Grenville to the Earl of Hereford, 20 July 1764, and Grenville to Halifax, 23 July 1764, ibid., pp. 397, 409–10; Halifax to all governors, 11 August 1764, PRO, C.O. 5/65, fols. 647–49.

73. Halifax to Penn, 18 October 1763, PRO, C.O. 5/1280, fols. 141–42; and Bedford to Grenville, 24 November 1746, *Grenville Papers,* 1:55.

74. A later ministry did try to establish these informal contacts with assemblymen, with the unfortunate result that the Virginia House of Burgesses publicly interpreted private assurances as formal pledges and made further demands for the repeal of American taxes. See the Earl of Hillsborough to Lord Botetourt, 18 January 1770, PRO, C.O. 5/1348, fols. 43–44. Grenville commented on the letter that began this controversy, Hillsborough's circular letter to colonial governors on 13 May 1769, in a speech to the House on 9 May 1770. Grenville's remarks reveal his sensitivity to the possibility that carelessly drafted official communications could contain embarrassing or harmful pledges that colonists could use to their own advantage. Grenville's speech, 9 May 1770, Cavendish Diaries, BL, Egerton MSS. 222, fol. 204.

75. [Cruwys], "American Stamp Office Law Bill," 29 October 1765, Hardwicke Papers, BL, Add. MSS. 35911, fols. 22–24. For discussion of the care and thoroughness of Whately's work, see E. Hughes, "The English Stamp Duties, 1664–1764," p. 258, and Chapter VIII.

Notes to Chapter VIII
Passing the Stamp Act

1. Significantly, Jenkinson made extracts from Massachusetts to Mauduit, 14 June 1764. Liverpool Papers, BL, Add. MSS. 38302, fol. 342. The assembly mistakenly believed Grenville had offered the colonies the chance to tax themselves.

2. Assembly of New York to Lt. Gov. Cadwallader Colden, 11 September 1764, in HEHL, "Copies of papers transmitted to the Privy Council office," Huntington Miscellany.

3. John Watts to Sir William Baker, 30 March 1765, and Watts to Robert Monckton, 11 August 1764, *Letter Book of John Watts of New York, Collections of the New York Historical Society* 61:341, 281. Watts later reported to Monckton "Mr. Charles' embarrassment with the colony's addresses, which were too warm, assuming, and tedious, better not presented." He added the news that Charles was "throwing up his agency," but his threatened resignation did not occur, and he remained New York's agent until his death in 1770. Watts to Monckton, 16 April 1765, ibid., p. 346.

4. Board of Trade to the King, 11 December 1764, PRO, C.O. 5/920, fols. 187–89; P. D. G. Thomas, *British Politics and the Stamp Act Crisis: The First Phase of the American Revolution, 1763–1767,* pp. 87–88.

5. Harrison to Temple, 12 January 1765, *Bowdoin-Temple Papers,* pp. 44–45.

6. "Mr. Secretary Whately's general plan," [6 December 1764], Hardwicke Papers, BL, Add. MSS. 35910, fols. 310–23. (The endorsement on this document dates it as 17 December 1764, but [Cruwys], "American Stamp Office Law Bill," 29 October 1765, ibid., 35911, fol. 22, makes it clear that it was read 6 December.) E. Hughes has published most of this document as an appendix to "The English Stamp Duties,

1664–1764," pp. 259–64, with the exception of Whately's recommendations concerning the distribution of the stamps, which will be discussed in Chapter IX.

7. Grenville's speech, 9 March 1764, *Ryder Diary,* p. 234; Whately, "general plan," [6 December 1764], Hardwicke Papers, BL, Add. MSS. 35910, fol. 311.

8. Hardwicke Papers, BL, Add. MSS. 35910, fols. 311–15.

9. Ibid., fol. 313; and Grenville to Knox, 16 August 1768, George Grenville Letterbooks, HEHL, ST 7, ii.

10. Whately, "general plan," [6 December 1764], Hardwicke Papers, BL, Add. MSS. 35910, fols. 311–12.

11. Ibid., fols. 313–15. Whately was concerned about the possibility that the charter and proprietary governments would claim that their grants were not mesne conveyances, and thus a stamp duty on provincial grants would amount to the Crown's obtaining a second fee for the land after granting it absolutely to the province or the proprietors and losing all rights to the land. To forestall this possibility, Whately recommended that the duties on all grants be equal and that they be "confounded" together. His use of *confound* may be understood to mean "to mix up or mingle so that the elements become difficult to distinguish or impossible to separate." *OED.*

12. Whately, "general plan," [6 December 1764], Hardwicke Papers, BL, Add. MSS. 35910, fol. 316. "Heads of the stamp duties proposed for the colonies," [n.d.], PRO, T. 1/433, fol. 308, tends to bear out Whately's contention that on an average, duties on Americans were 25 to 33 percent lower than those on Englishmen, in Whately to Temple, [February 1765], *Bowdoin-Temple Papers,* p. 50.

13. Whately, "general plan," [6 December 1764], Hardwicke Papers, BL, Add. MSS. 35910, fol. 316–17. The final version of the bill incorporated these suggestions with one exception. The Treasury exempted "appeals etc. from before a single justice of the peace" from these duties. This doubtless was intended to preserve the right of appeal to poor litigants, the most likely to be involved in this sort of small claims court.

14. Appendix C.

15. Ibid.

16. See Cal Winslow, "Sussex Smugglers," in *Albion's Fatal Tree: Crime and Society in Eighteenth-Century England,* ed. Douglas Hay et al., pp. 119–21, 140–47, and Hughes, "English Stamp Duties," for evidence of Englishmen's inclination to avoid paying taxes.

17. Whately to Temple, [February 1765], *Bowdoin-Temple Papers,* p. 50.

18. Ingersoll to Fitch, 11 February 1765, *Ingersoll Papers,* p. 314. Since Grenville told the House that he exempted "justices of the peace and militia officers" because this "was an objection to the stamp law in Jamaica," possibly many of Ingersoll's successful recommendations were supported by other sources as well. 6 February 1765, *Ryder Diary,* p. 256

19. Ingersoll to Fitch, 11 February 1765, *Ingersoll Papers,* p. 314. Cf. Whately, "general plan," [6 December 1764], Hardwicke Papers, BL, Add. MSS. 35910, fols. 314–15, with 5 Geo. 3, c. 12.

20. Whately to Temple, [February 1765], *Bowdoin-Temple Papers,* p. 50; and "Heads of the stamp duties proposed for the colonies," [n.d.], PRO, T. 1/433, fol. 408.

21. Jenkinson to Hallowell, 13 July 1765, Liverpool Papers, BL, Add. MSS. 38305. fol. 13. Ingersoll's hope that Americans would not "find [the stamp tax] more distressing than the people here in power are aware of" perhaps indicates that Whately had told him that these were relatively light taxes and that Americans would soon discover the same. Ingersoll to Fitch, 11 February 1765, *Ingersoll Papers,* p. 314.

22. Ingersoll to Whately, 6 July 1764, *Ingersoll Papers,* pp. 295–301. If Ingersoll

talked about these points with Whately, then he quickly discovered the futility of making them. "The point of the authority of Parliament to impose such a tax, I found on my arrival here was so fully and universally yielded, that there was not the least hopes of making any impressions that way." Ingersoll to Fitch, 11 February 1765, ibid., p. 306.

23. For Grenville's concern over the impending renewal of debate over general warrants, see Walpole to Mann, 13 January 1765, *Walpole's Correspondence,* 22:274; Grenville to Sir William Meredith, 19 January 1765, *Additional Grenville Papers,* pp. 241–42. See also Grenville's comments to the King just before the debate. Mrs. Grenville's Diary, 25 January 1765, *Grenville Papers,* 3:116. There is no record of his ever expressing similar concerns over the stamp tax. Indeed, Jenkinson observed to Hallowell on 12 January 1765 that the protests of New York and Massachusetts had harmed the colonial cause and turned all serious politicians against them. *Jenkinson Papers,* p. 346.

24. See "Extracts out of American charters, 1764," George Grenville Papers relating to the Peace of Paris, HEHL, STG Box 12; and Mansfield to Grenville, 24 December 1764, *Grenville Papers,* 2:478.

25. Jenkinson's letter has not survived, but his requests are clearly revealed in the body of Pownall to Jenkinson, 26 December 1764, Liverpool Papers, BL, Add. MSS. 38203, fol. 328. For Jenkinson's speech draft, see Appendix C.

26. *Regulations,* pp. 109–11.

27. Garth to South Carolina, 8 February 1765, in Sir Lewis Namier, "Charles Garth and His Connections," p. 649. Because most of the communications from the colonies to the agents on the proposed stamp tax have been lost, historians have had to take Garth's word about these messages. One anonymous source wrote to a correspondent in New York that "two of the colony agents only had any authority from their constituents to offer an equivalent to be raised by the colonies themselves, the others being instructed to oppose the bill by presenting petitions from the assemblies." Extract of letters from London, 2, 7, and 10 February 1765, *New York Mercury,* 10 May 1765. The *Annual Register* noted that no colony authorized its agent to consent to a stamp tax "or to offer any compensation for it," but also recounted that "two of the agents . . . answered for the colonies they served bearing their proportion of the stamp duty by methods of their own; but, when questioned, confessed that they had no authority to undertake for any particular sum." *Annual Register* 8:33.

28. Ingersoll to Fitch, 11 February 1765, *Fitch Papers,* p. 324. This letter and a later one from Ingersoll to Fitch on 6 March 1765 are the chief sources for the discussions at this meeting. Jackon's letter to Fitch on 9 February was a short one, which dealt only with the parliamentary debate of 6 February and his plans to introduce petitions against the stamp bill. His letter of 9 March repeated arguments similar to those ascribed to Grenville by Ingersoll, but without mentioning the source. See ibid., pp. 316–17, 340–42. His letters to Pennsylvania during this period have been lost. Franklin only discussed his meetings with Grenville in letters written much after the event, when he had reason to describe a Grenville "besotted with his stamp scheme" and unwilling to listen to reason. For example, see Franklin to Joseph Galloway, 11 October 1766, *Franklin Papers,* 13:449. Garth concentrated on describing his activities in Parliament in the greatest detail. See his letters during February 1765 in Namier, "Charles Garth and His Connections," pp. 649–52.

29. For other accounts of this meeting, see Thomas, *British Politics,* p. 78; Jack M. Sosin, *Agents and Merchants: British Colonial Policy and the Origins of the American Revolution, 1763–1775,* pp. 59–60; Michael Kammen, *A Rope of Sand: The Colonial Agents, British Politics, and the American Revolution,* pp. 112–13; and Edmund S.

Morgan, "The Postponement of the Stamp Act," pp. 371–73. Kammen and Morgan both believed that Grenville was less than candid with the agents; Sosin and Thomas argued that he realized the agents were merely playing for time and exposed their strategy with his questions and comments. None of these historians noticed the interesting differences between his remarks to the agents and his speech to the House.

30. Ingersoll to Fitch, 9 February 1765, *Fitch Papers*, p. 324. Garth's letter to South Carolina on 8 February 1765 was printed with some changes to disguise the author's identity in the *South Carolina Gazette* on 20 April, in the *Providence Gazette* on 11 May, in the *New York Mercury,* the *New York Gazette,* and the *Boston Post-Boy* on 13 May, so his account of Grenville's assurance "of his readiness and desire to pursue such measures only as might give universal satisfaction, but that he was bound in honor to Parliament to call for the resolution of last year" was widely disseminated in America. Colonial printers did, however, excise Garth's comment that Grenville "spoke to us with great tenderness and regard for the happiness of the colonies."

31. Ingersoll to Fitch, 11 February 1765, *Fitch Papers,* p. 324.

32. Jackson to Fitch, 9 February 1765; and Ingersoll to Fitch, 11 February and 6 March 1765, ibid., pp. 317, 321, 324–25, 336–37.

33. Franklin and Thomas Pownall to Grenville, 12 February 1765, *Franklin Papers,* 12:47–61. Ingersoll to Fitch, 11 February 1765, *Fitch Papers,* p. 324.

34. Appendix C; and Jenkinson to R. Wolters, 18 January 1765, *Jenkinson Papers,* p. 347.

35. Appendix C; and Jenkinson to R. Wolters, 18 December 1764, Liverpool Papers, BL, Add. MSS. 38304, fol. 108.

36. Appendix C. William Knox, who liked and admired Grenville, later wrote that he "wished to render every other part [of the empire] the mere instrument or conduit of conveying nourishment and vigor to it. . . . and every encouragement that he thought [Ireland or America] ought to receive, had no reference than the increase of the trade or revenue of [England]." Quoted in Leland J. Bellot, *William Knox: The Life and Thought of an Eighteenth-Century Imperialist,* p. 84.

37. Whately to Temple, 8 December 1764, Whately-Temple Letterbook, in George Grenville Papers, HEHL, STG Box 13(6).

38. Ingersoll to Fitch, 11 February 1765, *Fitch Papers,* pp. 324–25.

39. Ibid., p. 325. In *Extra-Official State Papers. Addressed to the Right Honourable Lord Rawdon . . . ,* 2:24–25, Knox recalled a similar version of this incident. Historians should not forget, though, that Whately had publicly declared in January 1765 in his pamphlet *Regulations,* p. 108, that the money raised by stamp duties would go only to defense; he had at the same time noted that it could have gone for other purposes, however. By not promising that all colonial revenue raised by parliamentary taxation would go to defense, Whately and Grenville preserved Parliament's freedom in this matter.

40. Jackson to Fitch, 9 February 1765, *Fitch Papers,* p. 317.

41. Ingersoll to Fitch, 6 March 1765, ibid., p. 338.

42. Ingersoll to Fitch, 11 February and 6 March 1765, ibid., pp. 325, 338. Morgan and Kammen criticized Grenville for asking the agents if they could determine the proportions. But as Thomas cogently argued, "The agents had gone specifically to ask for adoption of the method of requisitions, [so] the inquiry was therefore fair and logical." Thomas, *British Politics,* p. 78n.

43. Ingersoll to Fitch, 11 February 1765, *Fitch Papers,* p. 325.

44. Appendix C; *Regulations,* p. 102; Grenville's speech, 6 February 1765, *Ryder Diary,* pp. 225–26.

45. Ingersoll to Fitch, 6 March 1765, *Fitch Papers,* p. 337.

46. Ibid., pp. 337–38.

47. Harris Memorandum, 4 December 1764, in Thomas, *British Politics*, pp. 86–87.

48. Ingersoll to Fitch, 6 March 1765, *Fitch Papers*, pp. 338–39.

49. Ibid., pp. 339–40.

50. Ingersoll to Fitch, 11 February 1765, ibid., p. 325.

51. Halifax to Northumberland, 22 October 1763, *Additional Grenville Papers*, p. 57.

52. 10 January 1765, *Commons Journals*, 30:3–4; and Ingersoll to Fitch, 11 February 1765, *Fitch Papers*, pp. 321–23.

53. Grenville's speech, 6 February 1765, *Ryder Diary*, pp. 253–54. Unless specifically noted, all the quotations in this section are from Ryder's notes on this debate, ibid., pp. 253–56. For Grenville's investments, see H. Grenville to Grenville, 16 October 1759, George Grenville Papers, HEHL, STG Box 22(16).

54. Ryder may have omitted Grenville's discussion of this matter, for a comparison of his account with those of Ingersoll and Jackson reveals that he left out some favorable references to the colonies. Still, if Grenville had been openly critical of the colonies' failure to take advantage of this offer, surely Ingersoll and Jackson would have cited it in their letters to Connecticut. Another indication that Grenville passed over this point in his speech is that confusion in the House over his meaning when he said he had "inquired from North America whether they objected to this particular species of tax, and [had] not heard one gentleman propose any other," compelled him to announce he had "never received from any . . . assembly any approbation of this tax; . . . the case [had] been quite otherwise." *Ryder Diary*, pp. 256–57. It is perhaps possible that Grenville was so reticent not merely to spare the colonies' feelings, but also to avoid making any statement that might be construed in the future as meaning that the colonies had missed the opportunity this time to establish a precedent. Such a statement might be cited as supporting the creation of a precedent for prior consultation.

55. Ibid., pp. 253–54.

56. See Appendix C, which is clearer on Molyneaux's pamphlet than Ryder's notes. For a brief discussion of this pamphlet, see Francis Godwin James, *Ireland in the Empire, 1688–1770: A History of Ireland from the Williamite Wars to the Eve of the American Revolution* (Cambridge, Mass., 1973), pp. 38–43.

57. Jackson to Fitch, 9 February 1765, *Fitch Papers*, p. 317.

58. Ingersoll to Fitch, 11 February 1765, *Ingersoll Papers*, p. 309. Ingersoll's and Jackson's versions of Grenville's remarks and demeanor on 6 February are supported by an account of the debate sent to Newport, Rhode Island. "Grenville spoke with much moderation, expressed much concern at [the] undue spirit of the addresses, but foreswore to be particular, lest it exasperate the House, and requested that they proceed with coolness and moderation." *New York Gazette*, 6 May 1765.

59. Grenville's speech, 6 February 1765, *Ryder Diary*, p. 255. A merchant in London who was clearly privy to negotiations with the Treasury on a variety of colonial issues during February–April 1765 (for instance, his remarks in this letter betray a familiarity of the meeting with Grenville over the American quartering act in early April) believed one of the major arguments for the passage of the tax was "the provocation given by the clamor made in America, and by Americans here, of independence in the article of taxation, whence the Administration thought it highly necessary to establish in this instance the right of sovereignty in this kingdom over the colonies, lest dropping the bill . . . should be construed hereafter as an acknowledgement of that independence." "Letter from a considerable merchant in London to his friend in Connecticut," 9 April 1765, *Boston Post-Boy*, 8 July 1765. For a similar statement, see Franklin to Charles Thomson, 11 July 1765, *Franklin Papers*, 12:207.

60. On 21 February 1766, Jenkinson remarked to the House, "A proposition was

made to the colonies to propose some other duty, and the colonies did make another proposal, but it was not agreed to by the rest, and therefore the resolution of the year 1764 was carried into execution in 1765." *Ryder Diary*, p. 305. From this account, one cannot tell what Jenkinson was referring to. Connecticut's assembly suggested in May 1764 an import duty on Negroes and a tax on the fur trade. But before this news could reach England, Whately had already written Ingersoll that a stamp tax "must be allowed to be as general an imposition as can be devised, and . . . seems preferable to a tax upon Negroes." In his reply, Ingersoll did not mention the tax on Negroes, doubtlessly because he regarded it as a lost cause. See Lawrence Henry Gipson, *The British Empire before the American Revolution*, 10:236–37; Whately to Ingersoll, [Spring 1764], and Ingersoll to Whately, 6 July 1764, *Ingersoll Papers*, pp. 294–301. In July 1764, the Board of Trade proposed a duty on the fur trade. Richard Jackson criticized this proposal as too difficult to collect and evidently killed it. See "Plan for the future management of the Indian trade," and Jackson's comments on it, [July 1764], Shelburne Papers, WLCL, 107:321–28, 347–63. Jenkinson may have been referring to these suggestions in February 1766. No one from the colonies, however, mentioned them to Grenville, and thus he was justified in saying on 6 February 1765 he had heard nothing from there. Also, Jenkinson may have been referring to the proposal by Franklin and Thomas Pownall for raising a revenue by issuing paper currency in the colonies. That proposal was made to Grenville on 12 February 1765, six days after he made this statement. *Franklin Papers*, 12:51–61.

61. Appendix C begins with this argument. Interestingly, Grenville felt that it would be better to conclude with it.

62. For Beckford's and Barré's speeches, see *Ryder Diary*, pp. 256–57, 258, 260.

63. Whately to Temple, [February 1765], *Bowdoin-Temple Papers*, p. 49. Ingersoll noted that of all the speakers against the bill, "Beckford . . . only seemed to deny the authority of Parliament." Ryder's account of Beckford's speech corroborates this impression, yet it also reveals that he stopped short of an unequivocal declaration that Parliament was violating the colonies' constitutional rights.

64. Ingersoll to Fitch, 11 February 1765, *Ingersoll Papers*, p. 312.

65. Garth to South Carolina, 17 February 1765, Namier, "Charles Garth and His Connections," p. 651.

66. 15 February 1765, *Commons Journals*, 30:147–48; Garth to South Carolina, 17 February 1765, Namier, "Charles Garth and His Connections," p. 651; and Jackson to Fitch, 9 March 1765, *Fitch Papers*, p. 341. Robert Charles "received a petition from his constituents [in New York] with orders to present the same, but which was conceived in terms so inflammatory that he could not prevail on any one Member of the House to present it." Ingersoll to Fitch, 6 March 1765, *Ingersoll Papers*, p. 317. For a discussion of the right of subjects to petition the House, see P. D. G. Thomas, *The House of Commons in the Eighteenth Century*, pp. 17–19.

67. 15 February 1765, *Commons Journals*, 30:147. Almost surely the agents were aware of the plans of the London merchants who traded to the West Indies, and they may have felt that this petition was the least exceptionable, and thereby the most likely to be heard, and that the House's agreeing to hear this petition would dispose the members more favorably to hearing the others. Richard Jackson, who hoped "to obtain some alteration" in the Sugar Act, had "concerted some measures for that purpose with some of the principal merchants of London" by early February 1765. Perhaps Jackson also explained to the merchants that he planned to defer presenting Connecticut's petition against the stamp tax until just before the second reading of the bill because

"the presenting [of] it then will do more service than it would have done before."
Jackson to Fitch, 9 February 1765, *Fitch Papers,* p. 317. Certainly Rose Fuller was
aware of a version of the agents' plans before the debate, for he remarked on 15
February that "he [had] heard that some of the agents were for being heard at the bar of
the House by counsel upon the matter of the right of Parliament to tax America."
Ingersoll to Connecticut Assembly, 18 September 1765, *Ingersoll Papers,* p. 336.

68. 15 February 1765, Harris Diary, quoted in Thomas, *British Politics,* p. 94.
Meredith had agreed to introduce Montagu's petition, and almost certainly he and the
agent had settled on this argument as a persuasive one before the day's debate began.
The inclusion of this argument in Harris's notes indicates that Meredith stressed it in his
remarks. Those same notes also reveal that Grenville believed it was essential to deny the
validity of this point. For Grenville's remarks on 6 February, see *Ryder Diary,* p. 254.

69. Ingersoll to Fitch, 6 March 1765, *Ingersoll Papers,* pp. 315–16. Horace Walpole
also remembered that Grenville and his supporters strongly objected to receiving the
petition, "as it was a petition against a money-bill." Walpole, *Memoirs of George III,*
2:56. Grenville and Jeremiah Dyson, who also spoke for the administration, were well
aware that some precedents could be cited in favor of receiving these petitions. In a
manual of the House's procedures and practices that was written during 1762–1763,
probably by Grenville or Dyson, and preserved in Jenkinson's files, the author observed
that "though perhaps no precedent can be shown for receiving a petition directly
against a money bill," several precedents could be found for receiving petitions against
parts of such bills and against "the mode of raising the money." The author also noted
that the petition the House heard in 1733 against Sir Robert Walpole's proposed excise
taxes "was as bold, not to say as saucy a one, as ever came before that House." To
prevent the friends of America from taking advantage of these precedents, Grenville and
Dyson insisted that the rule of 8 March 1733 had wholly superseded earlier decisions of
the House. For the quotation, see Catherine Strateman, ed., *The Liverpool Tractate: An
Eighteenth-Century Manual on the Procedure of the House of Commons,* p. 63; for attribu-
tions of authorship, see ibid., pp. xii–xviii, and Thomas, *House of Commons,* p. 8n. For a
full discussion of this rule, see ibid., pp. 69–71.

70. Ingersoll to Fitch, 6 March 1765, *Ingersoll Papers,* p. 316.

71. Ibid. See also Walpole, *Memoirs of George III,* 2:56.

72. Whately to Temple, 12 June 1765, *Bowdoin-Temple Papers,* p. 60.

73. Jackson to Fitch, 9 March 1765, *Fitch Papers,* p. 341.

74. Thomas's summary of Harris's notes of the debate on Montagu's petition indicates that Grenville did not speak. Walpole's account corroborates this and further
reveals that Grenville confined himself to comments on the procedural question during
the discussion of the merchants' petition. Thomas, *British Politics,* pp. 95–96; Walpole,
Memoirs of George III, 2:56.

75. Thomas, *British Politics,* p. 96; and Ingersoll to Connecticut Assembly, 18
September 1765, *Ingersoll Papers,* p. 336.

76. Ingersoll to Fitch, 6 March 1765, *Ingersoll Papers,* p. 317. The reporter for the
London Magazine claimed that the margin on each question on the petitions was 245 to
49, but this is probably a mistaken reference to the vote of 6 February. *London Magazine*
34 (1765): 447.

77. See Yorke to Grenville, 17 February 1765, quoted in Franklin B. Wickwire,
British Subministers and Colonial America, 1763–1783, p. 191; and Ingersoll to Fitch, 6
March 1765, *Ingersoll Papers,* p. 318.

78. For a description of these changes, see Thomas, *British Politics,* pp. 96–97.

Notes to Chapter IX
"Of Emolument and of Influence"

1. See Whately to Temple, 5 November 1764, *Bowdoin-Temple Papers*, p. 38. For a good account of these deliberations, see Jack M. Sosin, "A Postscript to the Stamp Act: George Grenville's Revenue Measures, A Drain on Colonial Specie?"

2. John Shy, *Toward Lexington: The Role of the British Army in the Coming of the American Revolution*, pp. 241–44; and Lord Colville to John Cleveland, 17 January 1762, PRO Adm. 1/482, fols. 205–6.

3. Grenville to Whately, 11 April 1765, HEHL, George Grenville Letterbooks, ST 7, ii. Grenville declared his intentions to the House on 13 February; see P. D. G. Thomas, *British Politics and the Stamp Act Crisis: The First Phase of the American Revolution, 1763–1767*, p. 99. For a description of the procedure the Treasury finally used, see Sosin, "Postscript to the Stamp Act," p. 920.

4. Thomas, *British Politics*, p. 87. For the ministry's original plan to lay the papers before Parliament after the enactment of the stamp tax, see Edward Sedgwick to Edward Weston, 14 February 1765, Historical Manuscripts Commission, *Weston Underwood MSS.*, p. 382.

5. Charles Lloyd, *The conduct of the late Administration examined*, pp. 13–16, 22.

6. Ingersoll to Fitch, 11 February 1765, *Fitch Papers*, p. 321.

7. Thomas explained the ministry's failure to present the papers as "an apparent act of negligence by . . . Halifax." *British Politics*, p. 87. Lloyd's pamphlet contradicts this version of events. Even if Halifax was forgetful, it is significant that the Treasury made no effort to jog his memory. On other matters relating to the colonies that men at the Treasury wanted expedited, they requested that the appropriate departments act quickly. See, for example, Jenkinson to Grenville, 13 April 1765, *Jenkinson Papers*, p. 361; and Jenkinson to Pownall, 19 March 1765, PRO, T. 27/29, fol. 145.

8. Whately, "general plan," [6 December 1765], Hardwicke Papers, BL, Add. MSS. 35910, fol. 321. Cruwys's notations on this conference indicate that the Treasury accepted Whately's proposals without making exceptions, so Grenville evidently gave initial approval to these arrangements regarding the distributorships. [Cruwys], "American Stamp Office Law Bill," 29 October 1765, ibid., 35911, fol. 22. It is interesting to note that someone wrote in *Lloyd's Evening Post* on 19 December 1764 that the American stamp tax had "been found impractical as to the mode of collection in that country, [and] is now laid aside." Perhaps some friend of America heard a garbled version of Whately's concern over problems that could arise in the administration of the act and put the most optimistic construction possible on that concern. There is no evidence that the Treasury ever considered dropping the scheme for these reasons. The writer in *Lloyd's* added, "In lieu [of a stamp tax], an additional duty, we hear, is proposed to be laid on stationery wares imported to America from England." There is no evidence that Grenville's Treasury ever considered such a tax. Jenkinson did say, "There is a particular propriety in this [stamp] tax, . . . for the colonies need not and perhaps ought not to be supplied with paper but from Great Britain." See Appendix C. Again, perhaps a friend of America heard a confused version of a statement similar to this one.

9. See McCulloh to Jenkinson, 12 December 1763, *Jenkinson Papers*, p. 229; McCulloh to [Grenville], [n.d.], BL, Liverpool Papers, Add. MSS. 38339, fol. 153; and Barons to Jenkinson, 6 February 1764, ibid., 38202, fols. 83–84. Barons had enough influence at Whitehall to persuade the General Post Office to appoint him deputy postmaster general for the southern colonies in January 1765. *Franklin Papers*, 12:121n., 280.

10. Franklin to Josiah Tucker, 26 February 1774, *The Writings of Benjamin Franklin*, ed. A. H. Smyth, 6:200–1.

11. Ingersoll to Connecticut Assembly, 18 September 1765, *Ingersoll Papers*, p. 338. Alison Gilbert Olson has made the interesting observation that before the 1760s, "The British government was responsive to local pressures throughout the empire in a way that kept attempted law enforcement from getting too far out of line with public opinion anywhere." "Parliament, Empire, and Parliamentary Law, 1776," in J. G. A. Pocock, ed., *Three British Revolutions, 1641, 1688, 1776* (Princeton, 1980), p. 295. Perhaps the decision to make Americans the distributors was a conscious effort on the part of the Treasury to incorporate that flexibility into the administration of the stamp tax.

12. See Ingersoll to *Connecticut Gazette*, 6 September 1765, quoted in Lawrence Henry Gipson, *American Loyalist: Jared Ingersoll*, p. 145n. For Whately's interest in America, see Whately to Ingersoll, [Spring 1764], *Ingersoll Papers*, pp. 292–93.

13. Whately, "general plan," [6 December 1764], Hardwicke Papers, BL, Add. MSS. 35910, fol. 322.

14. The *OED* defines this use of *considerable* as "worthy of consideration or regard; important; of consequence or distinction; highly regarded or esteemed."

15. See *Regulations*, p. 94, for Whately's observation that "the due execution of [the laws] is become obnoxious to those who have been suffered to contemn them with impunity." (The definition of *contemn* in the *OED* determined my selection of words in the sentence in the text.) *Regulations* was written during December–January 1764–1765, so these considerations were familiar to Whately as he worked on the Stamp Act. For an indication that others shared the interpretation, see Jenkinson to Wolters, 18 January 1765, *Jenkinson Papers*, pp. 347–48.

16. *Regulations*, pp. 94, 4.

17. 9 March 1764, *Ryder Diary*, p. 235; E. Hughes, "The English Stamp Duties, 1664–1764," pp. 246–47; and "State of the revenues arising from stamps," [1764], Liverpool Papers, Add. MSS. 38338, fols. 125–71.

18. Ingersoll to Fitch, 9 March 1765, Jared Ingersoll, *Mr. Ingersoll's Letters Relating to the Stamp Act*, p. 28. Ingersoll made this comment in an explanatory footnote to the copy of this letter in this privately distributed pamphlet. The footnote was not reprinted in *Ingersoll Papers*.

19. Ingersoll to the *Connecticut Gazette*, 10 September 1765, *Ingersoll Papers*, p. 332. The only surviving accounts of these meetings are in Ingersoll's papers and in Franklin to Tucker, 26 February 1774, *Writings of Franklin*, ed. Smyth, 6:200–1. Both agree on all essentials, even down to many of the words Grenville and Whately used. Both men were defending themselves against the charge that they had solicited the office for themselves. Franklin convincingly demonstrated his innocence in his letter to Tucker, and other papers in Ingersoll's files prove his innocence. See Ingersoll to Whately, 2 November 1765; Ingersoll to Jackson, 3 November 1765; and Jackson to Ingersoll, 22 March 1766, *Ingersoll Papers*, pp. 353, 357–58, 383. For independent evidence that Trecothick named the distributor for New York, see James McEvers to Trecothick, August 1765, PRO, T. 1/439, fol. 63. The approximate time of the meetings may be established by Ingersoll's note to Fitch on 9 March, "'Tis said it is intended to give the business of collecting and paying the stamp duty to Americans in [their] respective colonies," and by the fact that Whately was out of town earlier in March. See Ingersoll to Fitch, 9 March 1765, *Ingersoll Papers*, p. 323; and Grenville to Whately, 3 March 1765, HEHL, George Grenville Letterbooks, ST 7, ii.

20. Franklin to Tucker, 26 February 1774, *Writings of Franklin*, ed. Smyth, 6:200–1. Robert Charles, agent for New York, of course had no opportunity to name a distribu-

tor, since Grenville had given that favor to Trecothick, who had been the spokesman for the North American merchants. But the eventual appointment of Philip DeLancey, Jr., as an inspector of stamps suggests that Charles was given this patronage. For Charles's relationship with the DeLanceys, see Nicholas Varga, "Robert Charles: New York Agent, 1748–1770," pp. 216–20, 229–32.

21. Lawrence Henry Gipson, *The British Empire before the American Revolution,* 10:277; and Whately to Temple, 10 May 1765, *Bowdoin-Temple Papers,* p. 55.

22. Ingersoll to *Connecticut Gazette,* 10 September 1765, *Ingersoll Papers,* p. 332.

23. See ibid. for an account of the meeting and for proof of Trecothick's knowledge about the bond. For evidence that Trecothick served as McEvers's security, see McEvers to Trecothick, 26 August 1765, PRO, T. 1/439, fol. 65.

24. See the contemporary definition of *discreet* in the *OED.*

25. Franklin to Tucker, 26 February 1774, *Writings of Franklin,* ed. Smyth, 6:200. For a similar statement, see Ingersoll to Connecticut Assembly, 19 September 1765, *Ingersoll Papers,* pp. 335–37.

26. Ingersoll to Fitch, 11 February, 6 March 1765, *Ingersoll Papers,* pp. 313, 322.

27. "A letter from London," *Maryland Gazette,* 22 August 1765.

28. Ingersoll to Fitch, 6 March 1765, *Ingersoll Papers,* p. 322.

29. Ingersoll to Connecticut Assembly, 19 September 1765, ibid., p. 338; Franklin to Tucker, 26 February 1774, *Writings of Franklin,* ed. Smyth, 6:200; and Ingersoll to Fitch, 6 March 1765, *Ingersoll Papers,* p. 322.

30. Trecothick's words are taken from Ingersoll to Connecticut Assembly, 19 September 1765, *Ingersoll Papers,* p. 338. The contemporary definition of *favor* may be found in the *OED.*

31. Franklin to Tucker, 26 February 1774, *Writings of Franklin,* ed. Smyth, 6:201. Interested observers in London and Philadelphia interpreted Grenville's offering this patronage to Franklin rather than to Thomas Penn, the proprietor of the colony, as a sign that the First Lord favored the ongoing efforts of Franklin and his friends to persuade the British government to make Pennsylvania a royal colony. Grenville certainly was aware of Franklin's mission, but there is no evidence to support the conjecture that he was demonstrating his approval of it by allowing Franklin to name the distributor. See [Samuel Wharton] to Franklin, 27 May 1765, *Franklin Papers,* 12:145, 146n.

32. The agents did not ask Grenville for the privilege of naming the distributors, but they may have already considered the benefits of having Americans serve as distributors. *The London Chronicle* reported in its 16–19 February edition, "We are informed, since the plantation agents have failed in opposing the present duty . . . a motion is preparing to be made in the House that the commissioners for the receipt of this duty may be appointed from the natives of each province where the tax is to take place." If this information was accurate, the agents decided against introducing that motion.

33. "An Enemy to Hypocrisy" [James Mercer], *Virginia Gazette* (Purdie and Dixon), 18 July 1766; and George Mercer to the Marquis of Rockingham, 11 April 1766, in "Colonel George Mercer's Papers," ed. J. E. Tyler, p. 412. Lee did not deny that he had applied for the post. See Merrill Jensen, *The Founding of a Nation: A History of the American Revolution, 1763–1776,* p. 200.

34. James Mercer to the printers of the *Virginia Gazette,* 3 October 1766, *Virginia Gazette* (Purdie and Dixon).

35. Grenville's speech, 24 February 1766, Harris Diary, quoted in Thomas, *British Politics,* p. 100.

36. News of the assembly's appointment arrived after Ingersoll had reached London

and begun lobbying against the stamp tax. Whately must have learned of this mark of trust; perhaps he passed the news on to Grenville. Ingersoll to Fitch, 11 February 1765, *Ingersoll Papers*, p. 306. Moreover, Jackson had heard from Connecticut that the assembly, "being convinced of [Ingersoll's] skill, ability, and good disposition to serve the interest of this colony," had asked him to assist Jackson, and intended to "let Mr. Ingersoll know that his services therein will be gratefully accepted and rewarded." Perhaps Jackson passed this testimonial of present and future satisfaction with Ingersoll to the Treasury. Resolution of the Connecticut assembly, 11 October 1764, in *The Public Records of the Colony of Connecticut*, ed. Charles J. Hoadley, 12:299–300. Fitch communicated the sense of this resolution in a letter to Ingersoll that he enclosed in Fitch to Jackson, 7 December 1764, *Fitch Papers*, 305.

37. Whately to Temple, 10 May 1765, *Bowdoin-Temple Papers*, p. 52. A list of the distributors and dates of their appointments may be found in Gipson, *The British Empire before the American Revolution*, 10:277.

38. Lloyd, *The conduct of the late Administration*, pp. 13–14. Lloyd was referring to the difficulty of obtaining adequate securities for the distributors, a problem that greatly troubled the commissioners of the stamps during this time.

39. For the governor's opinion, see Sharpe to Calvert, 16 August 1765, *Archives of Maryland* 14:220. For the reference explaining that some friends of his in London had recommended Hood to the Treasury, see Sharpe to Gage, 6 September 1765, in J. Thomas Scharf, *History of Maryland from the Earliest Period to the Present Day*, 3 vols. (1879; reprint ed., Hatboro, Pa.: Tradition Press, 1967), 1:527. For the comments of the unknown observer on Hood, see "A letter from London," *Maryland Gazette*, 22 August 1765. For Hood's reference to his services, see "A letter from New York," 5 December 1765, ibid., 30 January 1766. The exact nature of Hood's services are unknown. For Calvert's involvement in recommending Hood, see again Sharpe to Calvert, 16 August 1765, *Archives of Maryland* 14:220. The other friends who recommended him are unknown, though perhaps his letter to Franklin on 23 September 1765, describing the conditions in Maryland that prompted his flight to New York, offers a clue. Because this is the only letter from him to Franklin in the first twelve volumes of the *Franklin Papers*, perhaps his writing to Franklin on this subject indicates that Franklin was one of those recommending his appointment. *Franklin Papers*, 12:278.

40. *North Carolina Gazette*, 20 November 1765; and Charles G. Sellers, Jr., "Private Profits and British Colonial Policy: The Speculations of Henry McCulloh," p. 550.

41. Jenkinson to Nugent, 29 June 1765, Liverpool Papers, BL, Add. MSS. 39305, fol. 12. For the connections between Garth, Colleton and Nugent, see Namier and Brooke, *House of Commons*, 2:238–39, 483–84; and ibid., 3:219. Apparently, the Treasury had a choice between Lloyd and Charles Woodmason, who was at that time a resident of Charleston and subsequently became an itinerant Anglican priest in the Carolina backcountry. See Richard J. Hooker, ed., *The Carolina Backcountry on the Eve of the Revolution: The Journal and Other Writings of Charles Woodmason, Anglican Itinerant*, pp. 49, 193.

42. Jenkinson to Nugent, 29 June 1765, BL, Liverpool Papers, Add. MSS. 38305, fol. 12. Woodmason did not fulfill these requirements, either. Although he was an officeholder and man of property in Charleston, he was not a native of America. See Hooker's introduction to *The Carolina Backcountry on the Eve of the Revolution*, pp. xii–xviii.

43. Grenville to Sandwich, 17 June 1765; Whately to Grenville, 19 June 1765; Bedford to Grenville, 8 July 1765; and Grenville Diary, 30 June, 1–9 July, *Grenville*

Papers, 3:50, 52, 69–70, 204–11. His suspicions of his probable successors are discussed in Chapter X.

44. Whately to Temple, 10 May 1765, *Bowdoin-Temple Papers,* p. 52. For evidence of Grenville's concern over relations with the King, see *Grenville Papers,* 3:38–71, 163–211.

45. Treasury minutes, 5 July 1765, PRO, T. 29/37, fols. 29–30.

46. Ibid.; and Hughes, "English Stamp Duties," pp. 246–47.

47. Whately to Temple, 10 May 1765, *Bowdoin-Temple Papers,* p. 52. *Account* in contemporary usage referred to esteeming, valuing, or thinking much of something. See the *OED.*

48. For Ingersoll's estimate, see Ingersoll to Whately, 28 January 1765, PRO, T. 1/433, fol. 410.

49. On 12 February 1766, Mercer testified before the House that he had calculated in 1765 that the tax would produce £12,000 a year in Virginia. *Ryder Diary,* p. 296. In the notes of this testimony in Newcastle's files, the reporter had Mercer commenting further that this was a Treasury calculation, not his. Newcastle Papers, BL, Add. MSS. 33030, fols. 128.

50. Both men accepted their appointments well before the Treasury decided on 5 July to raise the distributor's percentage of the gross receipts to 8 percent. Gipson, *The British Empire before the American Revolution,* 10:277. Hood later noted that his distributorship gave him "pleasing views of a genteel subsistence for life." "Letter from New York," 5 December 1765, *Maryland Gazette,* 30 January 1766.

51. Namier and Brooke, *House of Commons,* 2:538–40.

52. Treasury minutes, 5 July 1765, PRO, T. 29/37, fols. 29–30.

53. Grenville's speech, 6 February 1765, *Ryder Diary,* p. 256. For Whately's original estimate of the number of underdistributors, see "general plan," [6 December 1765], Hardwicke Papers, BL, Add. MSS. 35910, fol. 321.

54. Knox, *Extra-Official State Papers. Addressed to the Right Honourable Lord Rawdon . . . ,* 2:25–26. Knox claimed that colonial leaders were well aware of this consequence of a stamp tax, and this consideration helped inspire them to resist it. Interestingly, the man who commented unfavorably on the appointment of Hood as Maryland's distributor observed, "It gives too many here pleasure to find that, let them make what laws they please to cramp your trade and destroy your freedom, there are not wanting sycophants enough of your own country to sue for commissions to put those very laws in execution among their nearest relatives and friends." "A letter from London," *Maryland Gazette,* 22 August 1765.

55. Ingersoll to Fitch, 11 February 1765, *Ingersoll Papers,* pp. 313–14.

56. See ibid., especially Ingersoll's comment at the end of the letter; Franklin to David Hall, 8 June 1765, and Franklin to John Hughes, 9 August 1765, *Franklin Papers,* 12:171, 234–35; Jackson to Fitch, 9 March 1765, *Fitch Papers,* p. 342; and Garth to South Carolina, 8 February 1765, Sir Lewis Namier, "Charles Garth and His Connections," pp. 649–50.

57. Franklin to Hughes, 9 August 1765, *Franklin Papers,* 12:234–35. Ingersoll bluntly stated in *The Connecticut Gazette* on 10 September 1765 that the agitation against the Stamp Act "can answer no other public purpose except so to inflame the Mother Country against us that they will even refuse to treat with us on the subject of our burdens." *Ingersoll Papers,* p. 334.

58. Franklin to Hall, 8 June 1765, *Franklin Papers,* 12:171.

59. Jenkinson to Grenville, 11 April 1765, *Jenkinson Papers,* p. 359; and Grenville to Jenkinson, 13 April 1765. *Additional Grenville Papers,* p. 258.

60. Hallowell to Jenkinson, 3 May 1765, Liverpool Papers, BL, Add. MSS. 38339, fol. 118; Jenkinson to Grenville, 19 June 1765, *Jenkinson Papers*, p. 365; and Philip Lloyd to Jenkinson, 20 June 1765, Liverpool Papers, BL, Add. MSS. 38204, fol. 285.

Notes to Chapter X
Future American Revenue

1. Jackson to Fitch, 9 March 1765, *Fitch Papers*, p. 342.
2. Whately to Temple, 12 June 1765, *Bowdoin-Temple Papers*, p. 60.
3. Ibid.; Appendix C; and Ingersoll to Fitch, 6 March 1765, *Ingersoll Papers*, p. 320.
4. See Grenville's estimate to his colleagues at the Treasury on 4 December 1764, Harris Memorandum, quoted in P. D. G. Thomas, *British Politics and the Stamp Act Crisis: The First Phase of the American Revolution, 1763–1767*, pp. 86–87. The highest estimate of the produce of the molasses tax was apparently Whately's guess that £77,775 might be collected annually. See PRO, T. 1/434, fol. 52. When Grenville estimated on 4 December 1764 that colonial stamp duties would yield £100,000 a year, he also estimated the cost of the army at about £350,000 a year, which in his judgment would require England to send about £200,000 to America each year.
5. Whately to Temple, 5 November 1764, *Bowdoin-Temple Papers*, p. 38.
6. Whately, "general plan," [6 December 1764], Hardwicke Papers, BL, Add. MSS. 35910, fol. 316.
7. Appendix C.
8. Ingersoll to Fitch, 6 March 1765, *Ingersoll Papers*, p. 320.
9. Grenville's speech, 6 February 1765, *Ryder Diary*, p. 256.
10. *Regulations*, p. 100. For an official opinion that the growth of the American colonies would cause increased purchases of French molasses, and thus "the establishing . . . [of] proper duties thereon at a lower rate than at present, so as to diminish the temptation to smuggling, and the securing [of] the just collection of these duties, seems to be an object at this juncture of importance to the revenue," see Customs Commissioners to the Treasury, 16 September 1763, PRO, T. 1/426, fol. 289. For a similar opinion, see "A state of the present branches of the customs in America, with hints for their improvement," [after 25 December 1762], BL, Add. MSS. 38334, fols. 223–24.
11. Ingersoll to Fitch, 11 February 1765, *Ingersoll Papers*, p. 313. Jenkinson recalled a year later, "Grenville thought he had found a means which though small in its produce at present might in [the] future be very fruitful." 21 February 1766, *Ryder Diary*, p. 305.
12. 6 February 1765, *Ryder Diary*, p. 256.
13. Whately to Temple, 12 June 1765, *Bowdoin-Temple Papers*, p. 60. In 1765, Whately publicly noted, moreover, "I have been assured, that when experience has enabled us to give a little more perfection to [the American taxes], a large sum, perhaps £150,000, may be produced by [them]." [Whately], *Remarks on "The Budget"; or, a candid examination of the facts and arguments offered to the public in that pamphlet*, p. 25. When Horace Walpole wrote his description of colonial taxation, he recalled that Grenville "termed [his taxes] but an experiment towards further aid, and as such the Americans immediately understood it." There is no evidence from 1765 that corroborates this assertion that Grenville publicly or privately referred to the molasses duty and the stamp tax as experiments toward further aid during future years. Walpole wrote this passage in January 1769, and it is quite possible he was referring to statements Grenville may have made when he was out of office and critical of his successors for giving up this source of revenue. Walpole, *Memoirs of George III*, 2:51, 53.

14. Whately to Temple, 10 May 1765; Walpole, *Memoirs of George III*, 2:52; and [Cruwys], "American Stamp Office Law Bill," Hardwicke Papers, BL, Add. MSS. 35911, fol. 36.

15. Entries for 13 April and 24 May 1764 in Hardwicke Papers, BL, Add. MSS. 35911, fols. 33–34.

16. Franklin to Hall, 8 June 1765, *Franklin Papers*, 12:171. The "other amendments" referred to probably dealt with the legal enforcement of the Stamp Act and the Crown's power to recover debts. It seems hardly likely that the Treasury expected to make many changes in rates of specific stamps during the next session. The Act would not go into effect until 1 November, and sessions of Parliament had been ending in April. This schedule would leave little time for the discovery that a duty was oppressive, the transmission of this news to England, the analysis of this information at the Treasury, the preparation and introduction of a bill, and its passage through Parliament.

17. *Regulations*, p. 100.

18. Joseph Harrison to Temple, 12 January 1765, *Bowdoin-Temple Papers*, p. 43.

19. Jenkinson to Hallowell, 12 January 1765, *Jenkinson Papers*, p. 346.

20. *Regulations*, pp. 79–83.

21. Trecothick's account of this conversation with Grenville may be found in his testimony before the House of Commons on 11 February 1766, in Newcastle Papers, BL, Add. MSS. 33030, fols. 102–3. The member questioning him about this meeting clearly was Grenville. The accuracy of Trecothick's memory is supported by reports from London that "there is not like[ly] to be any alteration with respect to the molasses duty this session; the ministry chose first to have some experiment of its efficacy." *Boston Post-Boy*, 20 May 1765.

22. Ingersoll to Godfrey Malbone, 7 April 1765, *Ingersoll Papers*, p. 323.

23. *Regulations*, pp. 83–84. In 1766, Grenville criticized the Rockingham administration for doing, in his opinion, precisely that—changing policies on the basis of ex parte testimony. Though clearly partisan, his comments reveal his dislike for this type of procedure in principle, due to his perception of the dangers of following it. James West to Newcastle, 30 April 1766, Newcastle Papers, BL, Add. MSS. 32975, fol. 56.

24. For evidence that Whately and Jenkinson would have continued soliciting these opinions, see Whately to Temple, 12 June and 12 July 1765, *Bowdoin-Temple Papers*, pp. 60, 65; and Jenkinson to Hallowell, 12 January 1765, and 13 July 1765, *Jenkinson Papers*, pp. 345–47, and Liverpool Papers, BL, Add. MSS. 38304, fols. 13–14.

25. See Whately, "general plan," [6 December 1764], Hardwicke papers, BL, Add. MSS. 35910, fol. 320; and Franklin to Hall, 8 June 1765, *Franklin Papers*, 12:171. The Treasury had agreed to lower the duty to one shilling during the debate in committee over the bill on 18 February 1765, but through error, the amendment Grenville accepted then was not written into the bill that passed the House.

26. Ingersoll to Fitch, 6 March 1765, *Ingersoll Papers*, p. 322.

27. Whately to Temple, 4 November 1764, *Bowdoin-Temple Papers*, p. 38.

28. Jasper Mauduit to Massachusetts, 26 May 1764, in Edmund S. Morgan, ed., *Prologue to Revolution: Sources and Documents on the Stamp Act Crisis, 1764–1766*, p. 27; and Grenville's speech, 6 February 1765, *Ryder Diary*, p. 255.

29. West to Newcastle, 30 April 1766, Newcastle Papers, BL, Add. MSS. 32975, fol. 56.

30. Jenkinson to Wolters, 18 January 1765, *Jenkinson Papers*, pp. 347–48. For similar comments, see *Regulations*, p. 80; and Treasury to the King, 4 October 1763, PRO, T. 1/430, fol. 332.

31. See Treasury minutes, 23 April and 18 May 1765; and Edward Stanley to Jenkinson, 14 May 1765; PRO, T. 29/36, fols. 159–60, 173; and S.P. 37/22, no. 5b.

32. Whately, "general plan," [6 December 1764], BL, Add. MSS. 35910, fol. 321. For Whately's eagerness to hear the sentiments of Americans on the law, see Whately to Temple, 12 June 1765, *Bowdoin-Temple Papers,* p. 60.

33. Franklin to Hall, 8 June 1765, *Franklin Papers,* 12:171.

34. [Cruwys], "American Stamp Office Law Bill," 13 April and 23 May 1765, Hardwicke Papers, BL, Add. MSS. 35911, fols. 33–34.

35. [John Dickinson], *Letters From a Farmer in Pennsylvania to the Inhabitants of the British Colonies* (Philadelphia, 1768), Letter 2, in Merrill Jensen, ed., *Tracts of the American Revolution, 1763–1776,* p. 136.

36. Whately to Temple, 12 June 1765, *Bowdoin-Temple Papers,* p. 60.

37. Ingersoll to Fitch, 6 March 1765, *Ingersoll Papers,* p. 322.

38. For example, see Garth to South Carolina, 5 June 1764, in Namier, "Charles Garth and His Connections," p. 646, and the response of Trecothick to the news about the distributors, in Ingersoll to *Connecticut Gazette,* 10 September 1765, *Ingersoll Papers,* pp. 332–33.

39. The quotations are from "A letter from a considerable merchant in London to his friend in Connecticut," 9 April 1765, in the *Boston Post-Boy,* 8 July 1765. For a good account of the negotiations on these matters, see Thomas, *British Politics,* pp. 110–12.

40. Jenkinson enclosed a copy of Hallowell to Jenkinson, 3 May 1765, now found in Liverpool Papers, BL, Add. MSS. 38339, fol. 118, in his letter to Grenville of 19 June 1765, *Jenkinson Papers,* p. 365. Hallowell had informed Jenkinson, "Most people [in Boston] realize that they have done themselves harm by their disrespectful behavior."

41. The Treasury to the King, 4 October 1763, PRO, T. 1/430, fol. 333.

42. Ingersoll to Fitch, 6 March 1765, *Ingersoll Papers,* p. 322.

43. See Grenville Diary, 24 July 1764, *Grenville Papers,* 2:507; and the King to Conway, 18 February 1767, in George III, *The Correspondence of King George the Third from 1760 to December 1783,* ed. Sir John Fortescue, 1:450. For a good account of Grenville's efforts to reduce civil list expenditures, see E. A. Reitan, "The Civil List, 1761–77: Problems of Finance and Administration," especially pp. 187–88, 196–97.

44. George III, "Memorandum," [November–December 1765], *Correspondence of King George the Third,* 1:164; and *Additions and Corrections to Sir John Fortescue's Edition of the Correspondence of King George the Third (Vol. I),* ed. Sir Lewis Namier, p. 38.

45. See John Brooke, *King George III,* pp. 102–22.

46. Grenville to Temple, 6 July 1765, *Additional Grenville Papers,* p. 292. For the King's several versions of his decision, see *Correspondence of King George the Third,* 1:162–77.

47. Grenville to Bedford, 7 July 1765, *Additional Grenville Papers,* p. 294.

48. Grenville Diary, 10 July 1765, *Grenville Papers,* 3:215. Horace Walpole's sources told him that during the climactic debate on the repeal of the Stamp Act on 21 February 1766, Grenville again used the image of a jewel, but in an interestingly different context. "Grenville . . . pushed the Ministers home with giving up the brightest jewel of the Crown, the right of taxation. How would they justify it to His Majesty? How to future Administrations?" Walpole, *Memoirs of George III,* 2:211.

49. Grenville Diary, 10 July 1765, *Grenville Papers,* 3:215–16. Grenville's concern about a "slackness in the execution" perhaps offers a clue to the decisions in early July to issue warrants as stamp distributors to Dr. William Houston and, in particular, to Caleb Lloyd, who did not meet the First Lord's criteria for that post. Perhaps these decisions were inspired by his knowledge that a ministerial change was imminent and his fear that

the Rockinghams might leave the distributors' places vacant for months. For another version of Grenville's conference with the King, see Sandwich to Bedford, 10 July 1765, *Bedford Correspondence*, 3:309–10.

Notes to Chapter XI
"The Author of all the Troubles"

1. Whately to Grenville, 8 August 1765, *Grenville Papers*, 3:78; and Grenville to Nugent, 13 August 1765, George Grenville Letterbooks, HEHL, ST 7, ii.

2. Whately to Grenville, 13 August 1765, *Grenville Papers*, 3:78; Grenville to Whately, 13 August 1765, George Grenville Letterbooks, HEHL, ST 7, ii.

3. Grenville to Nugent, 13 August 1765, George Grenville Letterbooks, HEHL, ST 7, ii. Grenville's assumption that the ministry would respond firmly was initially correct. Curiously, he did not guess that they would also try to embarrass him. Paul Langford, *The First Rockingham Administration, 1765–1766*, p. 79.

4. Grenville to Lord Lyttleton, 20 August 1765, George Grenville Letterbooks, HEHL, ST 7, ii.

5. Grenville to Nugent, 13 August 1765, George Grenville Letterbooks, HEHL, ST 7, ii.

6. Whately to Grenville, 17 October 1765, *Grenville Papers*, 3:100. Whately's information was accurate.

7. This was the prediction of Francis Bernard, which he expressed in letters of 31 August and 7 September 1765 to Halifax. See PRO, C.O. 5/755, fols. 295, 313. Burke later remembered about those days the feeling that "no act was better calculated to execute itself. [Grenville] thought it would do [so], Governor Bernard, in the very heat of the tumults, thought it would do [so], and why should the present administration be more diffident of the executive principle of the act than those who had themselves the making and [executing of] it?" Burke, speech draft, [1766], Burke Papers, Northamptonshire Record Office, A, xxvii–52.

8. Whately to Grenville, 25 October 1765, quoted in Michael Kammen, *A Rope of Sand: The Colonial Agents, British Politics, and the American Revolution*, p. 239. It is interesting to note the similarity between this prediction and the opinions of Colonel Mercer in 1765. Mercer thought then, "From the necessity an opposition to the law would reduce the colonies to, and the absurdity, as I conceived it, of their union in any particular point, [that] the act would enforce itself." Mercer to Rockingham, 11 April 1766, George Mercer, "Colonel George Mercer's Papers," ed. J. E. Tyler, p. 412.

9. Grenville to Botetourt, 3 November 1765, George Grenville Letterbooks, HEHL, ST 7, ii.

10. Whately to Grenville, 8 November 1765, *Grenville Papers*, 3:109. I have clarified the punctuation in this letter.

11. Grenville to Bedford, 28 November 1765, George Grenville Letterbooks, HEHL, ST 7, ii.

12. Conway to the King, 17 December 1765, George III, *The Correspondence of King George the Third from 1760 to December 1783*, ed. Sir John Fortescue, 1:201–2. Sir Gilbert Elliot, a prominent King's Friend, who was disposed to support Grenville on American matters, noted that the former First Lord made "several long angry speeches," even though, in Elliot's opinion, he had no intention of demanding a division on his amendment. Ironically, the fervor of his convictions cost him valuable

support. A more moderate amendment would have gained the voices and votes of Elliot and others, perhaps even Charles Townshend. Whately learned this, but Grenville, fully occupied by careful preparations for the debate, did not talk to his lieutenant until it was too late to change. See [Elliot], "Memorandum," [14 December 1765], National Library of Scotland, Minto Papers, Early Family Papers, MSS. 11032, fols. 65–66.

13. Walpole, *Memoirs of George III*, 2:168. For full accounts of these debates, see Langford, *The First Rockingham Administration*, pp. 132–36, and P. D. G. Thomas, *British Politics and the Stamp Act Crisis: The First Phase of the American Revolution, 1763–1767*, pp. 154–60.

14. Walpole, *Memoirs of George III*, 2:168. Walpole's source for this account was probably Conway. Grenville was probably making a comment similar to the one he made to the agents in February 1765: "He had pledged his word for offering the stamp bill to the House, [and] the House would hear all our objections and would do as they thought best." Ingersoll to Fitch, 11 February 1765, *Ingersoll Papers*, p. 313.

15. Ingersoll to Fitch, 6 March 1765, *Ingersoll Papers*, p. 319.

16. Grenville's speech, 3 February 1766, *Ryder Diaries*, p. 276.

17. Grenville's speech, 4 March 1766, ibid., p. 319.

18. For example, see Thomas, *British Politics*, p. 100.

19. See 5 Geo. 3, c. 32 and 33 in *Statutes at Large*, 26:300–5.

20. See George Rudé, *Wilkes and Liberty: A Social Study of 1763 to 1774*, pp. 16–36.

21. W. Oxford to Halifax, 11 September 1763, George Grenville Papers, HEHL, STG Box 19(3).

22. Grenville to Jenkinson, 22 August 1764, *Jenkinson Papers*, pp. 323–25.

23. The Treasury to the King, 4 October 1763, in *EHD*, 9:639.

24. Egremont to Ellis, 25 March 1763, PRO, S.P. 44/196, fol. 9. For a brief description of these riots, see Rudé, *Wilkes and Liberty*, p. 91.

25. Grenville to Botetourt, 3 November 1765, George Grenville Letterbooks, HEHL, ST 7, ii. In January 1765, Whately estimated the value of the trade to be around seven hundred thousand pounds annually. *Regulations*, p. 93.

26. For the Treasury's knowledge of the high cost of labor in America, see Jenkinson to Hallowell, 12 January 1765, *Jenkinson Papers*, p. 346.

27. Grenville to Hervey, 26 September 1766, George Grenville Letterbooks, HEHL, ST 7, ii. For an account of these riots, see George Rudé, *The Crowd in History: A Study of Popular Disturbances in France and England, 1730–1848*, pp. 38–45.

28. For example, see Ingersoll to Whately, 6 July 1764, *Ingersoll Papers*, pp. 297–98; and Massachusetts House of Representatives to Jasper Mauduit, [Summer 1764], in Bernard Bailyn, ed., *Pamphlets of the American Revolution: Volume I, 1750–1765*, pp. 479–80.

29. Ingersoll to Fitch, 6 March 1765, *Ingersoll Papers*, p. 320.

30. The Earl of Hardwicke to the Earl of Rochford, 28 January 1773, PRO, S.P. 37/10, fols. 9–10.

31. For an excellent, persuasive discussion of this, see Gary B. Nash, *The Urban Crucible: Social Change, Political Consciousness, and the Origins of the American Revolution.*

32. Ingersoll to Fitch, 6 March 1765, *Ingersoll Papers*, p. 320.

33. See Ingersoll to Whately, 6 July 1764, ibid., pp. 297–98; and Representation of Jasper Mauduit to the Treasury, 27 February 1764, PRO, T. 1/430, fol. 204.

34. Jenkinson to Hallowell, 12 January 1765, *Jenkinson Papers*, p. 346; and *Regulations*, pp. 61–67. For the strategy behind Grenville's use of bounties, see John L.

Bullion, "Honor, Trade, and Empire: Grenville's Treasury and 'the American Question,' 1763–1765," pp. 67–90; and Grenville to Knox, 16 August 1768, George Grenville Letterbooks, HEHL, ST 7, ii.

35. Grenville's speech, 6 February 1765, *Ryder Diaries*, p. 256.

36. For excellent descriptions of this development, see Harry S. Stout, "Religion, Communications, and the Ideological Origins of the American Revolution"; and Nash, *The Urban Crucible*, pp. 76–291.

37. Nash, *The Urban Crucible*, p. 290.

38. For an insight into the bitterness engendered by Hutchinson holding several offices, see John Adams's Diary, 15 August 1765, in *Diary and Autobiography of John Adams*, ed. L. H. Butterfield et al., 1:259–60.

39. James Otis, *The Rights of the British Colonies Asserted and Proved*, in Bailyn, ed., *Pamphlets of the American Revolution*, 1:443. For an account of the Otis-Hutchinson rivalry that is sympathetic to Hutchinson, see Bernard Bailyn, *The Ordeal of Thomas Hutchinson*, pp. 45–62; for one sympathetic to Otis, see Gary B. Nash, "Social Change and the Growth of Prerevolutionary Urban Radicalism," in Alfred F. Young, ed., *The American Revolution: Explorations in the History of American Radicalism*, pp. 18–27.

40. Ingersoll to Whately, 6 July 1764, *Ingersoll Papers*, pp. 297, 300. Ingersoll did influence Grenville to the point that he used the metaphor of a shoe pinching to describe the effect of a too-burdensome duty, but no further. Ingersoll to the Connecticut Assembly, 18 September 1765, ibid., p. 338. See the suggestive discussion of political rhetoric based on oral and egalitarian techniques in Stout, "Religion, Communications, and Ideological Origins," pp. 533–40.

41. [Franklin], *Remarks on a Late Protest Against the Appointment of Mr. Franklin as an Agent for this Province* (1764), *Franklin Papers*, 11:434.

42. Jackson to Fitch, 9 February 1765, *Fitch Papers*, p. 317.

43. "The City of Boston['s] . . . Instructions for Their Representatives," May 1764, printed as an appendix to Otis, *The Rights of the British Colonies*, in Bailyn, ed., *Pamphlets of the American Revolution*, 1:473. Bailyn identifies the author of them as Samuel Adams; ibid., 723.

44. See "Extracts from the assembly's . . . letter to their agent," [December 1764], Liverpool Papers, BL, Add. MSS. 38202, fols. 342–43; and Franklin to Pulteney, 12 March 1778, in Edmund S. Morgan, "The Postponement of the Stamp Act," pp. 390–91.

45. Otis, *The Rights of the British Colonies*, in Bailyn, ed., *Pamphlets of the American Revolution*, 1:448.

46. "The City of Boston['s] . . . Instructions to Their Representatives," an appendix to Otis, *The Rights of the British Colonies*, in ibid., pp. 471–72.

47. For example, see S. Adams to G——W——, 13 November 1765, Samuel Adams, *The Writings of Samuel Adams*, ed. H. A. Cushing, 1:35–36.

48. Andrew Oliver was Thomas Hutchinson's brother-in-law and a prominent member of the conservative faction in Boston. Interestingly, none of the nominees for the distributorships had participated prominently in 1764 in devising the most extreme colonial protests against parliamentary taxation.

49. For examples of the willingness of colonists to distribute stamps, see William Samuel Johnson to Ingersoll, 3 June 1765, *Ingersoll Papers*, pp. 324–25; Bailyn, *The Ordeal of Thomas Hutchinson*, p. 70; Martin Howard to Franklin, 14 May 1765, *Franklin Papers*, 12:129–30; and Beverly McAnear, "The Albany Stamp Act Riots," p. 486. William Knox later argued that patriot leaders feared that this patronage would undercut notions of independence in the colonies and that this fear helped to inspire

their resistance to the Stamp Act. *Extra-Official State Papers. Addressed to the Right Honourable Lord Rawdon . . .*,2:25–26.

50. As Bernard Bailyn has convincingly demonstrated, colonial patriots did believe that men in Britain and America were conspiring against colonists' liberties. See Bailyn, *The Ideological Origins of the American Revolution.*

51. Bailyn did not indicate whether or not these beliefs in conspiracy were well founded. At one point in his analysis, though, he came close to stating that the patriots' peculiar way of assessing the significances of political actions led them to mistake the intentions of the Grenville administration. Ibid., p. 95.

52. Ingersoll to William Livingston, 1 October 1765, *Ingersoll Papers,* p. 350; Ingersoll to Fitch, 6 March 1765, ibid., p. 322; and Thomson to Franklin, [24 September 1765], *Franklin Papers,* 12:279, a response to Franklin to Thomson, 11 July 1765, ibid., pp. 207–8. For North's observations, see his speech, 8 December 1768, Cavendish Diaries, BL, Egerton MSS. 215, fol. 302. Francis Bernard also noted two important causes of American resistance in 1765: Internal taxation was new to colonists and it "had no visible bounds set to it." Bernard presumed that these grounds for objection were so obvious that Grenville and his colleagues must have been cognizant of them. Bernard to Barrington, 23 November 1765, Edward Channing and A. C. Coolidge, eds., *The Barrington-Bernard Correspondence and Illustrative Matter 1760–1770,* p. 94.

53. For continuing opposition to the cockets, see James Parson to [?], 16 November 1767, Garth Correspondence, South Carolina Historical Society.

54. Temple to Whately, 10 September 1764, *Bowdoin-Temple Papers,* pp. 24–25; Harrison to Temple, 12 January 1764, ibid., pp. 44–45; Hallowell to Jenkinson, 10 November 1764, *Jenkinson Papers,* pp. 339–40. All these letters betray the authors' familiarity with colonial arguments against the tax, and Hallowell's suggestion for an ad valorem tax on British exports to the colonies had been popular in Massachusetts for many years. It is likely that colonists who discussed the state of trade and the new regulations with these men were aware of their criticism of the threepence duty.

55. See Customs Commissioners to the Treasury, 23 November 1764, PRO, T. 1/430, fol. 283. For the difficulties eighteenth-century officers regularly had with complicated forms, see Elizabeth E. Hoon, *The Organization of the English Customs System, 1696–1768,* p. 231.

56. See the comments of William Smith of New York: "When the Americans reflect upon the Parliament's refusal to hear their representations, when they read abstracts of the speeches within doors, and the ministerial pamphlets without, and find themselves tantalized and condemned, advantage taken of their silence heretofore, and remonstrances forbidden in time to come; and above all, when they see the prospect of immediate loads, arising from their connection with an overburdened nation, interested in shaking the weight off their own shoulders, and commanding silence in the oppressed beast upon which it is cast, what can be expected but discontent for a while, and in the end open opposition?" Smith to Monckton, 30 May 1765, in William Smith, *Historical Memoirs from 16 March 1763 to 9 July 1776 of William Smith,* ed. William H. W. Sabine, p. 29.

57. Temple to Whately, 10 September 1764, *Bowdoin-Temple Papers,* p. 25; and Hallowell to Sir Charles Knowles, 6 December 1765, Dartmouth Papers, Staffordshire Record Office, D 1778 ii. 121.

58. *Boston Gazette,* 12 August 1765.

59. Whately to Temple, 5 November 1764, *Bowdoin-Temple Papers,* pp. 36–37. It is also interesting to note that some people blamed the agents for the passage of the Stamp

Act. In Philadelphia, Franklin was accused of complicity in the formulation of this tax, and in New York, Robert Charles's enemies explained his coolness to the assembly's addresses by referring to his obligation to Grenville for his appointment as comptroller of the post office, a place he held during 1763–1765. See Hall to Franklin, 6 September 1765, *Franklin Papers*, 12:259; and Nicholas Varga, "Robert Charles: New York Agent, 1748–1770," p. 232. At least one observer in London found it "unaccountable" that the agents waited until after the stamp tax was introduced to present the petitions against it. According to this person, the agents had to "know the constant usage of Parliament, never to admit a petition against a money bill." *Boston Post-Boy,* 10 May 1765. Thomas Ruston, a native of Philadelphia who was studying medicine in Edinburgh, believed that Grenville "obtained the Act merely by browbeating our agents, and suppressing remonstrances." Years later, Burke speculated that the agents "must have appeared before Grenville like sheep before their shearer." See Ruston to J. Ruston, 3 March 1766, Miscellaneous Collections, WLCL; and Burke, a draft of comments on Israel Mauduit's pamphlet, [1775], Burke Papers, Sheffield Central Library, Bk. 6(d).

60. Ingersoll to *Connecticut Gazette,* 6 September 1765, quoted in Lawrence Henry Gipson, *American Loyalist: Jared Ingersoll,* p. 145n.; and Ingersoll to Connecticut Assembly, 18 September 1765, *Ingersoll Papers,* p. 338.

61. Edmund S. and Helen Morgan, *The Stamp Act Crisis,* pp. 152–53.

62. The Rockinghams later claimed that Grenville, by refusing to submit for Parliament's consideration the proceedings of the assemblies of Massachusetts and New York during 1764, had deliberately concealed the potential danger of resistance. Thomas, *British Politics,* pp. 225–26. For Grenville's response to this charge, see 4 March 1766, *Ryder Diary,* p. 319.

63. Johnson to Ingersoll, 3 June 1765, *Ingersoll Papers,* pp. 324–25.

64. Smith to Monckton, 30 May 1765, Smith, *Historical Memoirs,* ed. Sabine, p. 29.

65. Grenville to Hamilton, 31 December 1765, George Grenville Letterbooks, HEHL, ST 7, ii; and Namier and Brooke, *House of Commons,* 2:570.

66. The surprise of Grenville and his supporters is best shown by Bamber Gascoyne in a letter to John Strutt, 7 February 1766, Namier and Brooke, *House of Commons,* 2:488. The partisan Gascoyne overlooked the persuasiveness of the argument that enforcing the Stamp Act would ruin Britain's commerce with America and thus exacerbate to an unsupportable degree the recent decline in Britain's trade and manufacturing. Still, several observers who opposed Grenville in 1766 admitted the cogency of some of his arguments. See Walpole, *Memoirs of George III,* 2:211; Pitt's speech, 21 February 1766, *Ryder Diary,* pp. 307–8; and comments on Jenkinson's remarks on 21 February 1766, "Notes on the speakers in the Stamp Act debates," [21 February 1766], Burke Papers, Sheffield Central Library, Bk. 27(f).

67. Franklin to Joseph Fox, 24 February 1766, *Franklin Papers,* 13:168. At some later date, Franklin recalled that Grenville planned to "reduc[e] it to a stamp on commissions for profitable offices and on cards and dice." Ibid., p. 132n.

68. Whately, "general plan," [6 December 1764], Hardwicke Papers, BL, Add. MSS. 35910, fol. 319.

69. Conway's speech, 21 February 1766, *Ryder Diary,* p. 303.

70. Jenkinson's speech, 21 February 1766, ibid., p. 305.

71. Ruston to J. Ruston, 3 March 1766, Miscellaneous Collections, WLCL. One of these was probably James Coutts, the member for Edinburgh, an M.P. Ruston was on familiar terms with. See Ruston to J. Ruston, 10 March 1764, Thomas Ruston Papers, Library of Congress; and Ruston to J. Ruston, 1 September 1764, Transcripts of

Thomas Ruston Papers in the College of Physicians Library, Philadelphia, Pennsylvania, American Antiquarian Society. For the remark in Parliament, see Hans Stanley's speech, 24 February 1766, *Ryder Diary,* p. 312.

72. For two comprehensive accounts of the debates, see Thomas, *British Politics,* pp. 154–252; and Langford, *The First Rockingham Administration,* pp. 109–98. The vote to keep "repeal" in the motion on 21 February 1766 was 275 to 167.

73. This judgment is Walpole's, in *Memoirs of George III,* 4:125. It has been accepted by scholars of the period. Namier and Brooke, *House of Commons,* 2:543–44.

74. Grenville's speech, 26 January 1769, Cavendish Diaries, BL, Egerton MSS. 216, fol. 157. On one occasion, a minister did at least momentarily approve of one of Grenville's proposals. See Grenville's and Charles Townshend's speeches, 13 May 1767, *Ryder Diary,* p. 346.

75. 5 March 1770, Cavendish Diaries, BL, Egerton MSS. 221, fols. 38–40. For a description of Grenville's ideas about America after he left office that persuasively documents and analyzes his flexibility during that period, see Philip Lawson, "George Grenville and America: The Years of Opposition, 1765 to 1770."

76. Grenville's speeches, 5 March 1770, Cavendish Diaries, BL, Egerton MSS. 221, fol. 33; and 26 April 1770, BL, Egerton MSS. 222, fol. 25.

77. *Regulations,* p. 44.

78. Grenville to Nugent, 28 July 1765, *Additional Grenville Papers,* p. 313.

79. The quotation may be found in Paul Langford, *The Excise Crisis: Society and Politics in the Age of Walpole,* p. 43n.

Notes to Appendix A
McCulloh's "General Thoughts"

1. See McCulloh to Halifax, 10 December 1751, BL, Add. MSS. 11514, fols. 178–79; idem, [1755], Newcastle Papers, BL, Add. MSS. 33030, fols. 334–35; the editorial description of McCulloh to Jenkinson, 5 July 1763, in which McCulloh described an enclosure as "submitted to the Earl of Halifax in 1755," *Grenville Papers,* 2:374; [Cruwys], "Minutes taken on [a] conference with Mr. McCulloh," 12 October 1763, Bute Papers, BL, Add. MSS. 36226, fol. 357; P. D. G. Thomas, *British Politics and the Stamp Act Crisis: The First Phase of the American Revolution, 1763–1767,* pp. 70–71; and Jack P. Greene, " 'A Dress of Horror': Henry McCulloh's Objections to the Stamp Act." Joseph Albert Ernst's monumental research into British monetary planning turned up no similar suggestions during this period, so I am confident this scheme was unique to McCulloh. See *Money and Politics in America, 1755–1775: A Study in the Currency Act of 1764 and the Political Economy of Revolution,* pp. 78–80.

2. In the eighteenth century, *cede* signified the end of a formal process of surrender of territory. *OED.*

3. *Late* in eighteenth-century usage meant "recent in date; that has recently happened or occurred." The word could be applied to a period of years, as in "of late years." Ibid.

4. McCulloh, "Remarks with respect to the Collectors of the Customs in America," [n.d.], *Jenkinson Papers,* pp. 229–31. N. S. Jucker, the editor of the *Jenkinson Papers,* presumed that "Remarks" was enclosed with a letter McCulloh wrote to Jenkinson on 12 December 1763, probably because the two papers were filed together in Liverpool Papers, BL, Add. MSS. 38201, fols. 315–16. I suspect Jenkinson filed the papers together at some later date for his own convenience. As Jucker pointed out, "If McCulloh's 'Remarks' were written in December 1763, he seems to have been unaware

[Archibald] Kennedy [the collector of New York] had died on June 14." For reasons I discuss in this appendix and in n. 7, I think it was highly unlikely McCulloh was ignorant of this event.

5. See the editorial note on McCulloh to Jenkinson, 5 July 1763, *Grenville Papers,* 2:374.

6. See ibid.; Charles G. Sellers, "Private Profits and British Colonial Policy: The Speculations of Henry McCulloh," p. 550; Thomas, *British Politics,* pp. 70–71; and [Cruwys], "American Stamp Office Law Bill," entry for 4 October 1763, Hardwicke Papers, BL, Add. MSS. 35911, fol. 18.

7. News of Kennedy's death reached England in time to be included in the list of recent deaths in the August 1763 issue of the *London Magazine.* See *London Magazine* 32 (1763): 449. For Elliot's letter, see Sir Gilbert Elliot to Jenkinson, [endorsed 30 July 1763], Liverpool Papers, BL, Add. MSS. 38201, fol. 45. Sir Gilbert's brother did become collector at New York. Indeed, Grenville was apparently ready to promise the post to him in early November, making Jucker's assertion that "Remarks" was enclosed in the letter McCulloh wrote to Jenkinson on 12 December even more unlikely. That a man as well connected as McCulloh was at the Treasury and the customs house would be unaware both of Kennedy's death and Elliot's good fortune is inconceivable, and especially so because Andrew Elliot had been personally soliciting for that appointment during October and early November. Grenville to Sir Gilbert Elliot, 8 November 1763, George Grenville Letterbooks, HEHL, ST 7, i.

8. McCulloh to Jenkinson, 12 December 1763, *Jenkinson Papers,* p. 229.

9. [McCulloh] to Grenville, [1765], Liverpool Papers, BL, Add. MSS. 38339, fol. 153. The author of this letter is clearly McCulloh, for he describes his son as the collector of Beaufort in North Carolina, a post held by one of McCulloh's children. See John Cannon, "Henry McCulloch and Henry McCulloh," p. 73. McCulloh envisioned an important role for the inspectors and comptrollers of stamps, one that would amply reward his involvement in the preparation of the tax. He believed that these officers should not only monitor distributors' books and supervise the supply of stamps from England. "It will be found absolute necessary," he predicted, "to join the governor and the inspector and comptroller with the chief distributor in the nomination of such persons as are proper to act as deputy distributors." He justified this procedure by explaining if the distributor had "the sole choice of his deputies, it may not be easy to check . . . his accounts," and thus "he may . . . have it in his power to prefer his private interest for the public service." McCulloh, "Observations endeavoring to demonstrate that the course of business in use here with respect to the stamp duties cannot have a proper effect in America. Most humbly submitted to the consideration of the Right Honorable George Grenville," [March 1765], Liverpool Papers, BL, Add. MSS. 38339, fol. 188. Clearly, this argument did not impress Grenville. Moreover, the fact that McCulloh was not an American disqualified him from consideration for a place in the colonial administration of the Stamp Act.

10. The original document is in the George Grenville Papers, HEHL, STG Box 12(28).

Notes to Appendix B
Nathaniel Ware

1. John L. Bullion, "Escaping Boston: Nathaniel Ware and the Beginnings of Colonial Taxation, 1762–1763," *Huntington Library Quarterly,* in press.

2. Grenville to Walpole, 8 September 1763, *Grenville Papers,* 2:114.

3. Fremantle to Jenkinson, 3 January 1764, PRO, T. 1/429, no. 87; and Treasury Warrants, 1764, ibid., T. 11/27, fol. 224.

4. The only evidence I have uncovered about Ware's appointment is the notice of his death at Málaga in the *London Magazine* 36 (1767): 596. The introduction to Ware's "Observations on the British Colonies on the continent of America," *MHSC,* 1st ser. 1:66, mistakenly described him as the consul at Madeira and incorrectly gave the date of his death as "about the year 1769."

5. The original document is in the George Grenville Papers, HEHL, STG Box 12(14).

Notes to Appendix C
Jenkinson's Memorandum

1. *Jenkinson Papers,* p. 346. See Jenkinson's memorandum, "People of the colonies not taxable," [n.d.], ibid., pp. 442–43, for a similar statement.

2. Jenkinson to Wolters, 18 January 1765, ibid., p. 348.

3. Charles R. Ritcheson, "The Preparation of the Stamp Act," pp. 555–56.

4. *Statutes at Large,* 26:33.

5. The original document is in Liverpool Papers, BL, Add. MSS. 38339, fols. 131–35.

Bibliography

I. Manuscripts

As I noted in the Introduction, in common with other scholars of the period, I have found only a relatively small number of sources that bear directly on the formulation of the taxes on America at the Treasury during 1763–1765. These sources are described in the Introduction, cited and discussed in the notes and appendixes, and listed below. Also listed below are other sources I explored. In particular, I was interested in looking for information and opinions of the men in the army and navy who were to spend the American taxes, in the comments of important officials who dealt with the colonies during and after Grenville's tenure at the Treasury, and in the retrospective remarks made by prominent British politicians about the decisions of 1763–1765. Sir Lewis Namier once remarked, "I can hardly remember having come across contemporary materials, or any book reproducing those materials, which did not contribute something to my information." I share Sir Lewis's feeling, yet in these particular cases, I must concede that that something was most often of limited value and always had to be checked closely against documents relating more directly to Grenville's decisions.

For reasons beyond my control, in some areas my search never began. I never received from their respective owners permission to see the Bedford Papers and the diary and memoranda of James Harris. In the case of Bedford's manuscripts, this failure is not serious. I have seen the material in the Bedford Papers that relates to America and has been copied and deposited at the Library of Congress. That material reveals nothing about Grenville's thoughts and actions on American taxation. Moreover, many scholars have been through Bedford's political files for the same years, and their published work reveals that nothing of importance has been found there on colonial taxes. That that is so is not surprising: Grenville was determined not to permit Bedford to interfere in decisions on policies or patronage at the Treasury and thus did not confide in the Duke on American taxation. The Harris papers, however, are a serious loss to all scholars of the political history of the period. One can only hope that they will soon be reopened to students; until then, we all must rely on the descriptions made by the fortunate few who saw them in the past. In the near future, Harris's notes on debates in the House of Commons on colonial policy will be published in R. C. Simmons and P. D. G. Thomas, eds., *Proceedings and Debates of the British Parliaments Respecting North America, 1754–1783,* 6 vols. (Millwood, N.Y., 1982–). Unfortunately, the first volume of this series, which covers the years 1754–1764, arrived too late for me to use it in the preparation of this book. Had it been published earlier, it would have provided material from the Harris Diary that would have supplemented my descriptions and interpretations of debates in the House of Commons during 1763–1764. I saw nothing in Harris's notes that would have caused me to question the basic arguments of this book.

Three other sources familiar to students of British politics during the 1760s, though not listed below, must be noted as well. Due to constraints on my time during research trips to Britain, and due to my judgment that these papers would contain material of limited, if any, relevance to Grenville's decisions on American taxation, I did not examine the parliamentary diary and other papers of Sir Roger Newdigate at the Warwickshire County Record Office, the Strutt Papers at the Essex County Record office, or the Bute Manuscripts at the Central Library, Cardiff. The descriptions of the Newdigate collection by other historians indicate that the diaries make very few references to American taxation during the period 1763–1765, and those references have been thoroughly discussed, quoted from, and, in the case of the debate on the army on 4 March 1763, published. Nothing discovered so far in the Newdigate Manuscripts contradicts the narrative or interpretations in this book, and it is unlikely that anything startlingly new will be discovered there. The Strutt Papers are of particular interest to political historians of the 1760s because numerous letters from Bamber Gascoyne, a follower of Grenville during most of that period, to John Strutt are preserved in this collection. Gascoyne was a talented and contentious man, who had a knack for vivid, pungent descriptions of parliamentary debates and who was close enough to Grenville after 1765 to speak with some authority about reactions of the Grenvillites to various political problems. Unfortunately, for most of Grenville's tenure at the Treasury, Gascoyne was not a member of Parliament. His correspondence with Grenville, which may be found in Grenville's papers, is entirely devoted to his and the First Lord's efforts to find him a seat. They did not succeed until 16 January 1765. When Gascoyne did begin attending debates at the House later that month, he found that his official duties at the Board of Trade limited both his preparation for debates and attendance. Thus his regular letters to Strutt contain no information on the parliamentary discussions of American taxation during the period. Moreover, though he worked energetically at his official duties during this time, the Board of Trade was not consulted by Grenville on the important policy decisions on colonial taxation, so Gascoyne probably had no inside knowledge of proceedings at the Treasury. Certainly his private correspondence with Grenville does not indicate any exchange of views on that subject between the two men. And even if Gascoyne did have an insider's knowledge, it is doubtful he would have passed it along to Strutt, an Essex country gentleman who was his friend and political ally in county politics. Indeed, in the description of the holdings at the Essex County Record Office in John W. Raimo, ed., *A Guide to the Manuscripts Relating to America in Great Britain and Ireland: A Revision of the Guide Edited in 1961 by B. R. Crick and Miriam Alman* (Westport, Conn., 1979), the Strutt Papers are not listed at all. This is somewhat misleading, for these papers include several descriptions of and reactions to the debates over the Stamp Act during January–March 1766 by Gascoyne; still, that this collection has any authoritative material on the planning of colonial taxation is highly doubtful. Finally, Bute's papers at Cardiff are, from the standpoint of students of the period, tragically incomplete. He and George III carefully destroyed their correspondence during Grenville's tenure at the Treasury. What survived from earlier days has been published in a masterful edition by Romney Sedgwick. I suspect that even had this correspondence from 1763–1765 survived, it would reveal little about Grenville's plans for colonial taxation: Finance, after all, was neither Bute's forte nor a topic that interested him, and George III's published papers betray little interest on the King's part in the intricacies of taxation during this period. There are some papers in Bute's files relating to the colonies, but a descriptive list of them in Raimo, ed., *A Guide to Manuscripts Relating to America in Great Britain and Ireland* reveals nothing among these papers that relates directly to the Grenville program. Even if something directly relating to the taxation of America during 1763–1765 were there, it would still be doubtful that Bute would have passed it along to Grenville, given Grenville's suspicions that Bute was trying to exert undue influence on the Closet and the government. The political estrangement between the two men makes it highly unlikely that any authoritative material dealing with Grenville's program will ever be found misfiled in Bute's papers.

Indeed, it seems highly unlikely that new material from authoritative sources on Grenville's American taxes will be discovered anywhere. Rather, I suspect that if such documents ever existed, they have been lost—as the papers of Henry Seymour Conway and some of the Grenville papers have been—or are in the process of rapid deterioration resulting from either inattention if in private hands or reduction of personnel and cuts in budgets if in public depositories. Searches for such sources should and, I am certain, will continue. But the odds are that the best chance of achieving a fuller understanding of the Grenville program of American taxation lies in a close, careful analysis of materials whose existence is familiar to students of British politics in the 1760s.

A. In the British Library, London

Egerton MSS.
    Eg. MSS. 215–57, 3711, Cavendish Diaries
    Eg. MSS. 2659, Hutchinson Papers
Kings MSS.
    Kings MSS. 206
Stowe MSS.
    Stowe MSS. 264–65, Stamp Act Papers
Additional MSS.
    Add. MSS. 8133 B, C, Customs House Statistics
    Add. MSS. 11514, McCulloh essay
    Add. MSS. 12439–40 Circulars to American Governors
    Add. MSS. 21631–60, Bouquet Papers
    Add. MSS. 21671–95, 21728–29, Haldimand Papers
    Add. MSS. 22358–59, Buckinghamshire Papers
    Add. MSS. 30868–69, Wilkes Papers
    Add. MSS. 32679–3077, Newcastle Papers
    Add. MSS. 34419, Auckland Papers
    Add. MSS. 35349–916, Hardwicke Papers

Add. MSS. 36226, 36796, Bute Papers
Add. MSS. 38190–387, Liverpool Papers
Add. MSS. 41346–61, Martin Papers
Add. MSS. 42082–88, Grenville Papers
Add. MSS. 45728–30, Auckland Papers
Add. MSS. 46490–91, Auckland Papers
Add. MSS. 47053–54, Egmont Papers
Add. MSS. 47584, Villiers Journal
Add. MSS. 51318–400, Holland House Papers
Add. MSS. 57835, Grenville Papers
Add. MSS. 57927–28, Weston Papers

B. *In the Public Record Office, London*

Admiralty Papers
  Adm. 1/481–83, 3819, 3678–79, 3883
  Adm. 2/1057, 1333
Colonial Office Papers
  C.O. 5/4, 20, 62–67, 83, 755–58, 891, 920, 1071–72, 1097,
    1129–41, 1280, 1330–68
  C.O. 388/51–55
  C.O. 390/9
Gifts and Deposits
  P.R.O. 30/8/6–100, Chatham Papers
  P.R.O. 30/8/12/1, Ellenborough Papers
  P.R.O. 30/20, Rodney Papers
  P.R.O. 30/8/29/1–4, Granville Papers
  P.R.O. 30/8/43/1–2, Lowry Cole Papers (essays by James Harris)
  P.R.O. 30/8/47/14–22, Egremont Papers
Home Office Papers
  H.O. 49/1–2
State Papers, Domestic
  S.P. 37/7–10, 22
  S.P. 41/25–26
  S.P. 42/62
  S.P. 44/88, 138, 231
  S.P. 45/21
  S.P. 63/428–42
Treasury Papers
  T. 1/392–450
  T. 11/27–30
  T.27/28–30
  T. 28/1
  T. 29/30–40
War Office Papers
  W.O. 1/5–6
  W.O. 3/1–6, 23–25

W.O. 4/987, 1044
W.O. 34/99–109, 260

C. In other British libraries

Berkshire Record Office, Reading
  Braybrooke Papers
  Downshire Papers
  Hartley-Russell Papers
  Trumbull Additional Manuscripts
Bodleian Library, Oxford
  North Papers
Bury St. Edmonds and West Suffolk Record Office, Bury St. Edmonds
  Grafton Papers, Correspondence 1760–1766
  Hervey Papers
History of Parliament Trust, London
  Cavendish Diaries (translation of shorthand notes in BL, Egerton
    MSS. 254, 256).
House of Lords Record Office, London
  Items 200–300
Isle of Bute, Scotland
  Bute Papers in the possession of the Marquess of Bute
Manchester College Library, Oxford
  Hulton Letterbook, William Shepherd MSS., XVIII
National Library of Scotland, Edinburgh
  Minto Papers, Early Family Papers
National Maritime Museum, Greenwich
  Sandwich Transcripts
Northamptonshire Record Office, Northampton
  Burke Papers, A. vi–xxx (speech drafts)
  Northington Papers
Nottinghamshire Record Office, Nottingham
  Foljambe MSS., XIII
Nottingham University, Nottingham
  Mellish Papers
  Newcastle of Clumber Papers, Correspondence 1760–1766
  Portland Papers, Correspondence 1760–1766
Sheffield Central Library, Sheffield
  Rockingham Papers, R. 1/1–500, R. 21, R. 33, R. 38, R. 65
  Burke Papers, Bk. 6, 27
Staffordshire Record Office, Stafford
  Dartmouth Papers, Correspondence 1760–1766

D. In libraries in the United States

American Antiquarian Society, Philadelphia, Pennsylvania
  Ruston Papers

Henry E. Huntington Library, San Marino, California
  George Grenville Letterbooks, ST 7, i–ii
  George Grenville Papers, STG Boxes 1–30, 190–99
  George Grenville Papers relating to the Peace of Paris, STG Box 12
  Whately-Temple Papers, STG Box 13(6)
  Grenville Family Papers, STG Boxes 200–450
  Grenville Miscellany, L 9D9, L 9D10
  Huntington Miscellany, 513–2187, 31550–76
  Loudoun Papers
  Temple Correspondence
Library of Congress, Washington, D.C.
  Bedford Papers (transcripts of originals relating to America
    in the Bedford Record Office)
  Brickdale Diaries (transcripts of originals in Bristol University
    Library)
  Thomas Ruston Papers
South Carolina Historical Society, Charleston, S.C.
  Garth Correspondence
William L. Clements Library, Ann Arbor, Michigan
  Clinton Papers, Correspondence 1760–1766
  Dowdeswell Papers
  Gage Papers, English Series
  Knox Papers
  Lacaita-Shelburne Papers
  Lee Papers
  Lyttleton Papers
  Macartney Papers
  Melville Papers
  Miscellaneous Collections, 1746–1773
  Sackville-Germaine Papers
  Shadwell Papers
  Shelburne Papers
  Townshend-Brocklesby Papers
  Townshend (Charles) Papers
  Townshend (George) Correspondence
  Wedderburne Papers
  Wilkes Papers

II. Printed Primary Materials

A surprising amount of material relating to this period in British political history has been published. Students of this era should be aware, though, that some of the editorial standards of the nineteenth century fall far short of the standards of today. Fortunately, W. J. Smith's edition of *The Grenville Papers* is very good. Others, however, should be used with care, and checked against the original documents whenever possible.

ADAMS, JOHN. *Diary and Autobiography of John Adams.* Edited by L. H. Butterfield et al. Vol. 1. Cambridge, Mass., 1962.

ADAMS, SAMUEL. *The Writings of Samuel Adams.* Edited by H. A. Cushing. Vol. 1. New York, 1904.

ALBEMARLE, EARL OF. *Memoirs of the Marquis of Rockingham and his Contemporaries.* 2 vols. London, 1852.

[ALMON, JOHN.] *Biographical, Literary, and Political Anecdotes, of several of the most eminent persons of the present age, never before printed.* 3 vols. London, 1797.

ALMON, JOHN. *The Debates and Proceedings of the British House of Commons from 1743 to 1774.* 11 vols. London, 1766–1775.

BAILYN, BERNARD, ed. *Pamphlets of the American Revolution, 1750–1765.* Cambridge, Mass., 1965.

BEDFORD, JOHN, FOURTH DUKE OF. *Correspondence of John, Fourth Duke of Bedford, Selected from the Originals at Woburn Abbey.* Edited by Lord John Russell. 3 vols. London, 1842–1846.

BURKE, EDMUND. *The Correspondence of Edmund Burke.* Edited by Thomas W. Copeland et al. Vol. 1. Cambridge, 1958.

CALVERT, CECILIUS. "Cecilius Calvert Letters." Edited by William H. Browne et al. Vol. 14. *Archives of Maryland.* Baltimore, 1895.

CHANNING, EDWARD, and COOLIDGE, A. C., eds. *The Barrington-Bernard Correspondence and Illustrative Matter 1760–1770.* Cambridge, Mass., 1912.

COBBETT, WILLIAM, and HANSARD, T. C., eds. *The Parliamentary History of England from the Earliest Period to the Year 1803.* Vols. 15–29. London, 1813–1814.

DEBRETT, J. *The History, Debates, and Proceedings of Both Houses of Parliament . . . 1743 to . . . 1774.* 7 vols. London, 1792.

DODINGTON, GEORGE BUBB. *The Political Journal of George Bubb Dodington.* Edited by John Carswell and L. A. Dralle. Oxford, 1965.

FITCH, THOMAS. *The Fitch Papers: Correspondence and Documents During Thomas Fitch's Governorship of the Colony of Connecticut, 1754–1766. Collections of the Connecticut Historical Society.* Vol. 18. Hartford, 1920.

FITZMAURICE, LORD. *Life of William, Earl of Shelburne, Afterwards First Marquess of Lansdowne, with extracts from his papers and correspondence.* 2 vols. 2d rev. ed. London, 1912.

[FRANCIS, PHILIP.] *The Letters of Junius.* Edited by John Cannon. Oxford, 1978.

Franklin, Benjamin. *The Papers of Benjamin Franklin.* Edited by L. W. Labaree et al. 14 vols. New Haven, 1959–1970.

———. *The Writings of Benjamin Franklin.* Edited by A. H. Smyth. Vol. 6. New York, 1907.

GAGE, THOMAS. *The Correspondence of General Thomas Gage with the Secretaries of State, 1763–1775.* Edited by C. E. Carter. 2 vols. New Haven, 1931.

GARTH, CHARLES. "The Correspondence of Charles Garth." Edited by J. W. Barnwell. *South Carolina Historical and Genealogical Magazine* 26 (1925):65–92; 28 (1927):79–93; 29 (1928):41–48, 115–32, 212–30, and 295–305.

GEORGE III. *Additions and Corrections to Sir John Fortescue's Edition of the Correspondence of King George the Third (Vol. I)*. Edited by Sir Lewis Namier. Manchester, 1937.

———. *The Correspondence of King George the Third from 1760 to December 1783*. Edited by Sir John Fortescue. Vol. 1. London, 1927.

———. *Letters from George III to Lord Bute, 1756–1766*. Edited by Romney Sedgwick. London, 1939.

GRAFTON, DUKE OF. *Autobiography and Political Correspondence of Augustus Henry, Third Duke of Grafton, K.G. From Hitherto Unpublished Documents in the Possession of His Family*. Edited by W. R. Anson. London, 1898.

GRENVILLE, GEORGE. *Additional Grenville Papers, 1763–1765*. Edited by John R. G. Tomlinson. Manchester, 1962.

———. *The Grenville Papers: Being the Correspondence of Richard Grenville, Earl Temple, K.G., and the Right Honourable George Grenville, their friends and contemporaries*. Edited by W. J. Smith. 4 vols. London, 1852–1853.

HISTORICAL MANUSCRIPTS COMMISSION. *Dartmouth MSS*. 3 Vols. London, 1887–1896.

———. *Eyre Matcham MSS. Various MSS*. Vol. 6. London, 1906.

———. *5 Report*, pp. 215–60 (a catalog of Shelburne Papers now at the William L. Clements Library, Ann Arbor, Michigan). London, 1876.

———. *Knox MSS. Various MSS*. Vol. 6. London, 1906.

———. *Lothian MSS*. London, 1905.

———. *Report on the Manuscripts of Mrs. Stopford-Sackville*. Vols. 1–2. London, 1904.

———. *Rutland MSS*. Vol. 4. London, 1905.

———. *Townshend MSS. 11 Report*. Part 4. London, 1887.

———. *Weston Underwood MSS. 10 Report*. Part 1. London, 1885.

ILCHESTER, COUNTESS OF, and STAVORDALE, LORD, eds. *The Life and Letters of Lady Sarah Lennox, 1745–1826*. London, 1902.

ILCHESTER, EARL OF. *Henry Fox, First Lord Holland, His Family and Relations*. Vol. 2. London, 1920.

ILCHESTER, EARL OF, ed. *Letters to Henry Fox, Lord Holland, with a few addressed to his brother Stephen, Earl of Ilchester*. London, 1915.

INGERSOLL, JARED. "A Selection from the Correspondence and Miscellaneous Papers of Jared Ingersoll." Edited by F. B. Dexter. *Papers of the New Haven Colony Historical Society* 9 (1918):201–472.

JENKINSON, CHARLES. *The Jenkinson Papers, 1760–1766*. Edited by N. S. Jucker. London, 1949.

JENSEN, MERRILL, ed. *American Colonial Documents to 1776. English Historical Documents*, vol. 9. New York, 1955.

———, ed. *Tracts of the American Revolution, 1763–1776*. New York, 1967.

Journals of the Commissioners for Trade and Plantations 1704–1782. Vols. covering 1760–1766. London, 1920–1938.

Journals of the House of Commons. Vols. 28–30.

Journals of the House of Lords. Vols. 30–31.

KIMBALL, D. A., and QUINN, M. eds. "William Allen-Benjamin Chew Correspondence." *Pennsylvania Magazine of History and Biography* 90 (1966):202–26.

[KNOX, WILLIAM.] "A Project for Imperial Reform: Hints Respecting the Settlement For Our American Provinces, 1763." Edited by Thomas C. Barrow. *William and Mary Quarterly,* 3d ser. 24 (1967):108–26.

LABAREE, L. W., ed. *Royal Instructions to British Colonial Governors.* Vol. 2. New York, 1935.

McCULLOH, HENRY. " 'A Dress of Horror': Henry McCulloh's Objections to the Stamp Act." Edited by Jack P. Greene. *The Huntington Library Quarterly* 26 (1962–1963):253–62.

————. *Miscellaneous Representations Relative to Our Concerns in America, Submitted [in 1761] to the Earl of Bute, by Henry McCulloh.* Edited by William A. Shaw. London, 1905.

MASSACHUSETTS HISTORICAL SOCIETY. *The Bowdoin and Temple Papers. Collections of the Massachusetts Historical Society,* 6th ser. 9 (1897).

MAUDUIT, JASPER. "Mauduit Letters." *Collections of the Massachusetts Historical Society* 6 (1800):194–95.

————. "Mauduit Letters." *Collections of the Massachusetts Historical Society* 74 (1918).

MERCER, GEORGE. "Colonel George Mercer's Papers." Edited by J. E. Tyler. *Virginia Magazine of History and Biography* 60 (1952):405–20.

MINCHINTON, W. E., ed. *Politics and the Port of Bristol in the Eighteenth Century: The Petitions of the Society of Merchant Venturers, 1698–1803.* Bristol, 1963.

MORGAN, EDMUND S., ed. *Prologue to Revolution: Sources and Documents on the Stamp Act Crisis, 1764–1766.* Chapel Hill, N.C., 1959.

MORRIS, RICHARD, ed. *The American Revolution, 1763–1783: A Bicentennial Collection.* Columbia, S.C., 1970.

PICKERING, DANBY, ed. *The Statutes at Large from Magna Charta to . . . 1761 (continued to 1806).* Vol. 26. Cambridge, 1762–1807.

PITT, WILLIAM. *Correspondence of William Pitt, Earl of Chatham.* Edited by William Stanhope Taylor and John Henry Pringle. Vol. 2. London, 1838.

The Public Records of the Colony of Connecticut. Edited by Charles J. Hoadley. Vol. 12. Hartford, 1881.

RYDER, NATHANIEL. "The Parliamentary Diaries of Nathaniel Ryder, 1764–1767." Edited by P. D. G. Thomas. *Camden Miscellany Vol. xxiii.* Camden 4th ser. 7:229–351.

SANDWICH, EARL OF. *The Fourth Earl of Sandwich: Diplomatic Correspondence 1763–1765.* Edited by F. Spencer. Manchester, 1961.

SMITH, WILLIAM. *Historical Memoirs from 16 March 1763 to 9 July 1776 of William Smith.* Edited by William H. W. Sabine. New York, 1956.

STRATEMAN, CATHERINE, ed. *The Liverpool Tractate: An Eighteenth-Century*

Manual on the Procedure of the House of Commons [by George Grenville or Jeremiah Dyson]. New York, 1937.

WALPOLE, HORACE. *The Yale Edition of Horace Walpole's Correspondence.* Edited by W. S. Lewis. Vols. 1, 9–10, 15, 21–22, 28, 30–32, 35–36, 38–40. New Haven, 1937–1980.

[WARE, NATHANIEL.] "Observations on the British Colonies on the continent of America." [n.d.] *Collections of the Massachusetts Historical Society,* 1st ser. 1 (1792):66–84.

WATTS, JOHN. *Letterbook of John Watts of New York. Collections of the New York Historical Society* 61 (1928).

WOODMASON, CHARLES. *The Carolina Backcountry on the Eve of the Revolution: The Journal and Other Writings of Charles Woodmason, Anglican Itinerant.* Edited by Richard J. Hooker. Chapel Hill, N.C., 1953.

WRAXALL, NATHANIEL. *Historical Memoirs of My Own Time.* 2 vols. London, 1815.

YORKE, PHILIP C. *The Life and Correspondence of Philip Yorke, Earl of Hardwicke, Lord High Chancellor of Great Britain.* Vol. 3. Cambridge, 1913.

III. Pamphlets

When I surveyed the vast number of pamphlets published during this period, I chose to concentrate on those that were attributed to men closely associated with Bute's and Grenville's administrations, with the parliamentary opposition to those governments, or with the colonial agents. In addition, I read those pamphlets that contemporaries referred to in their correspondence as incisive or galling (depending on their politics), so some pamphlets that do not discuss America appear on this list. In the case of anonymous pamphlets concerning America, I read only those that went into multiple editions. I read these pamphlets at the Henry E. Huntington Library in San Marino, California. Many of them have been microfilmed and are accessible through use of Charles Evans, *American Bibliography: A Chronological Dictionary of all Books, Pamphlets, and Periodical Publications . . . From . . . 1639 . . . to 1820,* 13 vols. (1903; reprint ed., New York, 1941).

[ALMON, JOHN.] *A collection of interesting, authentic papers, relative to the dispute between Great Britain and America; showing the causes and progress of the misunderstanding from 1764 to 1777.* London, 1777.

———. *A letter to the Right Honourable George Grenville.* London, 1763.

An impartial examination of the conduct of the Whigs and Tories from the Revolution down to the present times. Together with considerations upon the state of the present political disputes. London, 1764.

A candid and fair examination of the remarks on the letter to two great men. Directed to the author of that piece. London, 1760.

A letter from a merchant who has left off trade to a Member of Parliament in which the case of British and Irish manufacture of linen, threads, and tapes, is fairly stated, and all the objections against the encouragement proposed to be given to that manufacture fully answered. London, 1738.

A plain and seasonable address to the freeholders of Great Britain on the present posture of affairs in America. London, 1766.

A state of the trade carried on with the French on the island of Hispaniola, by the merchants in North America, under color of flags of truce . . . . London, 1760.

A vindiction of the Whigs against the clamors of a Tory mob; with an address to the City. London, 1765.

Considerations on the American Stamp Act, and on the conduct of the minister who planned it. London, 1766.

The comparative importance of our acquisitions from France in America with remarks on a pamphlet entitled "an examination of the commercial principles of the late negotiations in 1761"; written before the preliminary articles, and may now serve as vindication of terms actually concluded. London, 1762.

The sentiments of an impartial Member of Parliament, upon the two following questions, 1. Whether Great Britain ought to be desirous of a peace in the present situation of her affairs? 2. What sort of a peace Great Britain has reason to expect? London, 1762.

[BOLLAN, WILLIAM.] The mutual interest of Great Britain and the American colonies considered, with respect to an act passed last session of Parliament for laying a duty on merchandize, etc. . . . London, 1765.

[BURKE, EDMUND.] An examination of the commercial principles of the late negotiation between Great Britain and France in 1761 in which the system of that negotiation with regard to our colonies and commerce is considered. London, 1762.

[BURKE, WILLIAM.] Remarks on the letter addressed to two great men. In a letter to the author of that piece. London, 1760.

[BUTLER, JOHN.] Serious considerations of the measures of the present administration. London, 1763.

[COOPER, GREY.] A candid answer to a late pamphlet, entitled "An honest man's reasons for declining to take any part in the new administration." London, 1765.

———. The merits of the new administration truly stated; in answer to the several pamphlets and papers published against them. London, 1765.

[DOUGLAS, JAMES.] A letter addressed to two great men on the prospect of peace; and on the terms necessary to be insisted upon in the negotiation. London, 1760.

———. Seasonable hints from an honest man on the present important crises of a new reign and a new Parliament. London, 1761.

[FOTHERGILL, JOHN.] Considerations relative to the North American colonies. London, 1765.

[FRANCIS, PHILIP.] A letter from the Cocoa-Tree to the country gentlemen. London, 1762.

[FRANKLIN, BENJAMIN.] The interest of Great Britain considered, with regard to her colonies, and to the acquisition of Canada and Guadeloupe . . . . London, 1760.

[GRENVILLE, GEORGE.] A reply to a letter addressed to the Right Honourable George Grenville, etc. In which the truth of the facts is examined, and the propriety *of the motto fully considered.* London, 1763.

[HARTLEY, DAVID.] *The Budget. Inscribed to the man who thinks himself minister.* London, 1764.

————. *The state of the nation, with a preliminary defense of The Budget.* London, 1765.

INGERSOLL, JARED. *Mr. Ingersoll's Letters Relating to the Stamp Act.* New Haven, 1766.

[INGERSOLL, JARED, SILLIMAN, EBENEEZER, and WYLLYS, GEORGE.] *Reasons why the British colonies in America should not be charged with internal taxes by authority of Parliament, humbly offered for consideration, in behalf of the colony of Connecticut.* New Haven, 1764.

[JENYNS, SOAMES.] *The objection to the taxation of our American colonies by the legislature of Great Britain, briefly considered.* London, 1765.

————. *A letter to a Member of Parliament, wherein the power of the British legislature, and the case of the colonists are briefly and impartially considered.* London, 1765.

————. *An appendix to "The Present State of the Nation," containing a reply to the observations on that pamphlet.* London, 1769.

[KNOX, WILLIAM.] *The claim of the colonies to an exemption from internal taxes imposed by authority of Parliament examined in a letter from a gentleman in London to his friend in America.* London, 1765.

————. *The controversy between Great Britain and her colonies reviewed . . . .* London, 1769.

————. *Extra-Official State Papers. Addressed to the Right Honourable Lord Rawdon . . . .* 2 vols. London, 1789.

————. *The present state of the nation: particularly with response to its trade, finances, etc., etc. Addressed to the King and both Houses of Parliament.* London, 1768.

[LLOYD, CHARLES.] *A Critical Review of the New Administration.* London, 1766.

————. *An honest man's reasons for declining to take any part in the new administration, in a letter to the Marquis of ———.* London, 1765.

————. *A defense of the majority in the House of Commons, on the question relating to general warrants . . . .* London, 1764.

————. *A true history of a late short administration.* London, 1766.

————. *The conduct of the late Administration examined.* London, 1767.

[MARRIOTT, SIR JAMES.] *Political considerations; being a few thoughts of a candid man at the present crisis. In a letter to a noble Lord retired from power.* London, 1762.

[MAUDUIT, ISRAEL.] *Considerations on the Present German War.* London, 1760.

————. *Some thoughts on the method of improving and securing the advantages which accrue to Great Britain from the Northern colonies.* London, 1765.

[MAUDUIT, JASPER.] *The legislative authority of the British Parliament with respect to North America, and the privileges of the assemblies there, briefly considered by Jasper Mauduit of the Inner Temple.* London, 1766.

———. *Short View of the History of the New England Colonies*. London, 1775.

[OTIS, JAMES.] *Considerations on behalf of the colonists, in a letter to a noble Lord.* London, 1765.

———. *The Rights of the British Colonies Asserted and Proved*. Boston, 1764.

[TOWNSHEND, CHARLES.] *A defense of the minority in the House of Commons, on the question relating to general warrants.* London, 1764.

[WHATELY, THOMAS.] *Considerations on the trade and finances of this Kingdom, and on the measures of administration with respect to those great national objects since the conclusion of the peace.* London, 1766.

———. *The regulations lately made concerning the colonies, and the taxes imposed upon them, considered.* London, 1765.

———. *Remarks on "The Budget"; or, a candid examination of the facts and arguments offered to the public in that pamphlet.* London, 1765.

[WRIGHT, J.] *The American negotiator: or the various currencies of the British colonies in America . . . .* London, 1761.

IV. Periodicals

I read the following periodicals and newspapers for the years 1762–1766, with particular concentration on short notices relating to American policy and letters from London.

Annual Register
Boston Gazette
Boston Evening Post
Boston Post-Boy
Gentleman's Magazine
Lloyd's Evening Post
London Chronicle
Maryland Gazette
New York Gazette
New York Mercury
North Briton
Pennsylvania Gazette
Providence Gazette
South Carolina Gazette (Timothy)
Virginia Gazette (Purdie and Dixon)

V. Secondary Sources

An enormous number of books and articles have discussed or mentioned the Grenville administration's colonial policies. What follows is not a list of those works—indeed, merely listing them might double the length of the present text—but a compilation of those works that I found most useful to an understanding of the workings of the worlds at Whitehall and Westminster, and in America, during this period. Thus, the list includes not only specialized studies, but also some surveys of the entire period of the American Revolution.

A. Books

ABBOT, W. W. *The Royal Governors of Georgia, 1754–1775*. Chapel Hill, N.C., 1959.

ALDEN, JOHN R. *General Gage in America*. Baton Rouge, 1948.

ANDREWS, CHARLES M. *The Colonial Period of American History*. Vol. 4. New Haven, 1938.

ARMYTAGE, FRANCES. *The Free Port System in the British West Indies*. London, 1953.

ASHTON, T. S. *Economic Fluctuations in England*. Oxford, 1959.

BAILYN, BERNARD. *The Ideological Origins of the American Revolution*. Cambridge, Mass., 1967.

————. *The Ordeal of Thomas Hutchinson*. Cambridge, Mass., 1974.

BARGAR, B. D. *Lord Dartmouth and the American Revolution*. Columbia, S.C., 1965.

BARROW, THOMAS C. *Trade and Empire: The British Customs Service in Colonial America, 1660–1775*. Cambridge, Mass., 1967.

BASYE, A. H. *The Lords Commissioners of Trade and Plantations, Commonly Known as the Board of Trade, 1748–1783*. New Haven, 1925.

BEER, G. L. *British Colonial Policy, 1745–1765*. New York, 1907.

BELLOT, LELAND J. *William Knox: The Life and Thought of an Eighteenth-Century Imperialist*. Austin, 1977.

BREWER, JOHN. *Party Ideology and Popular Politics at the Accession of George III*. Cambridge, 1976.

BREWER, JOHN, and STYLES, JOHN, eds. *An Ungovernable People: The English and Their Law in the Seventeenth and Eighteenth Centuries*. New Brunswick, N.J., 1980.

BROOKE, JOHN. *King George III*. London, 1972.

————. *The Chatham Administration, 1766–1768*. London, 1956.

BROWN, PETER. *The Chathamites*. London, 1967.

BROWNING, REED. *The Duke of Newcastle*. New Haven, 1975.

CHRISTIE, IAN R. *Crisis of Empire: Great Britain and the American Colonies 1754–1783*. London, 1966.

————. *Myth and Reality in Late-Eighteenth-Century British Politics and Other Papers*. London, 1970.

CHRISTIE, IAN R., and LABAREE, BENJAMIN W. *Empire or Independence, 1760–1776: A British-American Dialogue on the Coming of the American Revolution*. New York, 1976.

CLARK, G. N. *Guide to English Commercial Statistics, 1696–1782*. London, 1938.

CLARKE, DORA M. *British Opinion and the American Revolution*. 2d ed. New York, 1966.

————. *The Rise of the British Treasury: Colonial Administration in the Eighteenth Century*. New Haven, 1960.

CURREY, CECIL B. *Road to Revolution: Benjamin Franklin in England, 1765–1775*. New York, 1968.

DEANE, PHYLLIS, and COLE, W. A. *British Economic Growth, 1688–1959*. 2d ed. Cambridge, 1967.

DICKERSON, OLIVER M. *The Navigation Acts and the American Revolution*. Philadelphia, 1957.

DICKSON, P. G. M. *The Financial Revolution in England: A Study in the Development of Public Credit, 1688–1756*. New York, 1967.

ELLIOT, G. F. S. *The Border Elliots and the Family of Minto*. Edinburgh, 1897.

ERNST, JOSEPH ALBERT. *Money and Politics in America, 1755–1775: A Study in the Currency Act of 1764 and the Political Economy of Revolution*. Chapel Hill, N.C., 1973.

FORSTER, CORNELIUS P., O.P. *The Uncontrolled Chancellor: Charles Townshend and His American Policy*. Providence, R.I., 1978.

GIPSON, LAWRENCE HENRY. *American Loyalist: Jared Ingersoll*. New Haven, 1971.

————. *The British Empire before the American Revolution*. Vols. 7–11. New York, 1949–1965.

GREENE, JACK P. *The Quest for Power: The Lower House of Assembly in the Southern Royal Colonies, 1689–1776*. Chapel Hill, N.C., 1963.

GUTTRIDGE, GEORGE H. *English Whiggism and the American Revolution*. Berkeley, 1942.

————. *The Early Career of Lord Rockingham, 1730–1765*. University of California Publications in History, vol. 44. Berkeley, 1952.

HAY, DOUGLAS, et al., eds. *Albion's Fatal Tree: Crime and Society in Eighteenth-Century England*. New York, 1975.

HINKHOUSE, FRED J. *The Preliminaries of the American Revolution as seen in the English Press*. New York, 1926.

HOFFMAN, ROSS J. S. *The Marquis: A Study of Lord Rockingham*. New York, 1973.

HOON, ELIZABETH E. *The Organization of the English Customs System, 1696–1768*. New York, 1938.

HORN, DAVID BAYNE. *Great Britain and Europe in the Eighteenth Century*. Oxford, 1967.

JAMES, SIDNEY V. *Colonial Rhode Island: A History*. New York, 1975.

JARRETT, DEREK. *The Begetters of Revolution: England's Involvement with France, 1759–1789*. Totowa, N.J., 1973.

JENSEN, MERRILL. *The Founding of a Nation: A History of the American Revolution, 1763–1776*. Oxford, 1968.

JUDD, GERRIT P., IV. *Members of Parliament, 1734–1832*, Yale Historical Publications, 61. New Haven, 1955.

KAMMEN, MICHAEL. *A Rope of Sand: The Colonial Agents, British Politics, and the American Revolution*. Ithaca, N.Y., 1968.

————. *Empire and Interest: The American Colonies and the Politics of Mercantilism*. New York, 1970.

KEMP, BETTY. *King and Commons, 1660–1832*. London, 1957.

———. *Sir Francis Dashwood: An Eighteenth-Century Independent*. London, 1967.

KNOLLENBERG, BERNARD. *Origin of the American Revolution, 1759–1766*. Rev. ed. New York, 1965.

KOEBNER, RICHARD. *Empire*. Cambridge, 1961.

KURTZ, STEPHEN G., and HUTSON, JAMES H., eds. *Essays on the American Revolution*. Chapel Hill, N.C., 1973.

LANGFORD, PAUL. *The First Rockingham Administration, 1765–1766*. Oxford, 1973.

———. *The Excise Crisis: Society and Politics in the Age of Walpole*. Oxford, 1975.

LECKY, W. E. H. *A History of Ireland in the Eighteenth Century*. Vol. 2. London, 1913.

MILLER, JOHN C. *Origins of the American Revolution*. Rev. ed. Stanford, Calif., 1959.

MORGAN, EDMUND S., and MORGAN, HELEN M. *The Stamp Act Crisis*. Chapel Hill, N.C., 1953.

NAMIER, SIR LEWIS. *England in the Age of the American Revolution*. 2d ed. London, 1966.

———. *The Structure of Politics at the Accession of George III*. 2d ed. London, 1957.

NAMIER, SIR LEWIS, and BROOKE, JOHN. *Charles Townshend*. London, 1964.

NAMIER, SIR LEWIS, and BROOKE, JOHN, eds. *The History of Parliament: The House of Commons, 1754–1790*. 3 vols. Oxford, 1964.

NASH, GARY B. *The Urban Crucible: Social Change, Political Consciousness, and the Origins of the American Revolution*. Cambridge, Mass., 1979.

NORRIS, JOHN. *Shelburne and Reform*. London, 1963.

OLSON, ALISON G. *The Radical Duke: Career and Correspondence of Charles Lennox, Third Duke of Richmond*. Oxford, 1961.

OLSON, ALISON G., and BROWN, R. M., eds. *Anglo-American Political Relations, 1675–1775*. New Brunswick, N.J., 1970.

PARES, RICHARD. *King George III and the Politicians*. Oxford, 1953.

———. *War and Trade in the West Indies, 1739–1763*. 1937. Reprint. London, 1963.

———. *Yankees and Creoles*. London, 1956.

PENSON, LILLIAN M. *The Colonial Agents of the British West Indies*. Oxford, 1924.

PERKIN, H. J. *The Origins of Modern English Society, 1780–1880*. London, 1969.

RASHED, Z. E. *The Peace of Paris 1763*. Liverpool, 1951.

RITCHESON, CHARLES R. *British Politics and the American Revolution*. Norman, Okla., 1954.

ROBERTS, MICHAEL. *Splendid Isolation, 1763–1780*. The Stenton Lecture, 1969. Reading, 1970.

ROGERS, ALAN. *Empire and Liberty: American Resistance to British Authority, 1755–1763*. Berkeley, 1974.

ROSEVEARE, HENRY. *The Treasury: The Evolution of a British Institution.* New York, 1969.

RUDE, GEORGE. *The Crowd in History: A Study of Popular Disturbances in France and England, 1730–1848.* London, 1964.

———. *Wilkes and Liberty: A Social Study of 1763 to 1774.* Oxford, 1962.

SCHUMPETER, E. B. *English Overseas Trade Statistics, 1697–1808.* Oxford, 1960.

SHENTON, W. J. *English Hunger and Industrial Disorders: A Study of Social Conflict during the First Decade of George III's Reign.* Oxford, 1973.

SHY, JOHN. *A People Numerous and Armed: Reflections on the Military Struggle for American Independence.* Oxford, 1976.

———. *Toward Lexington: The Role of the British Army in the Coming of the American Revolution.* Princeton, 1965.

SOSIN, JACK M. *Agents and Merchants: British Colonial Policy and the Origins of the American Revolution, 1763–1775.* Lincoln, Nebr., 1965.

———. *Whitehall and the Wilderness: The Middle West in British Colonial Policy, 1760–1775.* Lincoln, Nebr., 1961.

THOMAS, P. D. G. *British Politics and the Stamp Act Crisis: The First Phase of the American Revolution, 1763–1767.* Oxford, 1975.

———. *The House of Commons in the Eighteenth Century.* Oxford, 1971.

THOMPSON, E. P. *Whigs and Hunters: The Origin of the Black Act.* New York, 1975.

UBBELOHDE, CARL. *The Vice-Admiralty Courts and the American Revolution.* Chapel Hill, N.C., 1960.

WICKWIRE, FRANKLIN B. *British Subministers and Colonial America, 1763–1783.* Princeton, 1966.

WIGGIN, LEWIS M. *The Faction of Cousins: A Political Account of the Grenvilles, 1733–1763.* Yale Historical Publications 49. New Haven, 1958.

B. Articles

BARROW, THOMAS C. "The American Revolution as a Colonial War for Independence." *William and Mary Quarterly,* 3d ser. 25 (1968):452–64.

———. "The Background to the Grenville Program, 1757–1763." *William and Mary Quarterly,* 3d ser. 22 (1965):93–104.

BULLION, JOHN L. "Escaping Boston: Nathaniel Ware and the Beginnings of Colonial Taxation, 1762–1763." *Huntington Library Quarterly,* in press.

———. "Honor, Trade, and Empire: Grenville's Treasury and 'the American Question,' 1763–1765." Ph.D. diss., The University of Texas at Austin, 1977.

CANNON, JOHN. "Henry McCulloch and Henry McCulloh," *William and Mary Quarterly,* 3d ser. 15 (1958):71–73.

CHRISTIE, IAN R. "The Cabinet During the Grenville Ministry." *English Historical Review* 73 (1958):86–92.

———. "William Pitt and American Taxation, 1766: A Problem of Parliamentary Reporting." *Studies in Burke and His Time* 57 (1976):167–79.

CRANE, V. W. "Benjamin Franklin and the Stamp Act." *Publications of the Colonial Society of Massachusetts* 32 (1933–1937): 56–77.

DAVIS, RALPH. "The Rise of Protection in England, 1689–1786." *Economic History Review*, 2d ser. 19 (1966):306–17.

ERICSON, FRED J. "The Contemporary British Opposition to the Stamp Act." *Papers of the Michigan Academy of Science, Arts, and Letters* 29 (1943):489–505.

ERNST, JOSEPH A. "Genesis of the Currency Act of 1764: Virginia Paper Money and the Protection of British Investments." *William and Mary Quarterly*, 3d ser. 22 (1965):33–74.

———. "The Currency Act Repeal Movement: A Study of Imperial Politics and Revolutionary Crisis, 1764–1767." *William and Mary Quarterly*, 3d ser. 25 (1968):177–211.

GRADISH, STEPHEN F. "Wages and Manning: The Navy Act of 1758." *English Historical Review* 93 (1978):46–67.

GREENE, JACK P. "An Uneasy Connection: An Analysis of the Preconditions of the American Revolution." In *Essays on the American Revolution*, edited by Stephen G. Kurtz and James H. Hutson, pp. 32–80. Chapel Hill, N.C., 1973.

———. "The Plunge of Lemmings: A Consideration of Recent Writings on British Politics and the American Revolution." *South Atlantic Quarterly* 67 (1968):141–75.

GREENE, JACK P., and JELLISON, RICHARD M. "The Currency Act of 1764 in Imperial-Colonial Relations, 1764–1776." *William and Mary Quarterly*, 3d ser. 18 (1961):484–518.

HAY, DOUGLAS. "Property, Authority, and the Criminal Law." In *Albion's Fatal Tree: Crime and Society in Eighteenth-Century England*, edited by Douglas Hay et al., pp. 17–64. New York, 1975.

HUGHES, E. "The English Stamp Duties, 1664–1764." *English Historical Review* 56 (1941):234–64.

JARRETT, DEREK. "The Regency Crisis of 1765." *English Historical Review* 85 (1970):282–316.

JERVEY, T. D. "Barlow Trecothick." *South Carolina Historical and Genealogical Magazine* 32 (1931):157–69.

JOHNSON, ALLEN S. "British Politics and the Repeal of the Stamp Act." *South Atlantic Quarterly* 62 (1963):169–88.

———. "The Passage of the Sugar Act." *William and Mary Quarterly*, 3d ser. 16 (1959):507–14.

LANGFORD, PAUL. "British Correspondence in the Colonial Press, 1763–1775: A Study in Anglo-American Misunderstanding before the American Revolution." In *The Press and the American Revolution*, edited by Bernard Bailyn and John B. Hench, pp. 273–313. Worcester, Mass., 1980.

LAPRADE, W. T. "The Stamp Act in British Politics." *American Historical Review* 35 (1930):735–57.

LAWSON, PHILIP. "George Grenville and America: The Years of Opposition, 1765 to 1770." *William and Mary Quarterly*, 3d ser. 37 (1980):561–76.

McANEAR, BEVERLY. "The Albany Stamp Act Riots." *William and Mary Quarterly*, 3d ser. 4 (1947):486–98.

MARSHALL, PETER. "Colonial Protest and Imperial Retrenchment: Indian Policy, 1764–1768." *Journal of American Studies* 5 (1971):1–17.

———. "The British Empire and the American Revolution." *Huntington Library Quarterly* 27 (1963–1964):135–45.

MINCHINTON, W. E. "The Stamp Act Crisis: Bristol and Virginia." *Virginia Magazine of History and Biography* 73 (1965):145–55.

MORGAN, EDMUND S. "Colonial Ideas of Parliamentary Power." *William and Mary Quarterly*, 3d ser. 5 (1948):311–41.

———. "The Postponement of the Stamp Act." *William and Mary Quarterly*, 3d ser. 7 (1950):353–93.

MUI, HOH-CHEUNG, and MUI, LORNA H. "Smuggling and the British Tea Trade before 1784." *American Historical Review* 74 (1968):44–73.

MURRIN, JOHN M. "The French and Indian War, the American Revolution, and the Counterfactual Hypothesis: Reflections on Lawrence Henry Gipson and John Shy." *Reviews in American History* 1 (1973):307–18.

NAMIER, SIR LEWIS. "Charles Garth and His Connections." *English Historical Review* 54 (1939):443–70, 632–52.

NASH, GARY B. "Social Change and the Growth of Prerevolutionary Urban Radicalism." In *The American Revolution: Explorations in the History of American Radicalism*, edited by Alfred F. Young, pp. 5–36. DeKalb, Ill., 1976.

OLSON, ALISON GILBERT. "Parliament, Empire, and Parliamentary Law, 1776." In *Three British Revolutions: 1641, 1688, 1776*, edited by J. G. A. Pocock, pp. 282–322. Princeton, 1980.

PENSON, L. M. "The London West India Interest in the Eighteenth Century." *English Historical Review* 36 (1921):373–92.

RAMSAY, J. F. *Anglo-French Relations, 1763–1770*. University of California Publications in History, vol. 17, no. 3, pp. 143–264. Berkeley, 1939.

REITAN, E. A. "The Civil List, 1761–77: Problems of Finance and Administration." *Bulletin of the Institute of Historical Research* 48 (1974):186–201.

RITCHESON, CHARLES R. "The Preparation of the Stamp Act." *William and Mary Quarterly*, 3d ser. 10 (1953):543–59.

SELLERS, CHARLES G., JR. "Private Profits and British Colonial Policy: The Speculations of Henry McCulloh." *William and Mary Quarterly*, 3d ser. 8 (1951):535–51.

SHERIDAN, R. B. "The Molasses Act and the Market Strategy of the British Sugar Planters." *Journal of Economic History* 17 (1957):62–83.

SHY, JOHN. "Thomas Pownall, Henry Ellis, and the Spectrum of Possibilities, 1763–1775." In *Anglo-American Political Relations, 1675–1775*, edited by Alison G. Olson and R. M. Brown, pp. 155–86. Brunswick, N.J., 1970.

SOSIN, JACK M. "A Postscript to the Stamp Act: Grenville's Revenue Measures, A Drain on Colonial Specie?" *American Historical Review* 62 (1958):918–23.

———. "Imperial Regulaton of Colonial Paper Money, 1764–1773." *Pennsylvania Magazine of History and Biography* 88 (1964):174–98.

STOUT, HARRY S. "Religion, Communicatons, and the Ideological Origins of the American Revolution." *William and Mary Quarterly*, 3d ser. 34 (1977):519–41.

STOUT, NEIL R. "Goals and Enforcement of British Colonial Policy, 1763–1775." *The American Neptune* 27 (1967):211–20.

THOMAS, P. D. G. "New Light on the Commons Debate of 1763 on the American Army." *William and Mary Quarterly*, 3d ser. 38 (1981):110–12.

VARGA, NICHOLAS. "Robert Charles: New York Agent, 1748–1770." *William and Mary Quarterly*, 3d ser. 18 (1961):211–35.

WARD, W. R. "Some Eighteenth Century Civil Servants: The English Revenue Commissioners, 1754–98." *English Historical Review* 70 (1955):25–54.

WATSON, J. S. "Parliamentary Procedure as a Key to the Understanding of Eighteenth Century Politics." *Burke Newsletter* 3 (1962):108–28.

WINSLOW, CAL. "Sussex Smugglers." In *Albion's Fatal Tree: Crime and Society in Eighteenth-Century England,* edited by Douglas Hay et al., pp. 119–66. New York, 1975.

Index

Adams, Samuel, 202, 284

Admiralty courts: and American smuggling, 73, 96; Treasury on, 73, 162; and the Stamp Act, 162; mentioned, 140

Agents, colonial: and molasses tax, 86–87; and the West Indian interest, 89–90; and Grenville, 91, 94–95, 170, 186–87, 189–90; and postponement of stamp tax, 114–15; and meetings with Grenville, 125–26, 128–32, 144–53, 171–72, 178–79, 181–83, 187, 269, 283; Grenville's 9 March 1764 speech, 125–26, 265; attempts to establish favorable precedents by, 129–31; Franklin on, 130–31; opposition to stamp tax by, 144–53, 158; Grenville's opinion of, 145–46, 152–53; on Grenville's attitudes toward the colonies, 145–48, 156–57; and requisitions, 149; and Grenville's recommendations to the colonies, 149–50, 152; objections to internal taxation by, 150–51; and colonial petitions, 160–62, 272–73, 286; and admiralty courts, 162; and payment of taxes in America, 164; and appointment of distributors, 169–75, 275–77; and colonial instructions against the stamp tax, 269; criticism of, 285–86; mentioned, 3–4, 8, 99, 105, 142, 183, 197–98. See also Charles, Robert; Franklin, Benjamin; Ingersoll, Jared; Mauduit, Isaac; Mauduit, Jared; Montagu, Edward

Allen, William, 111, 115, 263

Almon, John, 66, 235, 247

American Revenue Act of 1764, 93. See also Sugar Act

Army, British: and taxation of America, 14, 21–23, 34, 42, 150; role in America, 22, 36; in Ireland, 22–23, 35; cost of in America, 22, 279; and smuggling, British, 56; and smuggling, American, 73; Grenville on, 157–58, 279; Grenville on payments for, 164; quartering in America, 190; mentioned, 197–98. See also Ellis, Welbore, and Halifax, Earl of

Assemblies, American: British dissatisfaction with, 25–27; Grenville on, 94, 120–21, 127, 130, 132–33, 148–49, 158–59; on Grenville, 136; Jenkinson on, 147; mentioned, 124

Atholl, Duke of, and Isle of Man, 57–58, 244

Baker, Sir William: and molasses tax, 96–97; and drawback on linens, 110, 112; on Grenville, 196; mentioned, 136, 207, 267

Barbados: Grenville's investments on, 86, 154; mentioned, 25, 175

Barons, Benjamin, 166, 274

Barré, Isaac, 160

Barrow, Thomas C., 43, 246–47

Beckford, William: on American taxes, 35, 239–40; and molasses tax, 86; and McCulloh, 239; and postponement of stamp tax, 259; on internal taxation, 272; mentioned, 36, 114–15, 160

Bedford, Duke of: and peace in 1762, 11; and McCulloh, 239; mentioned, 12, 15, 27, 34, 44, 59, 62–63

Beer tax. See Taxes, British

Bernard, Francis, 180, 194, 282, 285

Bindley, John, 39–40, 240

Board of Trade: and American taxation, 26; and colonial protest, 137; mentioned, 26, 39, 74, 109–10, 116–17, 233, 241, 247, 255, 259

Boston, 39, 65–67, 81, 103, 157, 180, 185, 199–202, 205, 220, 247–50

Bristol, 92, 102, 111, 195, 255

Buckinghamshire, Earl of, 5

Burke, Edmund: on Grenville, 58–59, 61; on stamp tax, 282; mentioned, 286

Bute, Earl of: and George III, 5, 16–18, 51, 231; attitudes toward peace in 1762, 11; concern about national debt, 11, 16–17; and Grenville, 11, 13, 19–20, 44–51, 189, 242; and Townshend, 11–12; and making peace, 19–20; resignation of, 28, 37; and American taxation, 28–29; and linen tax, 31–32; on cider tax, 37; on Newcastle, 46–47; and Ware, 65–66, 81, 247; and the stamp tax, 107; ignorance of finance of, 234; and Dodington, 234; on Grenville and peace negotiations, 235; mentioned, 12, 14–16, 22–23, 25, 27–28, 31, 34–35, 40, 42, 44, 65, 191. See also Treasury

Calicoes, white: drawback on, 102, 111; and drawback on linen, 110; and British dyeing industry, 110–11, 113; Grenville and ad valorem tax on, 111–13. See also Drawback; Smuggling, American; Taxation of America; Taxes, American; and Treasury

Calvert, Cecelius, 174, 277

Canada, 22, 63, 247

Charles, Robert, 136–37, 267, 272, 275–76, 286

Charter colonies: and American smuggling, 67–68; Grenville on, 143, 148, 155–56; Jenkinson on, 144; Whately on, 144, 268; mentioned, 214

Christie, Ian R., 1, 43

Cider tax. *See* Taxes, British

Coffee tax. *See* Taxes, American

Colebrooke, Sir George, 257, 258

Colleton, J. E., 175

Colonial policy. *See* Imperial relationship, and Taxation, internal

Commercial crisis in Britain: impact of the German war on, 18; Grenville on, 18, 68–69; consensus in Bute's Cabinet on, 21; Townshend on, 234; mentioned, 2, 31

Colonial government, cost of American, 105, 157, 260

Commissioners of the Customs in England: and smuggling in England, 54, 56; and Grenville, 55–56, 246; and the American revenue, 64; reports to the Treasury by, 71–72, 78–79, 80, 84, 103, 214, 255, 279; and American customs service, 71–72, 78–79, 250; and smuggling, American, 72, 78–79, 84, 103; and the Treasury, 78–79, 246; on molasses tax, 78–80, 84, 279; on molasses trade, 78–79; and Ware, 220; and linen tax, 255; mentioned, 30–31, 58, 70, 75, 175, 211–12. *See also* Customs service, American, and Treasury

Commissioners of the Customs in Scotland, 56–57

Commissioners of the Excise in England, 52–54

Commissioners of the Stamps in England, 74, 109–10, 175–77, 188

Connecticut, 84, 155, 160, 162, 174, 176, 181, 190, 208, 271–72, 277

Conway, Henry Seymour, 209, 283

Country gentlemen, 34–35. *See also* Tories

Cruwys, Thomas: and preparation of stamp tax, 107–10, 117, 125, 134, 141, 256; and McCulloh, 257; mentioned, 76, 129, 184, 188, 266, 274

Currency, American: raising taxes by charging interest on, 2, 210, 272; Franklin on, 2, 146, 272; McCulloh on, 2, 108–9, 211; Grenville and raising a revenue by issuing, 108–9; British merchants' objections to, 109. *See also* Franklin, Benjamin, and McCulloh, Henry

Cust, Peregrine: and molasses tax, 90, 92; and linens, reexportation of, 102; and drawback on linens, 110–12; and linen tax, 255; mentioned, 252–53, 258

Customs service, American: problems with, 1, 3, 30, 33, 39, 41, 75, 78–79, 87–88, 98, 187, 211–12, 250; estimates of bribes paid to, 39, 84–85; Treasury reform of, 42, 71–72, 81, 96, 187–88, 211–12, 250; Grenville on, 63–64, 75, 249; Ware on, 65–66, 70, 75, 83; Whately on, 92, 168; reactions to Grenville's policies regarding, 205; McCulloh on, 211–12; mentioned, 165. *See also* Commissioners of the Customs in England, and Treasury

Customs service, English: and smuggling, 55–58; Grenville and, 55–56, 244; mentioned, 113

Dashwood, Sir Francis, 12–13, 30–33, 35–37

Debt, British national: impact on taxation by, 16–21; impact on the economy by, 16–21, 235; Grenville on, 17–18, 150, 157; mentioned, 11

Debt, colonial, 157

DeLancey, Philip, Jr., 276

Distilleries, American, 39, 82, 251

Distributors of stamps: American, 164–80 passim, 274–84 passim; Whately on, 195; Grenville on, 197; colonial reaction to appointments of, 202–3, 205–7; McCulloh on, 288; mentioned, 108, 187–89, 213–14, 257. *See also* Underdistributors of stamps, American

Dodington, George Bubb, 25, 234

Drawback. *See* Linens, foreign, and Reexportation of foreign goods to America

Dyer, Eliphalet, 115, 251

Dyson, Jeremiah, 12, 273

East India Company, 54, 56, 67, 102, 155

Egmont, Earl of, 118, 260

Egremont, Earl of: and American taxation, 26, 29; on Grenville and peace negotiations, 235; mentioned, 5, 14, 19, 25, 27, 39, 45, 49, 51, 63, 198, 233

Elliot, Andrew, 212, 288

Elliot, Sir Gilbert, 212, 282, 288

Ellis, Welbore, 14, 27, 34–36, 239

Financial crisis in Britain: impact on economy by, 16–21, 235; impact of the German war on, 18; Grenville on, 18; consensus in Bute's Cabinet on, 20–21; Townshend on, 234; mentioned, 2

Fitch, Thomas, 263, 269, 275, 277

Florida, 19–20, 22, 50, 253

Foreign policy. *See* France

Fox, Henry: character of, 13; and Grenville,

13, 37, 47–48; becomes Leader, 20; and
the King, 27–28; and Bute, 27–28;
mentioned, 24, 35, 38, 40, 44, 50–51,
191, 236, 241
France, 19, 27, 118–19, 133
Frankland, Sir Henry, 248, 250
Franklin, Benjamin: and tax on colonial
currency, 2, 146, 272; and meetings with
Grenville, 145–46; distributorship offered
to, 170; and distributors, 172, 275–77;
mentioned, 87, 126, 131, 171–72,
178–79, 184, 186, 188, 197, 201, 209,
230, 263–64, 269, 272, 286
Fuller, Rose, 37–39, 86, 161–62, 251, 273

Garth, Charles: and Grenville, 8; on
postponement of the stamp tax, 123,
129–32; on Grenville's 9 March 1764
speech, 125–26; on meetings with
Grenville, 129–32, 145, 266; petition
against stamp tax from, 160–62; and
appointment of distributor, 175; on
Grenville, 270; mentioned, 178, 232, 265
General warrants, 90–91, 95, 118, 143
George II, 17, 23
George III: and Bute, 5, 51, 231; and
Grenville, 13, 19–20, 45–51, 107,
175–76, 189, 191–92, 208, 242, 258; and
Townshend, 14, 40, 237; and national
debt, 16–17; and Fox, 20, 237; and the
postwar military establishment, 21–23; and
the stamp tax, 107; and Irish pensions,
119–20; and Dodington, 234; and
postponement of the stamp tax, 258;
mentioned, 12, 14, 15, 25, 28, 40, 153,
165, 197–98, 211
Glover, Richard, 110–11, 255, 258
Grenville, Richard. See Temple, Earl
Guadeloupe, 19, 247
Guinea: and molasses trade, 92; Treasury on
trade to, 252–53

Halifax, Earl of: and augmenting the army in
Ireland, 22–23; on assemblies, 25; on uses
of American revenue, 41, 94; and Ware,
65–66, 220, 247; and Irish pensions,
119–21; and circular to colonial governors,
133–35; and McCulloh, 246; mentioned,
6, 14, 20, 26–27, 49, 148, 164–65
Hallowell, Benjamin, 9, 180, 190, 205, 220,
224, 281, 285
Harris, James, 42, 51, 126–27, 265, 273
Harrison, Joseph, 184–85, 205
Havana, 19, 50
Hay, Douglas, 4, 257
Hillsborough, Earl of, 5, 267

Hervey, Lord, 210
Hood, Zachariah, 171, 174–75, 177, 277,
278
Houston, Dr. William, 175, 181
Hovering Act, 41, 54, 63
Hughes, John, 172, 179, 197
Hulton, Henry, 72–73, 77
Huske, John: and drawback on linens,
110–12; and postponement of stamp tax,
114–15, 121–22, 124–25, 259, 260–61,
261–62; mentioned, 99, 132
Hutchinson, Thomas, 200, 202, 284

Imperial relationship: with colonies, 2–3, 9,
75, 83, 120–21, 153–54, 180; with
Ireland, 119–20. See also Taxation,
internal, and Taxes, American
Ingersoll, Jared: and Whately, 8–9, 125,
141–42, 145, 167, 169, 184, 201, 206–7,
262, 277; and preparation of the Stamp
Act, 8, 141–42, 268; and Grenville, 8,
154, 201, 203–4, 277, 284; and meetings
with Grenville, 145–46, 148; on Grenville,
156–57; and stamp distributorship, 167,
169–70, 172, 206–7, 275–77; and
estimate of produce of stamp tax, 176–77;
and molasses tax, 185; on internal taxation,
203; on stamp tax, 256, 262–64; on
significance of postponement of stamp tax,
261–62; on Grenville's 6 February 1765
speech, 271; on colonial protests, 278;
mentioned, 160, 166, 171–72, 174, 178,
196–97, 208, 266, 268–69, 272
Ireland: plans for augmenting the army in,
35; imperial relationship with, 114,
119–20; mentioned, 26, 54, 57, 156, 270
Irish parliament, 10, 23, 119–20, 153, 156,
167

Jackson, Richard: and Grenville, 8, 180, 251;
and molasses tax, 84–85, 87–88, 252; on
American customs service, 85; and
postponement of stamp tax, 114; and
Grenville's speech of 9 March 1764, 126;
on internal taxation, 126; and meetings
with Grenville, 145–48; on bad effects of
stamp tax, 147; on Grenville, 156–57; on
colonial petitions, 162, 272–73; on future
taxes, 181; on Grenville's 6 February 1765
speech, 271; on tax on fur trade, 272; and
appointment of distributors, 277;
mentioned, 103, 125, 171, 174, 178, 180,
263, 269
Jamaica: Grenville's investments on, 154;
mentioned, 161
Jenkinson, Charles: and Grenville, 7;

personal characteristics of, 9, 232; and colonial ideas about imperial relationship, 9; on Britain's financial state, 18–19, 235; on the navy in America, 22; and the molasses tax, 37–38, 80, 85, 185, 240; on smuggling, 53, 64; and McCulloh, 64–65, 211–12, 214; and Ware, 66, 248; on uses for American revenue, 94; on law enforcement in America, 97; on colonial manufacturing, 102, 224; and removal of the drawback on reexported foreign goods, 101–3, 224, 255; on stamp tax, 104, 141, 146–47, 274, 279; and preparation of the stamp tax, 104, 107, 125, 133–34, 224–25, 266; and political implications of an American stamp tax, 106; and ad valorem tax on white calicoes, 111; on Grenville's 9 March 1764 speech, 127; on internal taxation, 143–44; on assemblies, 147; on uses of colonies, 147, 224; on colonial obligations, 150; and collection of American revenue, 164; and appointment of distributors, 175; on the poor in America, 182; defense of stamp act by, 209; on labor costs in America, 224; as reporter of debates, 239–40; and postponement of stamp tax, 259; on meetings with agents, 266; on petitions against stamp tax, 269; on colonial alternatives to the stamp tax, 271–72; mentioned, 9, 12–13, 27, 34–36, 39, 54–56, 66, 71–72, 76, 85, 87, 95, 104, 156, 180–81, 186, 212, 250, 258, 273, 287. See also Treasury
Jensen, Merrill, 251
Johnson, Allen S., 250–51, 253
Johnson, William Samuel, 208
Jucker, N. S., 287–88

Kennedy, Archibald, 212, 288
Kinnoul, Lord, 30
Knox, William: and Grenville, 5, 235; and postponement of stamp tax, 115; on appointment of distributors, 178; on burdens of taxes in Britain, 235; on rice tax, 254; on meetings with Grenville, 265–66; on Grenville, 270; mentioned, 130–31

Labor in America, cost of: Oswald on, 32; Whately on, 140; Grenville on, 199; Jenkinson on, 224; mentioned, 103, 198
Land speculation in America, 30, 138–39
Land tax. See Taxes, British
Langford, Paul, 263
Law enforcement in America: poor record of,

3, 97; political importance of, 3, 190–91, 193–96; Whately on, 168, 275
Lee, Richard Henry, 173, 276
Linens, British, 102
Linens, foreign: removing drawback on, 31–33, 101–2, 110–11; drawback paid on, 102; Grenville's modification of drawback on, 111–13
Linen tax. See Taxes, American
Lloyd, Caleb, 175, 277, 281
Lloyd, Charles, 165, 174, 231, 274, 277

McCulloh, Henry: and exchequer bills of union, 2, 65, 108–9, 211; and Jenkinson, 64–65, 211–14; on smuggling in North America, 67–68; and Grenville, 67–68, 70, 74, 211–14, 288; estimate of smuggling from Europe by, 67–68, 198; on political implications of American smuggling, 69; plan to hinder smuggling by, 69–70, 72, 212–13; and the stamp tax, 74, 76; on American political ideas, 75, 83, 120; on customs officers, 84, 211–12; on volume of molasses trade, 85, 251; on wine tax, 100; on advantages of a stamp tax, 104, 249; and preparation of stamp tax, 104, 106–10, 134, 141, 213–14, 260; and Cruwys, 106–10, 257; requests for office by, 212–14, 287–88; and Beckford, 239; and Bedford, 239; and Halifax, 246, 256, 287; on distributors, 288; mentioned, 71, 75, 95, 116, 129, 166, 175, 246
Madeira, 100–1, 254, 288
Mansfield, Earl of, 14–15, 16, 18, 27, 143
Manufacturing, American: and the linen drawback, 32; Whately on, 102; Grenville on, 102, 199; Jenkinson on, 102, 224; mentioned, 198
Manufacturing, British: effect of taxation on, 16–17; importance of colonial trade to, 23–25, 66–69, 74; and linen, 31; Whately on, 97; Grenville's concern over, 113
Martin, Samuel, 12, 18, 31, 240
Maryland, 155, 157, 171, 174, 177, 188, 277
Massachusetts: assembly of, on Grenville, 136; mentioned, 41, 97, 123, 131, 142, 145, 165, 169, 201–2, 205–6, 269, 286
Mauduit, Israel, 88–89, 90, 95, 97, 126, 129, 241, 265
Mauduit, Jasper: and molasses tax, 41, 88–89, 252, 254; on Grenville's moderation, 95; on postponement of the stamp tax, 123, 262; on Grenville's 9 March 1764 speech, 125–26; mentioned, 90–91, 95–97, 126, 136, 145, 241, 265

Mercer, George, 173, 177, 278, 282
Merchants, in America, 112
Merchants, in Britain: importance of colonial trade to, 23–25; and linen trade, 31, 164; and colonial currency, 109; opposition to stamp tax by, 159, 161, 169; and Grenville, 186–87, 190; and petitions against stamp tax, 272–73; mentioned, 240
Meredith, Sir William, 161, 273
Molasses Act of 1733, 37–42, 80, 156, 240–41
Molasses tax: 78–98 passim; 251–54 passim; mentioned, 1, 31, 40–42, 69, 73, 99, 101, 131, 138, 182, 185–86, 187–88, 193, 196, 199, 203–4, 211, 230, 240, 246–47, 279, 280. See also Treasury
Molyneaux, William, 156
Montagu, Edward: and postponement of stamp tax, 114, 123; and Grenville's 9 March 1764 speech, 125; petition against stamp tax from, 160–62; and appointment of distributors, 173; mentioned, 126, 273
Morgan, Edmund S., 207, 264–65, 270
Morgan, Helen M., 207

Namier, Sir Lewis, 1, 177, 242
Navy Act of 1758, 60, 245
Navy Board, 59–60, 260
Navy, British: postwar strength in American waters of, 22; Grenville and reduction of, 27; and smuggling in Britain, 54–57, 253; and smuggling in North America, 63, 73, 75–76, 96, 195; and French rearmament, 118–19; increase in appropriations to, 119; Grenville on, 157, 249, 260; mentioned, 164, 197–98
Newcastle, Duke of: and Grenville, 5, 47–48, 243; on Fox, 13; mentioned, 12, 17–18, 28–30, 36, 45–47, 49, 65, 192, 278
Newdigate, Sir Roger, 5, 34, 239
Newfoundland, 19, 22, 27, 63, 89, 118
New York, 67, 103, 136, 142, 145, 157, 165, 169–70, 199, 212, 269, 277, 286
North Carolina, 25, 107, 157, 174–75, 260
North, Lord: and American taxes, 30; on internal taxation, 204; criticized by Grenville, 209–10; mentioned, 12, 66, 233
Northumberland, Earl of: and Irish pensions, 119–21; and Grenville, 120; mentioned, 134
Norton, Sir Fletcher, 184, 188
Nugent, Robert, 175, 193–95, 210

Oliver, Andrew, 169, 202, 206, 284
Olson, Alison Gilbert, 275

Oswald, James: on the German war, 18; and drawback on linen, 31; and the linen tax, 31–33, 238; mentioned, 12, 13, 34, 42, 101, 241
Otis, James, on Grenville, 202; mentioned, 137, 200, 202

Pelham, Henry, 59–60
Pennsylvania, 25, 84, 155, 157, 188, 202
Petitions: against tax bills, 114; ordinary colonial, 124; colonial, against stamp tax, 143–45, 160–62, 272–73, 281, 286; Grenville against hearing colonies', 161, 273; significance of unsuccessful colonial, 204–5; Grenville's reaction to colonial, 231; and rule of 8 March 1733, 273; effect on opinion in Britain of, 274, 281; Parliament's refusal to hear, 285; and the agents' handling of, 286; criticism of Grenville's handling of, 286
Philadelphia, 103, 172, 199, 212, 286
Pimento tax. See Taxes, American
Pitt, Thomas, Jr.: opinion of Grenville, 6–8, 243, 266; mentioned, 51, 56
Pitt, William: Grenville's estrangement from, 5; on the peace treaty, 35–36; on the army in America, 36; mentioned, 17, 19, 24–25, 28, 35, 37, 45, 48–49, 52, 60, 109, 123, 143, 191, 231, 235
Plantation duties. See Taxes, American
Politics, colonial: popular accusations against Grenville, 136, 203–4; changes in, 200–1; Grenville's ignorance of changes in, 201, 206–7; conservatives' reaction to Grenville's policies, 204–5; reaction to distributors, 205–7
Post Office Act, 156
Poverty: American, 67, 139–40, 182, 199; British, 16–17
Pownall, John, 143–44, 156
Precedents: and colonial pretensions to power, 4; Grenville's desire to create favorable, 4; and pensions on the Irish establishment, 10, 119–20; and the agents, 121, 129–31, 160–62; Grenville's efforts to avoid binding, 121–22, 124–25, 128–34, 148, 158, 161–62, 189, 267, 273
Privy Council, 73, 114, 137, 165
Prosperity, American: political implications of, 5, 74–77, 97–98, 183–84, 190–91; economic implications of, 23–25, 37–38, 68–69; consensus in Britain on, 23–25, 182–85, 198–99
Public opinion, colonial: misgivings about Britain, 3, 114–17, 123–24, 145–53, 189–91, 193–96, 201–7, 272, 278,

285–86; importance of influencing, 4;
Grenville's efforts to influence, 3–4, 91,
106, 115, 117, 122–24, 127–28, 131,
136–37, 145–54, 156–57, 159, 164–69,
171–72, 178–79, 185, 189–90, 194,
230–31, 271; impact of evasion of British
law upon, 99–100; agents on, 115,
146–53; against the stamp tax, 136,
193–96, 201–7, 285–86; Treasury concern
over, 142
Puerto Rico, 19, 20, 50

Quitrents. *See* Taxes, American

Reexportation of foreign goods to America:
drawback on, 42, 102, 196; removing
drawback on, 101–4, 109; parliamentary
reaction to removing drawback on,
110–12; Jenkinson on removal of
drawback on, 224
Requisitions, colonial: as alternative to stamp
tax, 144–47, 270; Grenville on, 146, 149;
Grenville's objections to, 158–59
Rhode Island, 67, 155, 188
Rice trade, 100. *See also* Taxes, American
Rigby, Richard, 11, 15–16, 27, 30, 34
Riots: American, 197; English, 197–99
Ritcheson, Charles R., 224–25, 261
Rockingham administration: Grenville's
concern over colonial policy of, 192–96,
280–82; on Grenville, 286; mentioned,
174, 187, 230
Rockingham, Marquis of, 192, 195, 211
Royal African Company, 92
Rum: West Indian manufacture of, 83–84,
250; French distilling of, 88–89; trade in,
92, 183; Treasury decision on French, 89;
West Indian interest in, 90; in Britain, 97
Ryder, Nathaniel: on Grenville, 232;
mentioned, 7–8, 225, 257, 262, 271–72

Sandwich, Earl of, 241
Scotland, 57–58
Shelburne, Earl of, 6, 32, 236, 241
Shy, John, 247
Silliman, Ebeneezer, 256, 263
Slaves, 257, 264, 272
Smith, William, 208, 285
Smuggling, American: as illicit trade with
France, 22, 62–63; from Gulf of St.
Lawrence, 22; with the enemy, 25; of
linen, 32, 111; of foreign molasses, 38–39,
78–83, 250–51; Grenville on, 58, 62–63,
74–75, 93, 206; estimates of volume from
Europe of, 67–69, 198, 248, 283; Ware
on, 67–68, 80–83; McCulloh on, 67–68;

Whately on, 68, 184; political implications
of, 69; commercial implications of, 69;
McCulloh's plan to hinder, 69–70;
Treasury orders on, 71–73; and estimates
of volume of molasses trade, 82, 85–86; of
foreign linens, 103; Jenkinson on, 147; *See
also* Treasury
Smuggling, British: causes of, 52–53, 244;
Grenville's efforts against, 44, 52–58;
political implications of, 53, 55, 100, 244;
from Isle of Man, 57–58; and courts, 162
Society of Merchant Venturers in Bristol,
112
Sosin, Jack M., 250–51, 253, 261–62, 270
South Carolina, 100, 107, 126, 130,
160–61, 174–75, 277
Stamp Act Congress, 194, 208
Stamp tax, American: 99–210 passim,
254–288 passim; mentioned, 65, 73–74,
76, 95. *See also* Cruwys, Jenkinson,
McCulloh, Treasury, Whately
Stamp taxes, other. *See* Taxes, British
Stationery tax. *See* Taxes, American
Subdistributors of stamps. *See*
Underdistributors of stamps
Sugar Act, 98, 148, 156, 185, 190, 211, 224,
250, 272. *See also* American Revenue Act
of 1764
Surveyors-General in America, 70

Taxation, internal, Parliamentary right of:
colonists' opinions on, 115; Grenville on,
115–16, 143–44, 154–56, 232, 281;
agents on, 121, 150–51; Jackson on, 126;
Grenville's efforts to achieve unanimity on,
143; Mansfield on, 143; Jenkinson on,
143–44; Whately on, 144; popularity in
Parliament of, 160, 269; Ingersoll on, 203;
North on, 204; effect of colonial protests
against, 271; Beckford on, 272; Bernard
on, 285; mentioned, 106
Taxation, principles of: and equality, 37,
237; Grenville and, 76, 87, 99–100, 157,
165, 187, 224–25; Whately on, 96–97,
101, 137–38, 141; Grenville and ad
valorem, 111–13; Jenkinson on, 235;
Weston and, 237
Taxation of America: political significance of,
4–5, 96–101, 105–6, 185–96, 281; first
Treasury discussion of, 28–29; popularity
in Parliament of, 29, 36, 42, 96, 122–23,
252; commercial considerations in
planning of, 37–40, 89–93, 96–98, 106–7,
137–42; customs reform and, 73–77;
information on, 76–77; Ware on, 83;
Grenville on uses for, 94–95, 147–48,

270; petitions against, 88–89, 160–62;
Halifax on uses for, 94; Jenkinson on uses
for, 94; Grenville on, 99–100, 116, 121,
127–28, 157, 187, 198–99, 231, 270;
McCulloh on weight of,107; agents'
concern over precedent of, 151; estimates
of total produce, 181–82; consequences of
colonial growth for, 183–84; criteria for
amendment of, 184–87; Whately on,
186–87, 270, 279; necessity of enforcing,
187–91; popular colonial politicians'
reaction to, 201–4; Knox on, 235;
Beckford on, 239–40. *See also* Taxation,
internal; Taxation, principles of; and Taxes,
American
Taxes, American: quitrents, 30; on linen,
31–33, 101–4, 111–13, 183, 238, 255;
plantation duties, 31, 33, 156; on rice,
100–1, 254; on wine, 100–1, 183; on
coffee, 101, 183; on pimento, 101; on the
fur trade, 264, 272; on stationary, 274. *See
also* Molasses tax; Stamp tax; Taxation,
internal; Taxation of America; and
Treasury
Taxes, British: controversies over, 3;
advantages to financiers from, 3; and the
economy, 16–21; on beer, 16–17, 20, 157,
187, 234; and the poor, 16–17; on land,
20, 29, 187; postwar burdens of, 20; new
in 1763, 33; on cider, 37–38, 40–41, 53,
76, 157, 187; on stamps, English, 37, 104,
129, 239; on stamps, Scottish, 92; on
luxuries, 101; on stamps, Jamaican, 126,
130, 263, 268
Temple, Earl (Richard Grenville): Grenville's
estrangement from, 5, 46, 51, 231, 242;
mentioned, 45
Temple, John, 9, 125, 147, 170, 174,
181–82, 184, 186, 205–6, 266
Temple, Sir William, 231
Thomas, P. D. G., 43, 76, 94, 109, 122,
239, 258–59, 261–62, 266–67, 270, 274
Thomson, Charles, 204
Tod, William, 31, 101–4, 238, 255–56, 258
Tories, 34–35, 148
Townshend, Charles: plan for American
taxation by, 11; on the German war, 18;
on assemblies, 25; and the molasses tax,
38–42, 63, 91, 96; and Bindley, 39, 240;
and smuggling in America, 63; on Britain's
financial and commercial crises, 234;
mentioned, 14–15, 26–27, 35, 48, 241,
243, 283
Townshend, George, 35
Trade, North American: importance to

Britain of, 2, 23–25, 31, 68–69, 137,
140–42, 182; Grenville on, 116
Trade, West Indian: Grenville on, 24, 50;
Pitt on, 24
Treasury: initial discussions of American
taxes in, 28–29, 34, 38, 42; and American
customs service, 30–31, 33, 70–73, 188,
211–12; and drawbacks on reexported
foreign goods, 33, 102–3, 255; Grenville
becomes First Lord of, 42, 44–45, 51–52;
and smuggling in Britain, 54–55, 57; and
British customs service, 55–57; Grenville
as junior Lord of, 59, 134; and smuggling
in North America, 63, 103; and the
American revenue, 64, 164; orders against
smuggled manufactured goods from, 72;
and memorial of 4 October 1763, 73, 75,
130, 243; and admiralty courts, 73, 162;
on smuggled molasses, 80; and reducing
the molasses tax, 84–93; and legislation
against French rum, 89; and the wine tax,
100–1; and Whately's report of 6
December 1764, 137–41; preparation for
House debates on stamp tax by, 142–44;
and stamp distributors, 172–77, 188,
274–75; and decisions against new taxes
after Stamp Act, 180–84; on the poor in
America, 182–83; and criteria for
amending American taxes, 184–87; and
necessity of enforcing American taxes,
187–91; and the customs commissioners,
246
Trecothick, Barlow, 169–70, 172, 185, 190,
275–76, 280–81
Turner, Sir John, 12, 240

Underdistributors of stamps, American, 166,
208, 288

Virginia: resolutions against stamp tax from,
193–94; Grenville on resolves of, 193–94;
mentioned, 107, 109, 160, 173, 177

Walpole, Horace: on Grenville, 8, 257, 279,
281; mentioned, 5, 273, 283
Walpole, Sir Robert, 37, 210, 273
Ware, Nathaniel: background of, 65–67, 81,
247–48, 250; estimate of smuggling from
Europe by, 67–68, 198; on American
customs service, 65–66, 75, 83–84; and
Halifax, 65–66, 220, 247; and Bute, 66,
247; on smuggling in North America,
66–70, 72; and contacts with North and
Jenkinson, 66; and Grenville, 67–68, 70,
74, 81–83, 220–21; and the molasses tax,

74, 80–83; on American political ideas, 75; on molasses trade, 80–83, 85; and his report of 22 August 1763, 80–84, 246–47, 251; on wine tax, 100; ordered to America, 250; mentioned, 71, 95, 246

Watts, John, 267

Weare, Mesech, 247

Wedderburne, Alexander, 245

West Indian interest: and the Molasses Act, 38; and molasses tax, 78, 86–90, 253; and Grenville, 86–91; and molasses trade, 86–87; and the sugar trade, 86, 251; and petitions against stamp tax, 272–73

West Indies, British, 72, 98, 139

West Indies, French: dependence on North American colonies of, 78–80; and molasses trade, 79; See also Rum

Weston, Robert, 237

Whately, Thomas: on political implications of American taxation, 5, 98, 106; and Grenville, 7, 9, 210; and Ingersoll, 8, 125, 141–42, 145, 167, 169, 184, 206–7, 262, 277; on the financial crisis in Britain, 21; on smuggling in North America, 68, 74, 80, 85, 184, 283; on importance of North American trade, 69; on molasses tax, 88, 91–93, 96, 186, 251–52, 279; on principles of taxation, 96–97, 101, 137–38, 141; on British manufacturers, 97; on colonial reaction to taxation, 97; on removing drawbacks on reexported foreign goods, 102; on colonial manufacturing, 102; and preparation of stamp tax, 117, 134–35, 137–42, 209, 266–68; and John Temple, 125; and report of 6 December 1764, 137–41, 165–66, 182; on American poverty, 139–40, 182; on internal taxation, 144; on colonial obligations, 150; on colonial petitions, 162; and collection of American revenue, 164; and appointment of stamp distributors, 165–72, 174, 176–78, 188, 195, 274–75; and underdistributors, 166, 176–78; on future taxes, 181, 184; on amending taxes after 1765, 184; on colonists' response to taxation, 185–87; on colonial response to the Stamp Act, 193–95; on Grenville's colonial policy, 210; on tax on slave importations, 257, 272; on stamp tax, 257, 268; on uses for American revenue, 270; on law enforcement, 275; on American taxation, 279; mentioned, 3, 95, 110–11, 142, 147, 160, 162, 175, 186, 206, 225, 230, 269, 283

Wickwire, Franklin B., 255

Wilkes, John, 197

Wine trade, 100. See also Taxes, American

Wood, William, 76–77

Wraxall, Nathaniel, 232, 257–58

Wyllys, George, 256, 263

Yorke, Charles, 23, 161–62, 234